プロジェクトアームズ

PROJECT ARMS

The Second Revelation □ Evil Eye

vol. 4

Project Arms
The Second Revelation: Evil Eye
vol. 4
Action Edition

Created by Ryoji Minagawa and Kyoichi Nanatsuki

English Adaptation/Lance Caselman
Translator/Katy Bridges
Touch-up & Lettering/Kathryn Renta
Cover and Graphics Design/Sean Lee
Editor/Andy Nakatani

Managing Editor/Annette Roman
Editor in Chief/William Flanagan
Production Manager/Noboru Watanabe
Sr. Dir. of Licensing and Acquisitions/Rika Inouye
VP of Marketing/Liza Coppola
Sr. VP of Editorial/Hyoe Narita
Publisher/Seiji Horibuchi

Published by VIZ, LLC
P.O. Box 77010
San Francisco, CA 94107

Action Edition
10 9 8 7 6 5 4 3 2 1
First printing, March 2004

CONTENTS

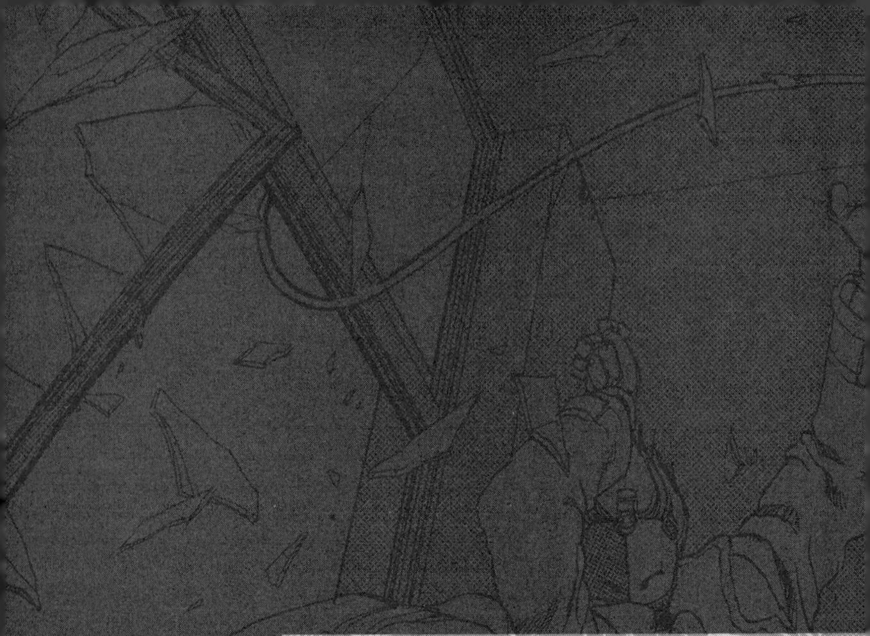

Story thus far

Ryo Takatsuki, Hayato Shingu, and Takeshi Tomoe are Arms—kids who have been implanted with nanotech limb enhancements that cause their arms to transform into grotesquely deformed and out of control superweapons. Venturing off to Abumisawa village to discover the secrets of their past, they find out that they are caught in the middle of a power struggle within the secret organization known as Egrigori. In the ensuing battle, when Ryo's childhood friend Katsumi goes up in flames, he loses control and his entire being transforms into the ferocious Jabberwock...

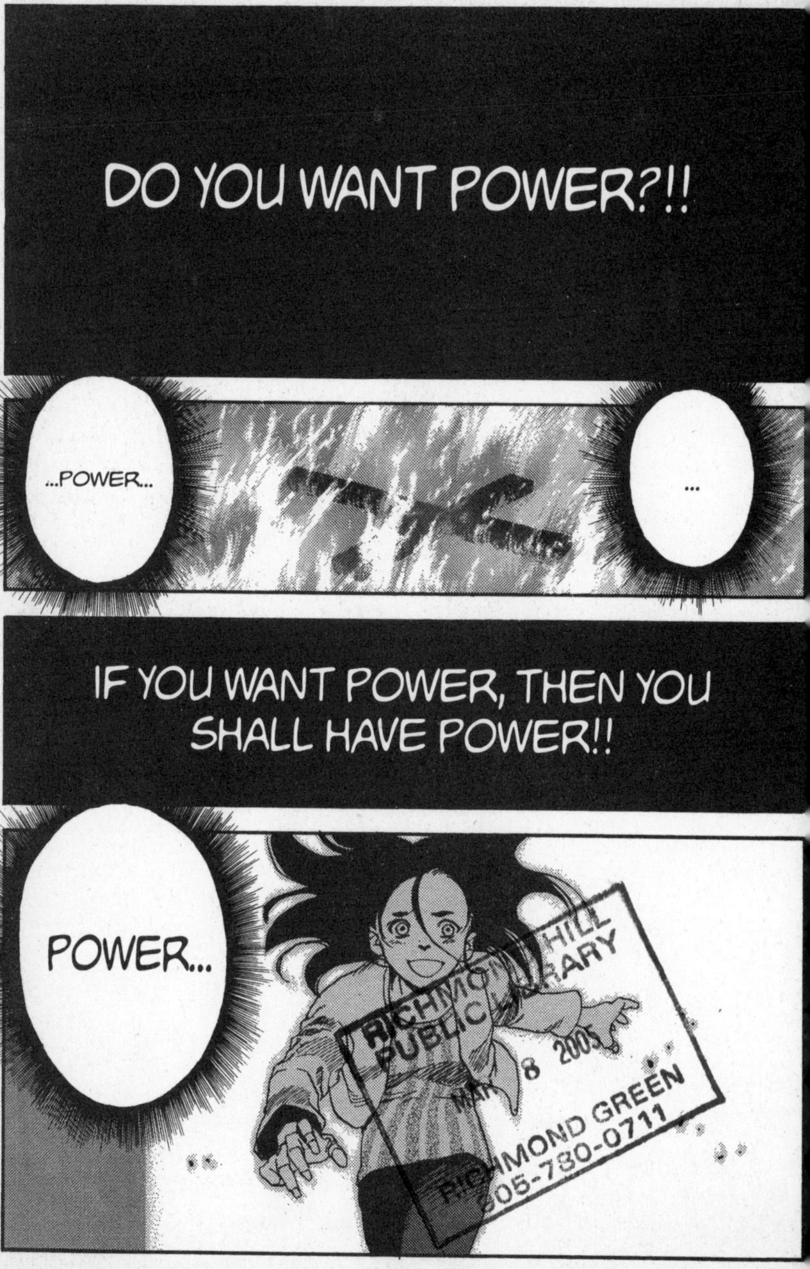
DO YOU WANT POWER?!!
...
...POWER...
IF YOU WANT POWER, THEN YOU SHALL HAVE POWER!!
POWER...

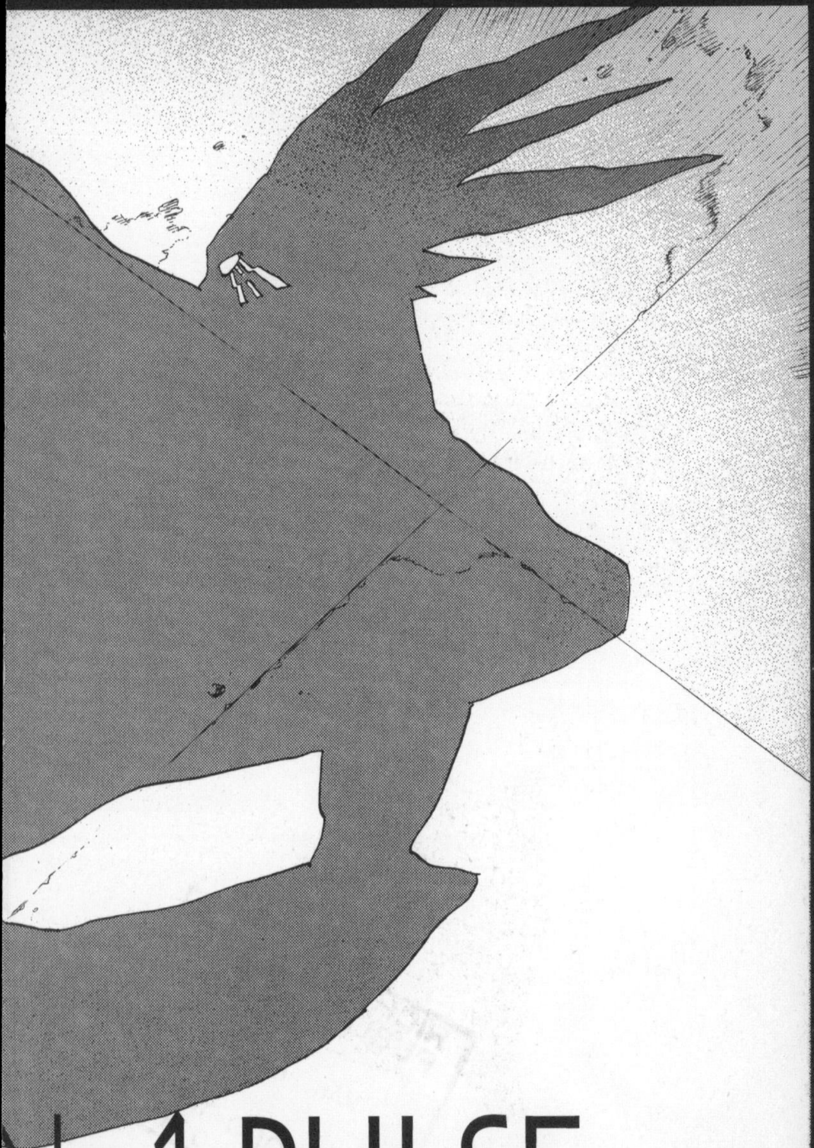

No.1 PULSE

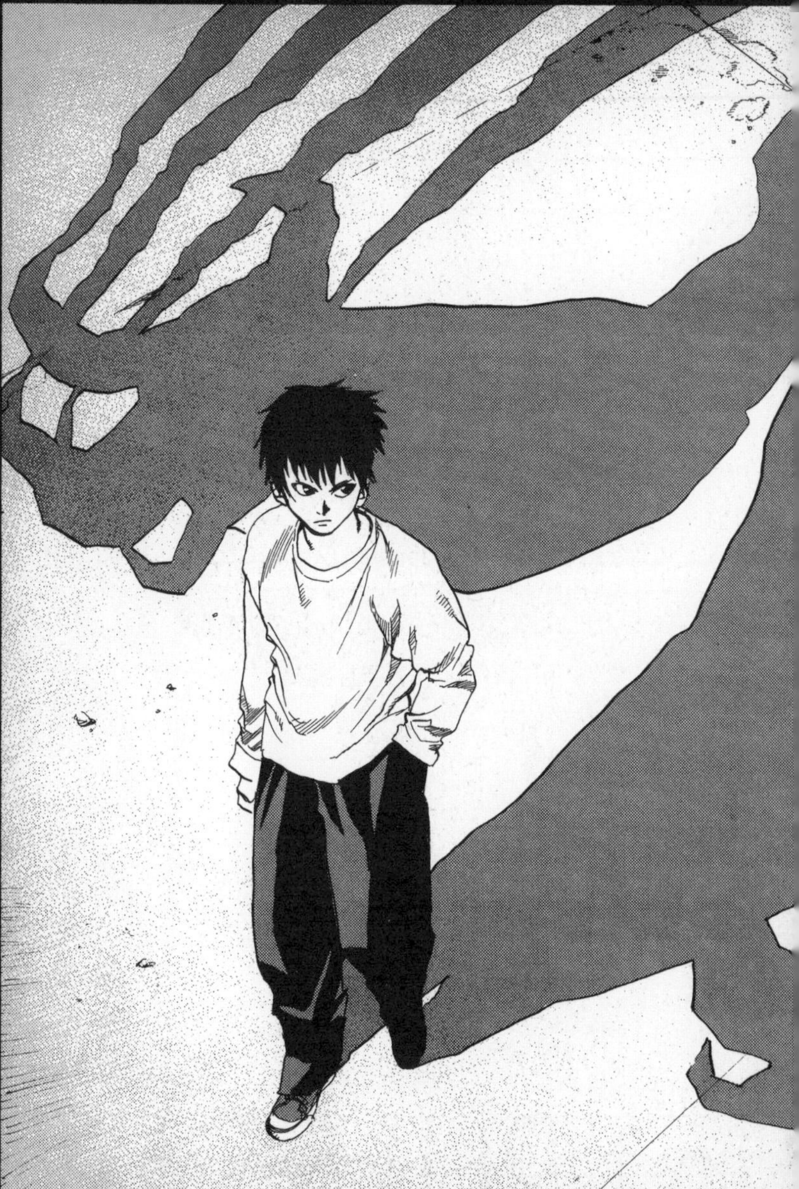

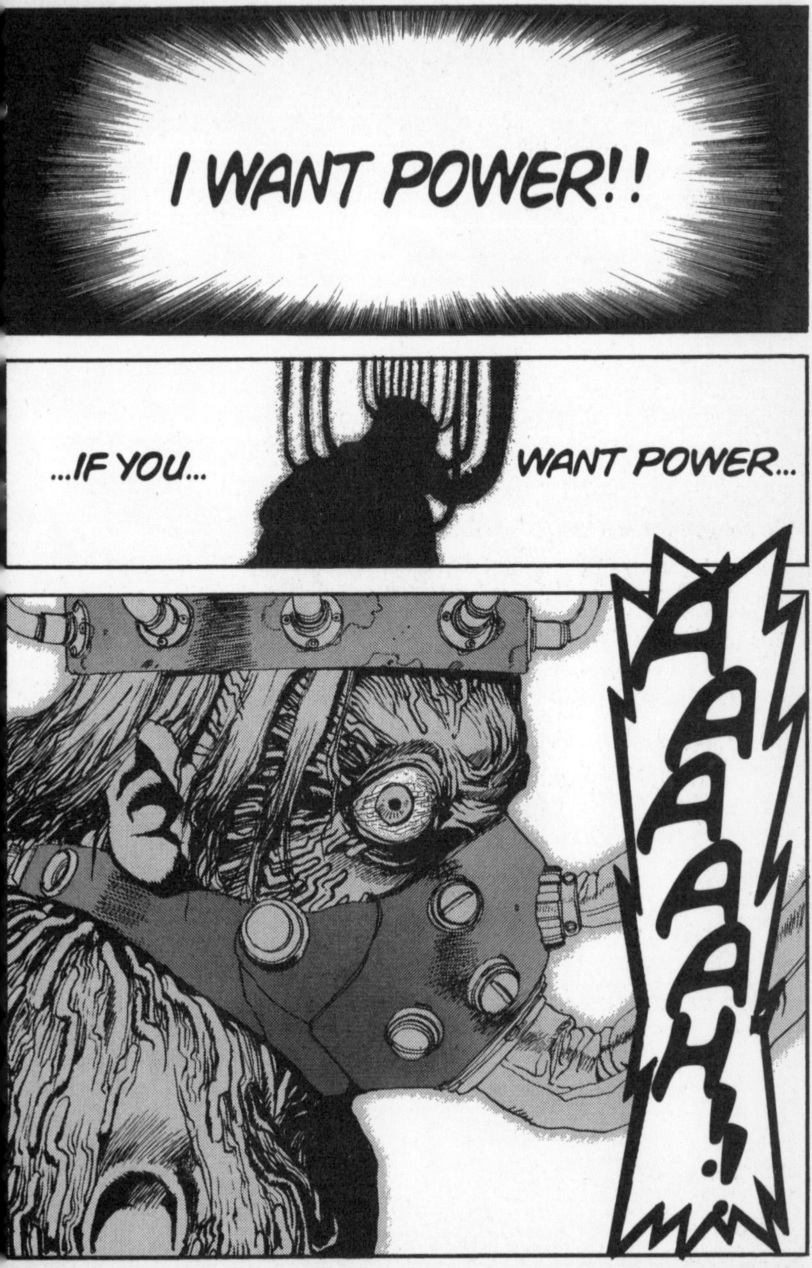
I WANT POWER!!
...IF YOU...
WANT POWER...
AAAAAAH!!

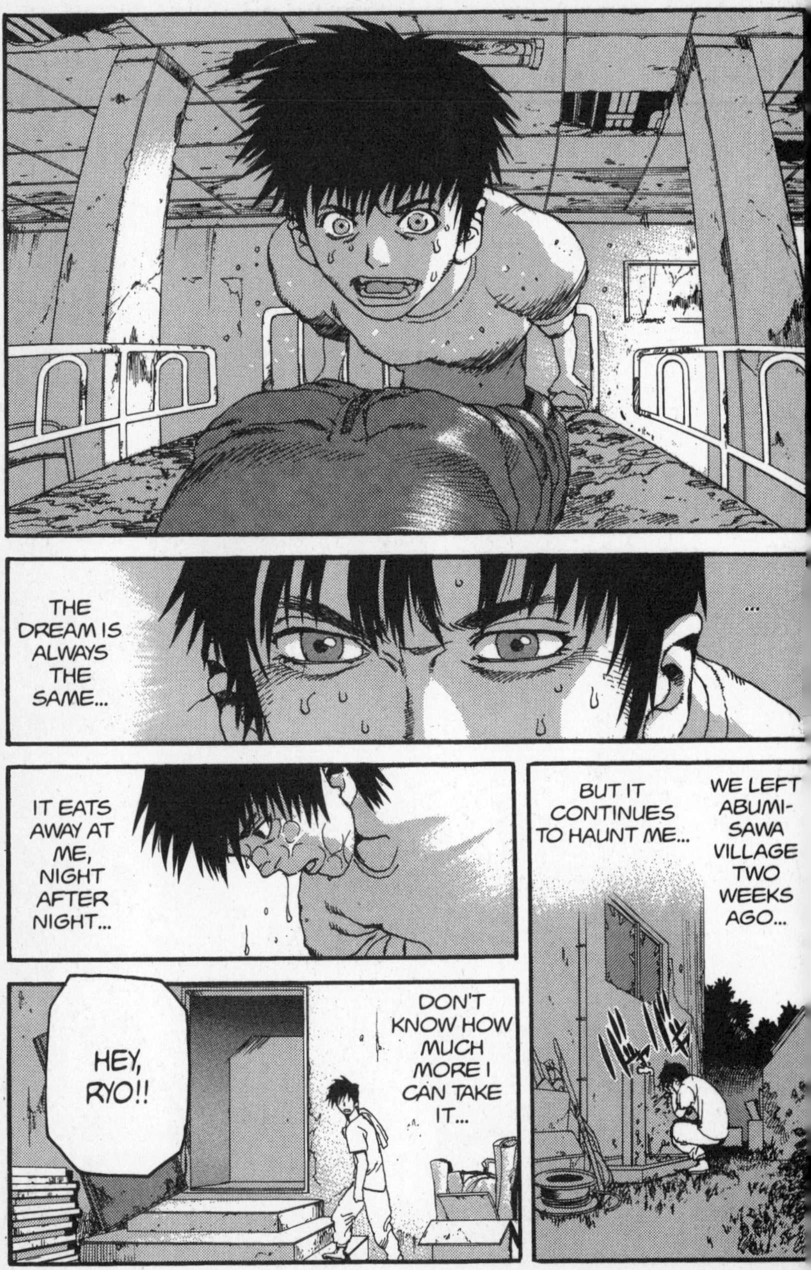
THE DREAM IS ALWAYS THE SAME...
...
IT EATS AWAY AT ME, NIGHT AFTER NIGHT...
WE LEFT ABUMI-SAWA VILLAGE TWO WEEKS AGO...
BUT IT CONTINUES TO HAUNT ME...
DON'T KNOW HOW MUCH MORE I CAN TAKE IT...
HEY, RYO!!

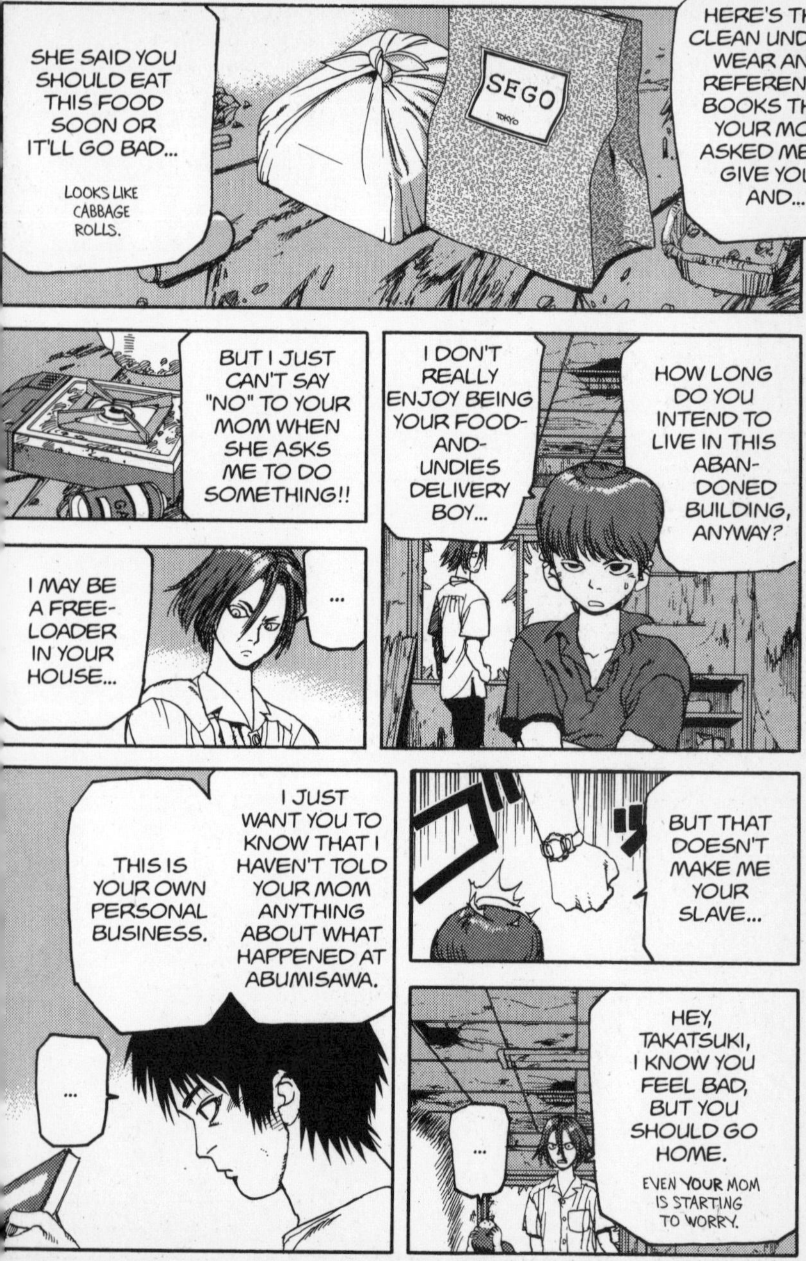
HERE'S THE CLEAN UNDER-WEAR AND REFERENCE BOOKS THAT YOUR MOM ASKED ME TO GIVE YOU... AND...
SEGO
TOKYO
SHE SAID YOU SHOULD EAT THIS FOOD SOON OR IT'LL GO BAD...
LOOKS LIKE CABBAGE ROLLS.
HOW LONG DO YOU INTEND TO LIVE IN THIS ABAN-DONED BUILDING, ANYWAY?
I DON'T REALLY ENJOY BEING YOUR FOOD-AND-UNDIES DELIVERY BOY...
BUT I JUST CAN'T SAY "NO" TO YOUR MOM WHEN SHE ASKS ME TO DO SOMETHING!!
...
I MAY BE A FREE-LOADER IN YOUR HOUSE...
BUT THAT DOESN'T MAKE ME YOUR SLAVE...
HEY, TAKATSUKI, I KNOW YOU FEEL BAD, BUT YOU SHOULD GO HOME.
EVEN YOUR MOM IS STARTING TO WORRY.
...
I JUST WANT YOU TO KNOW THAT I HAVEN'T TOLD YOUR MOM ANYTHING ABOUT WHAT HAPPENED AT ABUMISAWA.
THIS IS YOUR OWN PERSONAL BUSINESS.
...

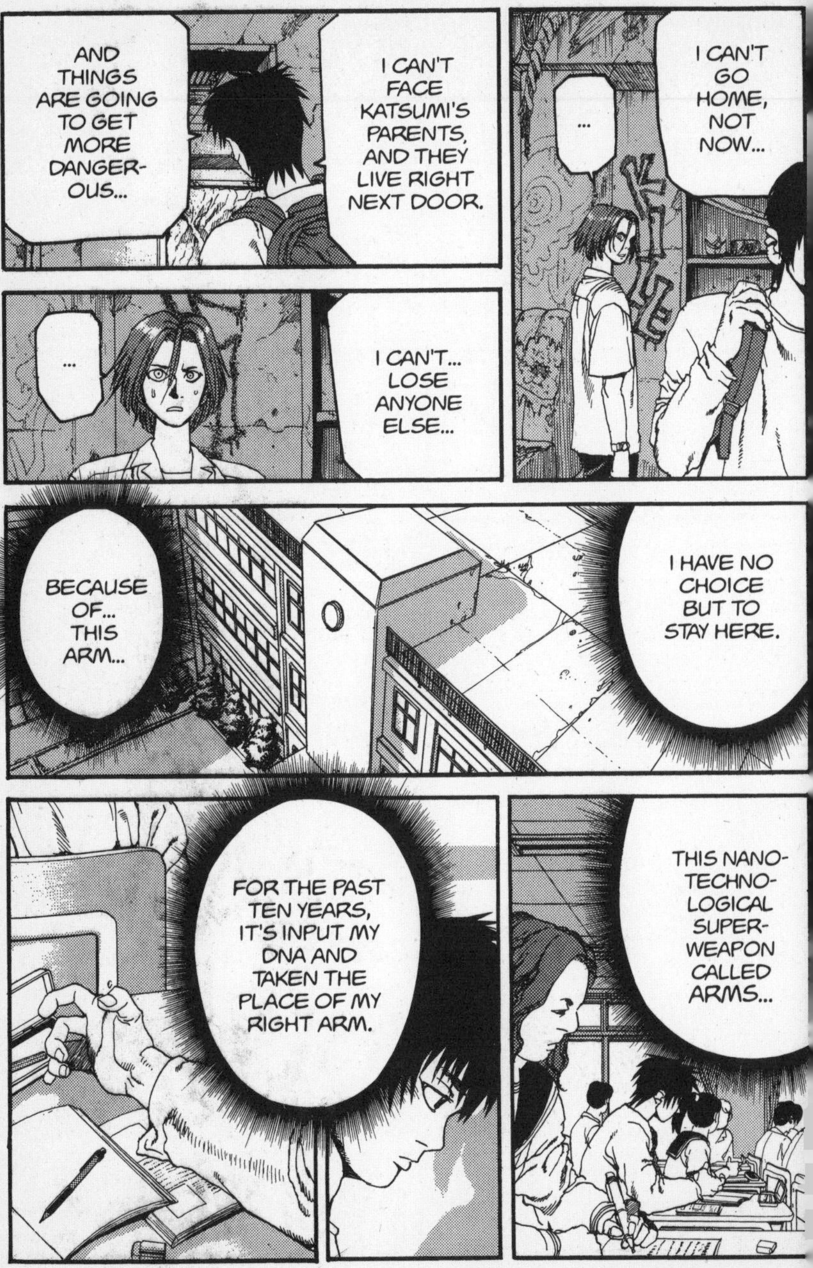
I CAN'T GO HOME, NOT NOW...
...
I CAN'T FACE KATSUMI'S PARENTS, AND THEY LIVE RIGHT NEXT DOOR.
AND THINGS ARE GOING TO GET MORE DANGER-OUS...
I CAN'T... LOSE ANYONE ELSE...
...
I HAVE NO CHOICE BUT TO STAY HERE.
BECAUSE OF... THIS ARM...
THIS NANO-TECHNO-LOGICAL SUPER-WEAPON CALLED ARMS...
FOR THE PAST TEN YEARS, IT'S INPUT MY DNA AND TAKEN THE PLACE OF MY RIGHT ARM.

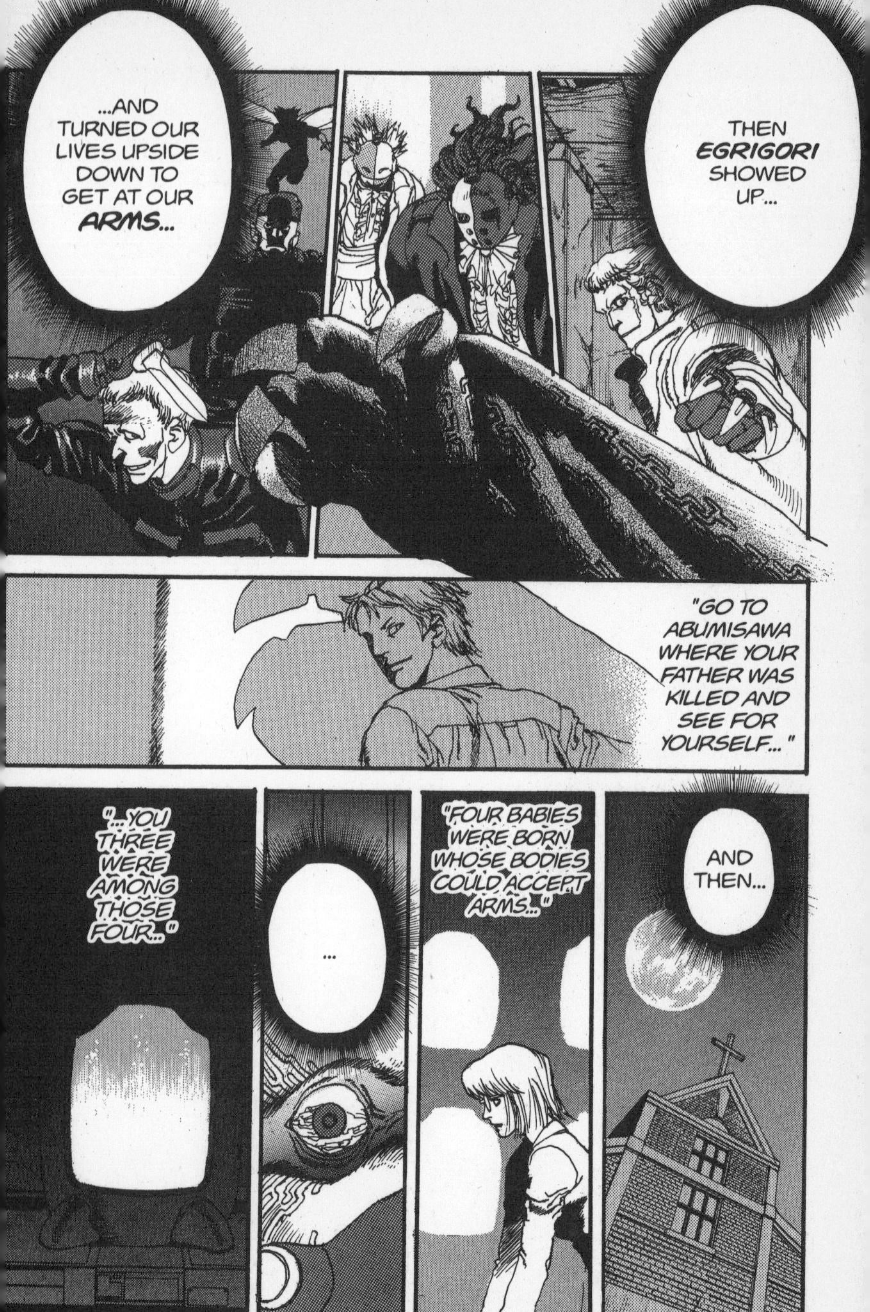
THEN *EGRIGORI* SHOWED UP...
...AND TURNED OUR LIVES UPSIDE DOWN TO GET AT OUR *ARMS*...
"GO TO ABUMISAWA WHERE YOUR FATHER WAS KILLED AND SEE FOR YOURSELF..."
AND THEN...
"FOUR BABIES WERE BORN WHOSE BODIES COULD ACCEPT ARMS..."
...
"...YOU THREE WERE AMONG THOSE FOUR..."

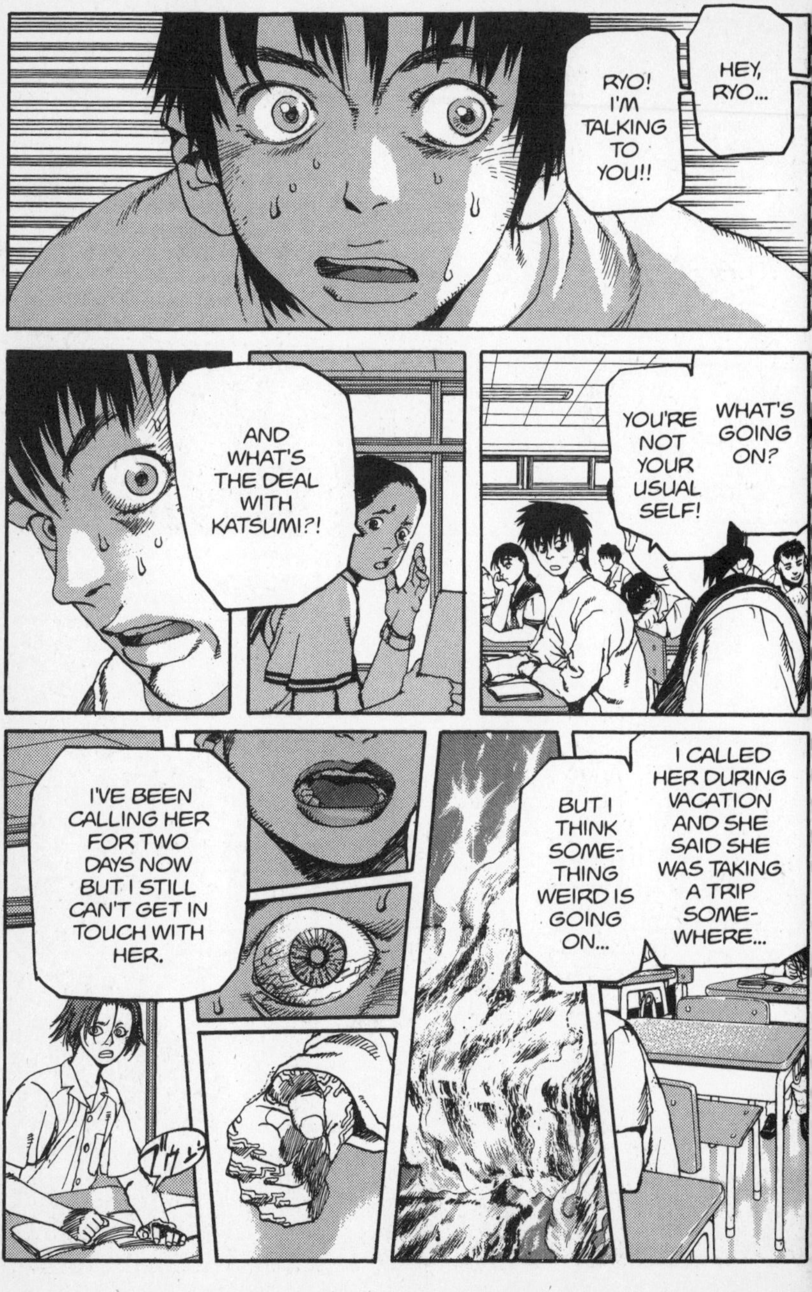
HEY, RYO...
RYO! I'M TALKING TO YOU!!
WHAT'S GOING ON?
YOU'RE NOT YOUR USUAL SELF!
AND WHAT'S THE DEAL WITH KATSUMI?!
I CALLED HER DURING VACATION AND SHE SAID SHE WAS TAKING A TRIP SOME-WHERE...
BUT I THINK SOME-THING WEIRD IS GOING ON...
I'VE BEEN CALLING HER FOR TWO DAYS NOW BUT I STILL CAN'T GET IN TOUCH WITH HER.

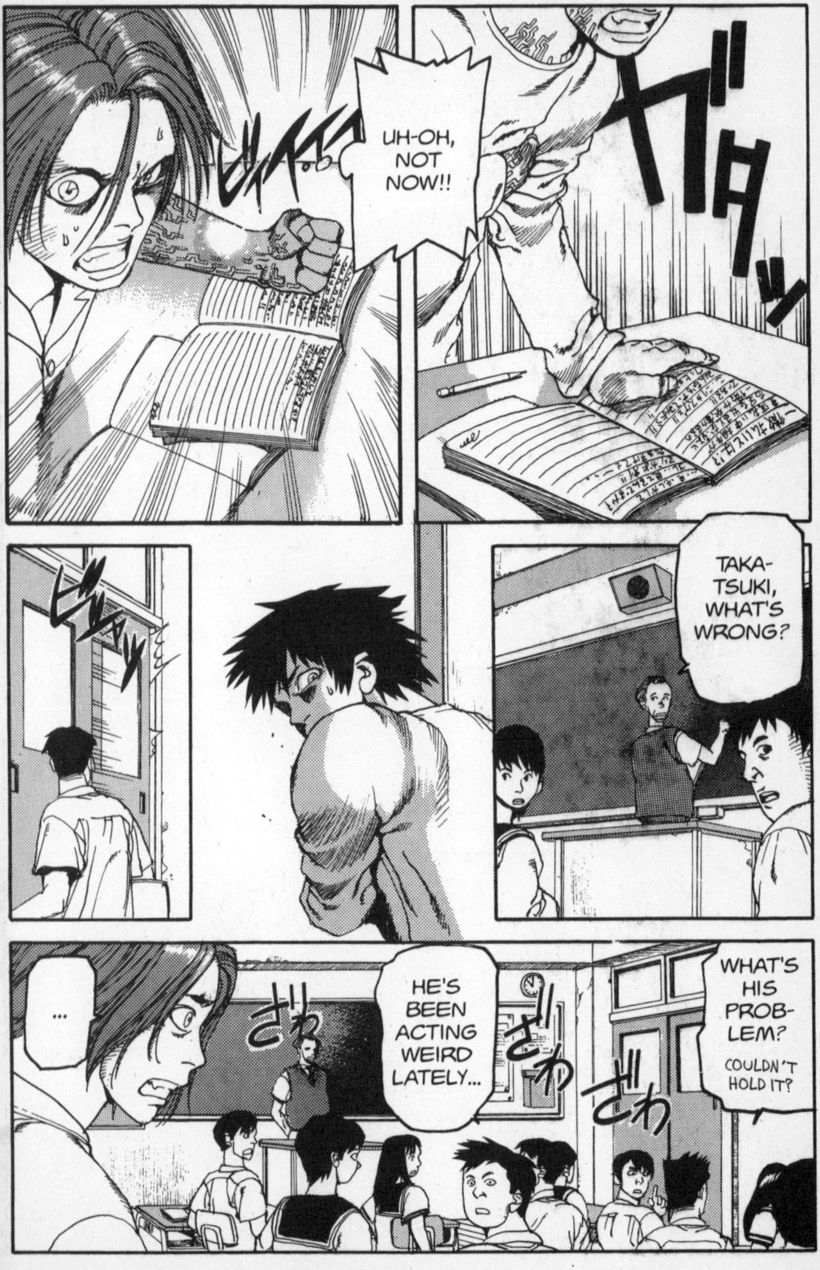
ガタッ
UH-OH, NOT NOW!!
TAKA-TSUKI, WHAT'S WRONG?
WHAT'S HIS PROB-LEM?
COULDN'T HOLD IT?
ざわ
ざわ
HE'S BEEN ACTING WEIRD LATELY...
ざわ
...

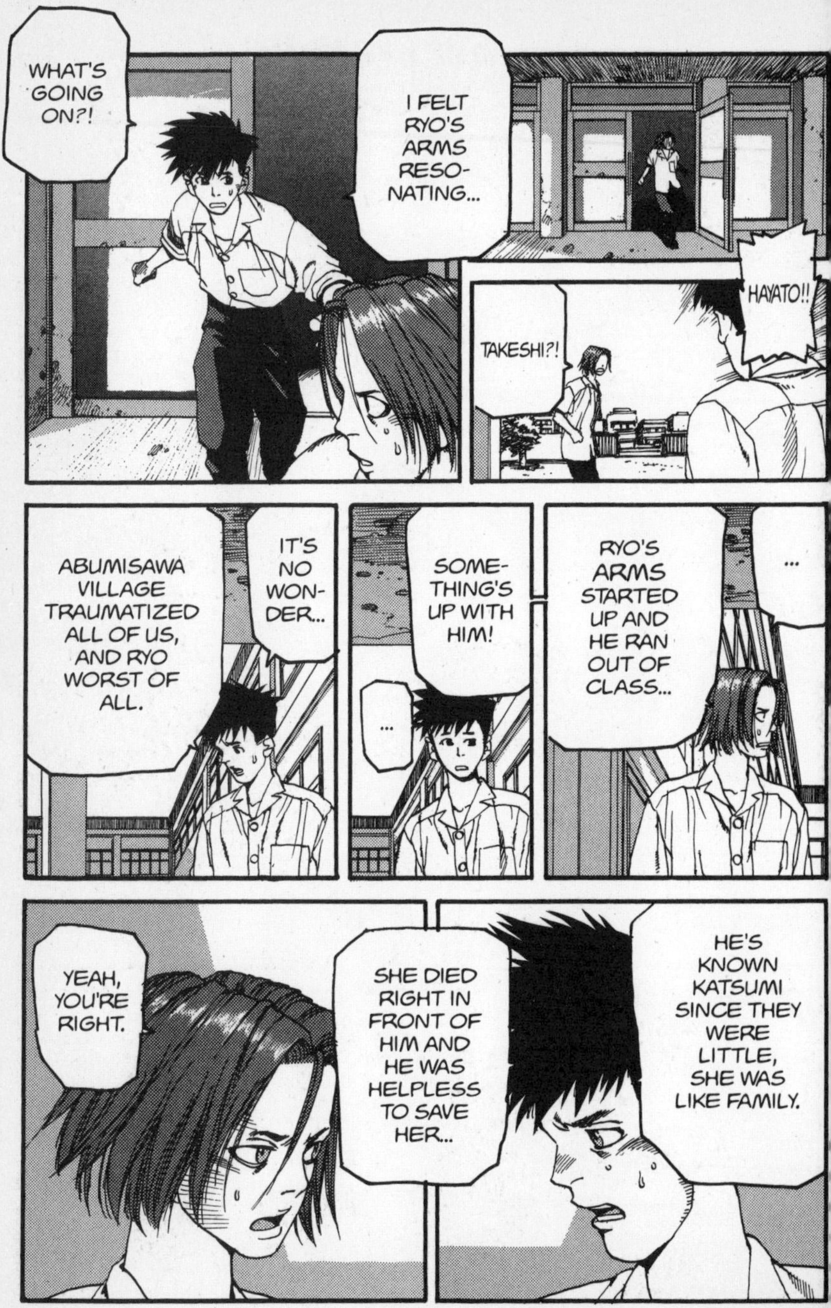
HAYATO!!
TAKESHI?!
WHAT'S GOING ON?!
I FELT RYO'S ARMS RESO-NATING...
RYO'S ARMS STARTED UP AND HE RAN OUT OF CLASS...
...
SOME-THING'S UP WITH HIM!
...
IT'S NO WON-DER...
ABUMISAWA VILLAGE TRAUMATIZED ALL OF US, AND RYO WORST OF ALL.
HE'S KNOWN KATSUMI SINCE THEY WERE LITTLE, SHE WAS LIKE FAMILY.
SHE DIED RIGHT IN FRONT OF HIM AND HE WAS HELPLESS TO SAVE HER...
YEAH, YOU'RE RIGHT.

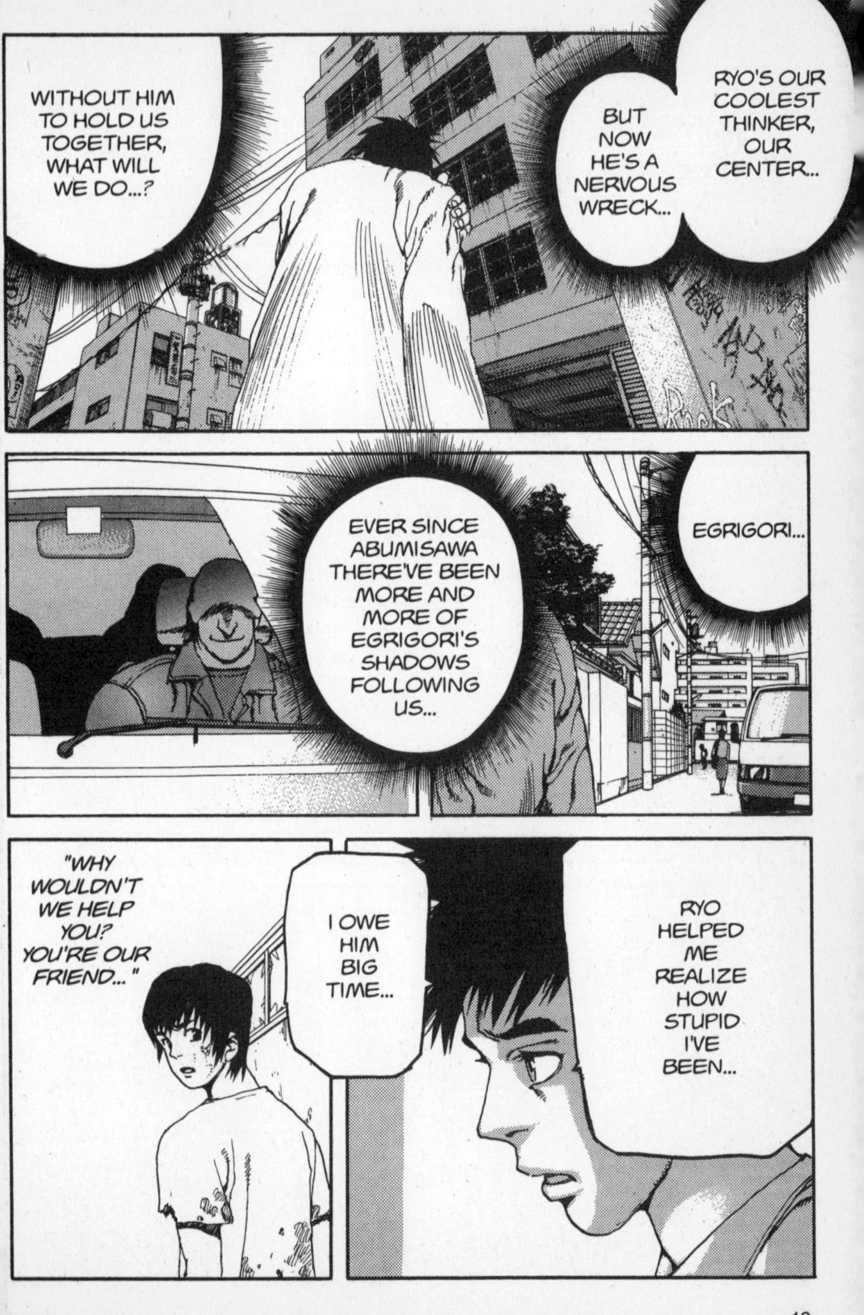
RYO'S OUR COOLEST THINKER, OUR CENTER...
BUT NOW HE'S A NERVOUS WRECK...
WITHOUT HIM TO HOLD US TOGETHER, WHAT WILL WE DO...?
EGRIGORI...
EVER SINCE ABUMISAWA THERE'VE BEEN MORE AND MORE OF EGRIGORI'S SHADOWS FOLLOWING US...
RYO HELPED ME REALIZE HOW STUPID I'VE BEEN...
I OWE HIM BIG TIME...
"WHY WOULDN'T WE HELP YOU? YOU'RE OUR FRIEND..."

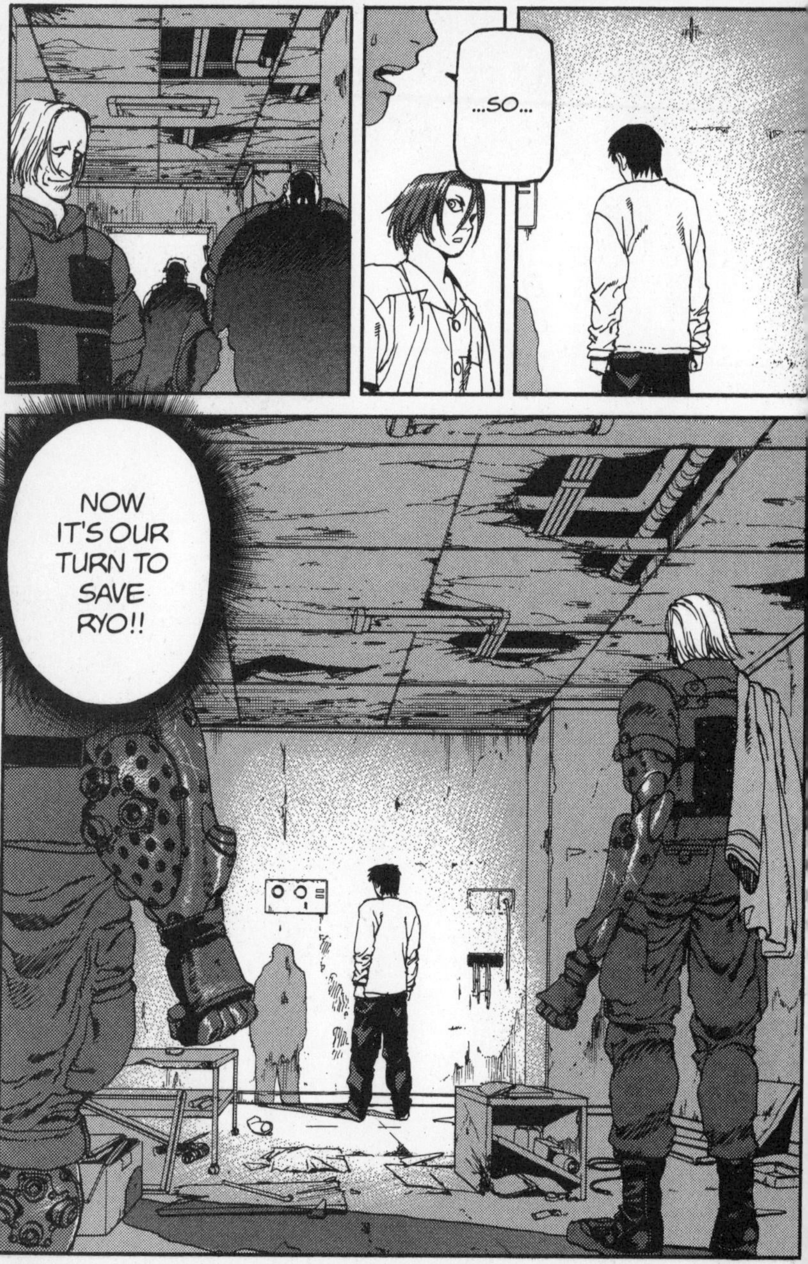
...SO...
NOW IT'S OUR TURN TO SAVE RYO!!

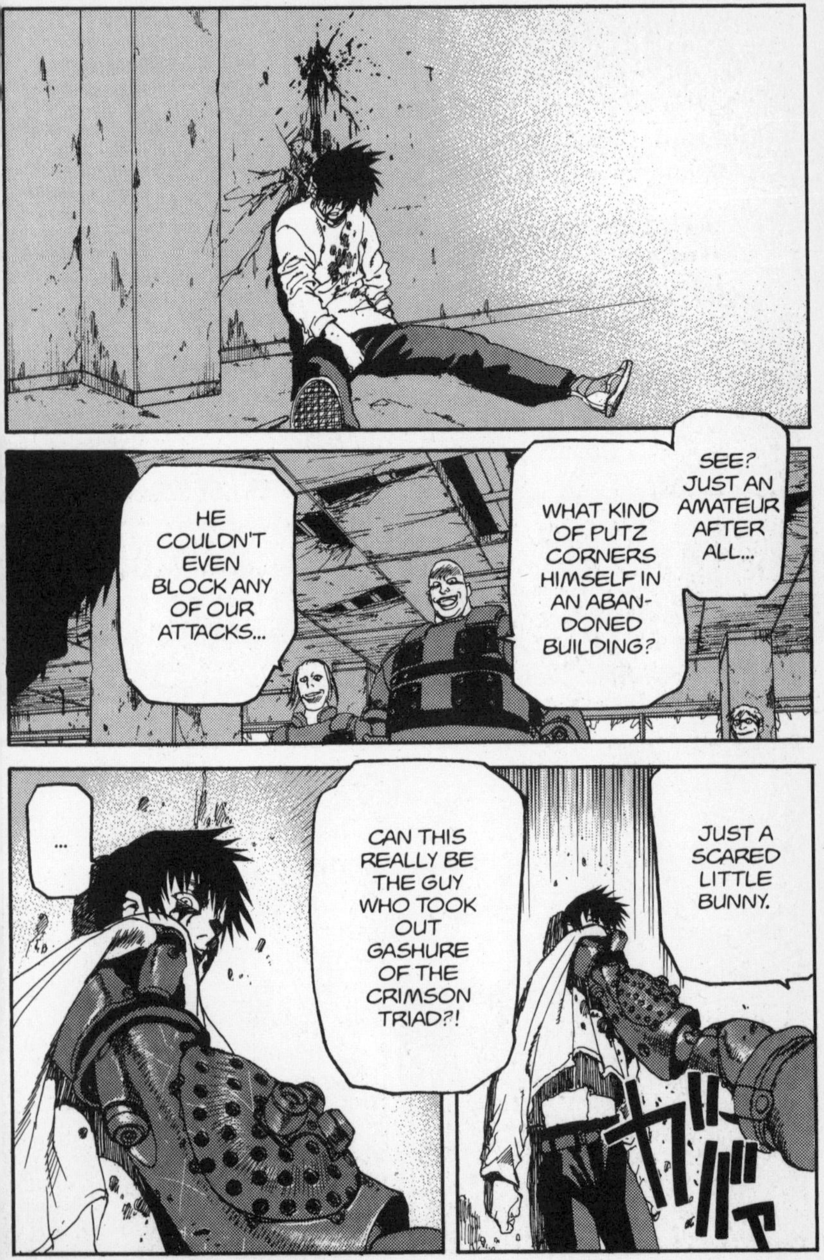
SEE? JUST AN AMATEUR AFTER ALL...
WHAT KIND OF PUTZ CORNERS HIMSELF IN AN ABANDONED BUILDING?
HE COULDN'T EVEN BLOCK ANY OF OUR ATTACKS...
JUST A SCARED LITTLE BUNNY.
CAN THIS REALLY BE THE GUY WHO TOOK OUT GASHURE OF THE CRIMSON TRIAD?!
...

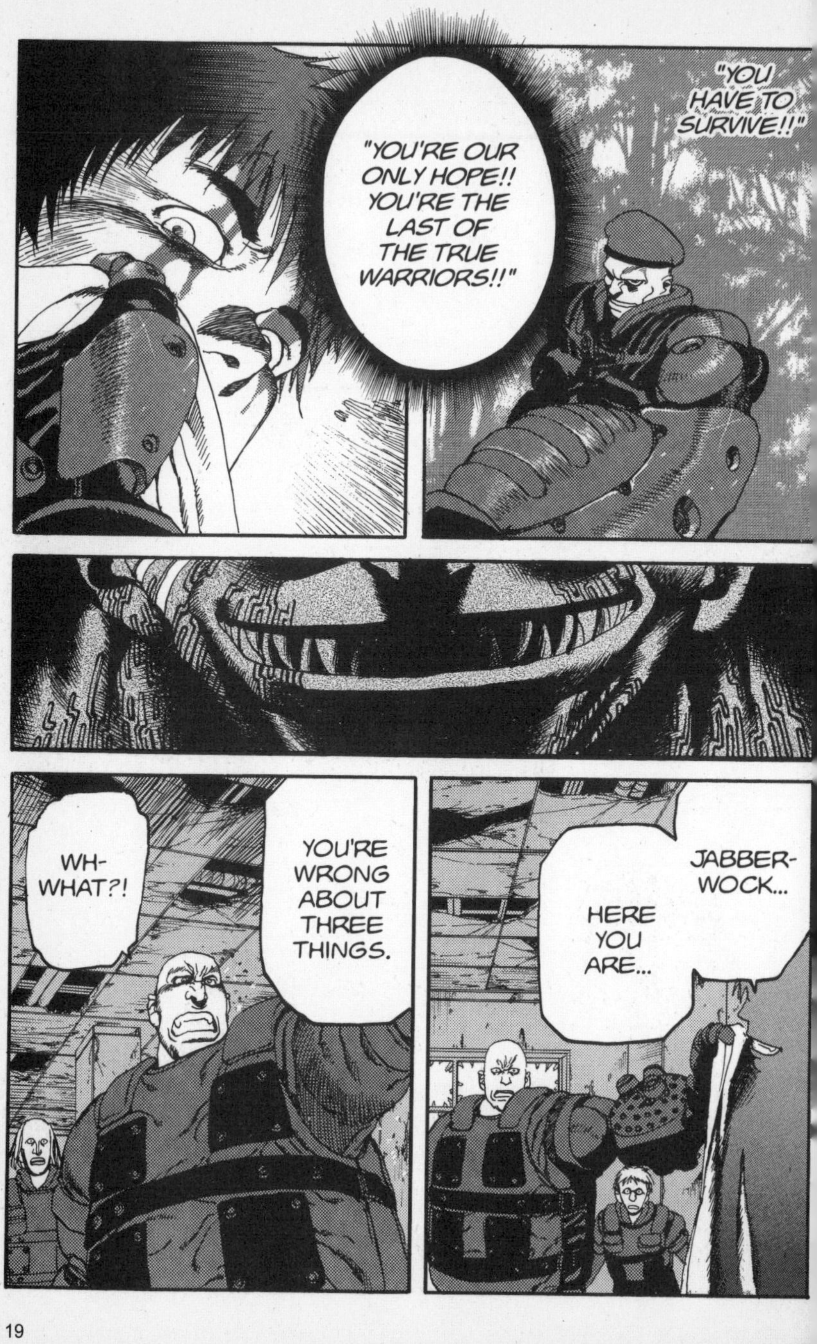
"YOU HAVE TO SURVIVE!!"
"YOU'RE OUR ONLY HOPE!! YOU'RE THE LAST OF THE TRUE WARRIORS!!"
JABBERWOCK...
HERE YOU ARE...
YOU'RE WRONG ABOUT THREE THINGS.
WH-WHAT?!

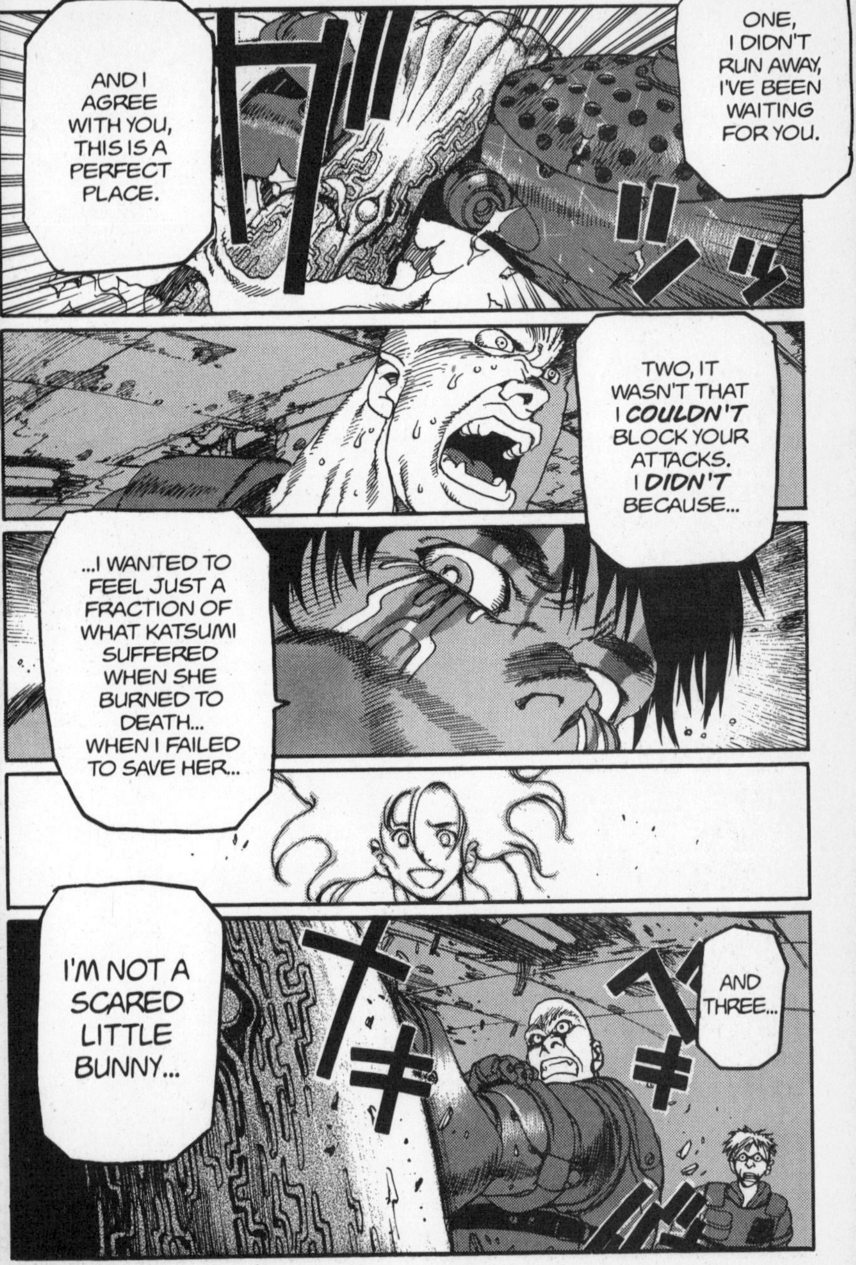
ONE, I DIDN'T RUN AWAY, I'VE BEEN WAITING FOR YOU.
AND I AGREE WITH YOU, THIS IS A PERFECT PLACE.
TWO, IT WASN'T THAT I **COULDN'T** BLOCK YOUR ATTACKS. I **DIDN'T** BECAUSE...
...I WANTED TO FEEL JUST A FRACTION OF WHAT KATSUMI SUFFERED WHEN SHE BURNED TO DEATH... WHEN I FAILED TO SAVE HER...
AND THREE...
I'M NOT A SCARED LITTLE BUNNY...

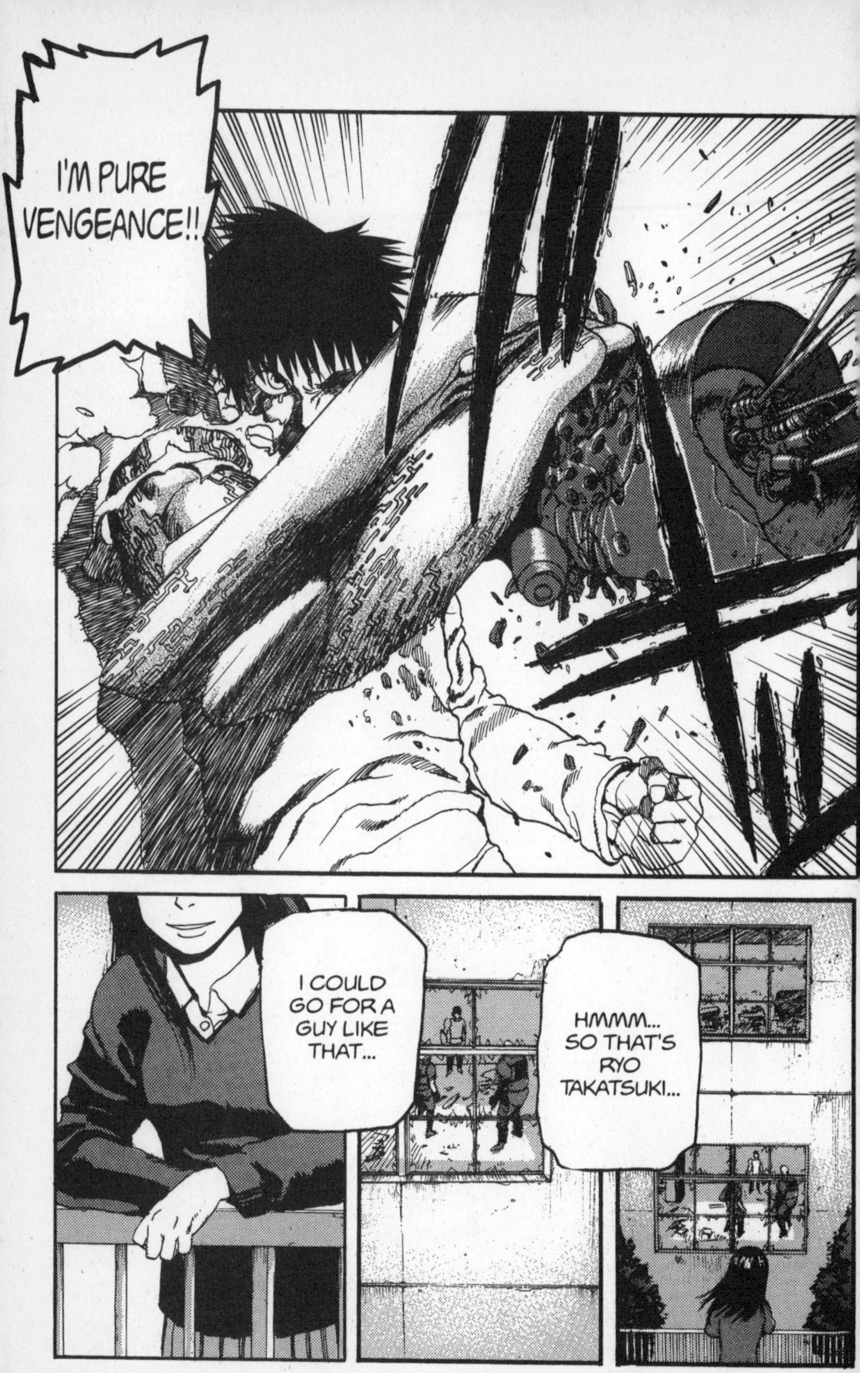
I'M PURE VENGEANCE!!
HMMM... SO THAT'S RYO TAKATSUKI...
I COULD GO FOR A GUY LIKE THAT...

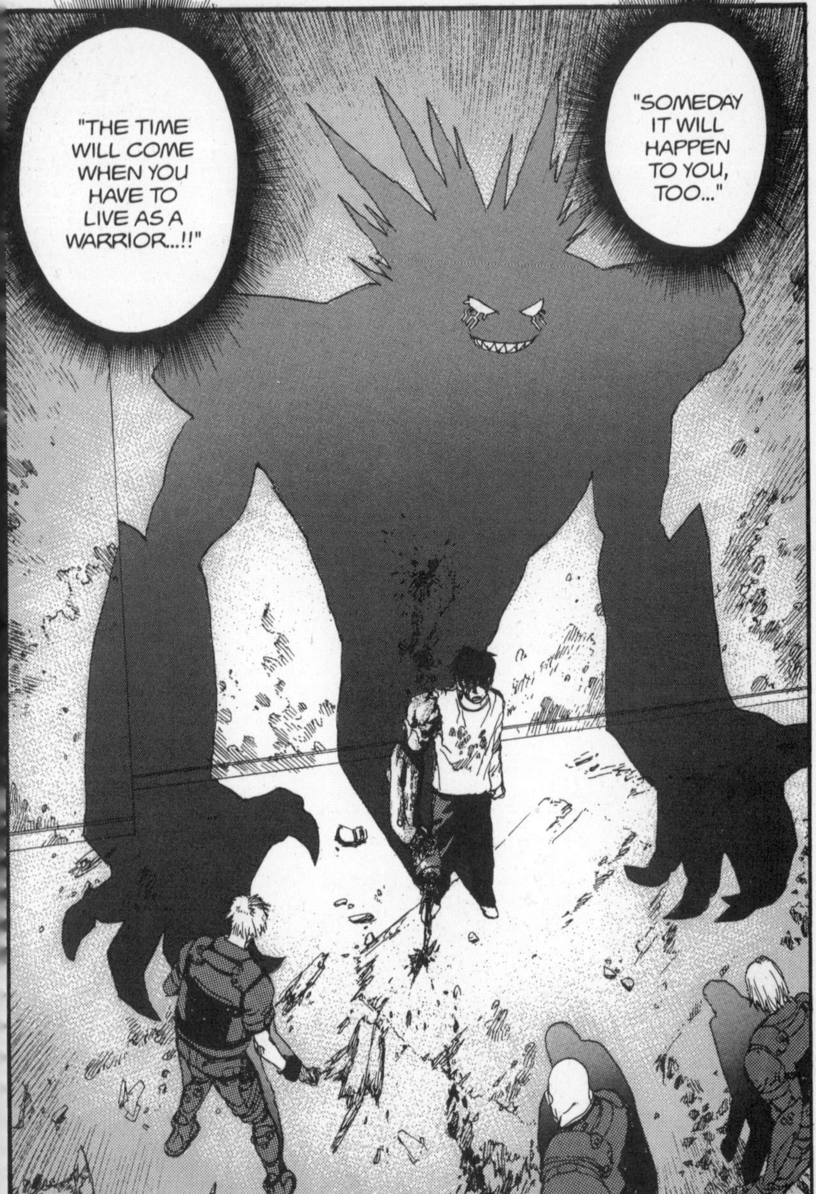
"SOMEDAY IT WILL HAPPEN TO YOU, TOO..."
"THE TIME WILL COME WHEN YOU HAVE TO LIVE AS A WARRIOR...!!"

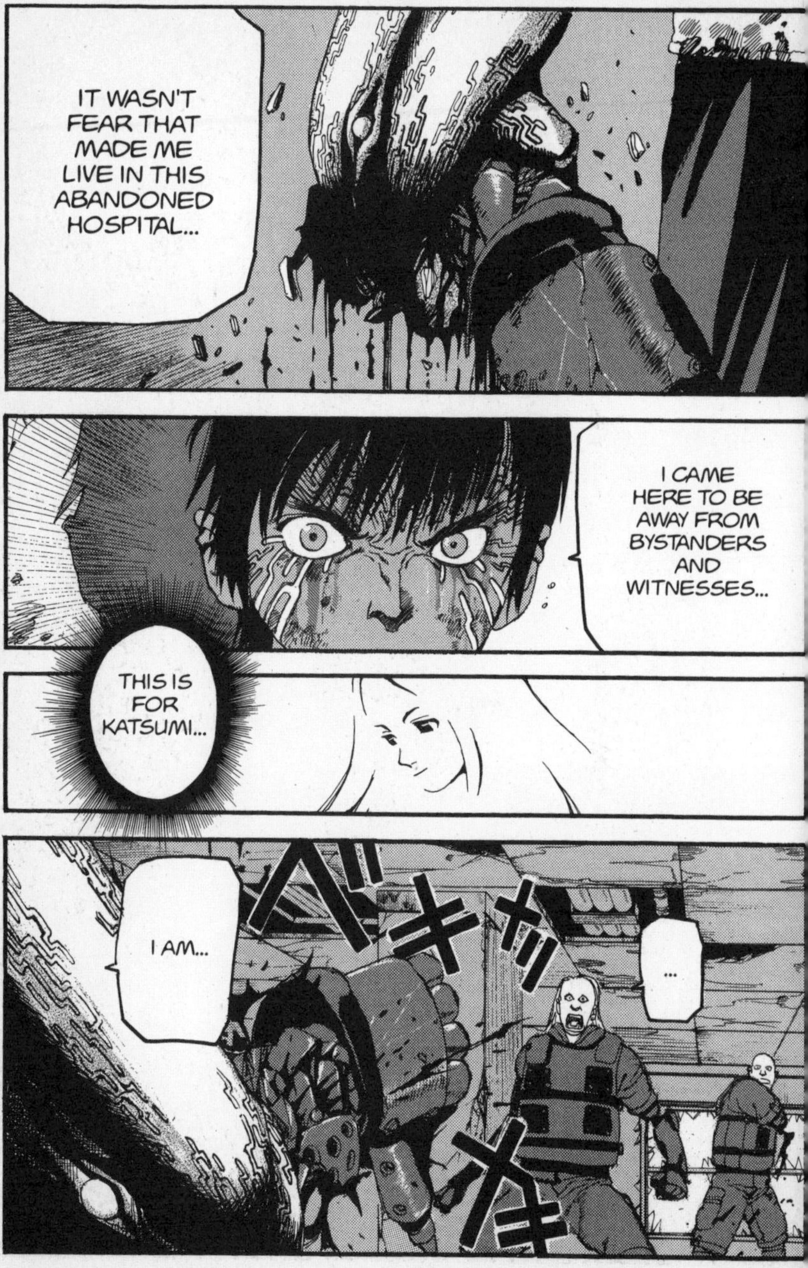
IT WASN'T FEAR THAT MADE ME LIVE IN THIS ABANDONED HOSPITAL...
I CAME HERE TO BE AWAY FROM BYSTANDERS AND WITNESSES...
THIS IS FOR KATSUMI...
ベキッ
I AM...
...
メキ

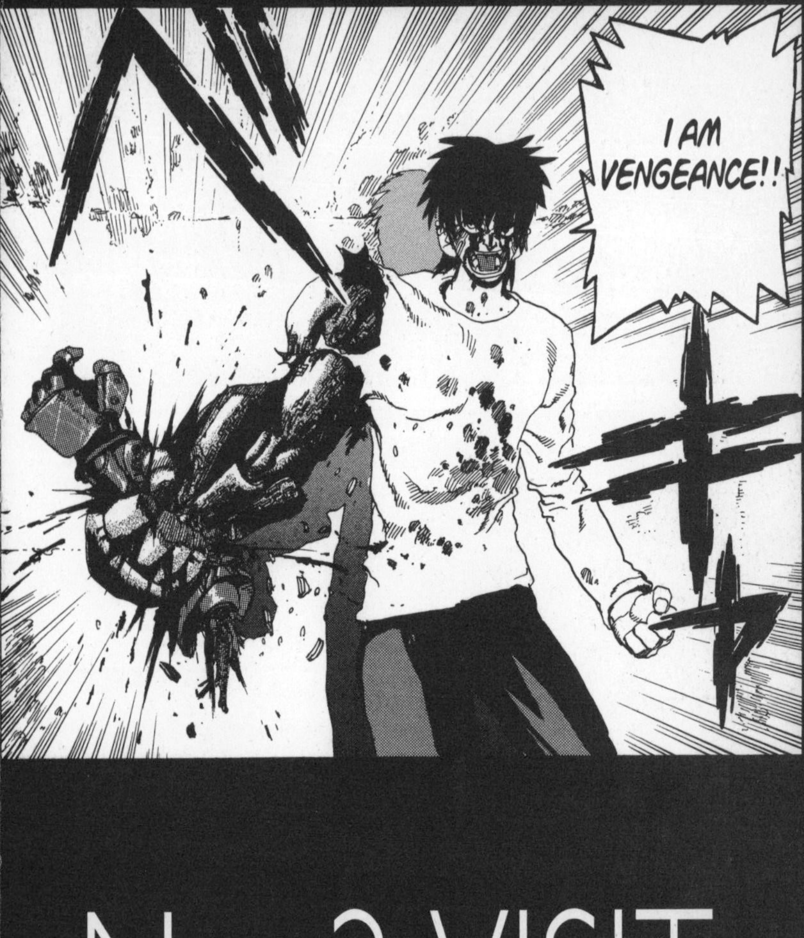
I AM VENGEANCE!!

No. 2 VISIT

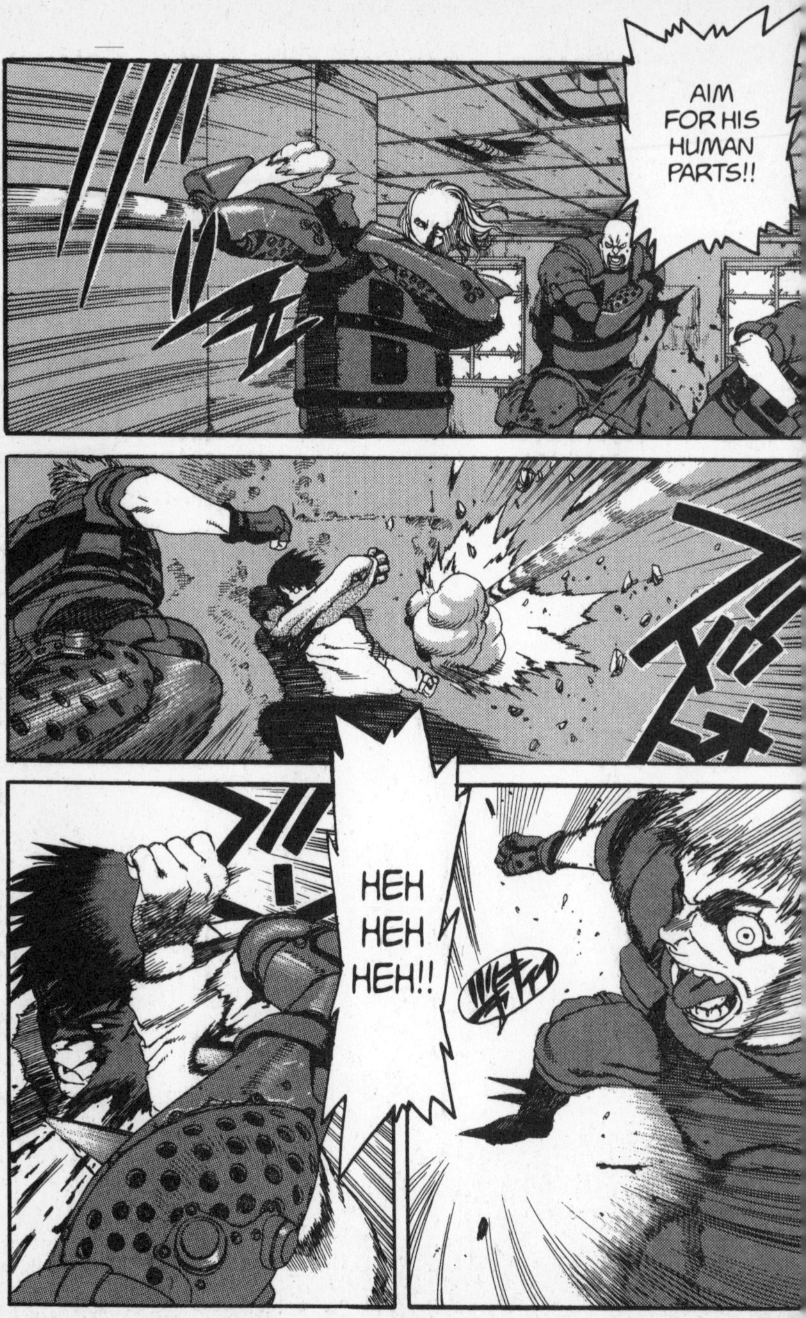
AIM FOR HIS HUMAN PARTS!!
HEH HEH HEH!!

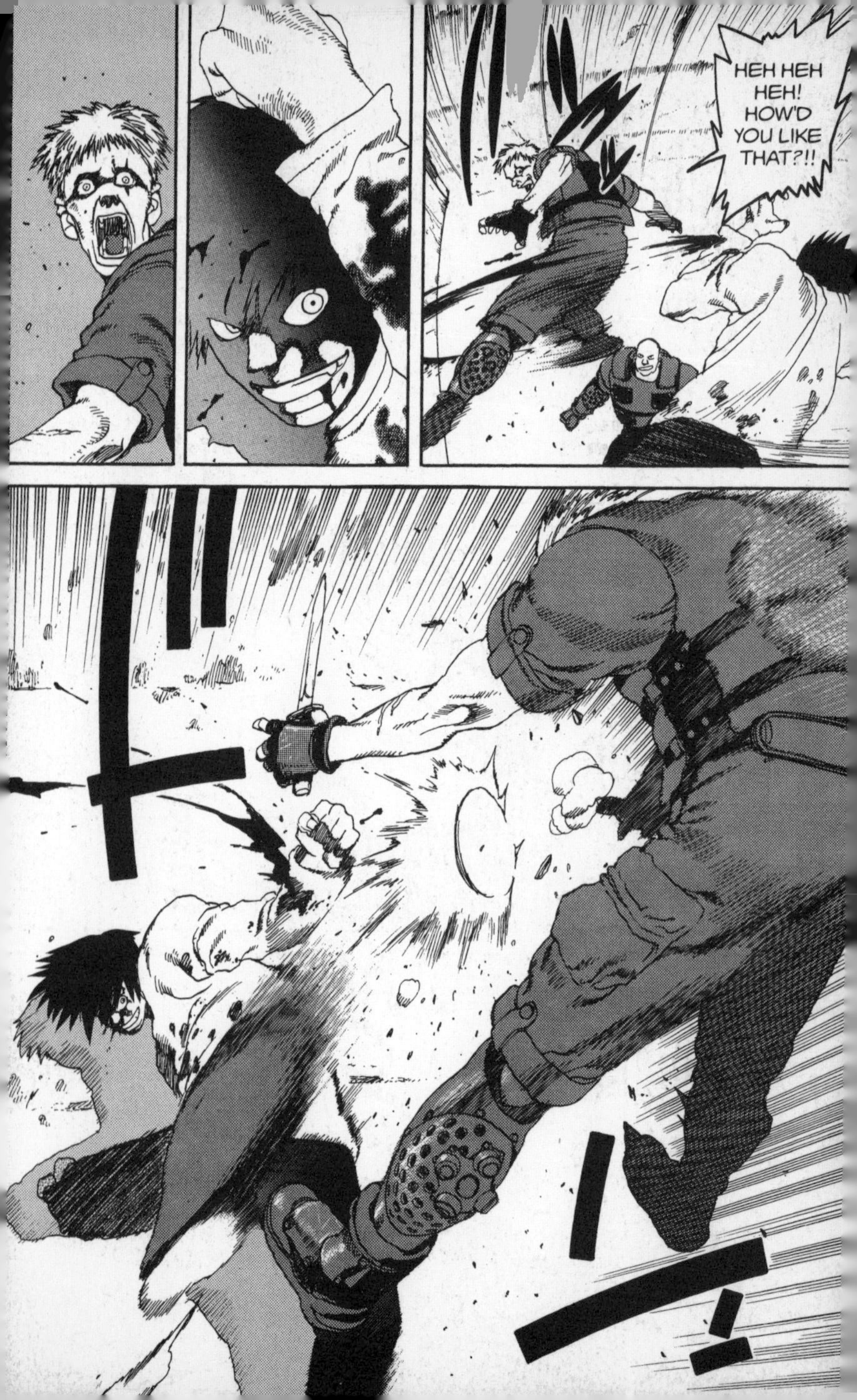
HEH HEH HEH! HOW'D YOU LIKE THAT?!!

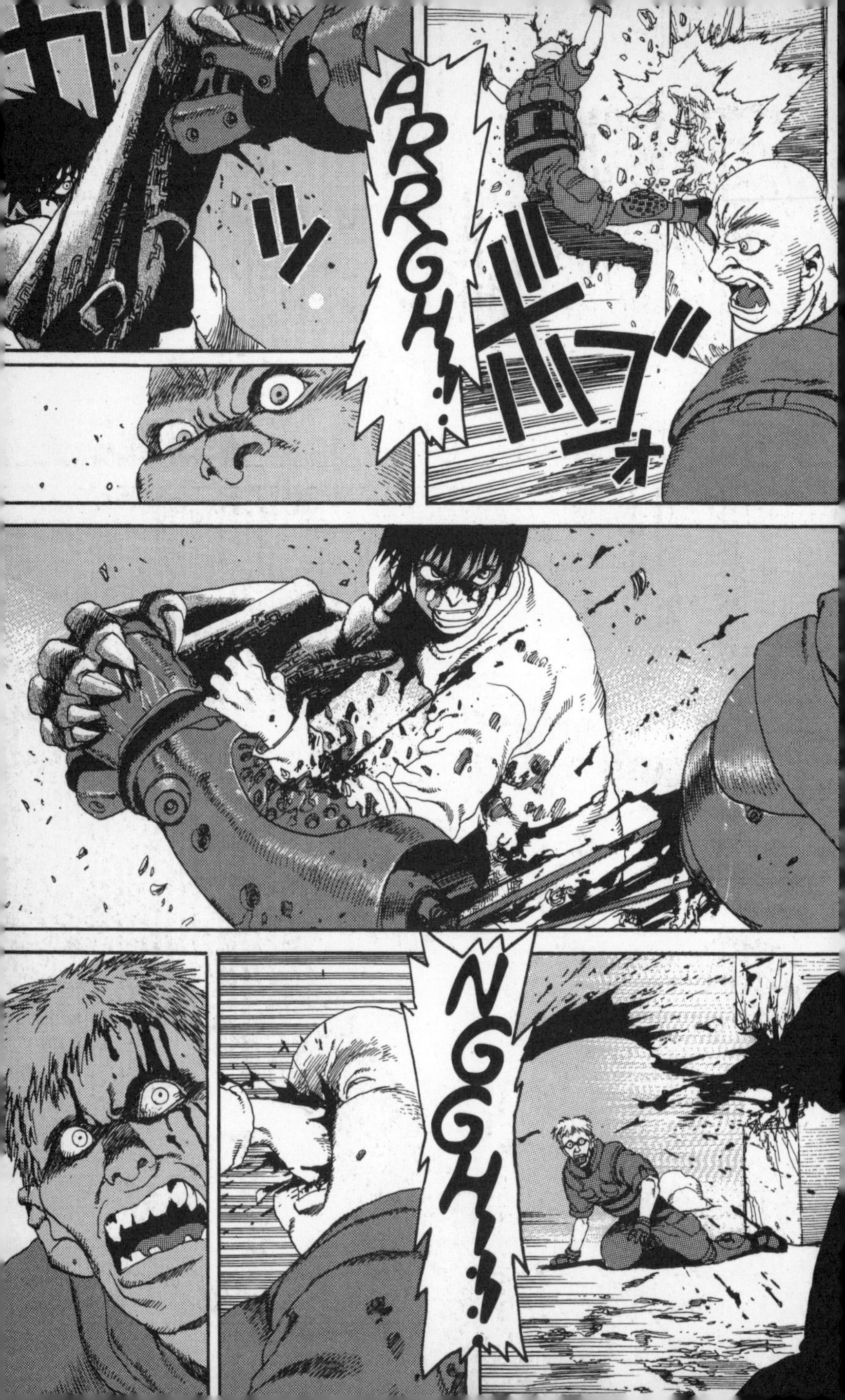
ボブォ
ARRGH...!!
ッ
NGGGH...!!

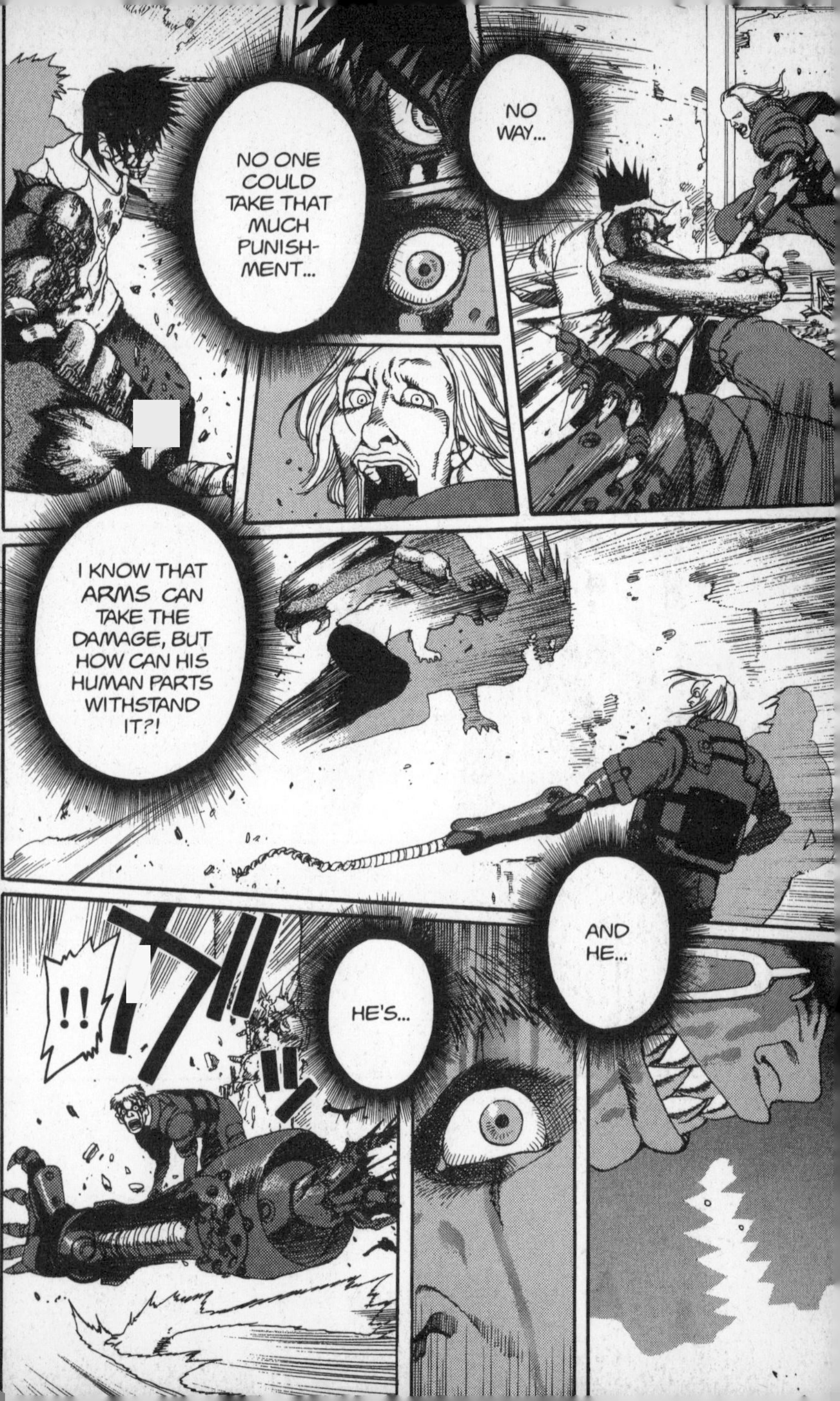
NO WAY...
NO ONE COULD TAKE THAT MUCH PUNISHMENT...
I KNOW THAT ARMS CAN TAKE THE DAMAGE, BUT HOW CAN HIS HUMAN PARTS WITHSTAND IT?!
AND HE...
HE'S...
!!

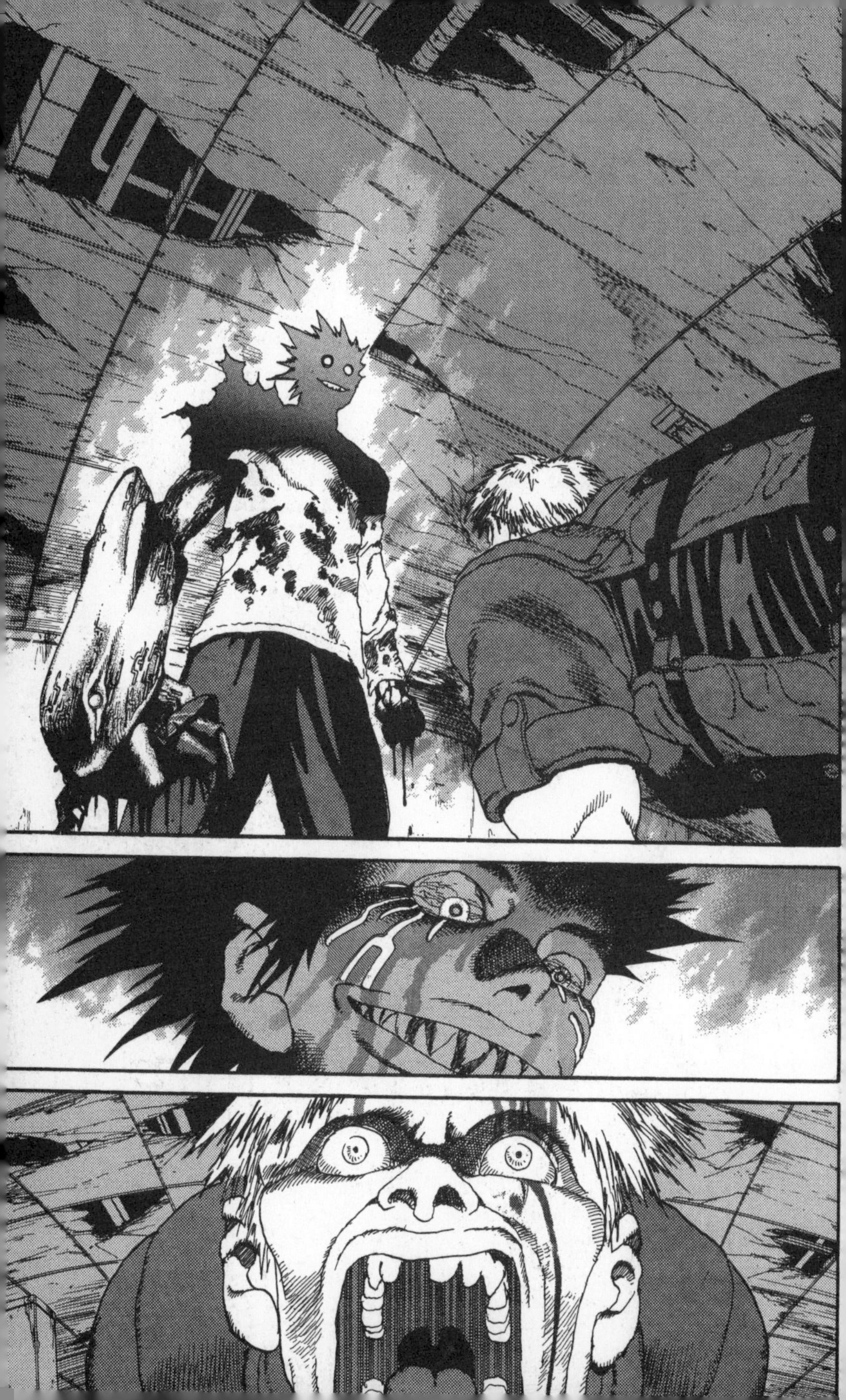

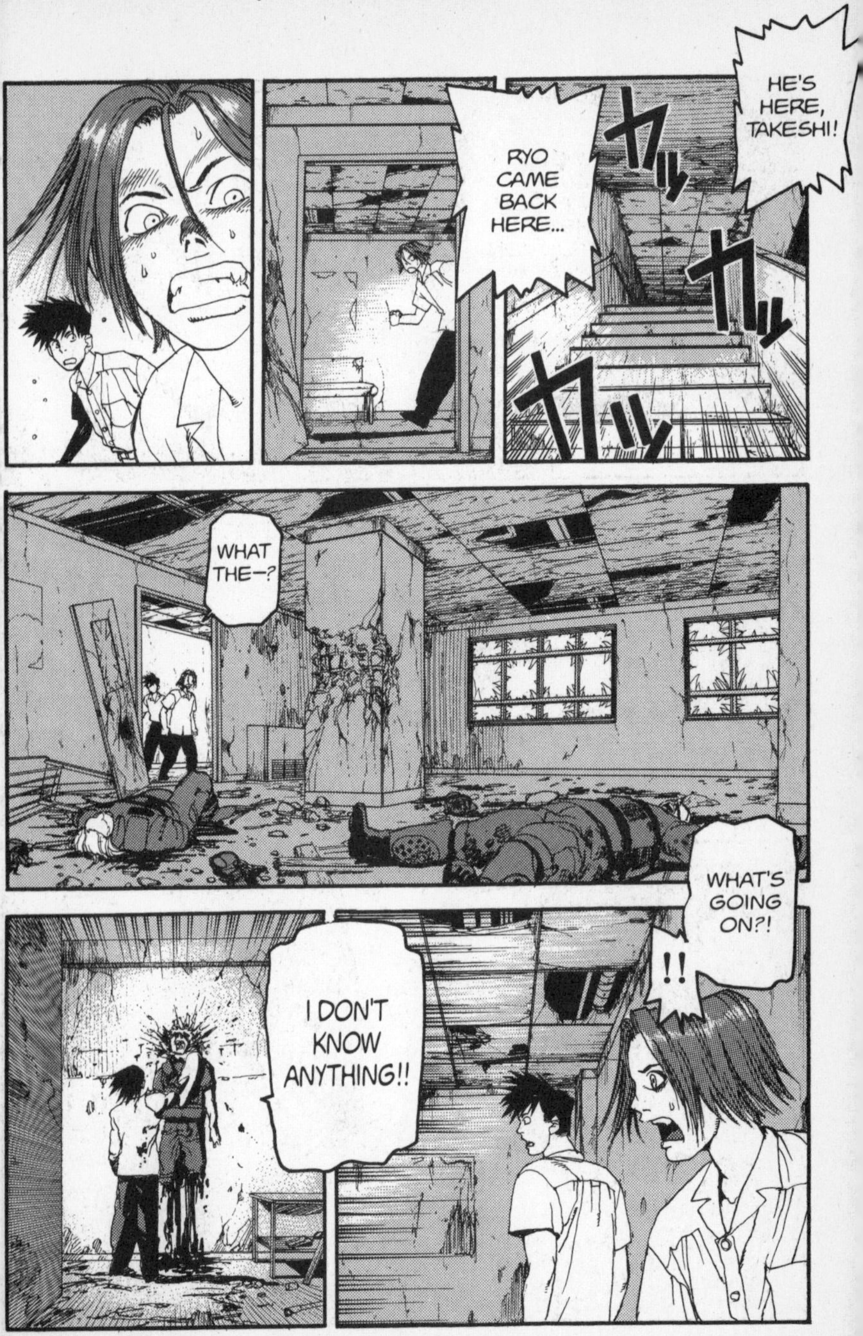
HE'S HERE, TAKESHI!
RYO CAME BACK HERE...
WHAT THE—?
WHAT'S GOING ON?!
!!
I DON'T KNOW ANYTHING!!

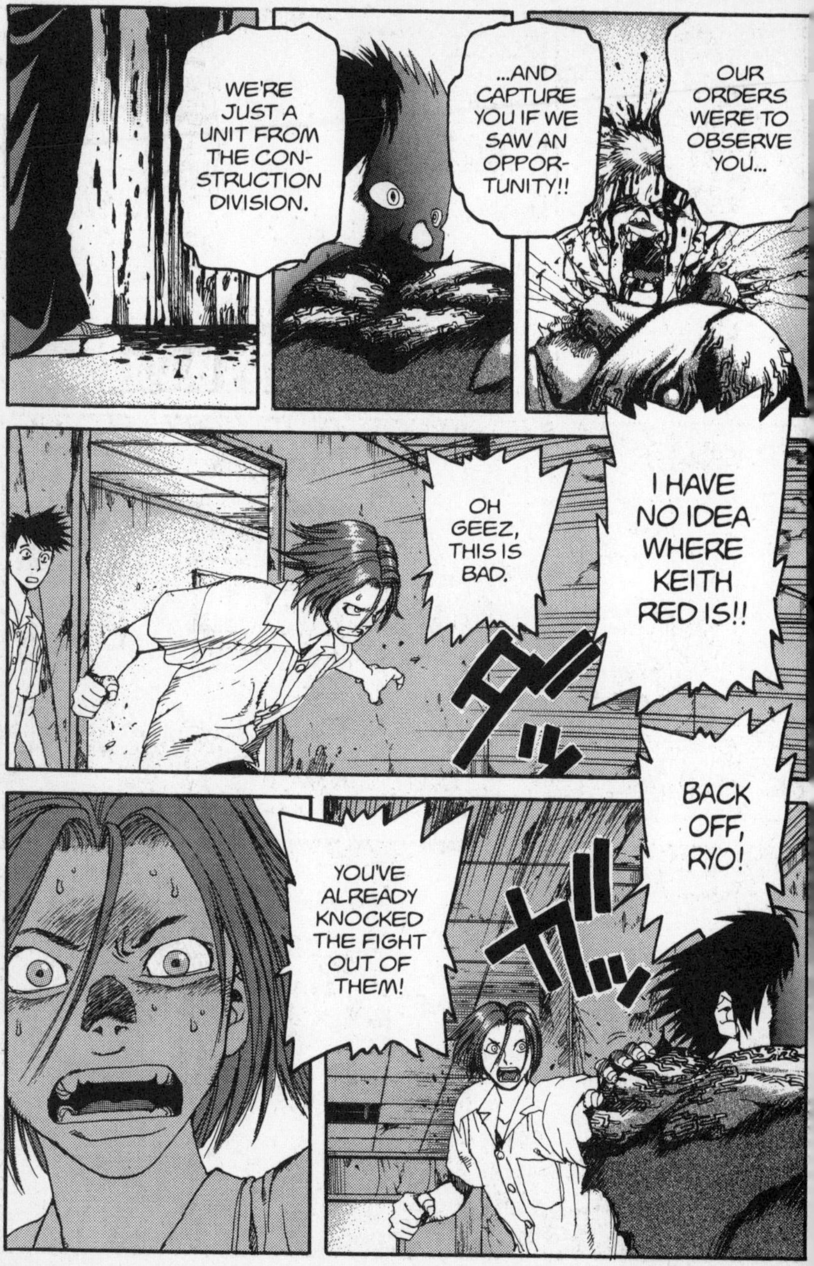
OUR ORDERS WERE TO OBSERVE YOU...
...AND CAPTURE YOU IF WE SAW AN OPPOR-TUNITY!!
WE'RE JUST A UNIT FROM THE CON-STRUCTION DIVISION.
I HAVE NO IDEA WHERE KEITH RED IS!!
OH GEEZ, THIS IS BAD.
ダッ
BACK OFF, RYO!
ガッ
YOU'VE ALREADY KNOCKED THE FIGHT OUT OF THEM!

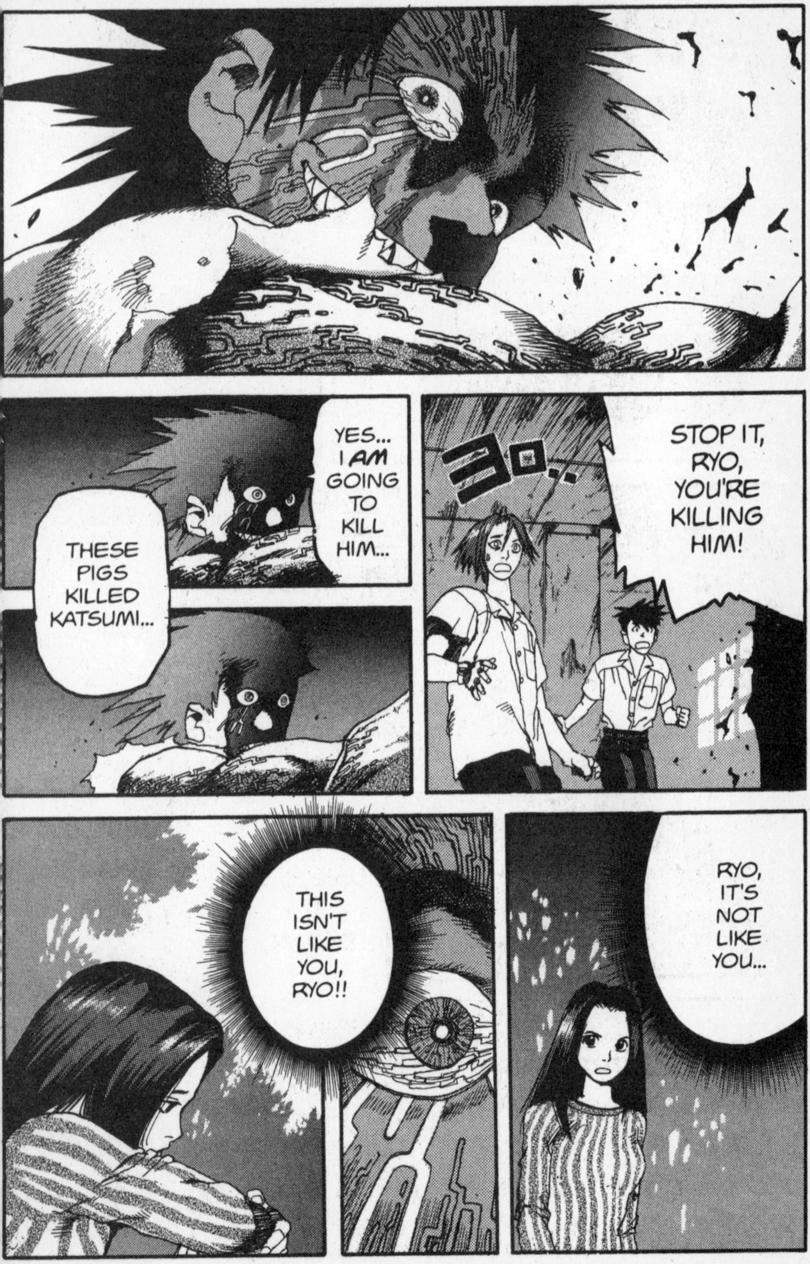
STOP IT, RYO, YOU'RE KILLING HIM!
YES... I AM GOING TO KILL HIM...
THESE PIGS KILLED KATSUMI...
RYO, IT'S NOT LIKE YOU...
THIS ISN'T LIKE YOU, RYO!!

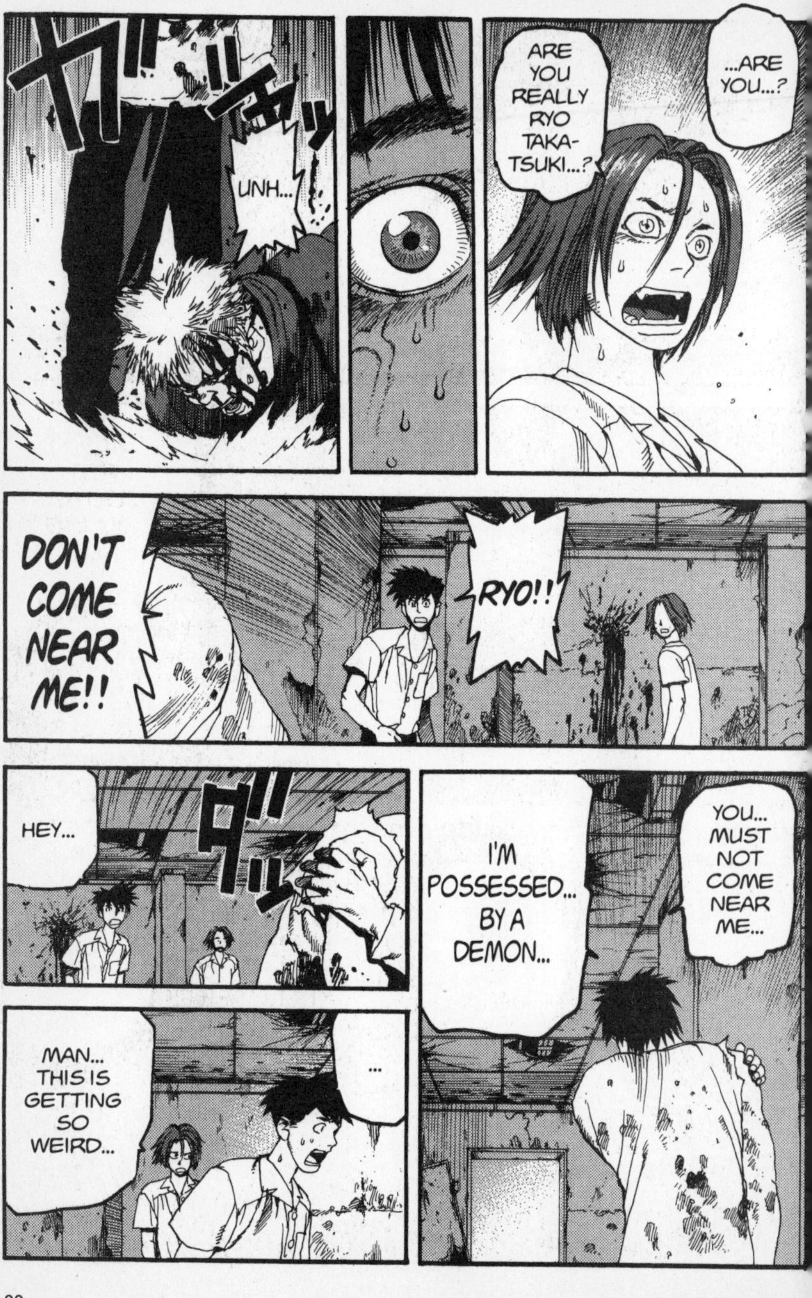
...ARE YOU...?
ARE YOU REALLY RYO TAKA-TSUKI...?
UNH...
RYO!!
DON'T COME NEAR ME!!
YOU... MUST NOT COME NEAR ME...
I'M POSSESSED... BY A DEMON...
HEY...
...
MAN... THIS IS GETTING SO WEIRD...

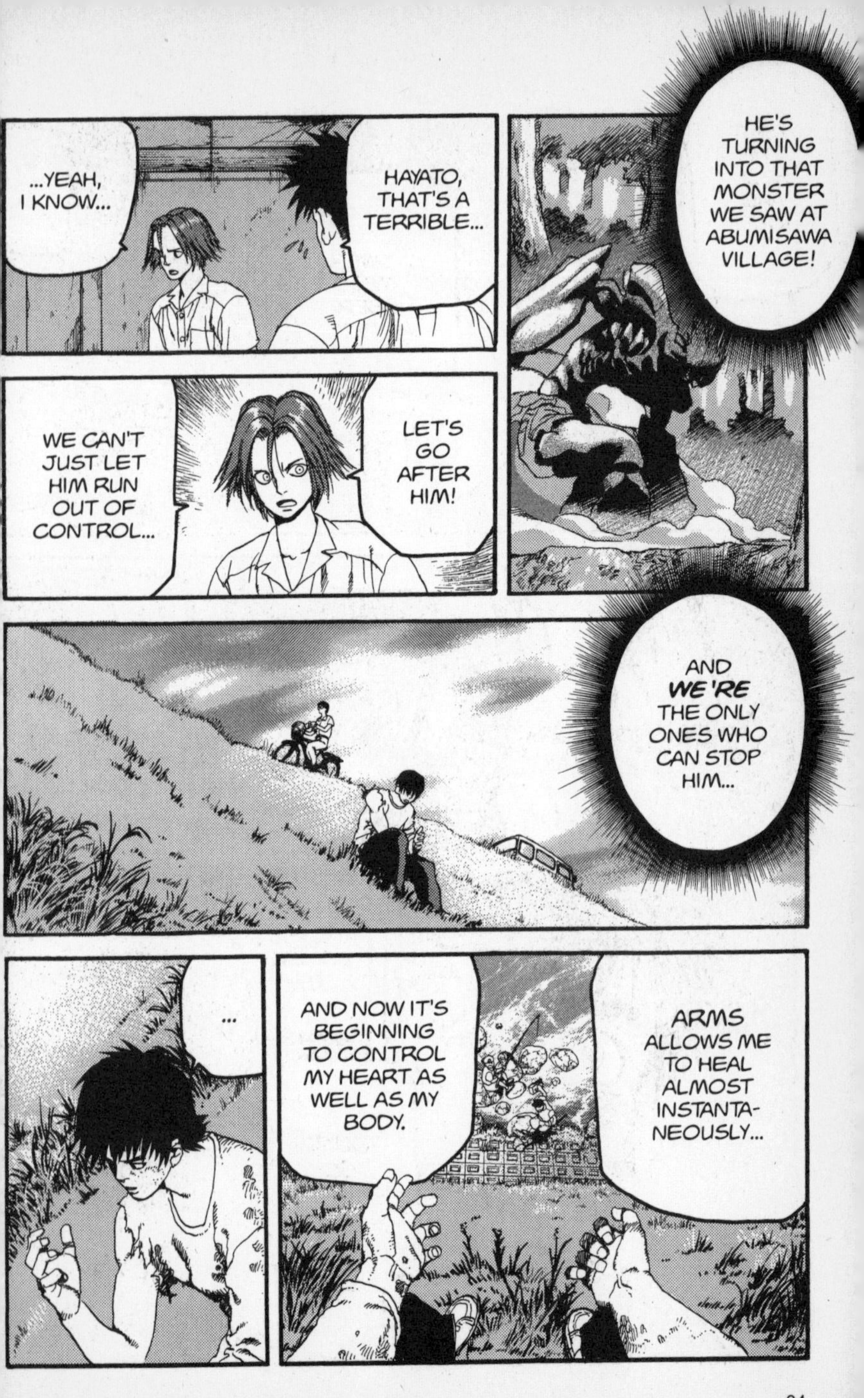
HE'S TURNING INTO THAT MONSTER WE SAW AT ABUMISAWA VILLAGE!
HAYATO, THAT'S A TERRIBLE...
...YEAH, I KNOW...
LET'S GO AFTER HIM!
WE CAN'T JUST LET HIM RUN OUT OF CONTROL...
AND **WE'RE** THE ONLY ONES WHO CAN STOP HIM...
ARMS ALLOWS ME TO HEAL ALMOST INSTANTA-NEOUSLY...
AND NOW IT'S BEGINNING TO CONTROL MY HEART AS WELL AS MY BODY.
...

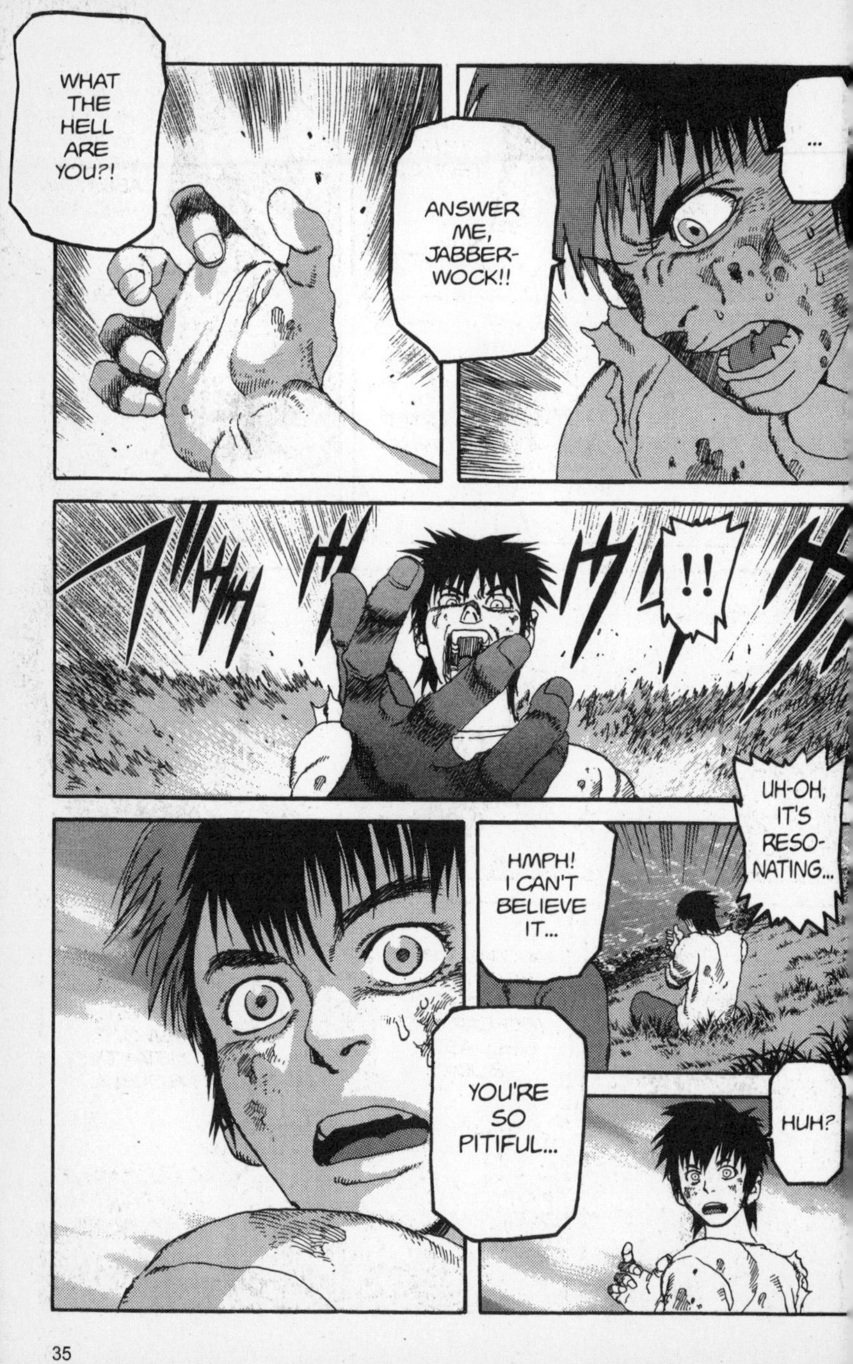
...
ANSWER ME, JABBER-WOCK!!
WHAT THE HELL ARE YOU?!
!!
UH-OH, IT'S RESO-NATING...
HMPH! I CAN'T BELIEVE IT...
YOU'RE SO PITIFUL...
HUH?

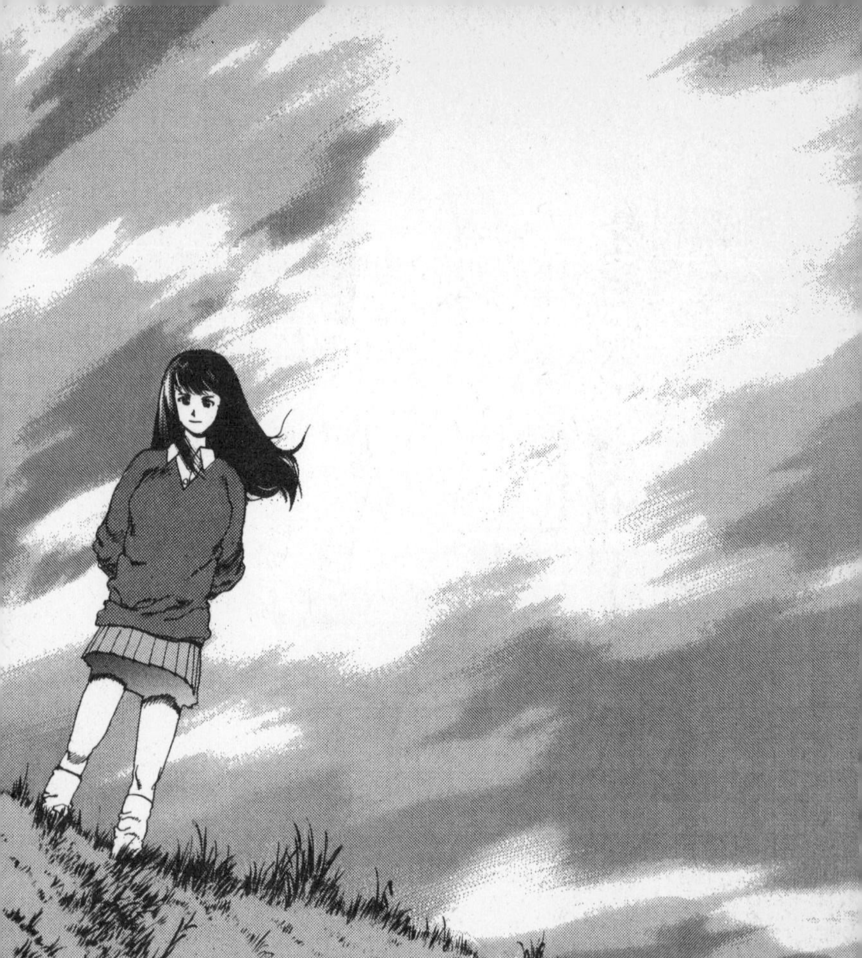
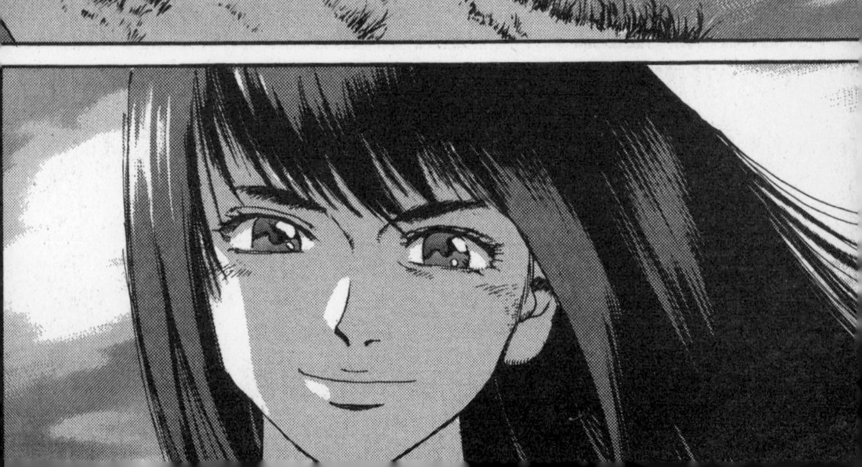

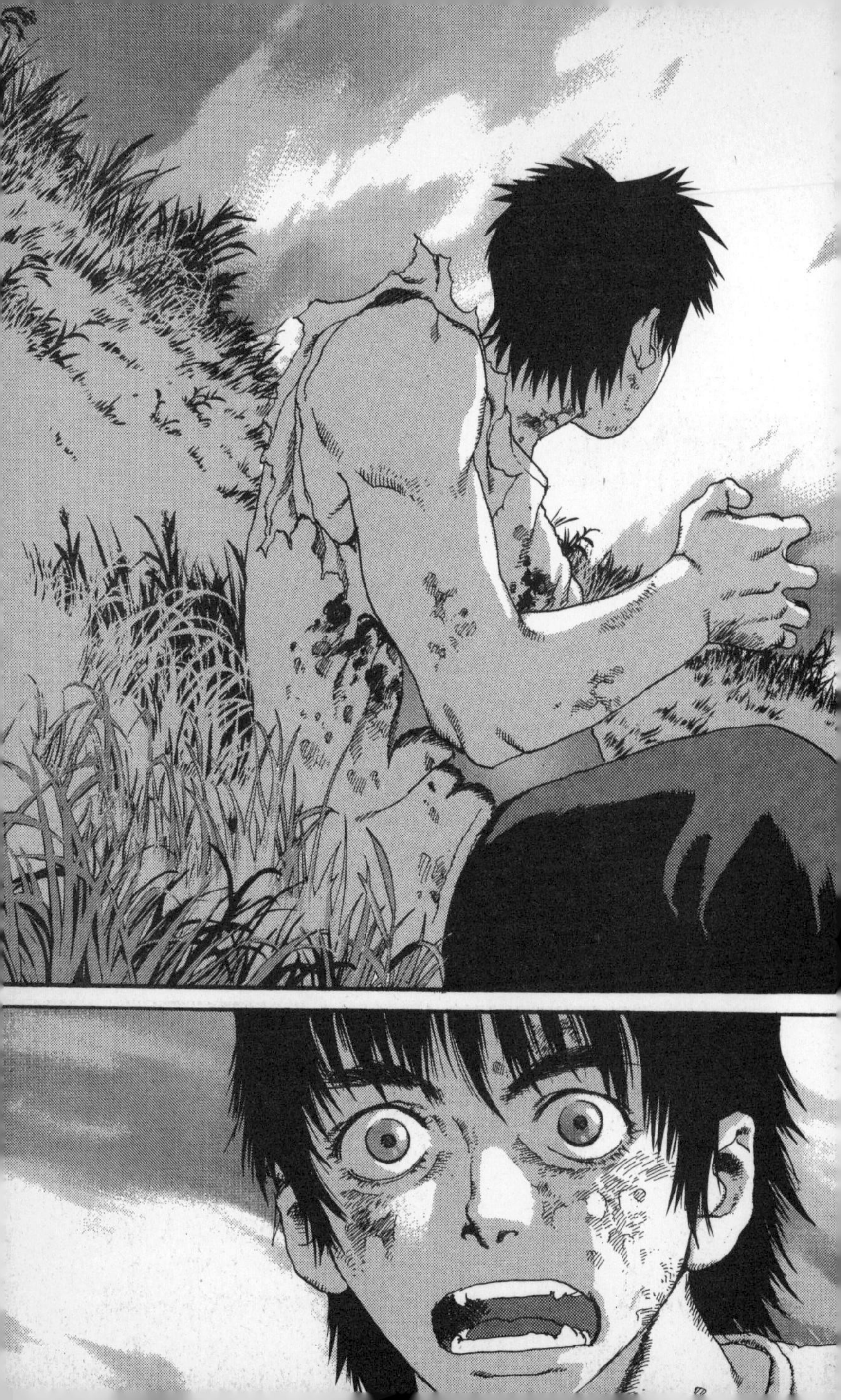

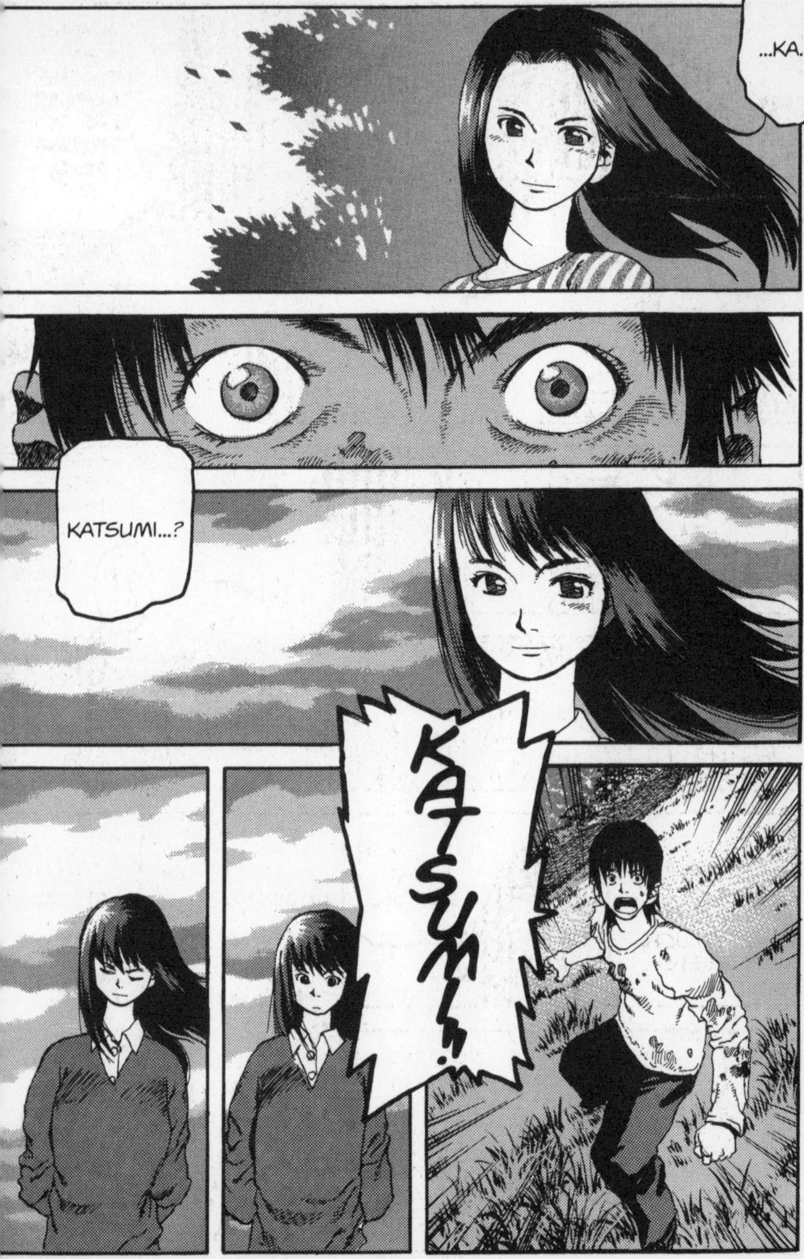
...KA...
KATSUMI...?
KATSUMI!!

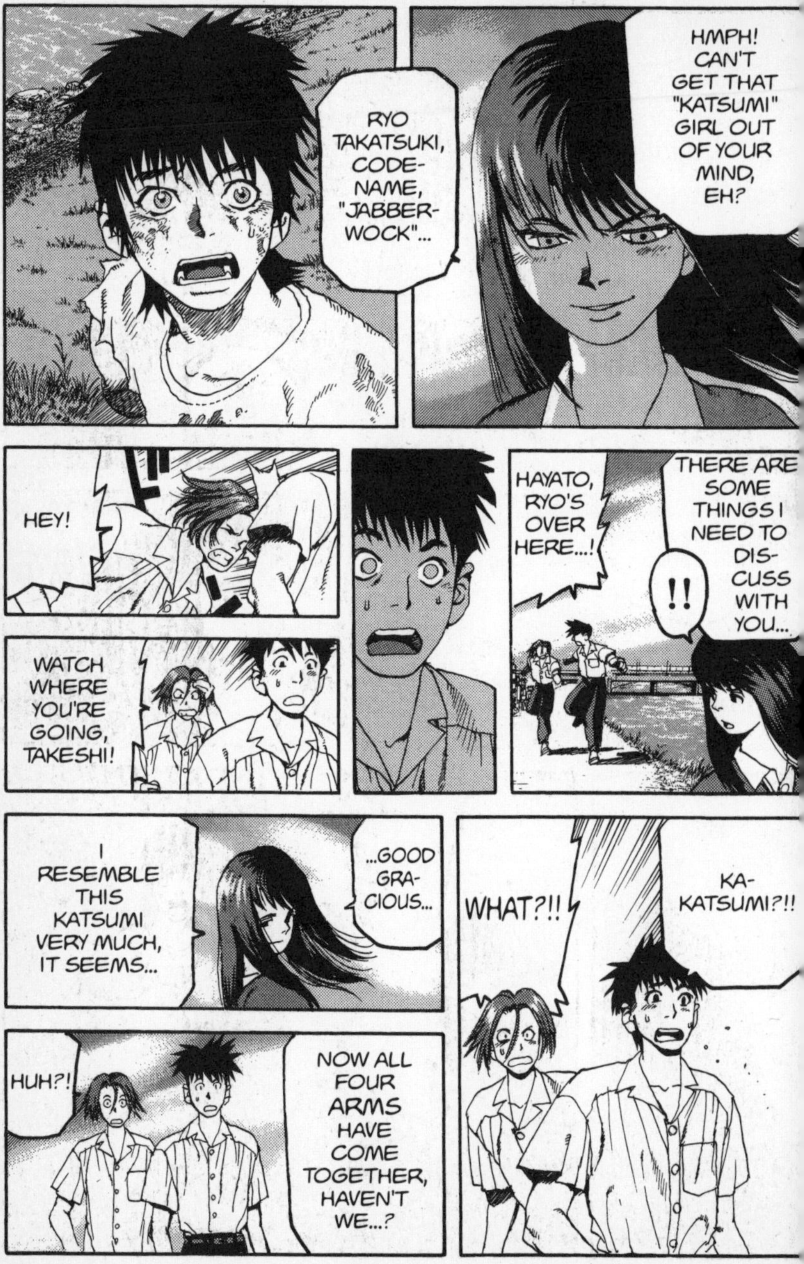
HMPH! CAN'T GET THAT "KATSUMI" GIRL OUT OF YOUR MIND, EH?
RYO TAKATSUKI, CODE-NAME, "JABBER-WOCK"...
THERE ARE SOME THINGS I NEED TO DIS-CUSS WITH YOU...
HAYATO, RYO'S OVER HERE...!
!!
HEY!
WATCH WHERE YOU'RE GOING, TAKESHI!
KA-KATSUMI?!!
WHAT?!!
...GOOD GRA-CIOUS...
I RESEMBLE THIS KATSUMI VERY MUCH, IT SEEMS...
NOW ALL FOUR ARMS HAVE COME TOGETHER, HAVEN'T WE...?
HUH?!

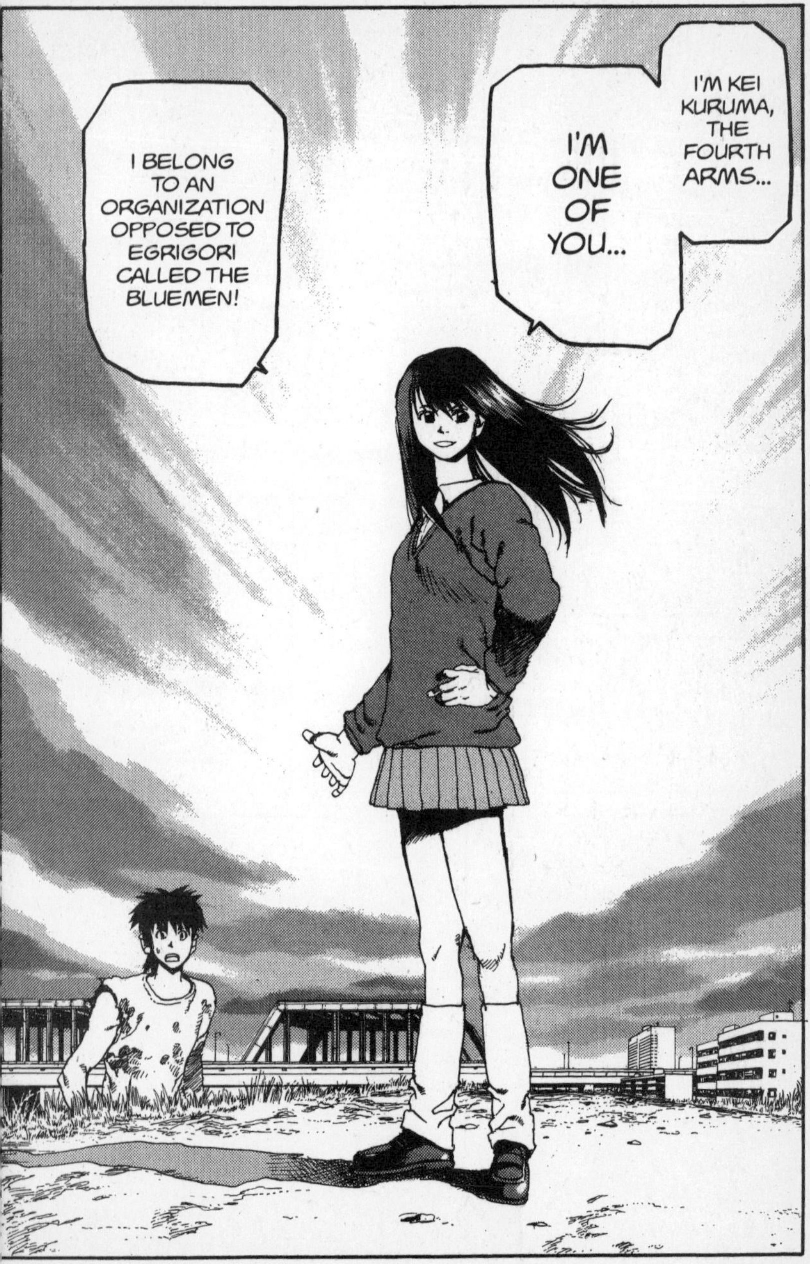
I'M KEI KURUMA, THE FOURTH ARMS...
I'M ONE OF YOU...
I BELONG TO AN ORGANIZATION OPPOSED TO EGRIGORI CALLED THE BLUEMEN!

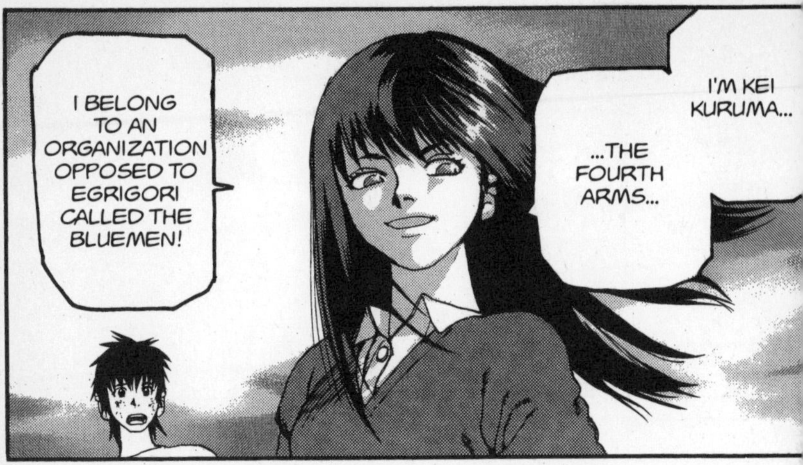
I'M KEI KURUMA...
...THE FOURTH ARMS...
I BELONG TO AN ORGANIZATION OPPOSED TO EGRIGORI CALLED THE BLUEMEN!

No. 3 EVIL EYE

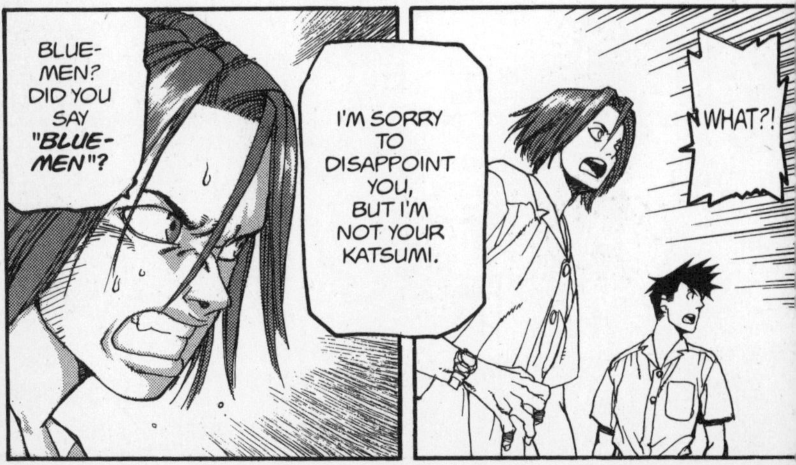
BLUE-MEN? DID YOU SAY "*BLUE-MEN*"?
I'M SORRY TO DISAPPOINT YOU, BUT I'M NOT YOUR KATSUMI.
WHAT?!

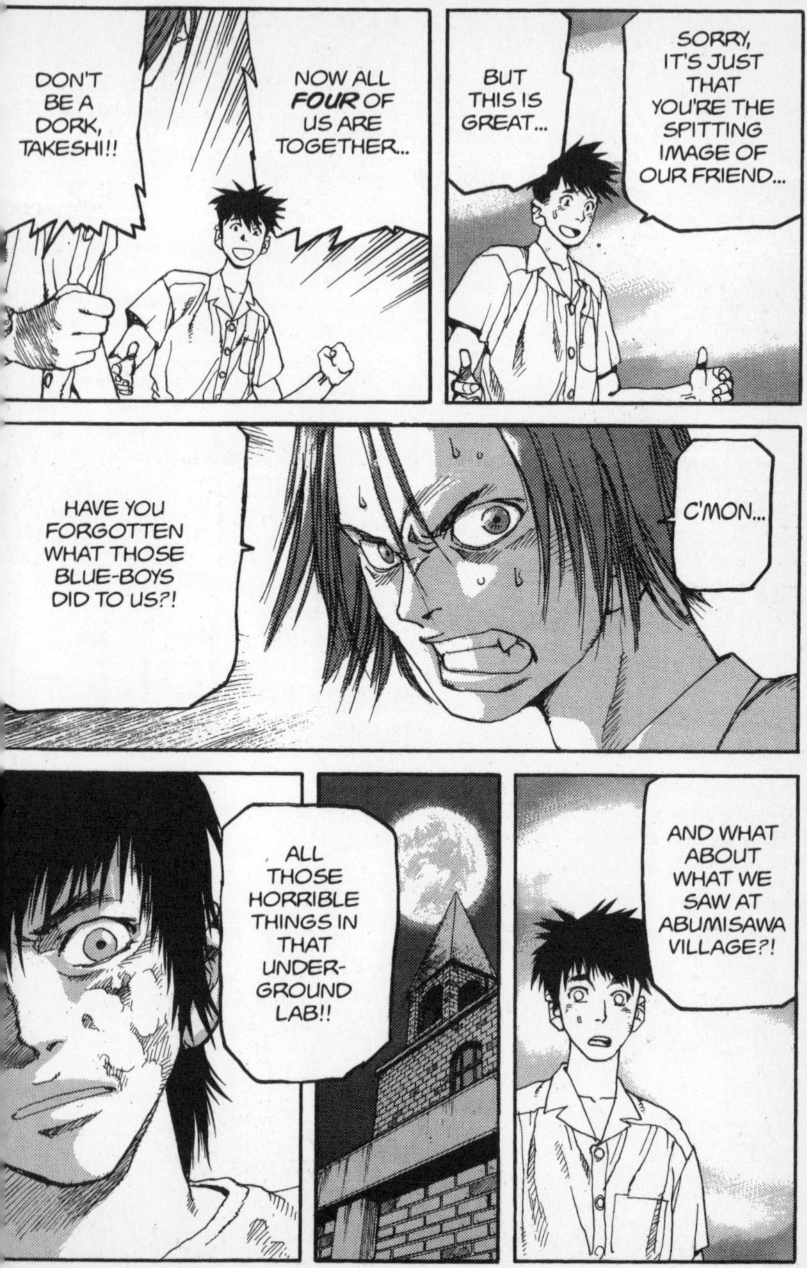
SORRY, IT'S JUST THAT YOU'RE THE SPITTING IMAGE OF OUR FRIEND...
BUT THIS IS GREAT...
NOW ALL **FOUR** OF US ARE TOGETHER...
DON'T BE A DORK, TAKESHI!!
C'MON...
HAVE YOU FORGOTTEN WHAT THOSE BLUE-BOYS DID TO US?!
AND WHAT ABOUT WHAT WE SAW AT ABUMISAWA VILLAGE?!
ALL THOSE HORRIBLE THINGS IN THAT UNDER-GROUND LAB!!

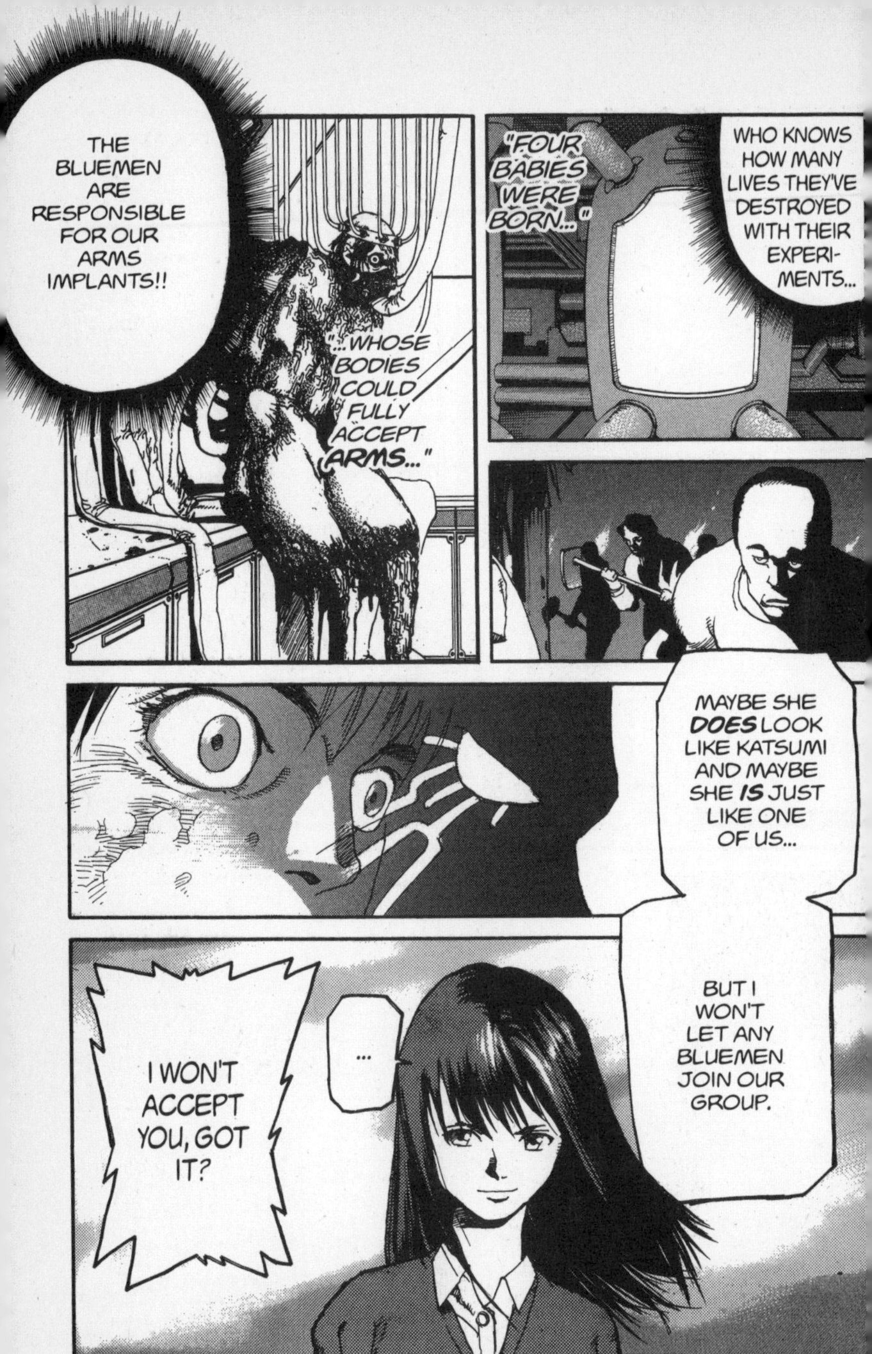
WHO KNOWS HOW MANY LIVES THEY'VE DESTROYED WITH THEIR EXPERI-MENTS...
"FOUR BABIES WERE BORN..."
THE BLUEMEN ARE RESPONSIBLE FOR OUR ARMS IMPLANTS!!
"...WHOSE BODIES COULD FULLY ACCEPT ARMS..."
MAYBE SHE DOES LOOK LIKE KATSUMI AND MAYBE SHE IS JUST LIKE ONE OF US...
BUT I WON'T LET ANY BLUEMEN JOIN OUR GROUP.
...
I WON'T ACCEPT YOU, GOT IT?

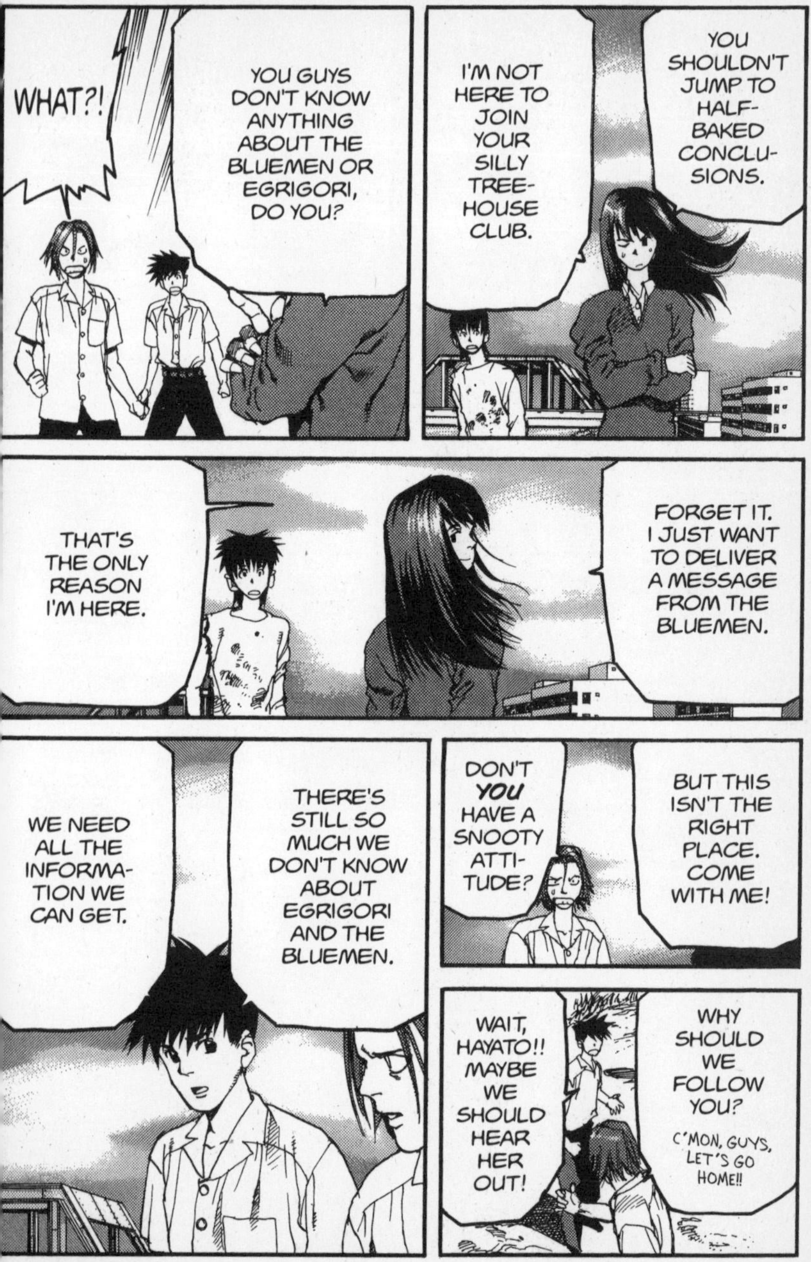
YOU SHOULDN'T JUMP TO HALF-BAKED CONCLUSIONS.
I'M NOT HERE TO JOIN YOUR SILLY TREE-HOUSE CLUB.
YOU GUYS DON'T KNOW ANYTHING ABOUT THE BLUEMEN OR EGRIGORI, DO YOU?
WHAT?!
FORGET IT. I JUST WANT TO DELIVER A MESSAGE FROM THE BLUEMEN.
THAT'S THE ONLY REASON I'M HERE.
BUT THIS ISN'T THE RIGHT PLACE. COME WITH ME!
DON'T *YOU* HAVE A SNOOTY ATTITUDE?
WHY SHOULD WE FOLLOW YOU?
C'MON, GUYS, LET'S GO HOME!!
WAIT, HAYATO!! MAYBE WE SHOULD HEAR HER OUT!
THERE'S STILL SO MUCH WE DON'T KNOW ABOUT EGRIGORI AND THE BLUEMEN.
WE NEED ALL THE INFORMATION WE CAN GET.

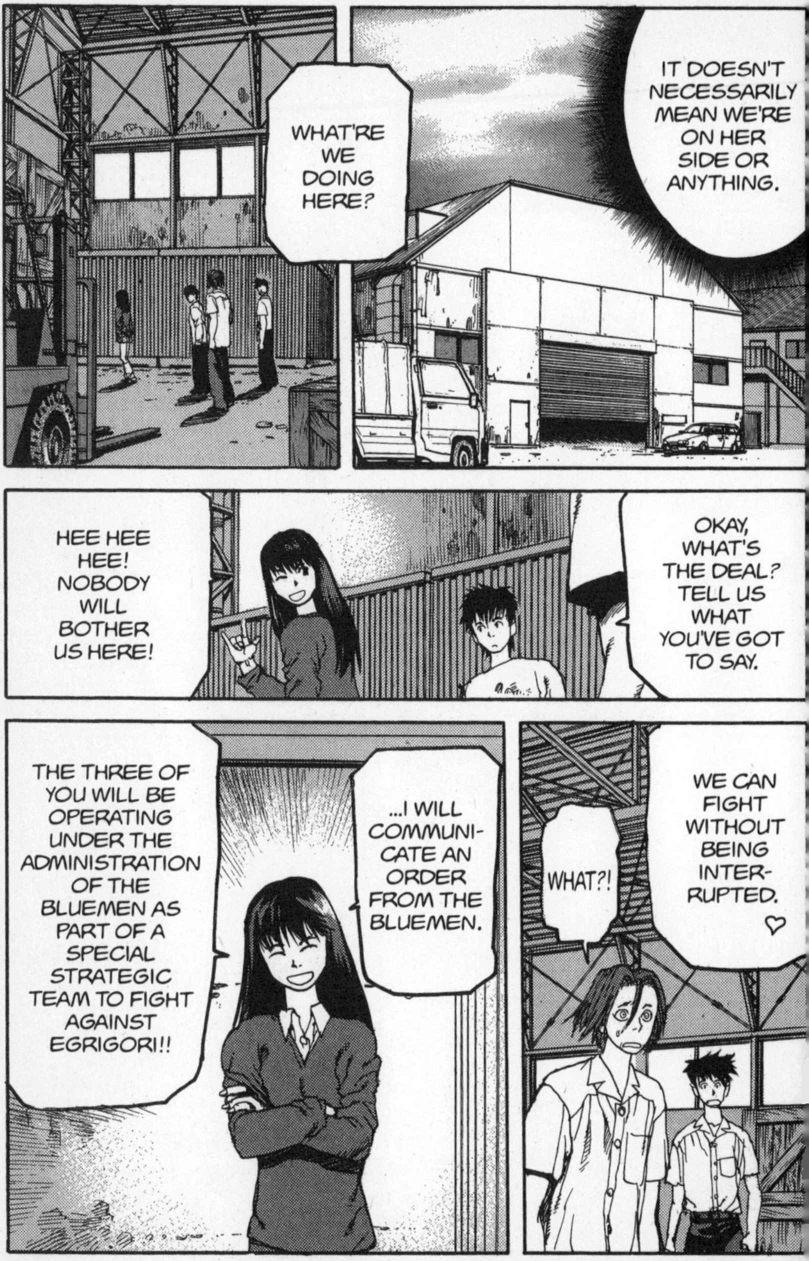
WHAT'RE WE DOING HERE?
IT DOESN'T NECESSARILY MEAN WE'RE ON HER SIDE OR ANYTHING.
HEE HEE HEE! NOBODY WILL BOTHER US HERE!
OKAY, WHAT'S THE DEAL? TELL US WHAT YOU'VE GOT TO SAY.
THE THREE OF YOU WILL BE OPERATING UNDER THE ADMINISTRATION OF THE BLUEMEN AS PART OF A SPECIAL STRATEGIC TEAM TO FIGHT AGAINST EGRIGORI!!
...I WILL COMMUNICATE AN ORDER FROM THE BLUEMEN.
WHAT?!
WE CAN FIGHT WITHOUT BEING INTERRUPTED. ♡

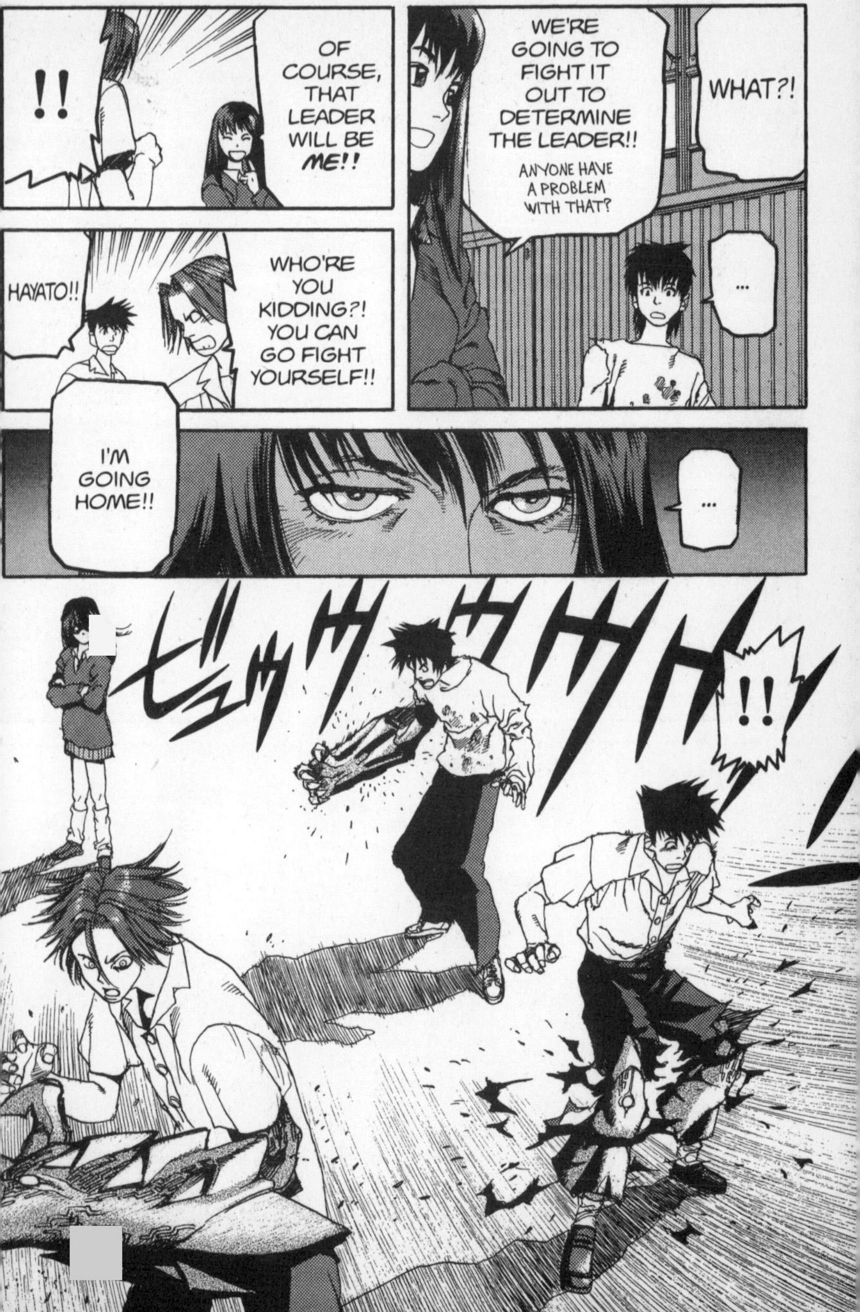
!!
OF COURSE, THAT LEADER WILL BE *ME!!*
WE'RE GOING TO FIGHT IT OUT TO DETERMINE THE LEADER!!
ANYONE HAVE A PROBLEM WITH THAT?
WHAT?!
...
HAYATO!!
WHO'RE YOU KIDDING?! YOU CAN GO FIGHT YOURSELF!!
I'M GOING HOME!!
...
ビュッ
!!

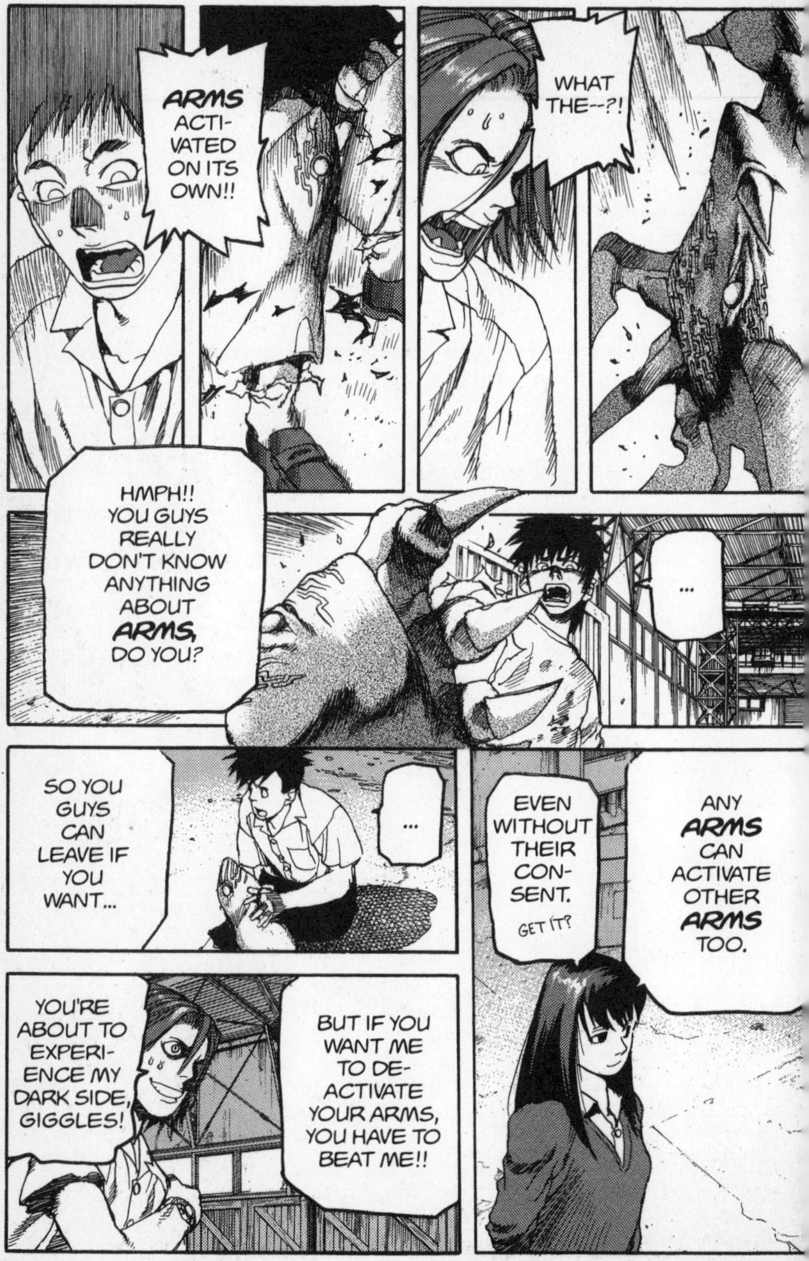
WHAT THE--?!
ARMS ACTIVATED ON ITS OWN!!
...
HMPH!! YOU GUYS REALLY DON'T KNOW ANYTHING ABOUT ARMS, DO YOU?
ANY ARMS CAN ACTIVATE OTHER ARMS TOO.
EVEN WITHOUT THEIR CONSENT.
GET IT?
...
SO YOU GUYS CAN LEAVE IF YOU WANT...
BUT IF YOU WANT ME TO DE-ACTIVATE YOUR ARMS, YOU HAVE TO BEAT ME!!
YOU'RE ABOUT TO EXPERIENCE MY DARK SIDE, GIGGLES!

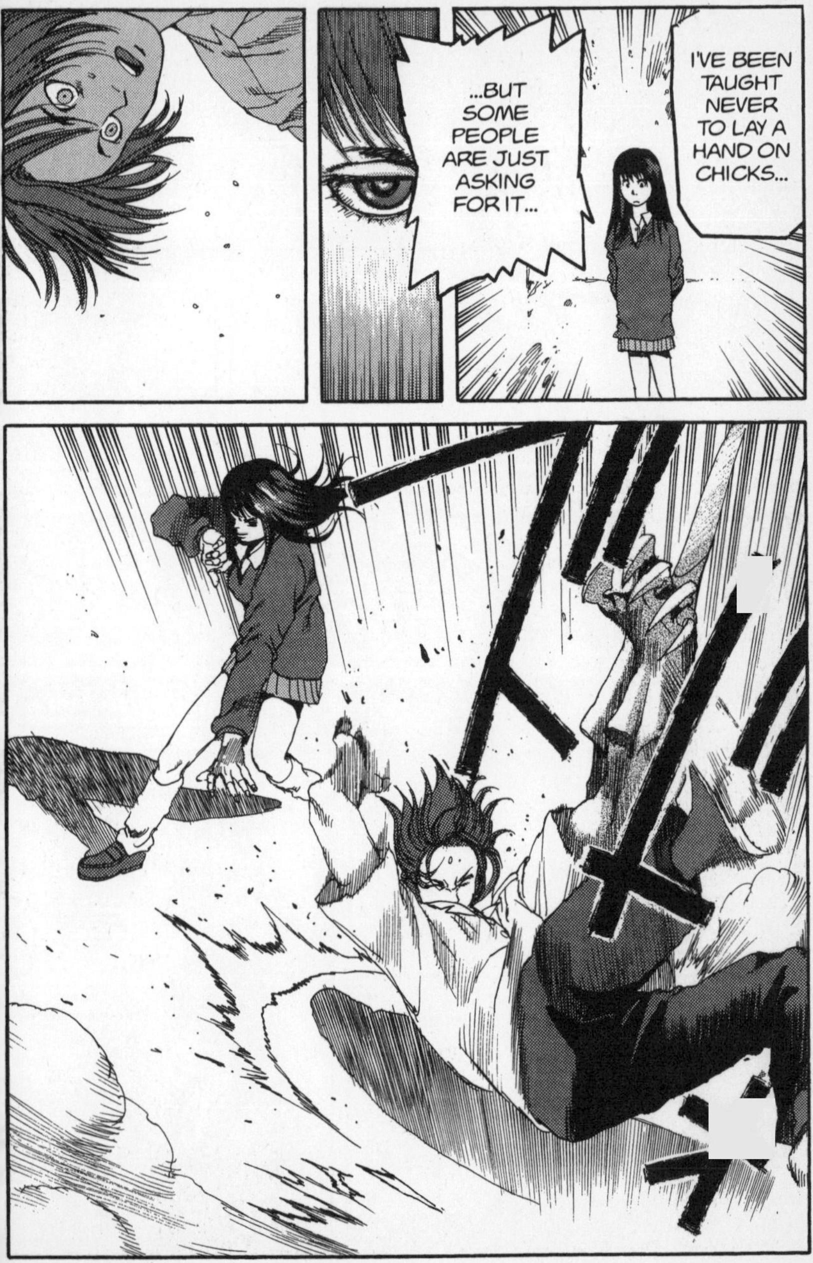
I'VE BEEN TAUGHT NEVER TO LAY A HAND ON CHICKS...
...BUT SOME PEOPLE ARE JUST ASKING FOR IT...

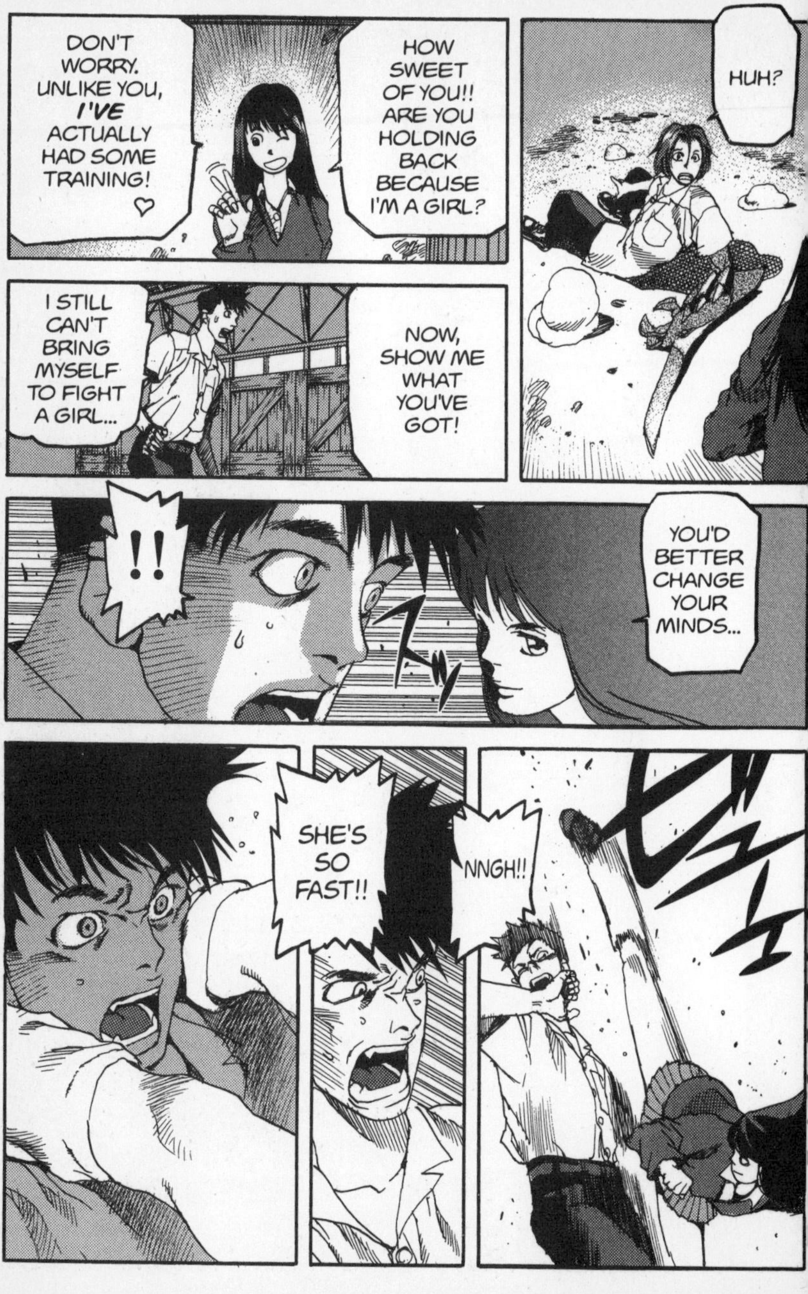
HUH?
HOW SWEET OF YOU!! ARE YOU HOLDING BACK BECAUSE I'M A GIRL?
DON'T WORRY. UNLIKE YOU, *I'VE* ACTUALLY HAD SOME TRAINING! ♡
NOW, SHOW ME WHAT YOU'VE GOT!
I STILL CAN'T BRING MYSELF TO FIGHT A GIRL...
YOU'D BETTER CHANGE YOUR MINDS...
!!
NNGH!!
SHE'S SO FAST!!

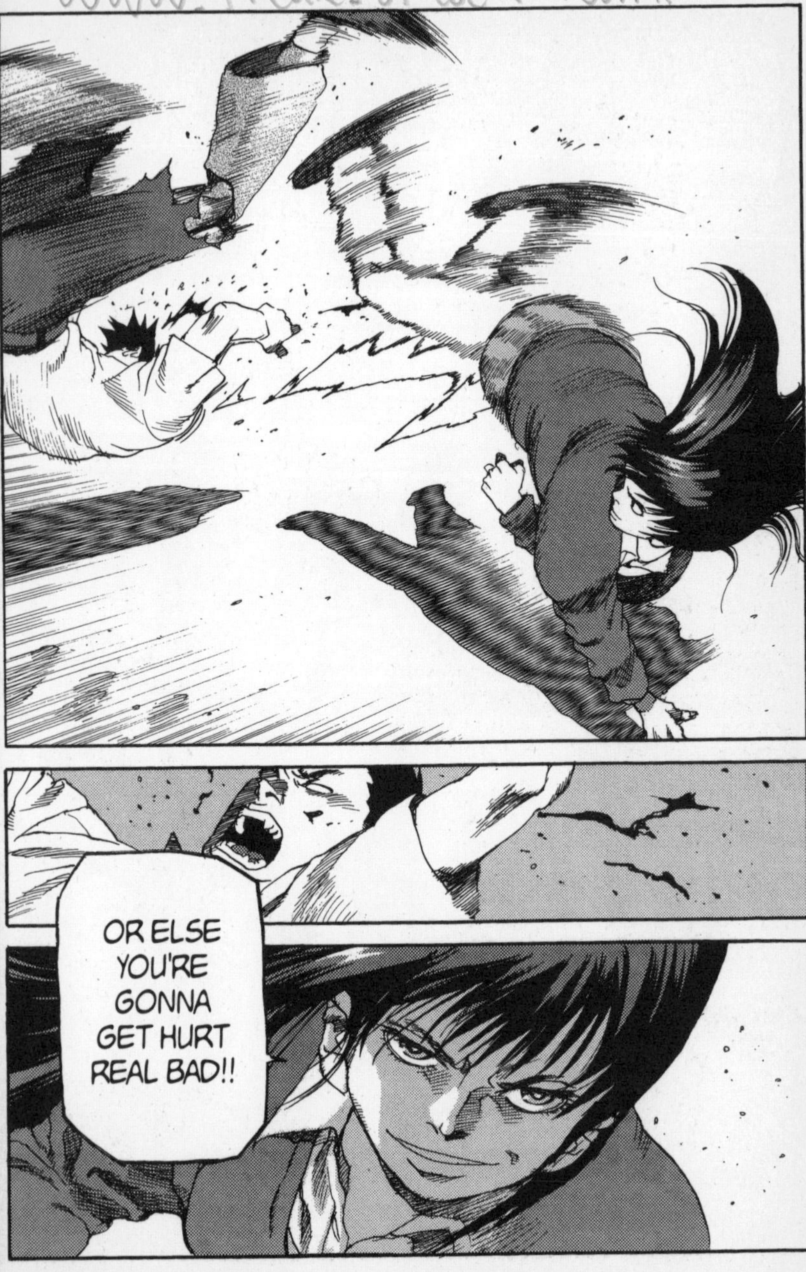
OR ELSE YOU'RE GONNA GET HURT REAL BAD!!

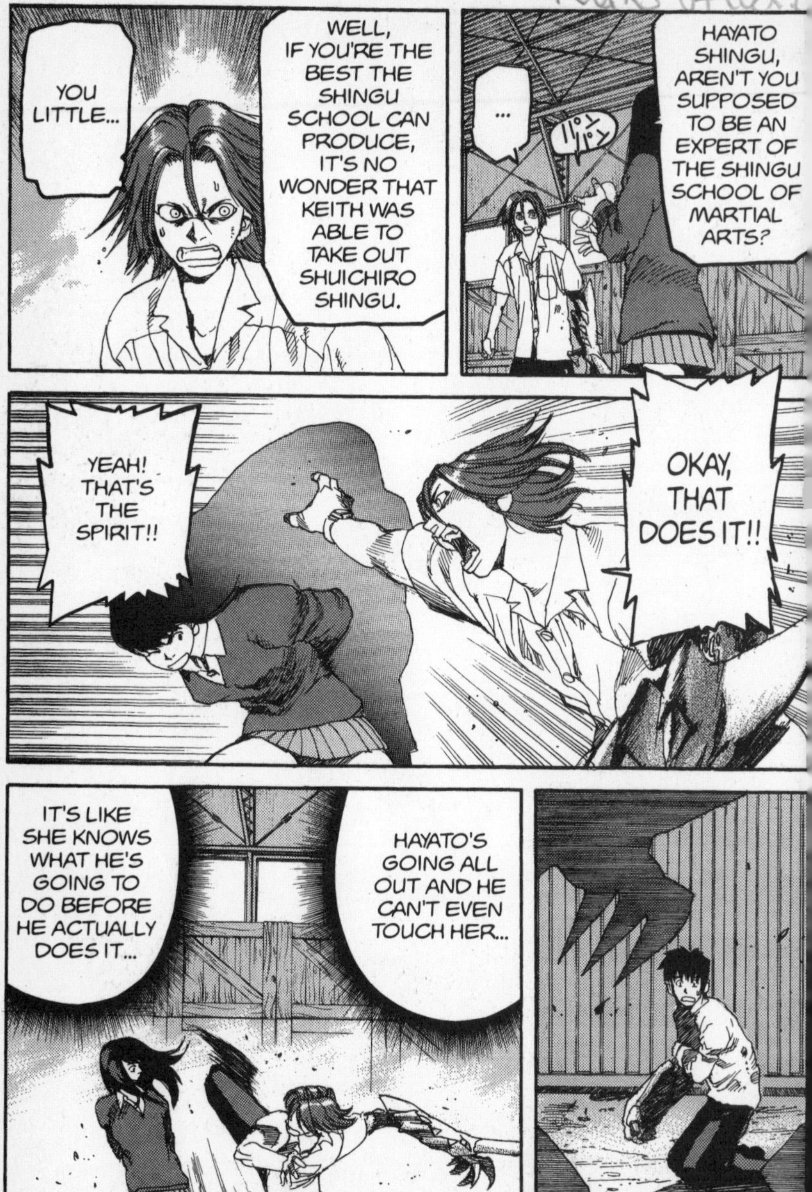
HAYATO SHINGU, AREN'T YOU SUPPOSED TO BE AN EXPERT OF THE SHINGU SCHOOL OF MARTIAL ARTS?
...
WELL, IF YOU'RE THE BEST THE SHINGU SCHOOL CAN PRODUCE, IT'S NO WONDER THAT KEITH WAS ABLE TO TAKE OUT SHUICHIRO SHINGU.
YOU LITTLE...
OKAY, THAT DOES IT!!
YEAH! THAT'S THE SPIRIT!!
HAYATO'S GOING ALL OUT AND HE CAN'T EVEN TOUCH HER...
IT'S LIKE SHE KNOWS WHAT HE'S GOING TO DO BEFORE HE ACTUALLY DOES IT...

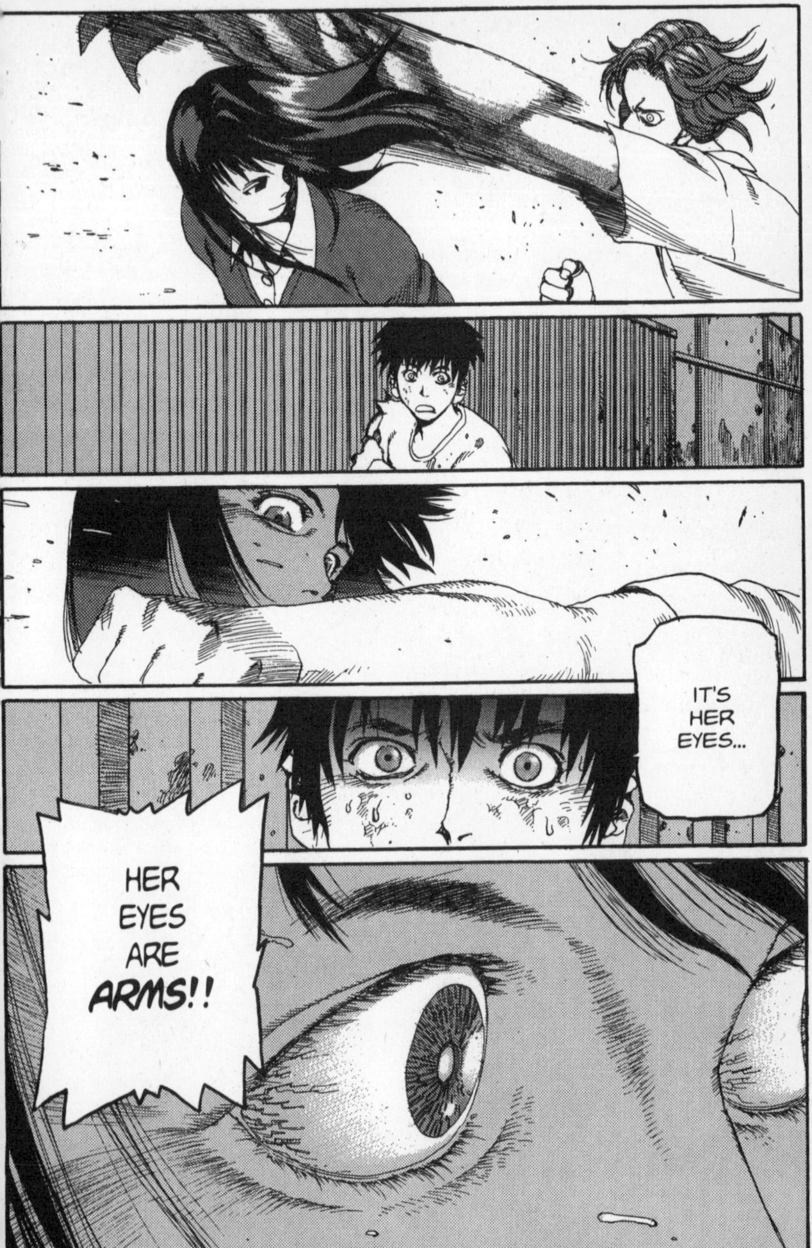
IT'S HER EYES...
HER EYES ARE ARMS!!

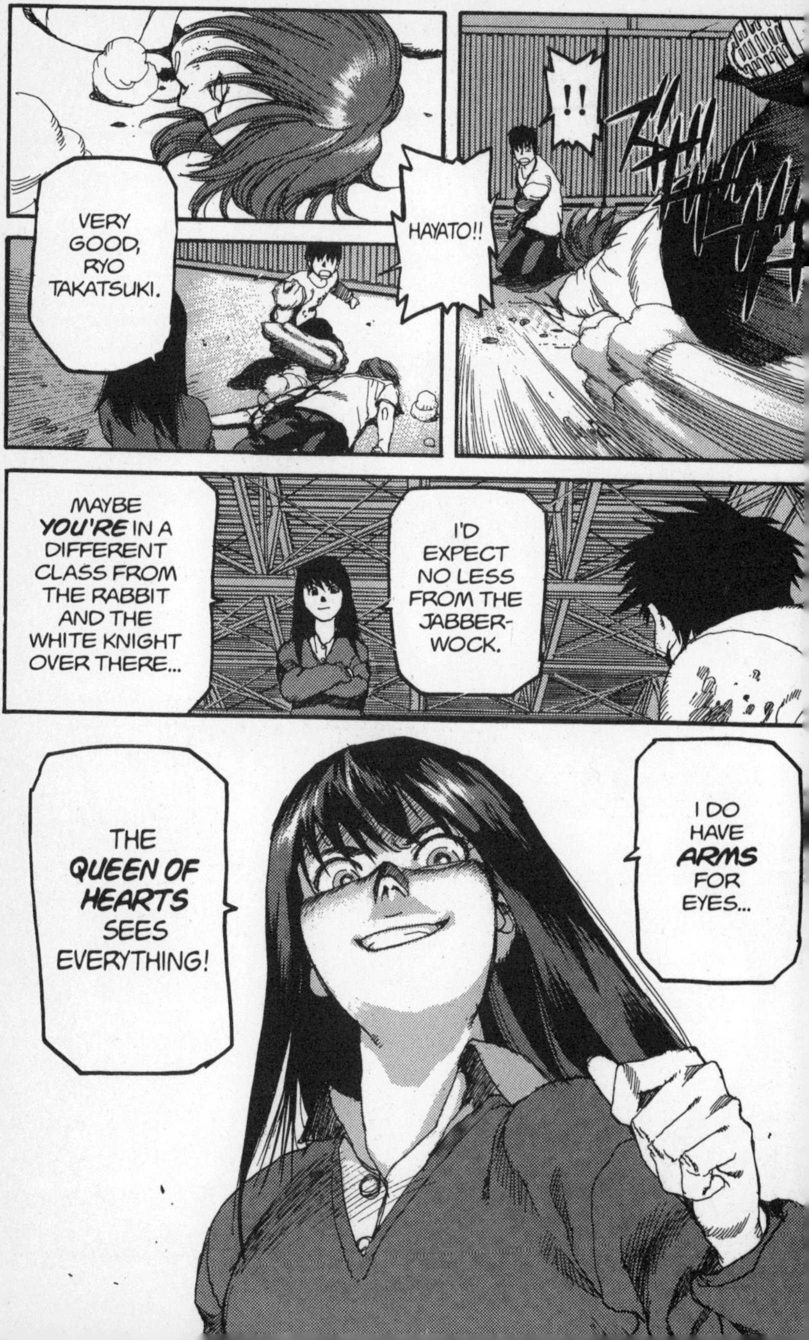
!!
HAYATO!!
VERY GOOD, RYO TAKATSUKI.
I'D EXPECT NO LESS FROM THE JABBER-WOCK.
MAYBE YOU'RE IN A DIFFERENT CLASS FROM THE RABBIT AND THE WHITE KNIGHT OVER THERE...
I DO HAVE ARMS FOR EYES...
THE QUEEN OF HEARTS SEES EVERYTHING!

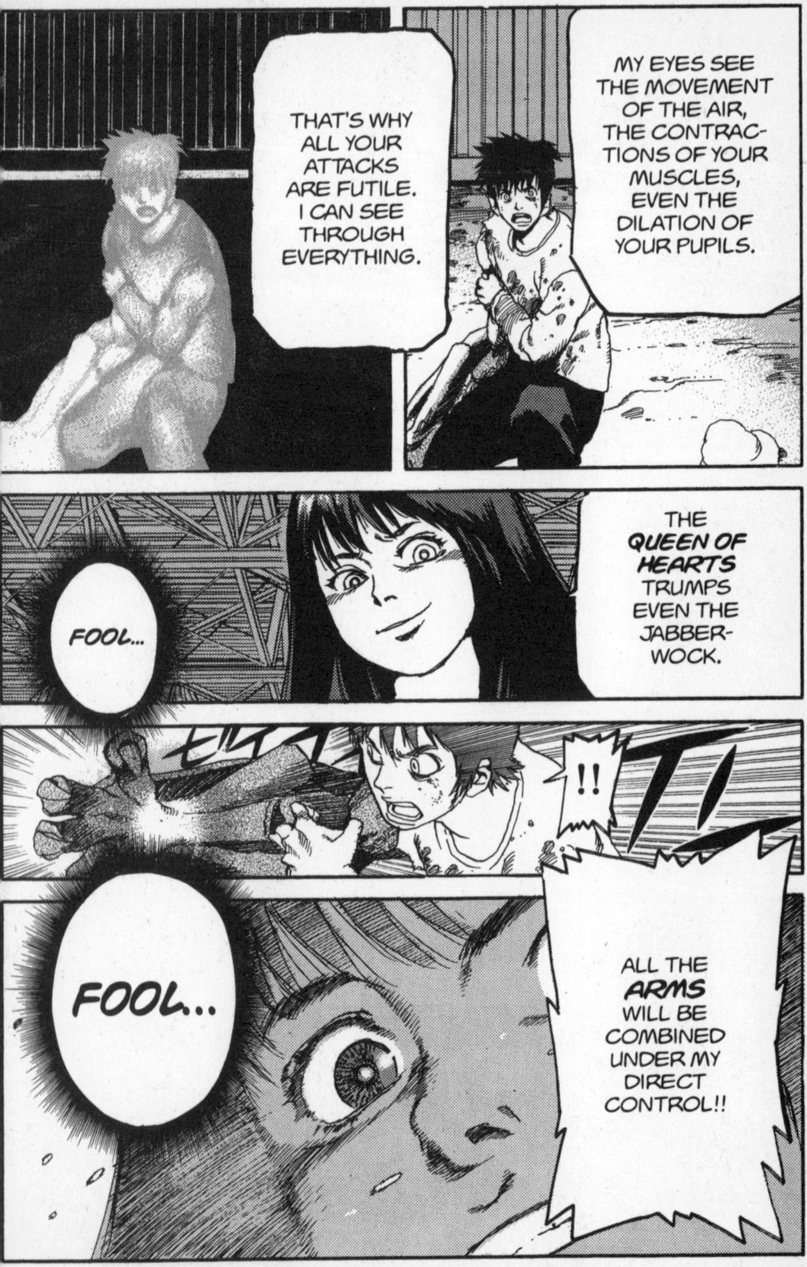
MY EYES SEE THE MOVEMENT OF THE AIR, THE CONTRACTIONS OF YOUR MUSCLES, EVEN THE DILATION OF YOUR PUPILS.
THAT'S WHY ALL YOUR ATTACKS ARE FUTILE. I CAN SEE THROUGH EVERYTHING.
THE ***QUEEN OF HEARTS*** TRUMPS EVEN THE JABBERWOCK.
FOOL...
!!
ALL THE ***ARMS*** WILL BE COMBINED UNDER MY DIRECT CONTROL!!
FOOL...

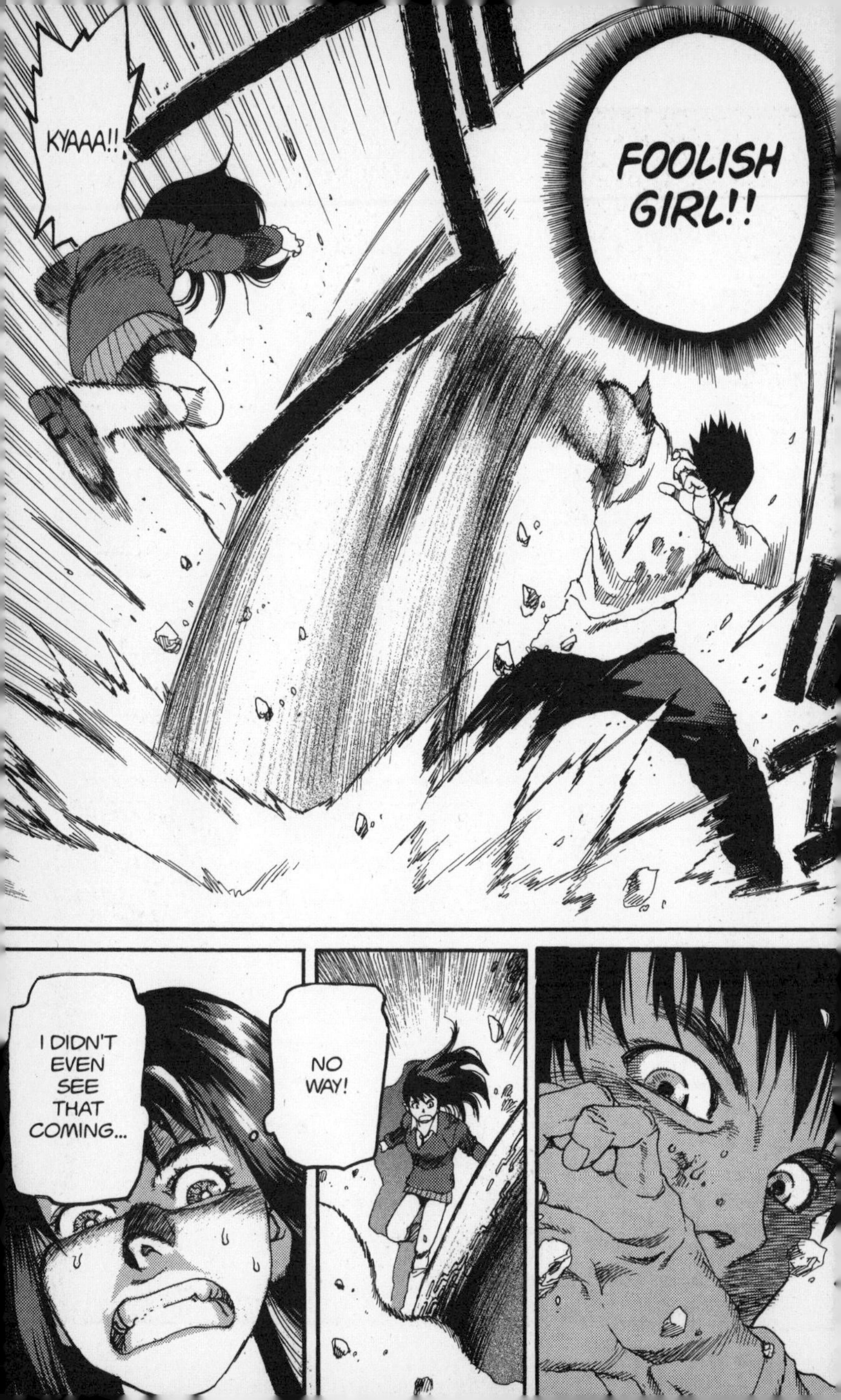
FOOLISH GIRL!!
KYAAA!!
NO WAY!
I DIDN'T EVEN SEE THAT COMING...

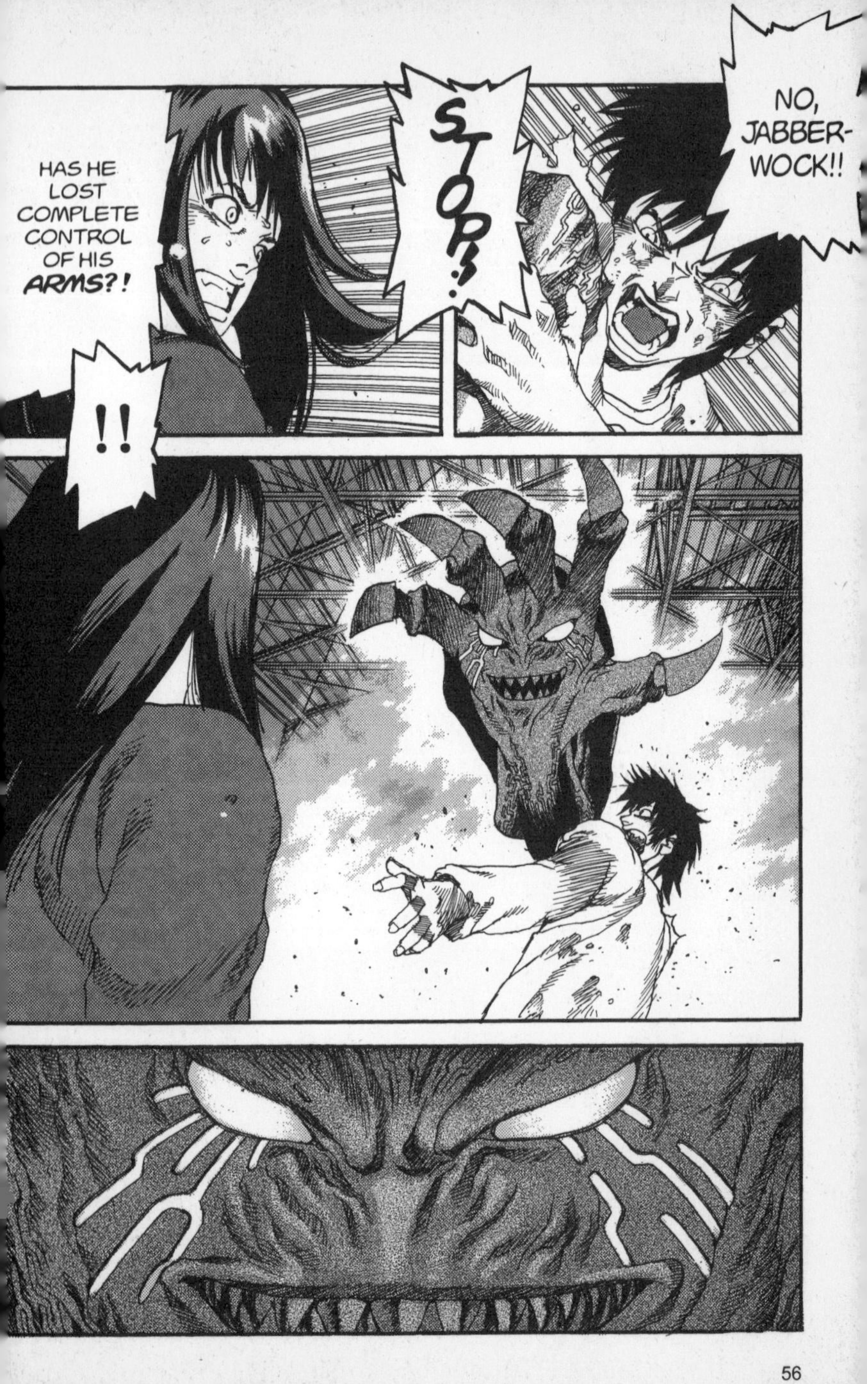
NO, JABBER-WOCK!!
STOP?!.
HAS HE LOST COMPLETE CONTROL OF HIS ARMS?!
!!

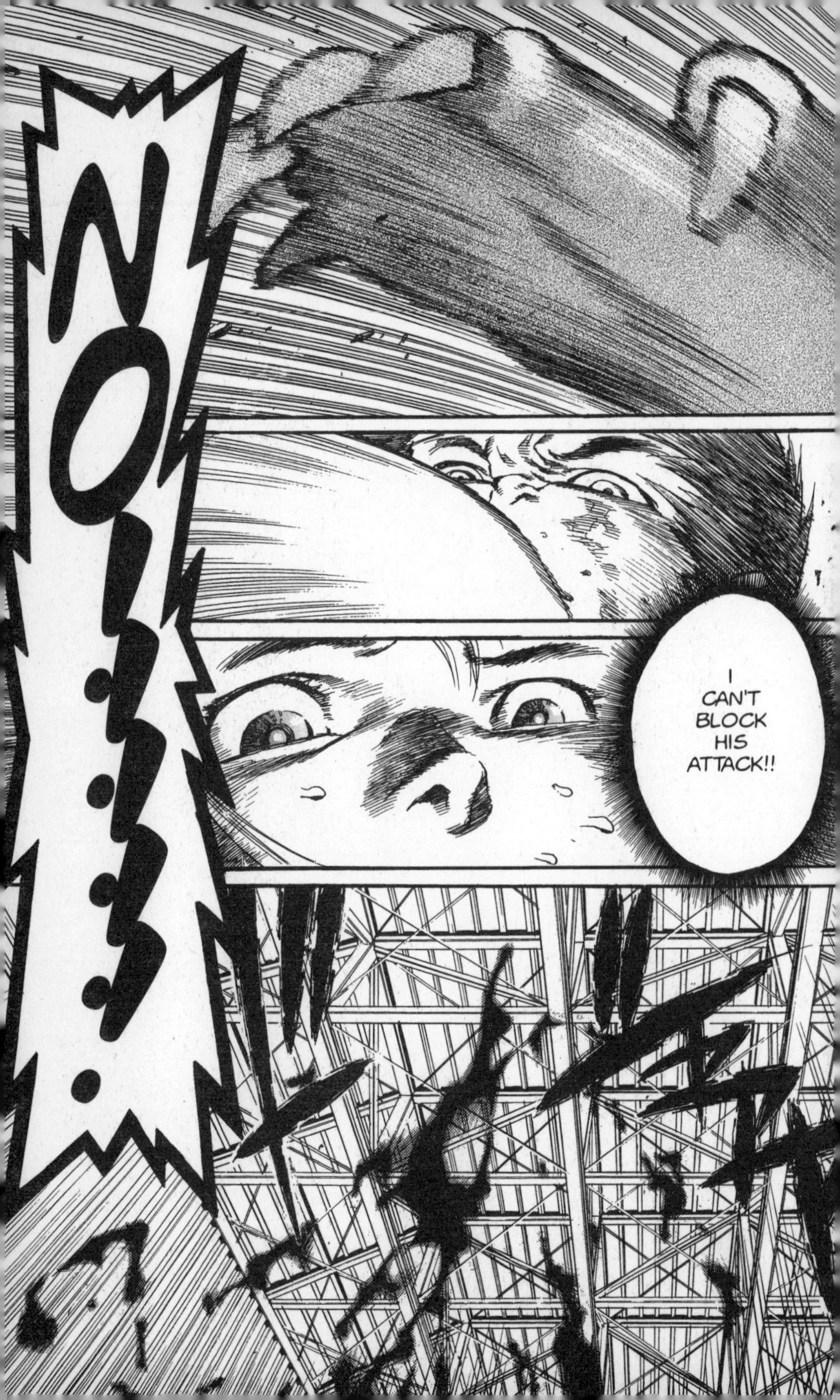
NO...!!
I CAN'T BLOCK HIS ATTACK!!

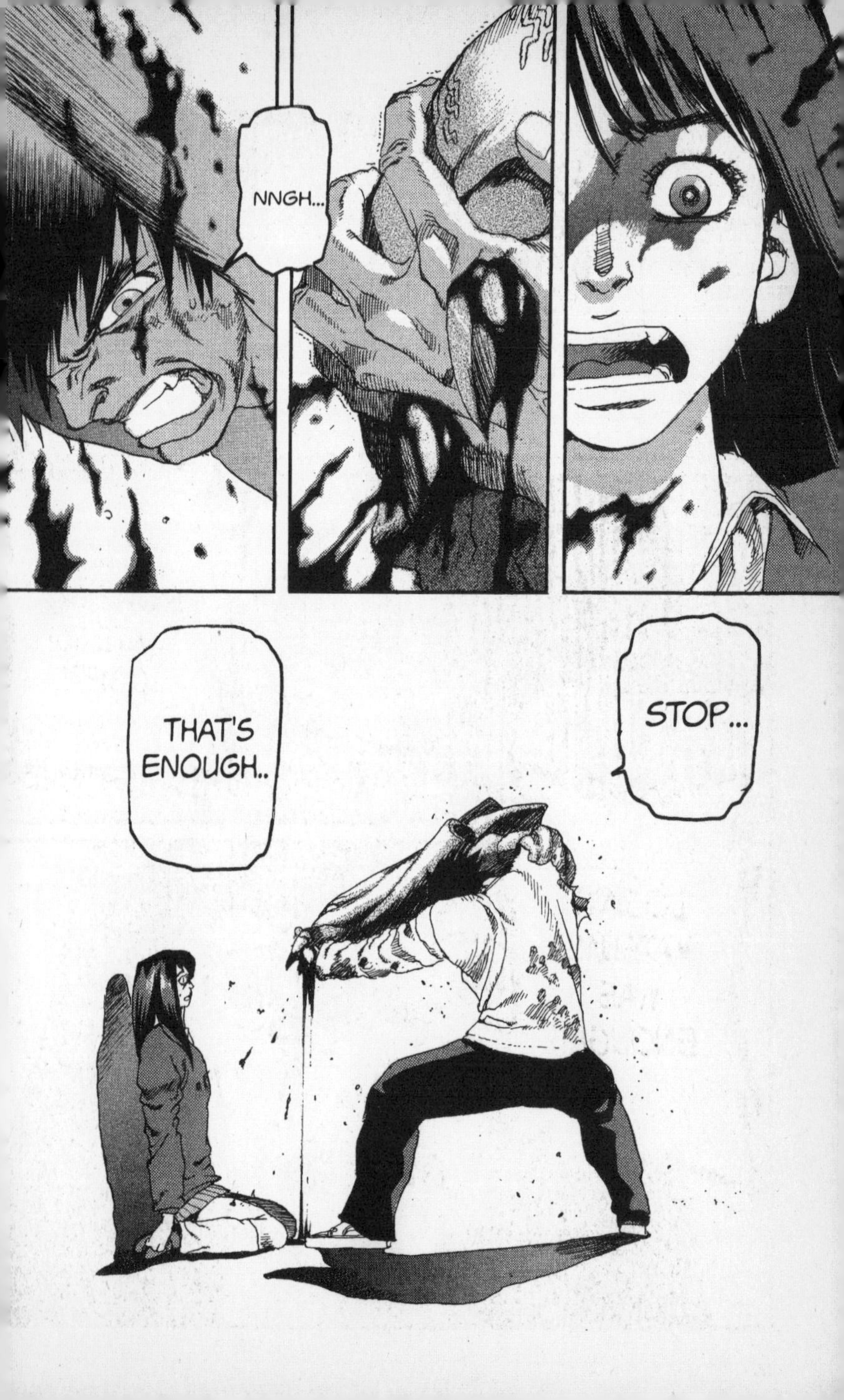
NNGH...
STOP...
THAT'S ENOUGH..

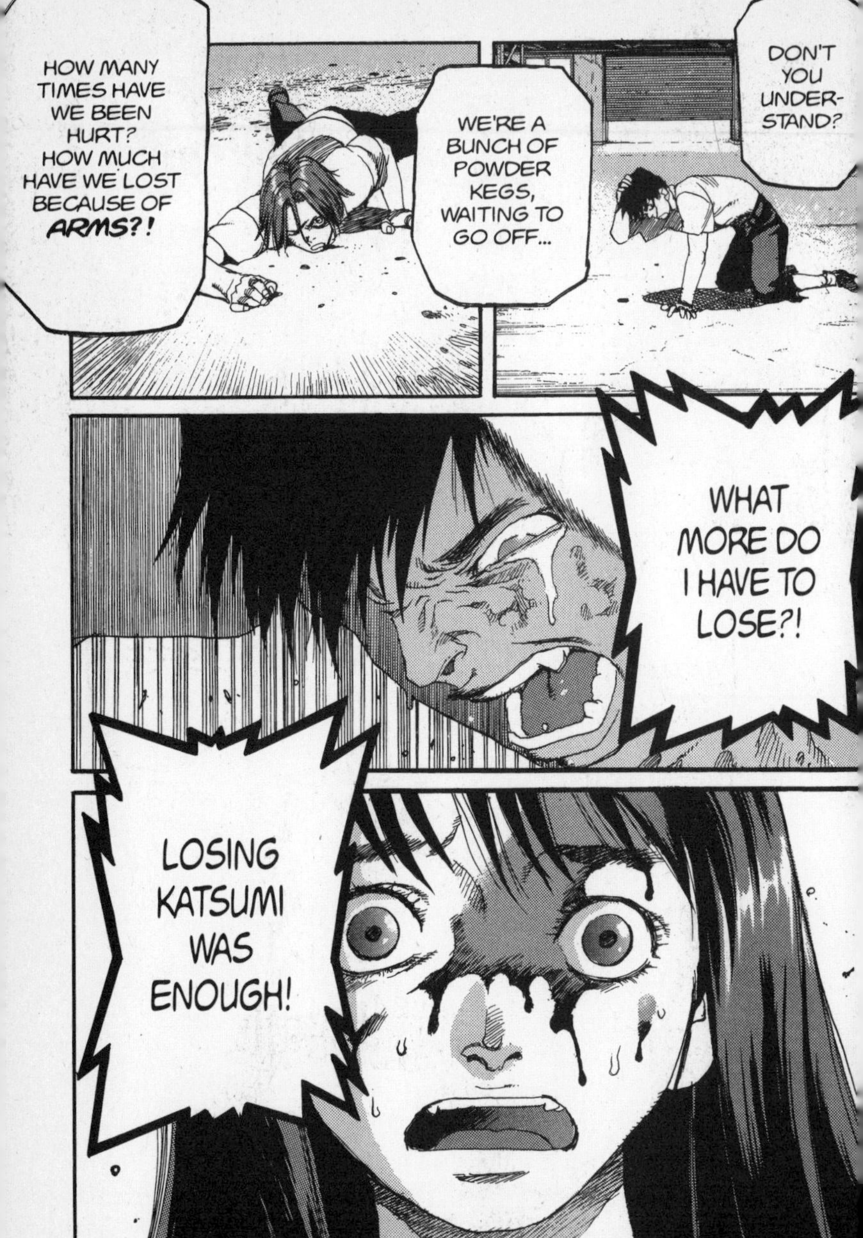
DON'T YOU UNDER-STAND?
WE'RE A BUNCH OF POWDER KEGS, WAITING TO GO OFF...
HOW MANY TIMES HAVE WE BEEN HURT? HOW MUCH HAVE WE LOST BECAUSE OF ARMS?!
WHAT MORE DO I HAVE TO LOSE?!
LOSING KATSUMI WAS ENOUGH!

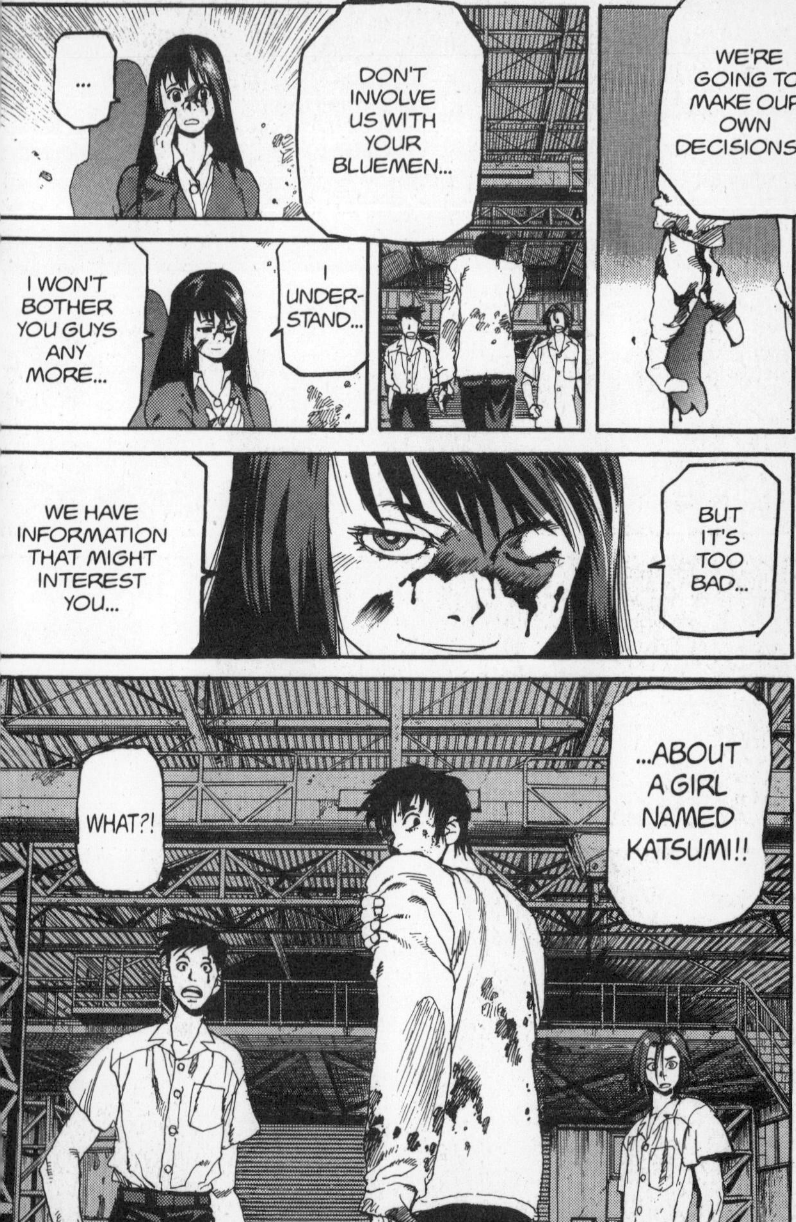
WE'RE GOING TO MAKE OUR OWN DECISIONS...
DON'T INVOLVE US WITH YOUR BLUEMEN...
...
I UNDER-STAND...
I WON'T BOTHER YOU GUYS ANY MORE...
BUT IT'S TOO BAD...
WE HAVE INFORMATION THAT MIGHT INTEREST YOU...
...ABOUT A GIRL NAMED KATSUMI!!
WHAT?!

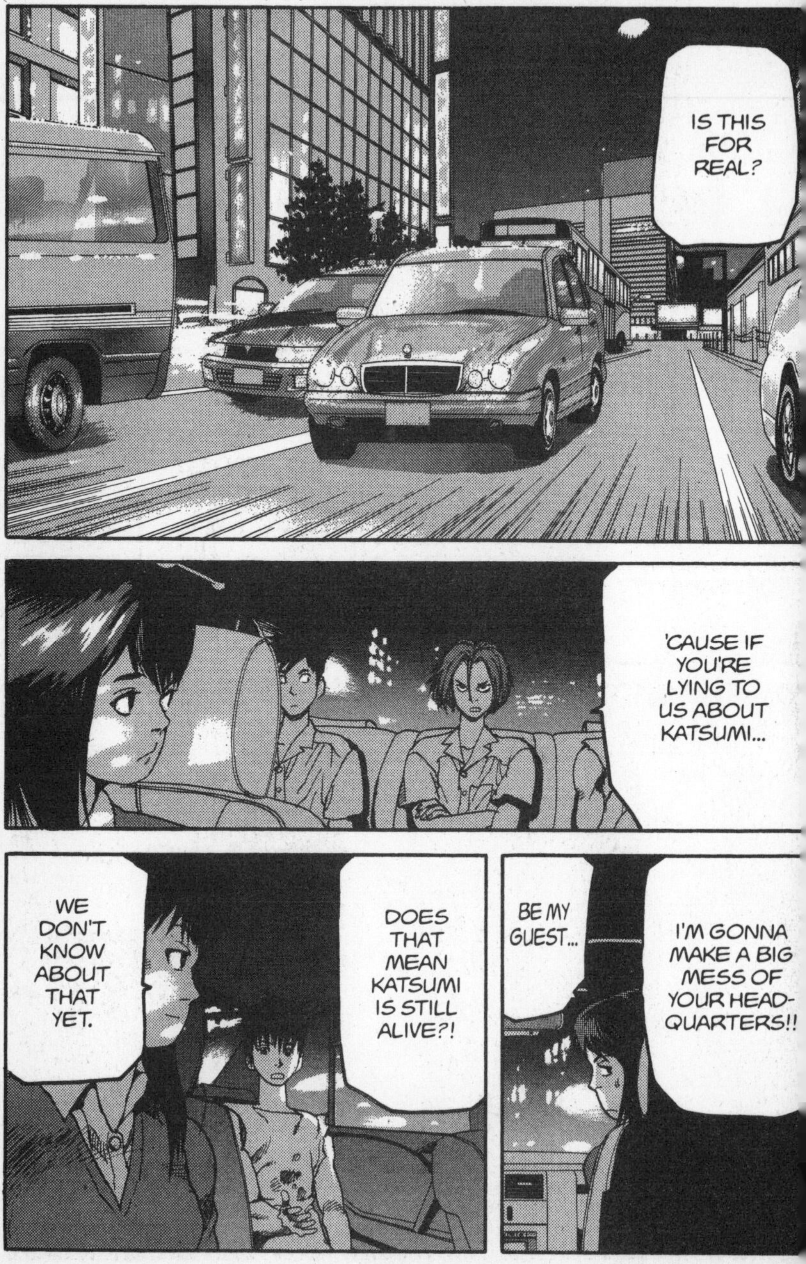
IS THIS FOR REAL?
'CAUSE IF YOU'RE LYING TO US ABOUT KATSUMI...
I'M GONNA MAKE A BIG MESS OF YOUR HEAD-QUARTERS!!
BE MY GUEST...
DOES THAT MEAN KATSUMI IS STILL ALIVE?!
WE DON'T KNOW ABOUT THAT YET.

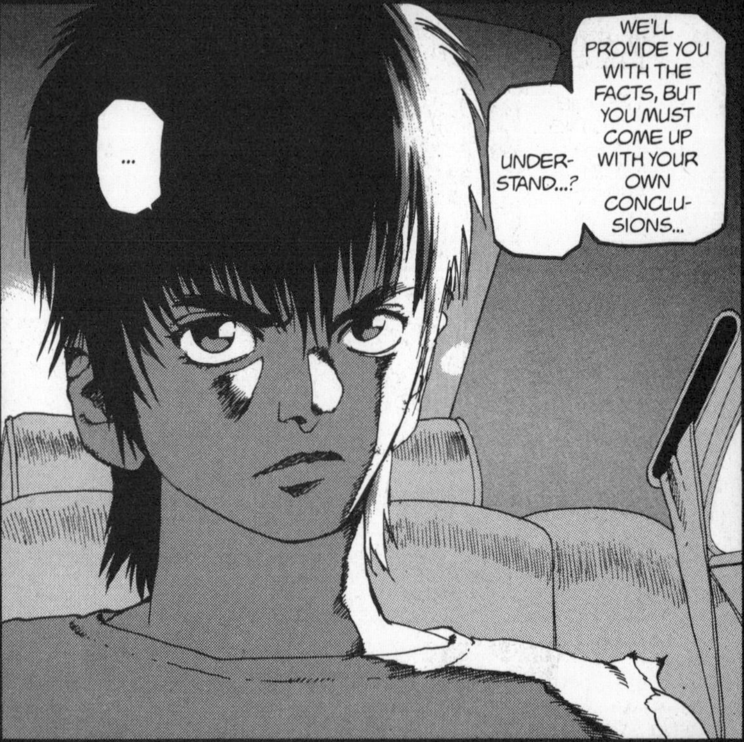
WE'LL PROVIDE YOU WITH THE FACTS, BUT YOU MUST COME UP WITH YOUR OWN CONCLU-SIONS...
UNDER-STAND...?
...

No. 4 THE BLUEMEN

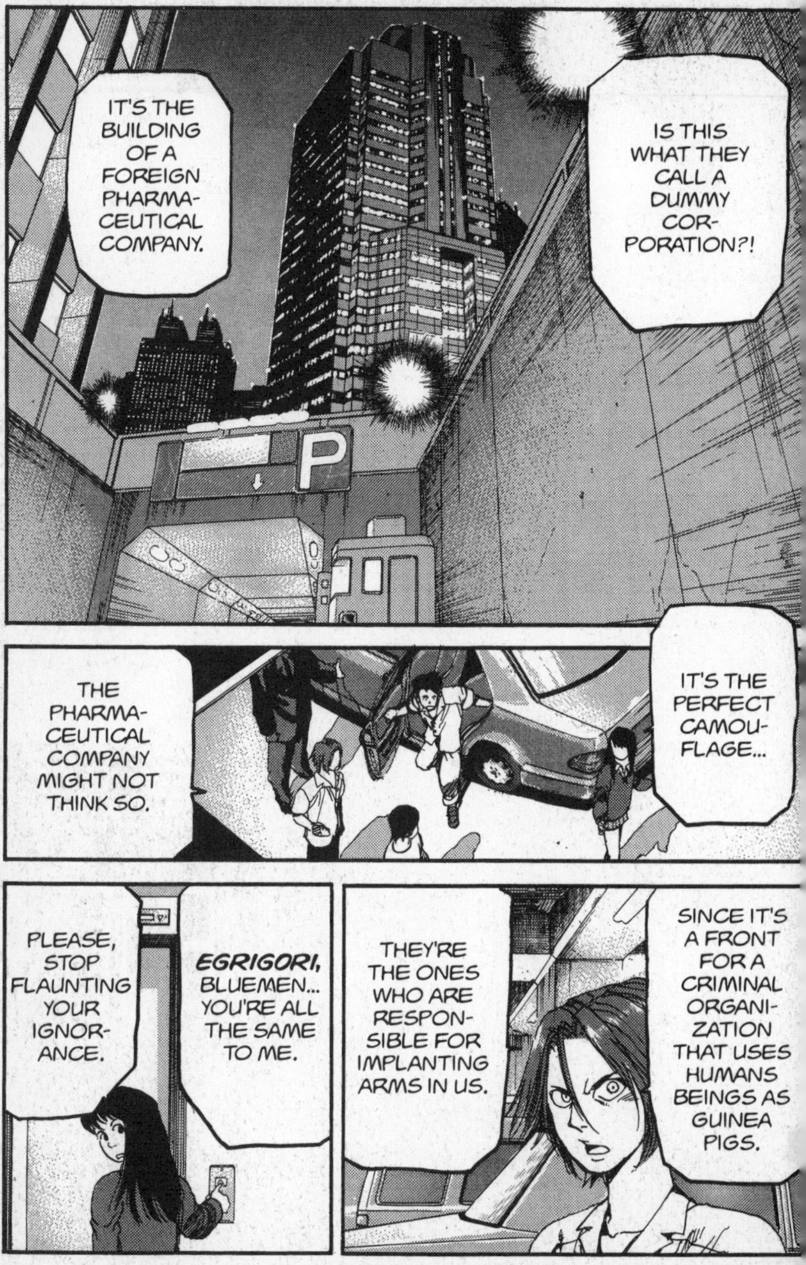
IS THIS WHAT THEY CALL A DUMMY CORPORATION?!
IT'S THE BUILDING OF A FOREIGN PHARMACEUTICAL COMPANY.
IT'S THE PERFECT CAMOUFLAGE...
THE PHARMACEUTICAL COMPANY MIGHT NOT THINK SO.
SINCE IT'S A FRONT FOR A CRIMINAL ORGANIZATION THAT USES HUMANS BEINGS AS GUINEA PIGS.
THEY'RE THE ONES WHO ARE RESPONSIBLE FOR IMPLANTING ARMS IN US.
EGRIGORI, BLUEMEN... YOU'RE ALL THE SAME TO ME.
PLEASE, STOP FLAUNTING YOUR IGNORANCE.

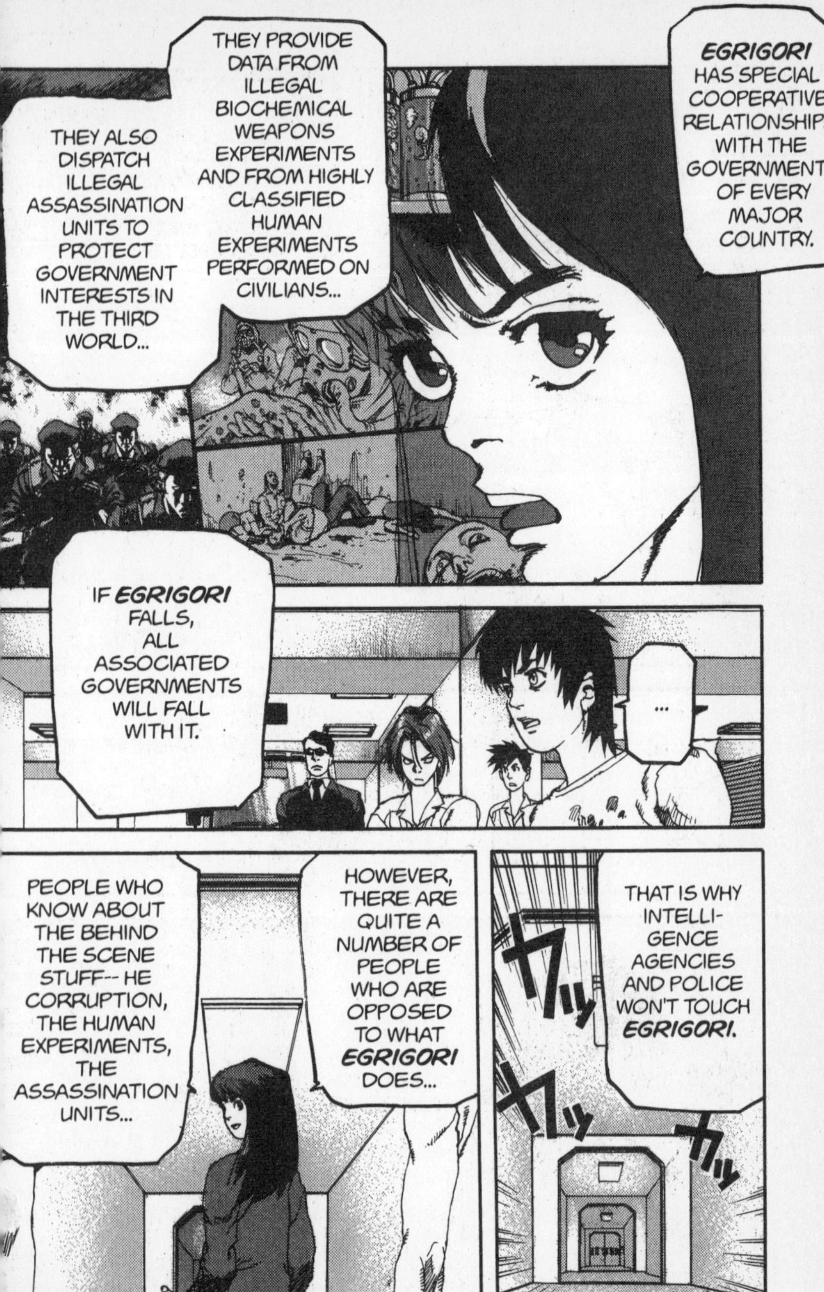
EGRIGORI HAS SPECIAL COOPERATIVE RELATIONSHIPS WITH THE GOVERNMENTS OF EVERY MAJOR COUNTRY.
THEY PROVIDE DATA FROM ILLEGAL BIOCHEMICAL WEAPONS EXPERIMENTS AND FROM HIGHLY CLASSIFIED HUMAN EXPERIMENTS PERFORMED ON CIVILIANS...
THEY ALSO DISPATCH ILLEGAL ASSASSINATION UNITS TO PROTECT GOVERNMENT INTERESTS IN THE THIRD WORLD...
IF EGRIGORI FALLS, ALL ASSOCIATED GOVERNMENTS WILL FALL WITH IT.
...
THAT IS WHY INTELLI-GENCE AGENCIES AND POLICE WON'T TOUCH EGRIGORI.
HOWEVER, THERE ARE QUITE A NUMBER OF PEOPLE WHO ARE OPPOSED TO WHAT EGRIGORI DOES...
PEOPLE WHO KNOW ABOUT THE BEHIND THE SCENE STUFF-- HE CORRUPTION, THE HUMAN EXPERIMENTS, THE ASSASSINATION UNITS...

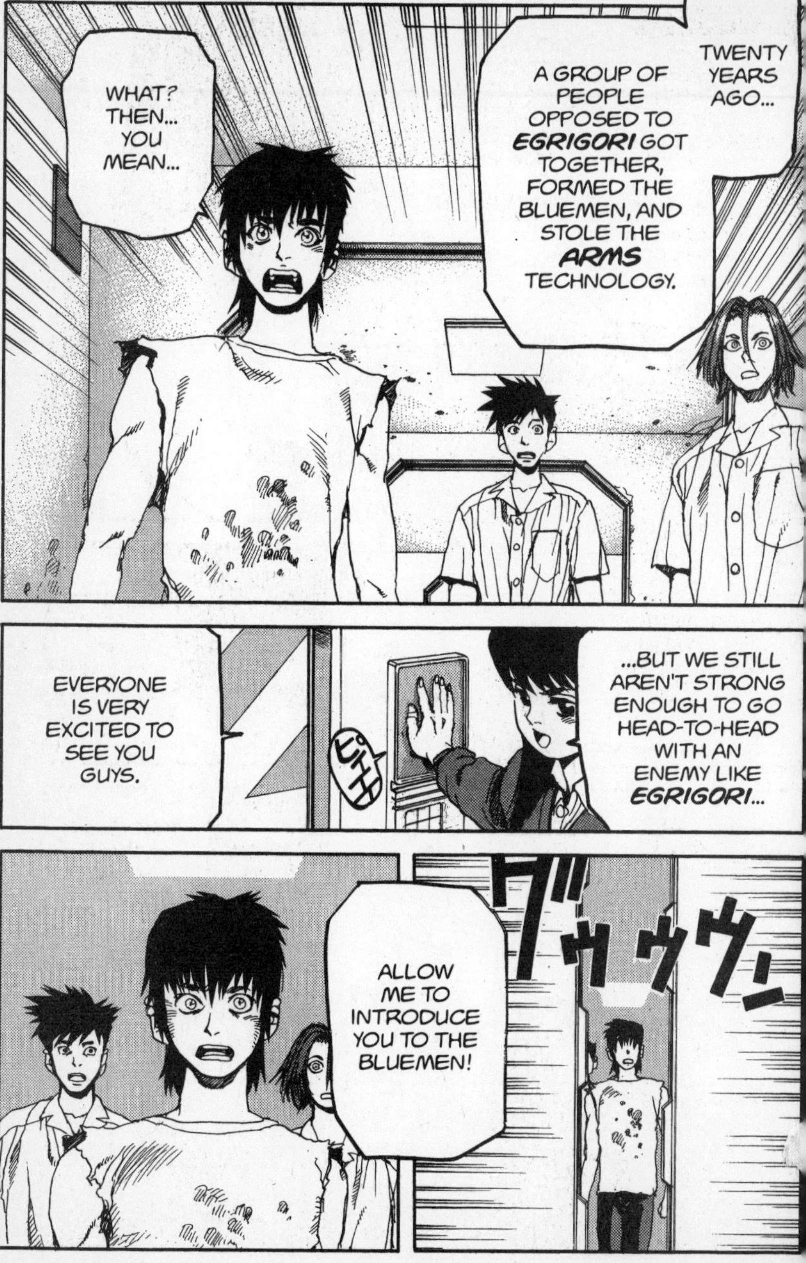
TWENTY YEARS AGO...
A GROUP OF PEOPLE OPPOSED TO EGRIGORI GOT TOGETHER, FORMED THE BLUEMEN, AND STOLE THE ARMS TECHNOLOGY.
WHAT? THEN... YOU MEAN...
...BUT WE STILL AREN'T STRONG ENOUGH TO GO HEAD-TO-HEAD WITH AN ENEMY LIKE EGRIGORI...
EVERYONE IS VERY EXCITED TO SEE YOU GUYS.
ALLOW ME TO INTRODUCE YOU TO THE BLUEMEN!

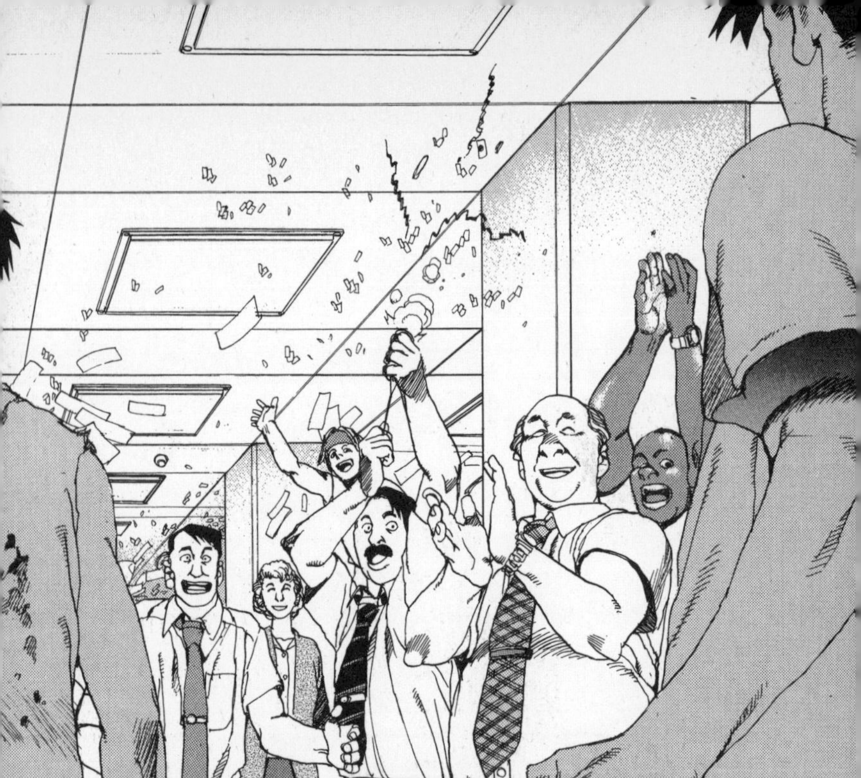

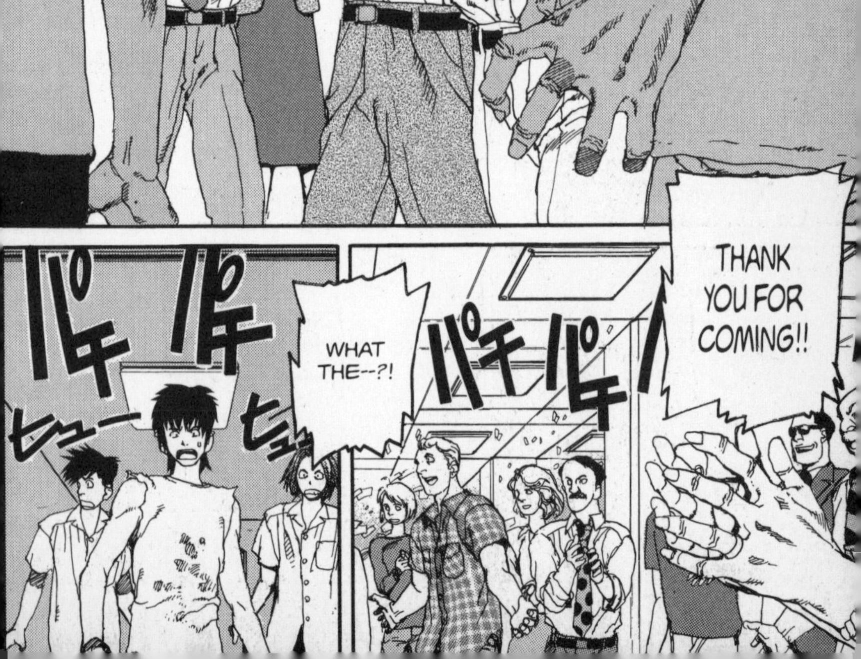
THANK YOU FOR COMING!!
パチパチ
WHAT THE--?!
パチ パチ
ヒュー ヒュー

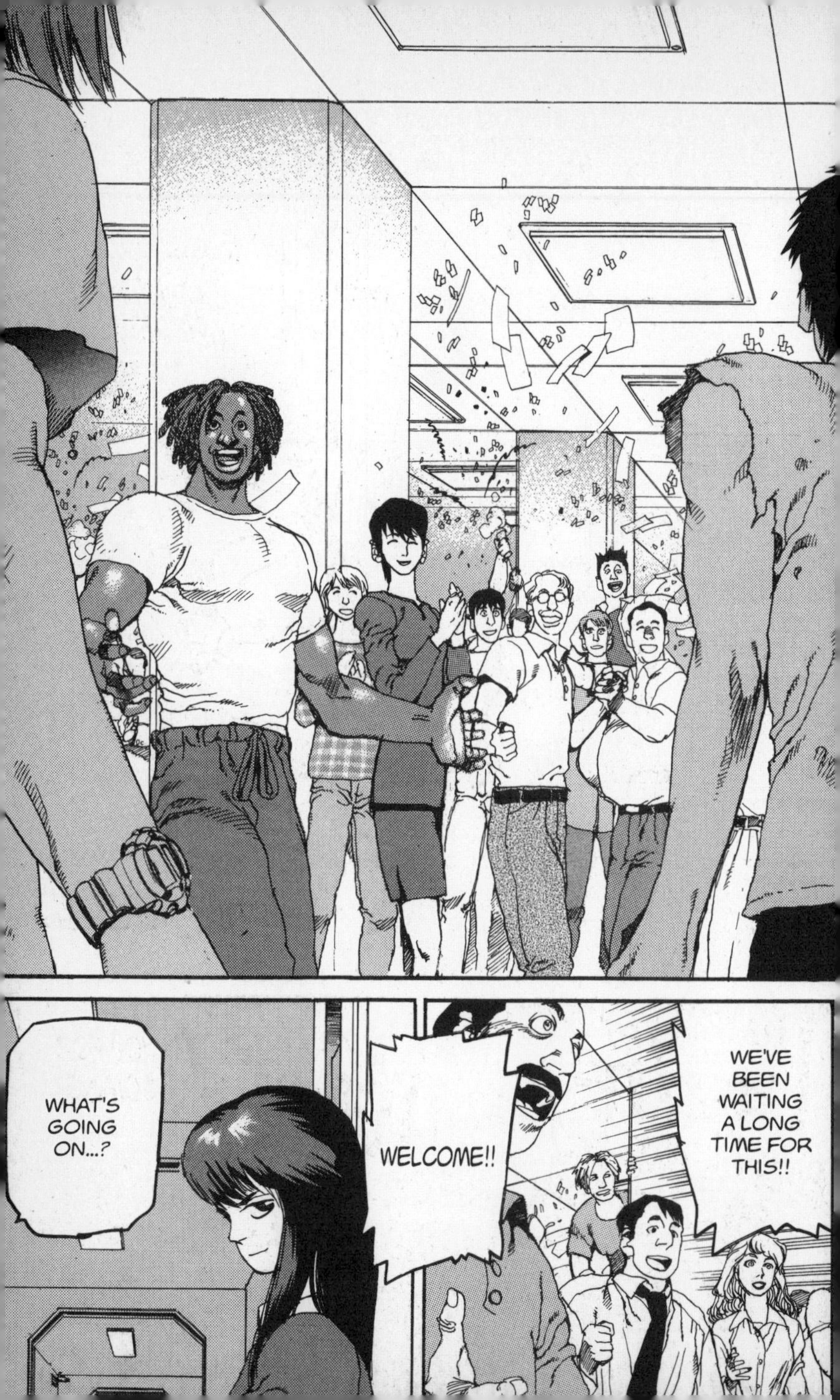
WE'VE BEEN WAITING A LONG TIME FOR THIS!!
WELCOME!!
WHAT'S GOING ON...?

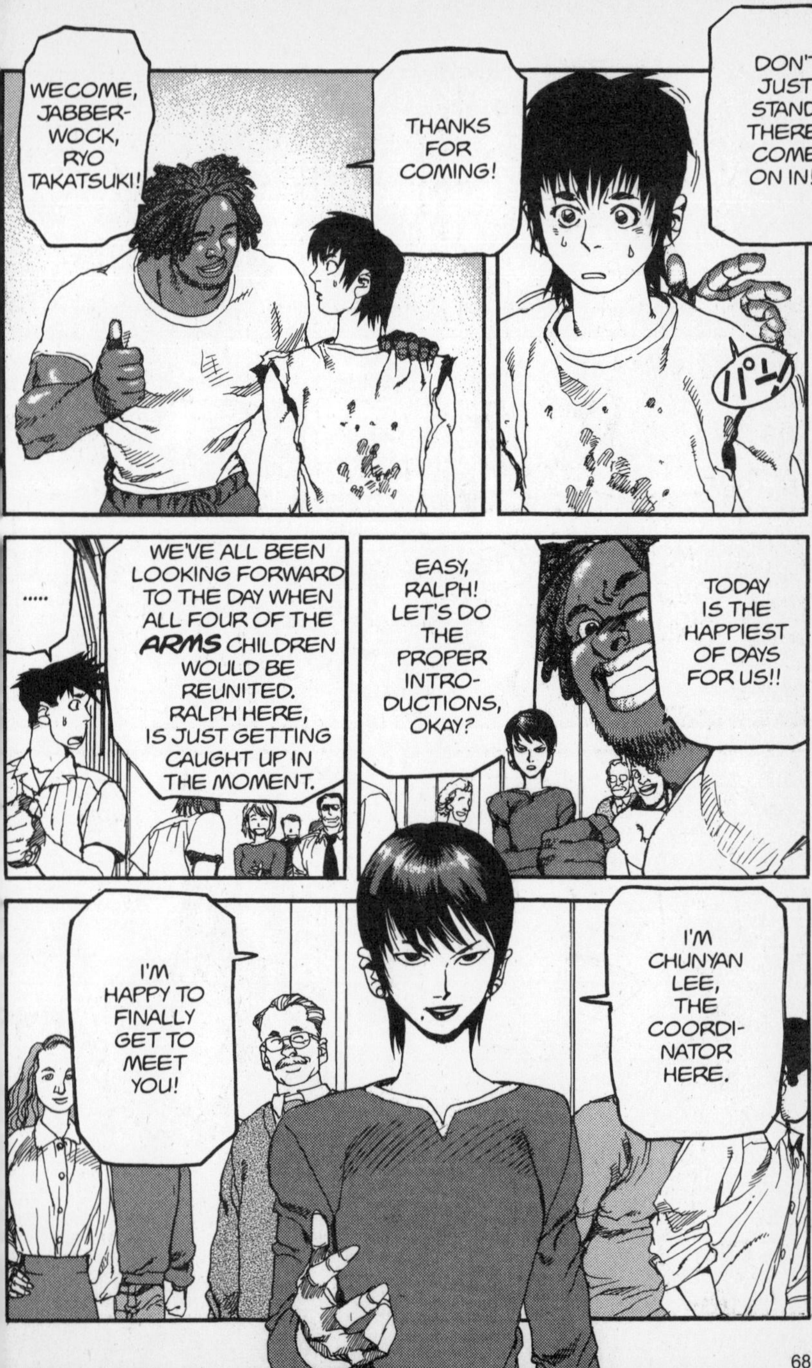
DON'T JUST STAND THERE, COME ON IN!!
パン!
WECOME, JABBER-WOCK, RYO TAKATSUKI!
THANKS FOR COMING!
TODAY IS THE HAPPIEST OF DAYS FOR US!!
EASY, RALPH! LET'S DO THE PROPER INTRO-DUCTIONS, OKAY?
WE'VE ALL BEEN LOOKING FORWARD TO THE DAY WHEN ALL FOUR OF THE ARMS CHILDREN WOULD BE REUNITED. RALPH HERE, IS JUST GETTING CAUGHT UP IN THE MOMENT.
.....
I'M CHUNYAN LEE, THE COORDI-NATOR HERE.
I'M HAPPY TO FINALLY GET TO MEET YOU!

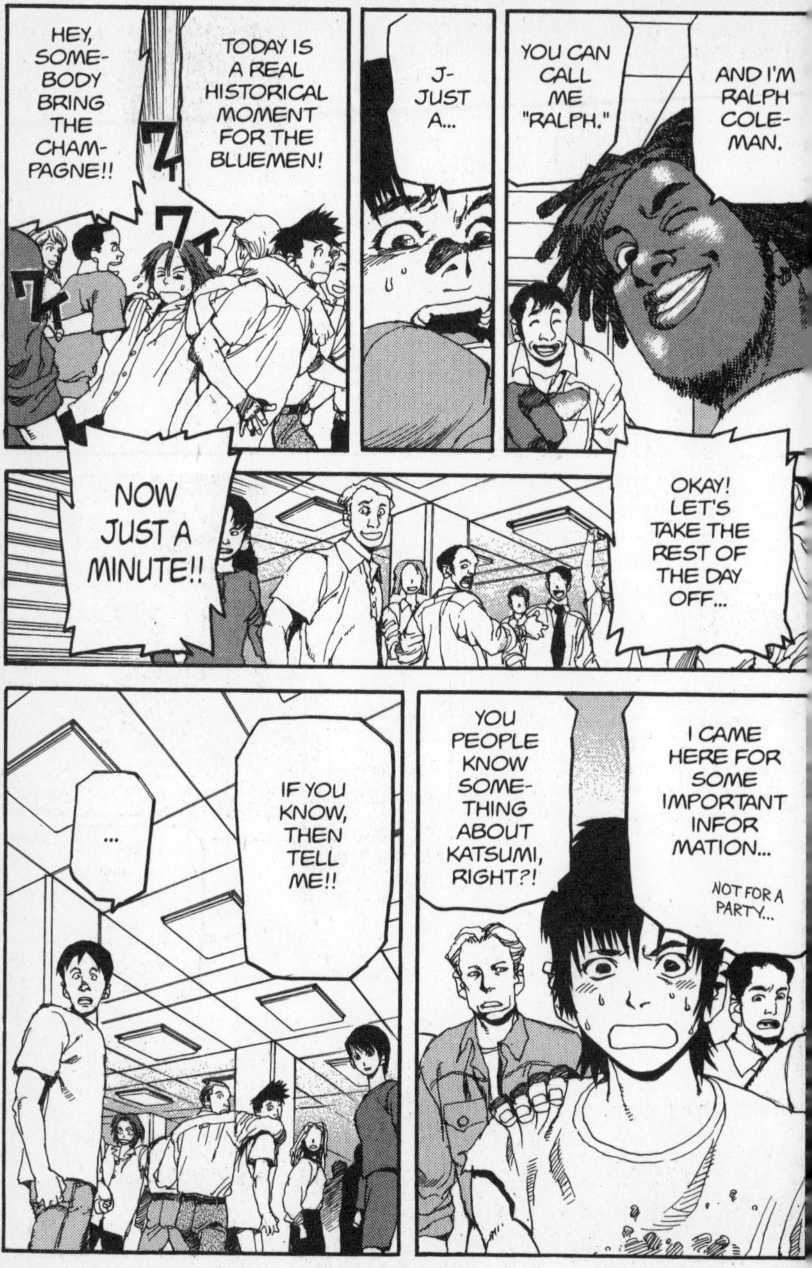
AND I'M RALPH COLE-MAN.
YOU CAN CALL ME "RALPH."
J-JUST A...
TODAY IS A REAL HISTORICAL MOMENT FOR THE BLUEMEN!
HEY, SOME-BODY BRING THE CHAM-PAGNE!!
OKAY! LET'S TAKE THE REST OF THE DAY OFF...
NOW JUST A MINUTE!!
I CAME HERE FOR SOME IMPORTANT INFOR MATION...
NOT FOR A PARTY...
YOU PEOPLE KNOW SOME-THING ABOUT KATSUMI, RIGHT?!
IF YOU KNOW, THEN TELL ME!!
...

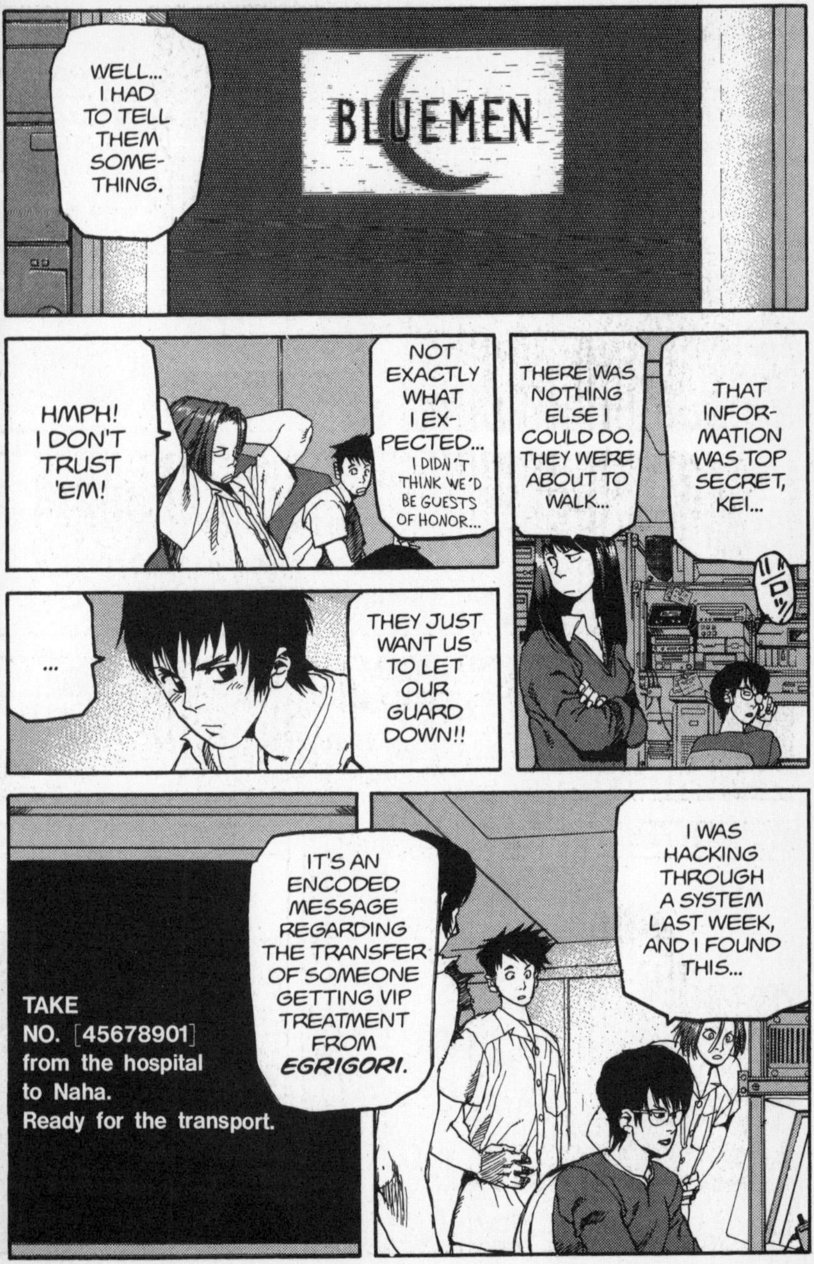

BLUEMEN
WELL... I HAD TO TELL THEM SOMETHING.
THAT INFORMATION WAS TOP SECRET, KEI...
THERE WAS NOTHING ELSE I COULD DO. THEY WERE ABOUT TO WALK...
NOT EXACTLY WHAT I EXPECTED... I DIDN'T THINK WE'D BE GUESTS OF HONOR...
HMPH! I DON'T TRUST 'EM!
THEY JUST WANT US TO LET OUR GUARD DOWN!!
...
I WAS HACKING THROUGH A SYSTEM LAST WEEK, AND I FOUND THIS...
IT'S AN ENCODED MESSAGE REGARDING THE TRANSFER OF SOMEONE GETTING VIP TREATMENT FROM EGRIGORI.
TAKE NO. [45678901] from the hospital to Naha. Ready for the transport.

TAKE
NO. [45678901]
from the hospital
to Naha.
Ready for the transport.

WE'LL JUST PUT IT THROUGH THE KEY CODE AND...

IT'S CODE.

TRANSFER NO. 45678901 FROM THE HOSPITAL TO NAHA... WHO'S 456-WHATEVER?!

039.SKW8..E8RH4HMS72IIH9U5/.:
QT8830../4//OPEM3994860-33.-/
55436::-741@29:572991
URRJI483WK2TEKKEN3/3IINK798W
0000-283669//.3.33@01.237↵
194JEI402/.:2U4U8EOY91AK6//
0E3333
55::4////[12345]/069.¥49:
495TUEE39JGI38:::22P@EI↓
8857.::.H.YL::@U:
29444158TIEJKEOW2059FHJG

KATSUMI·A Female age:16 blood:A

WHAT...?

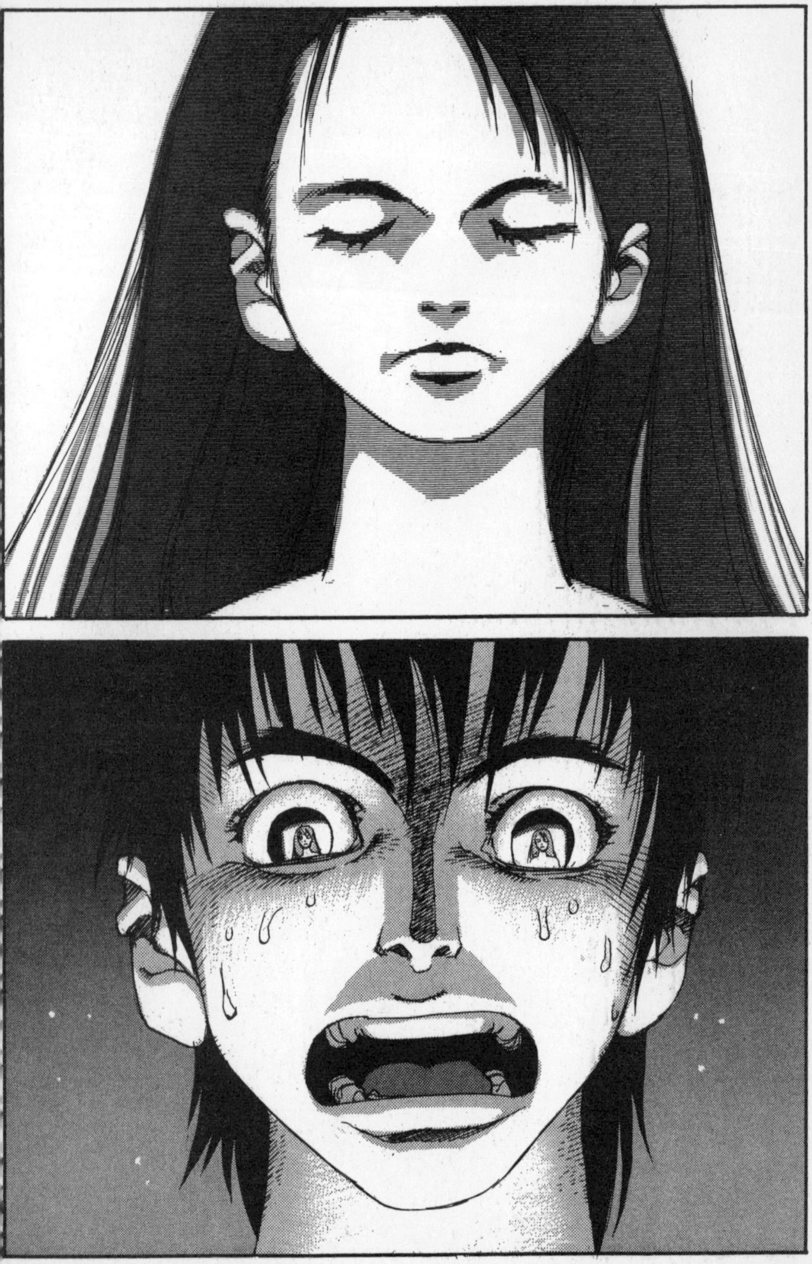

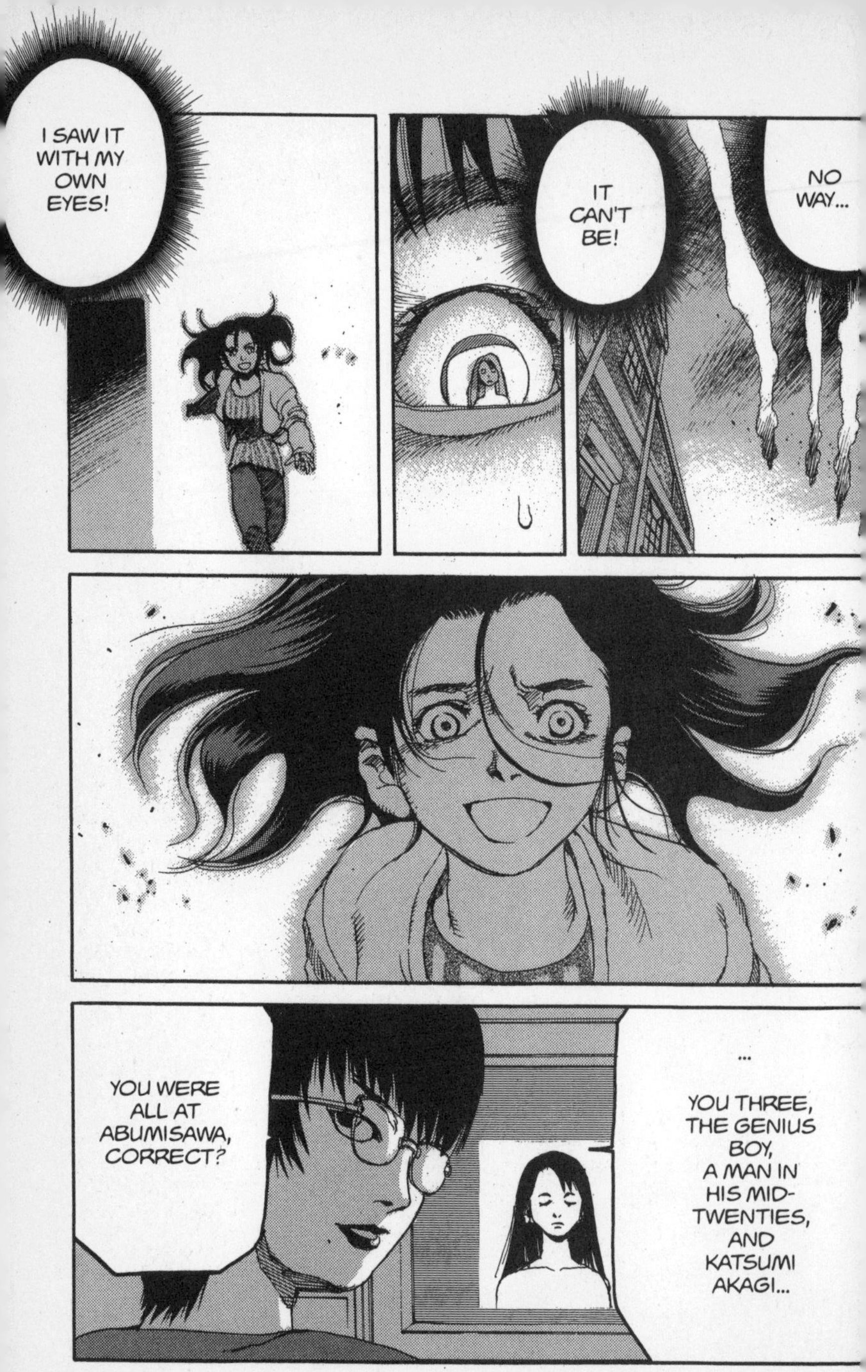
NO WAY...
IT CAN'T BE!
I SAW IT WITH MY OWN EYES!
...
YOU THREE, THE GENIUS BOY, A MAN IN HIS MID-TWENTIES, AND KATSUMI AKAGI...
YOU WERE ALL AT ABUMISAWA, CORRECT?

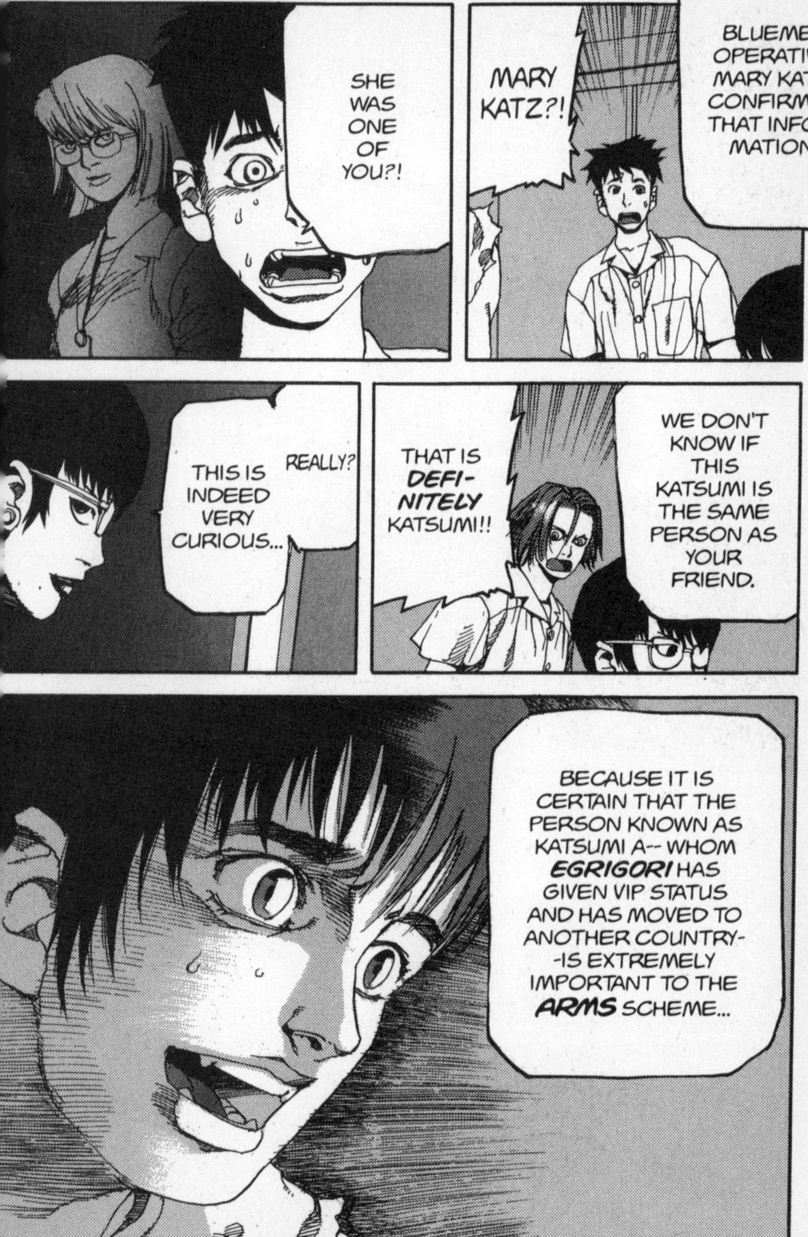
BLUEMEN OPERATIVE, MARY KATZ, CONFIRMED THAT INFORMATION.
MARY KATZ?!
SHE WAS ONE OF YOU?!
WE DON'T KNOW IF THIS KATSUMI IS THE SAME PERSON AS YOUR FRIEND.
THAT IS ***DEFINITELY*** KATSUMI!!
REALLY?
THIS IS INDEED VERY CURIOUS...
BECAUSE IT IS CERTAIN THAT THE PERSON KNOWN AS KATSUMI A-- WHOM ***EGRIGORI*** HAS GIVEN VIP STATUS AND HAS MOVED TO ANOTHER COUNTRY- -IS EXTREMELY IMPORTANT TO THE ***ARMS*** SCHEME...

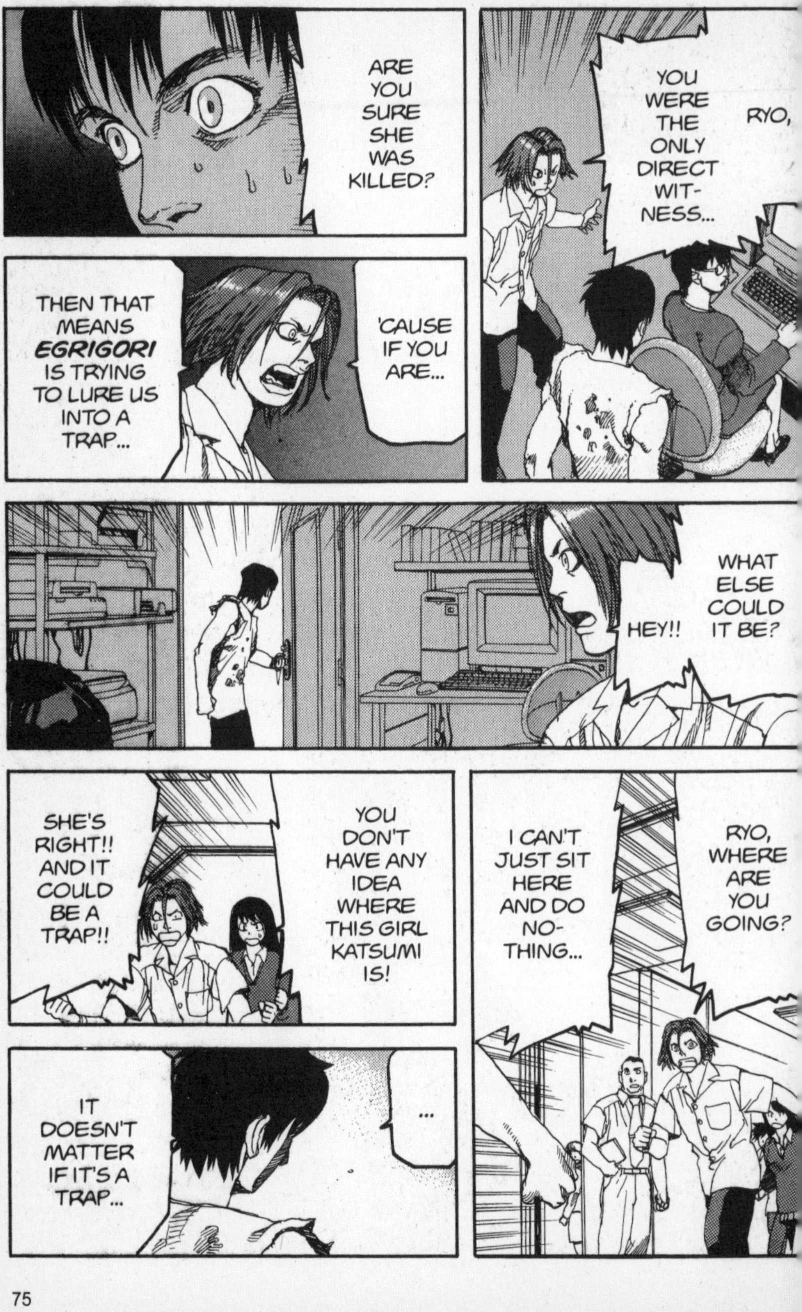
RYO,
YOU WERE THE ONLY DIRECT WIT- NESS...
ARE YOU SURE SHE WAS KILLED?
'CAUSE IF YOU ARE...
THEN THAT MEANS EGRIGORI IS TRYING TO LURE US INTO A TRAP...
WHAT ELSE COULD IT BE?
HEY!!
RYO, WHERE ARE YOU GOING?
I CAN'T JUST SIT HERE AND DO NO- THING...
YOU DON'T HAVE ANY IDEA WHERE THIS GIRL KATSUMI IS!
SHE'S RIGHT!! AND IT COULD BE A TRAP!!
...
IT DOESN'T MATTER IF IT'S A TRAP...

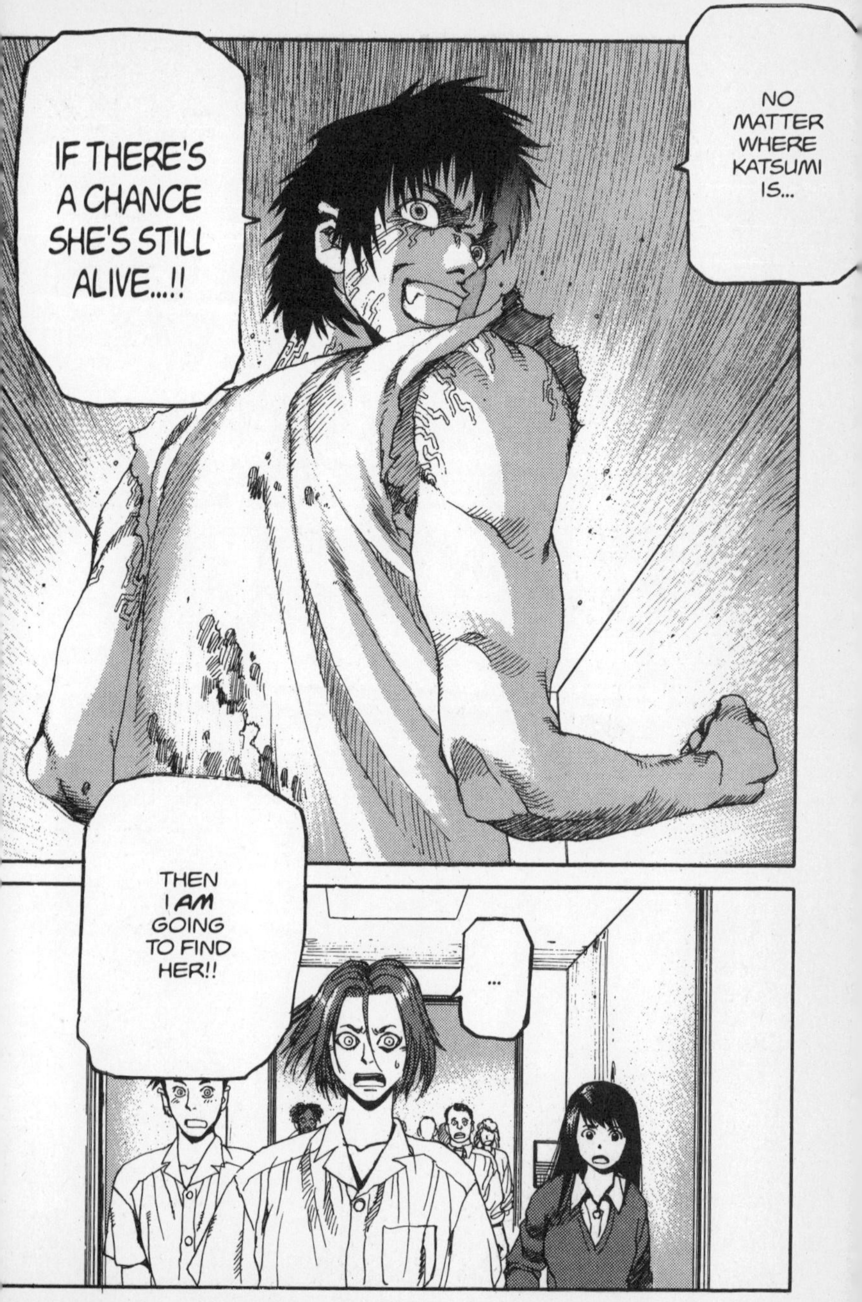
NO MATTER WHERE KATSUMI IS...
IF THERE'S A CHANCE SHE'S STILL ALIVE...!!
THEN I *AM* GOING TO FIND HER!!
...

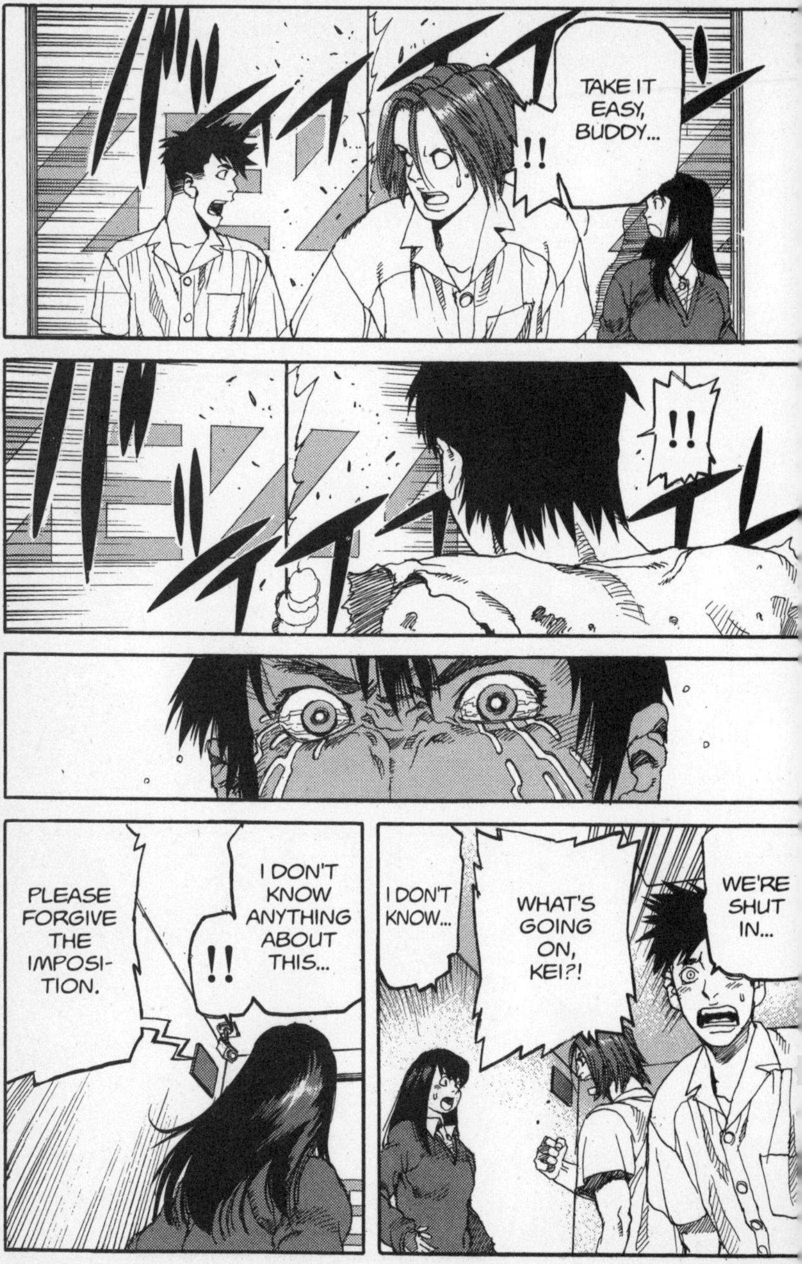
TAKE IT EASY, BUDDY...
!!
!!
WE'RE SHUT IN...
WHAT'S GOING ON, KEI?!
I DON'T KNOW...
I DON'T KNOW ANYTHING ABOUT THIS...
!!
PLEASE FORGIVE THE IMPOSITION.

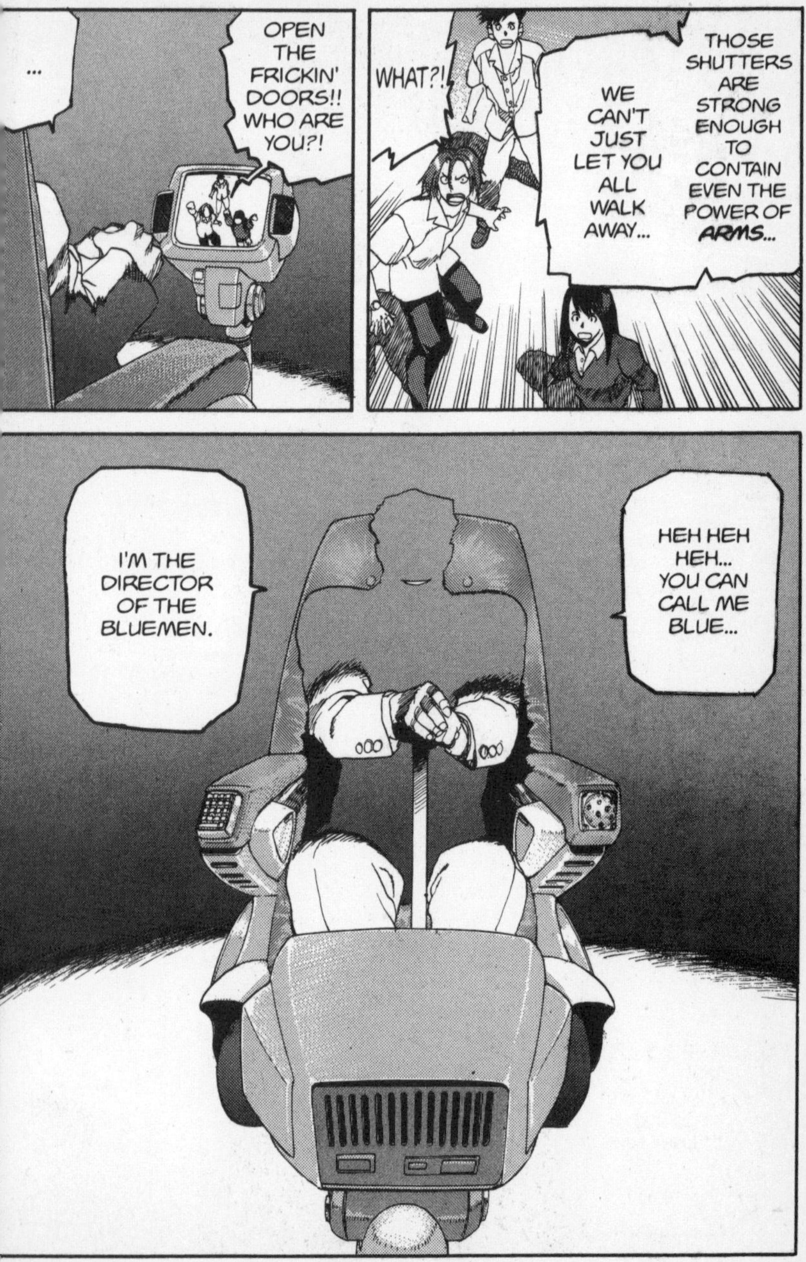
THOSE SHUTTERS ARE STRONG ENOUGH TO CONTAIN EVEN THE POWER OF ARMS...
WE CAN'T JUST LET YOU ALL WALK AWAY...
WHAT?!
OPEN THE FRICKIN' DOORS!! WHO ARE YOU?!
...
HEH HEH HEH... YOU CAN CALL ME BLUE...
I'M THE DIRECTOR OF THE BLUEMEN.

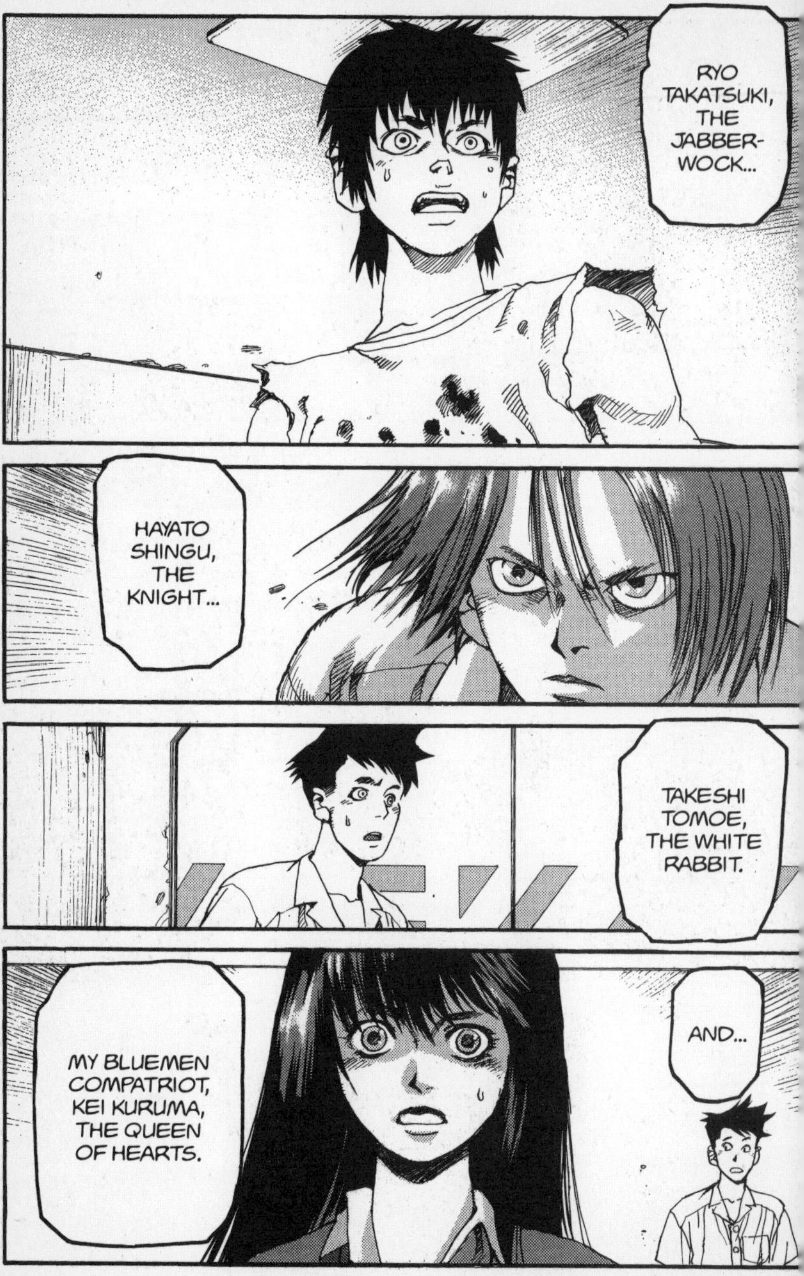
RYO TAKATSUKI, THE JABBER-WOCK...
HAYATO SHINGU, THE KNIGHT...
TAKESHI TOMOE, THE WHITE RABBIT.
AND...
MY BLUEMEN COMPATRIOT, KEI KURUMA, THE QUEEN OF HEARTS.

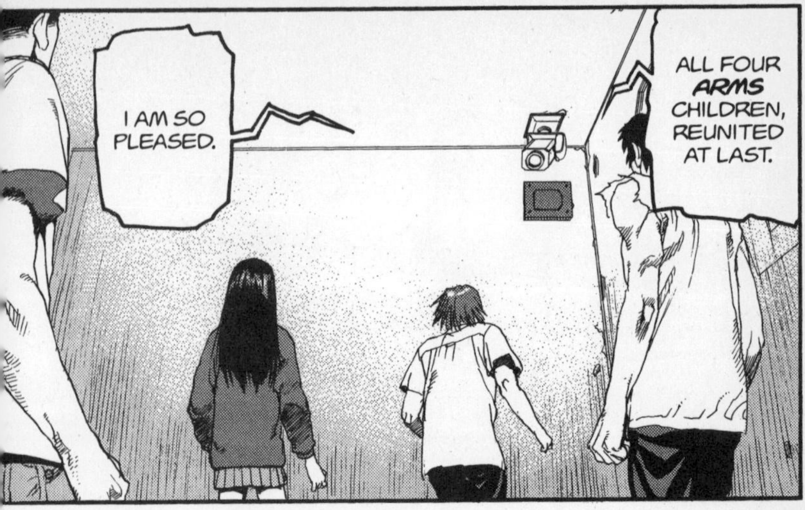
ALL FOUR ARMS CHILDREN, REUNITED AT LAST.
I AM SO PLEASED.

No. 5 WILL

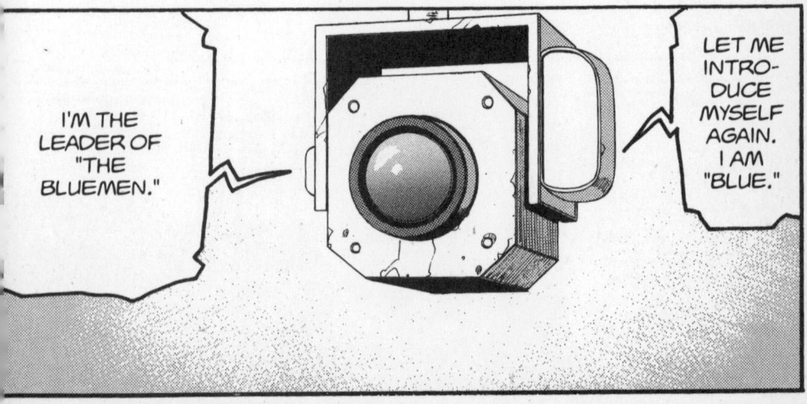
LET ME INTRO-DUCE MYSELF AGAIN. I AM "BLUE."
I'M THE LEADER OF "THE BLUEMEN."

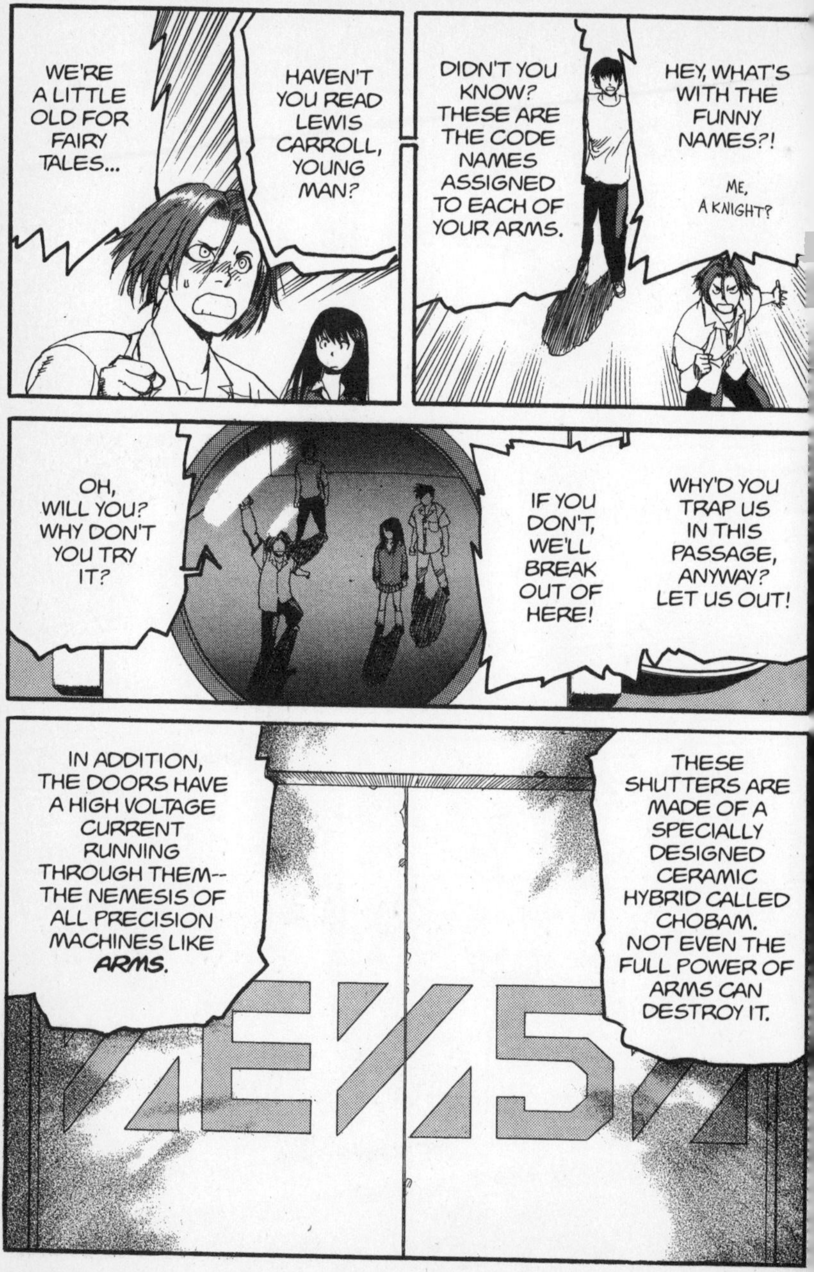
HEY, WHAT'S WITH THE FUNNY NAMES?!
ME, A KNIGHT?
DIDN'T YOU KNOW? THESE ARE THE CODE NAMES ASSIGNED TO EACH OF YOUR ARMS.
HAVEN'T YOU READ LEWIS CARROLL, YOUNG MAN?
WE'RE A LITTLE OLD FOR FAIRY TALES...
WHY'D YOU TRAP US IN THIS PASSAGE, ANYWAY? LET US OUT!
IF YOU DON'T, WE'LL BREAK OUT OF HERE!
OH, WILL YOU? WHY DON'T YOU TRY IT?
THESE SHUTTERS ARE MADE OF A SPECIALLY DESIGNED CERAMIC HYBRID CALLED CHOBAM. NOT EVEN THE FULL POWER OF ARMS CAN DESTROY IT.
IN ADDITION, THE DOORS HAVE A HIGH VOLTAGE CURRENT RUNNING THROUGH THEM--THE NEMESIS OF ALL PRECISION MACHINES LIKE ***ARMS***.

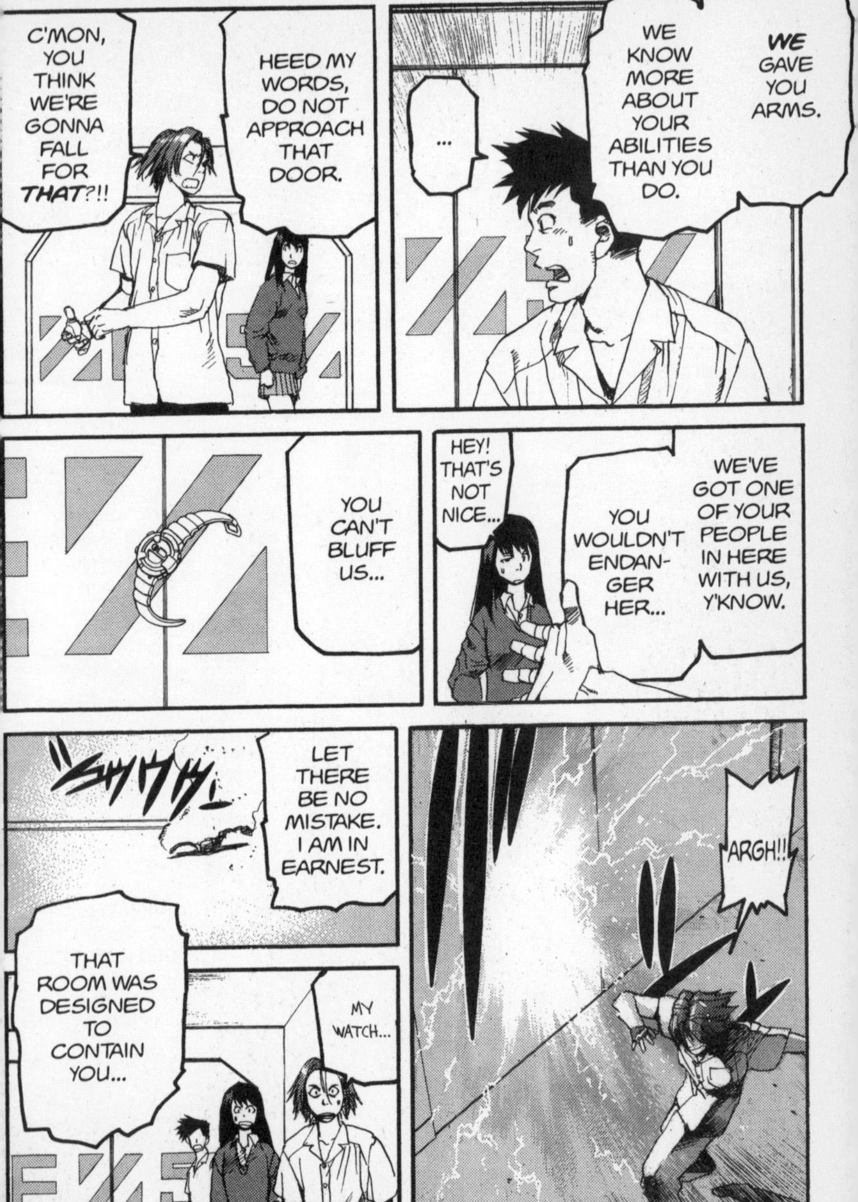
WE GAVE YOU ARMS.
WE KNOW MORE ABOUT YOUR ABILITIES THAN YOU DO.
...
HEED MY WORDS, DO NOT APPROACH THAT DOOR.
C'MON, YOU THINK WE'RE GONNA FALL FOR THAT?!!
WE'VE GOT ONE OF YOUR PEOPLE IN HERE WITH US, Y'KNOW.
YOU WOULDN'T ENDAN-GER HER...
HEY! THAT'S NOT NICE...
YOU CAN'T BLUFF US...
ARGH!!
LET THERE BE NO MISTAKE. I AM IN EARNEST.
THAT ROOM WAS DESIGNED TO CONTAIN YOU...
MY WATCH...

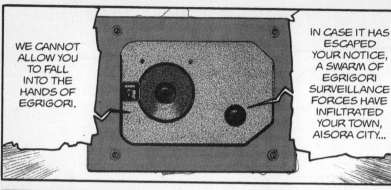

IN CASE IT HAS ESCAPED YOUR NOTICE, A SWARM OF EGRIGORI SURVEILLANCE FORCES HAVE INFILTRATED YOUR TOWN, AISORA CITY...
WE CANNOT ALLOW YOU TO FALL INTO THE HANDS OF EGRIGORI.
FOR TWENTY YEARS, THE BLUEMEN AND EGRIGORI HAVE WAGED BLOODY WAR OVER THE SECRETS OF ARMS...
COUNTLESS HAVE FALLEN...
ARMS IS THE FUTURE OF HUMANKIND... THE KEY TO OUR EVOLUTION!!
THE FATE OF ARMS TECHNOLOGY TAKES PRECEDENCE OVER THE WELFARE OF INDIVIDUALS.

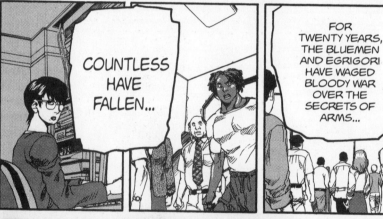

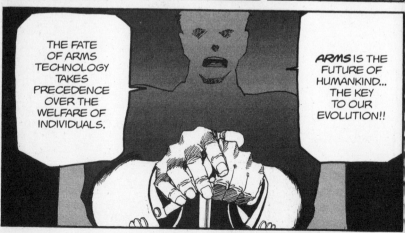

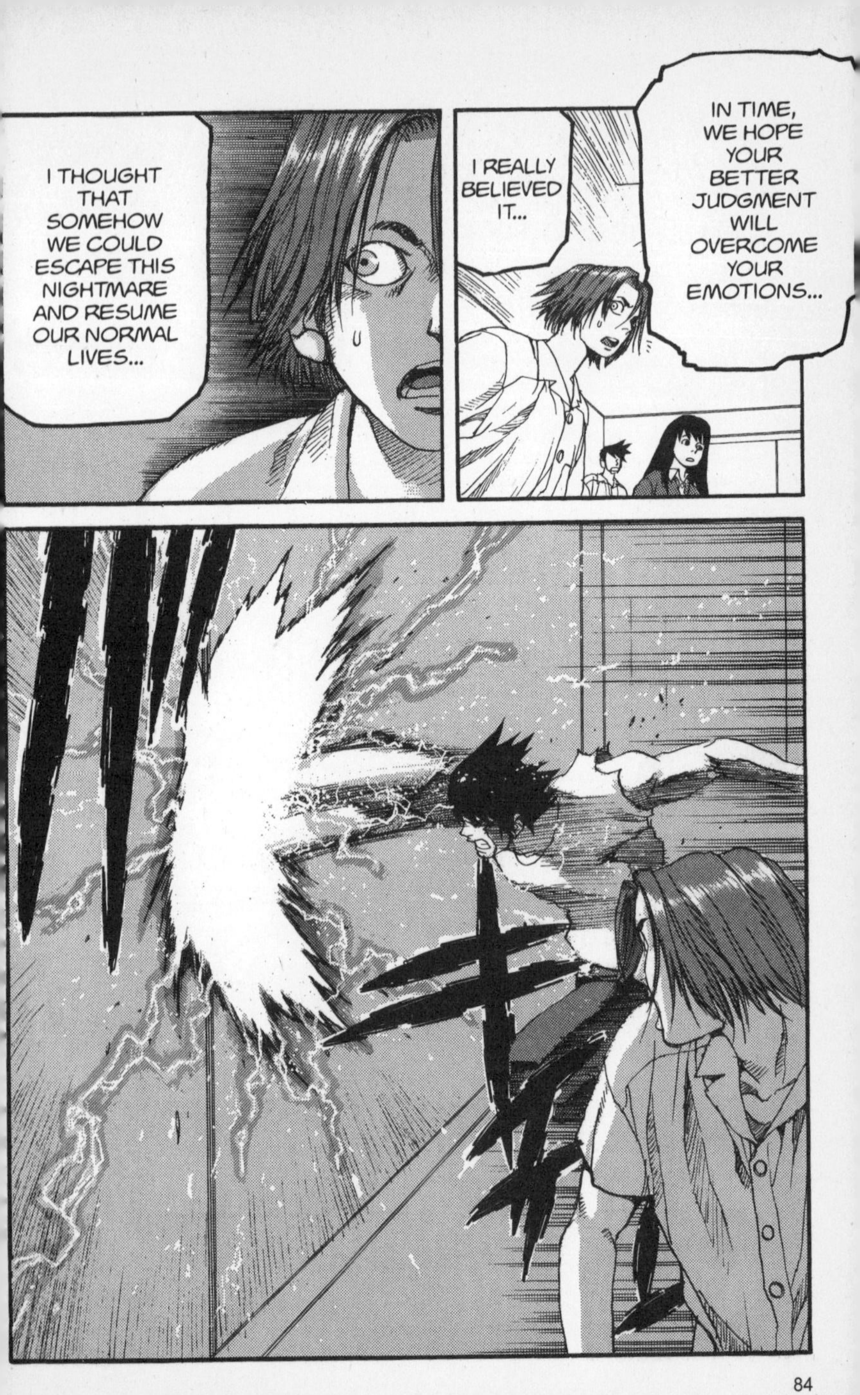
I THOUGHT THAT SOMEHOW WE COULD ESCAPE THIS NIGHTMARE AND RESUME OUR NORMAL LIVES...
I REALLY BELIEVED IT...
IN TIME, WE HOPE YOUR BETTER JUDGMENT WILL OVERCOME YOUR EMOTIONS...

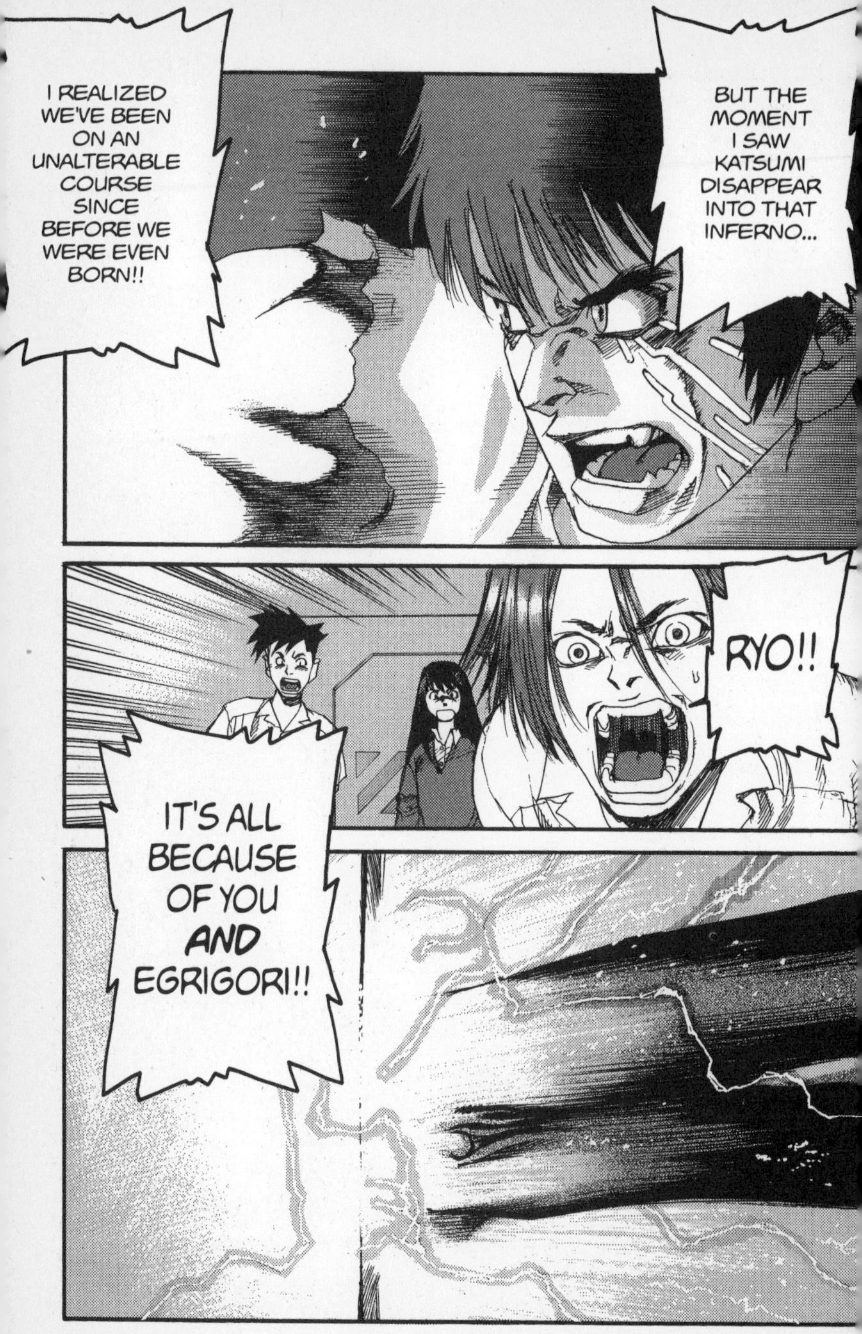
BUT THE MOMENT I SAW KATSUMI DISAPPEAR INTO THAT INFERNO...
I REALIZED WE'VE BEEN ON AN UNALTERABLE COURSE SINCE BEFORE WE WERE EVEN BORN!!
RYO!!
IT'S ALL BECAUSE OF YOU AND EGRIGORI!!

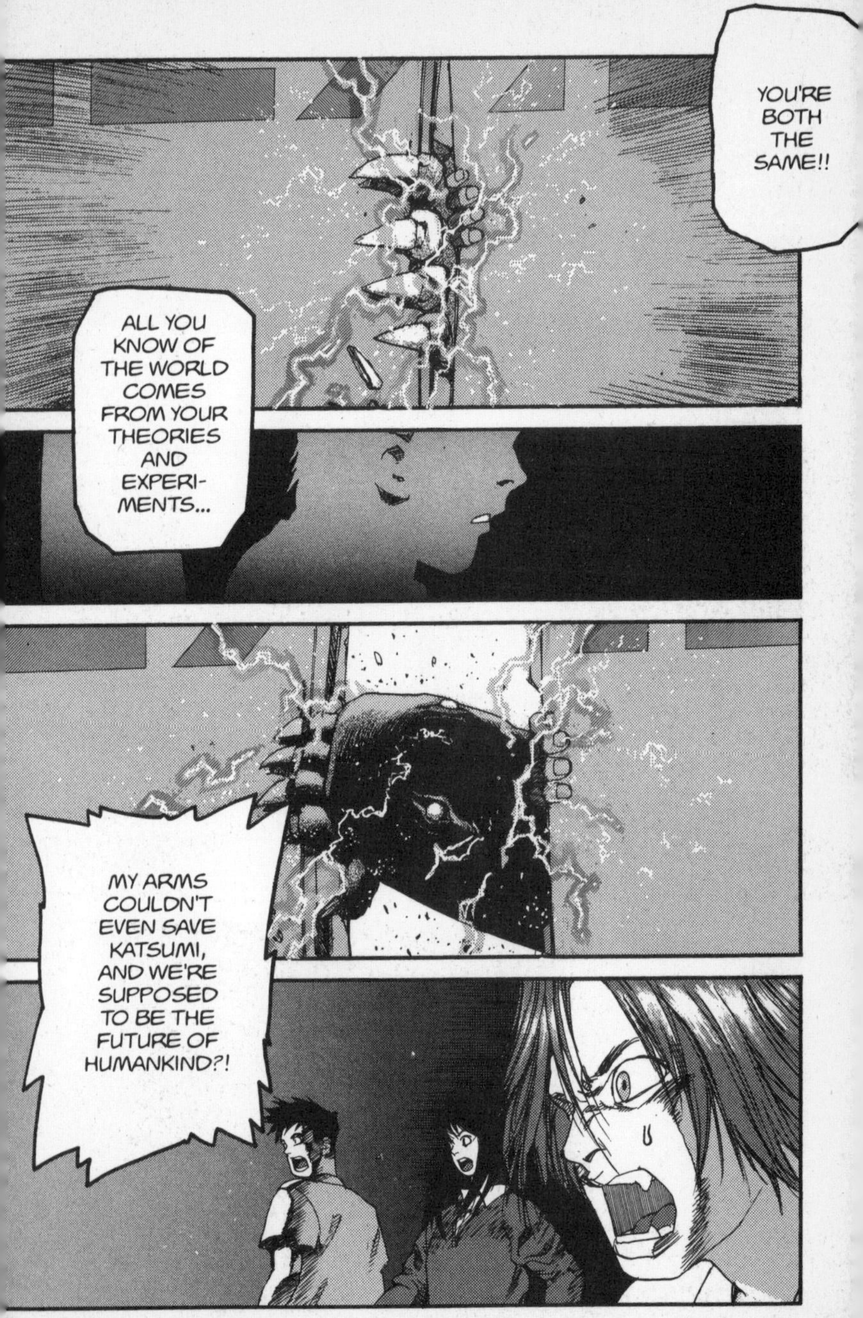
YOU'RE BOTH THE SAME!!
ALL YOU KNOW OF THE WORLD COMES FROM YOUR THEORIES AND EXPERI- MENTS...
MY ARMS COULDN'T EVEN SAVE KATSUMI, AND WE'RE SUPPOSED TO BE THE FUTURE OF HUMANKIND?!

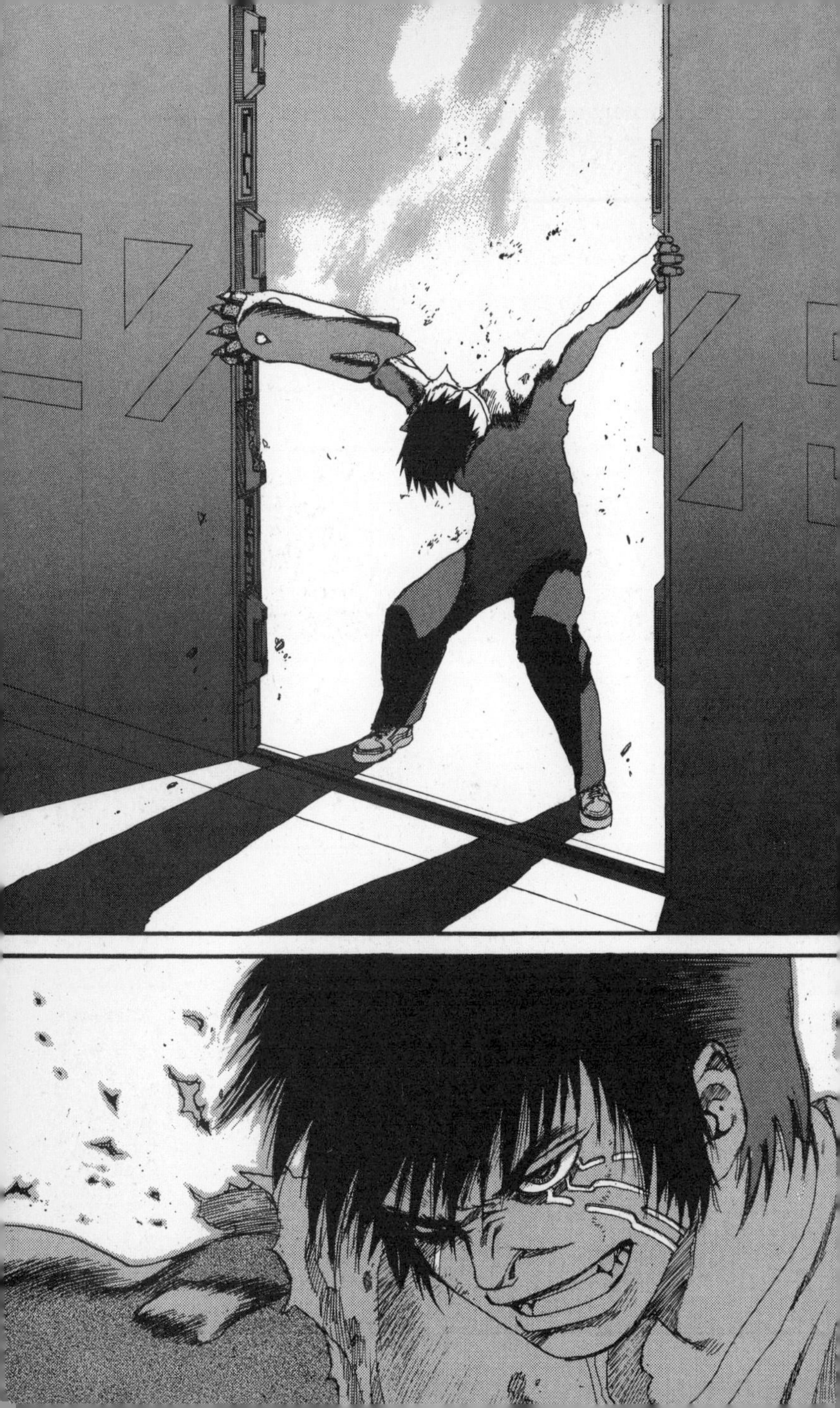

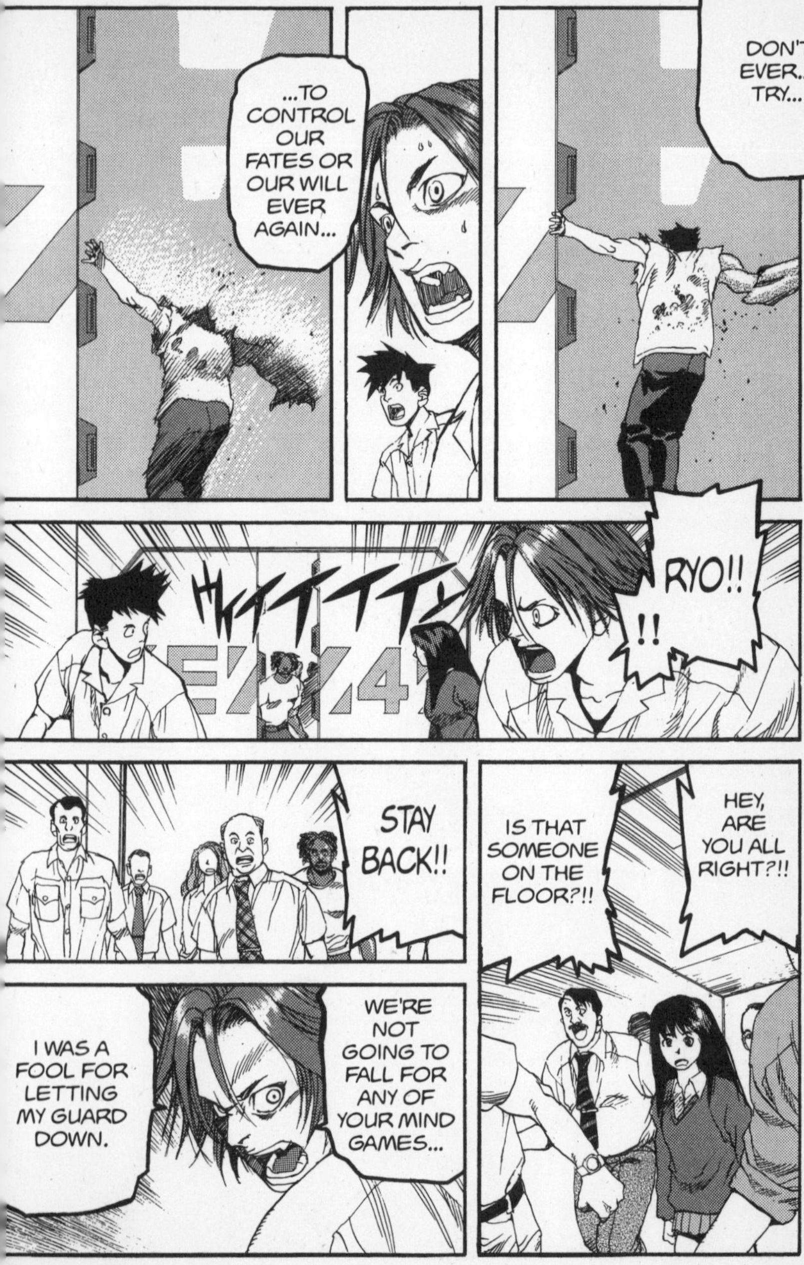
DON'T EVER... TRY...
...TO CONTROL OUR FATES OR OUR WILL EVER AGAIN...
RYO!!
!!
HEY, ARE YOU ALL RIGHT?!!
IS THAT SOMEONE ON THE FLOOR?!!
STAY BACK!!
WE'RE NOT GOING TO FALL FOR ANY OF YOUR MIND GAMES...
I WAS A FOOL FOR LETTING MY GUARD DOWN.

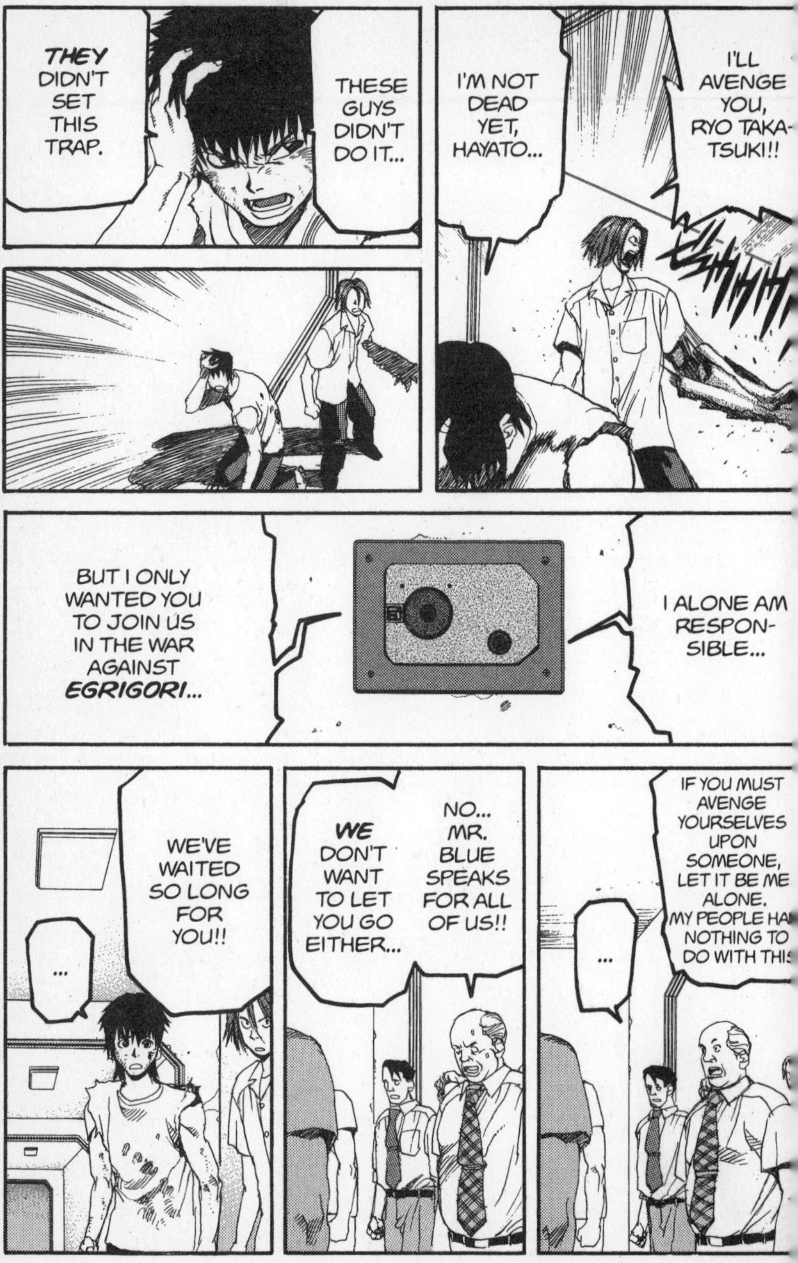
I'LL AVENGE YOU, RYO TAKA-TSUKI!!
I'M NOT DEAD YET, HAYATO...
THESE GUYS DIDN'T DO IT...
THEY DIDN'T SET THIS TRAP.
I ALONE AM RESPON-SIBLE...
BUT I ONLY WANTED YOU TO JOIN US IN THE WAR AGAINST *EGRIGORI*...
IF YOU MUST AVENGE YOURSELVES UPON SOMEONE, LET IT BE ME ALONE. MY PEOPLE HA NOTHING TO DO WITH THI
...
NO... MR. BLUE SPEAKS FOR ALL OF US!!
WE DON'T WANT TO LET YOU GO EITHER...
WE'VE WAITED SO LONG FOR YOU!!
...

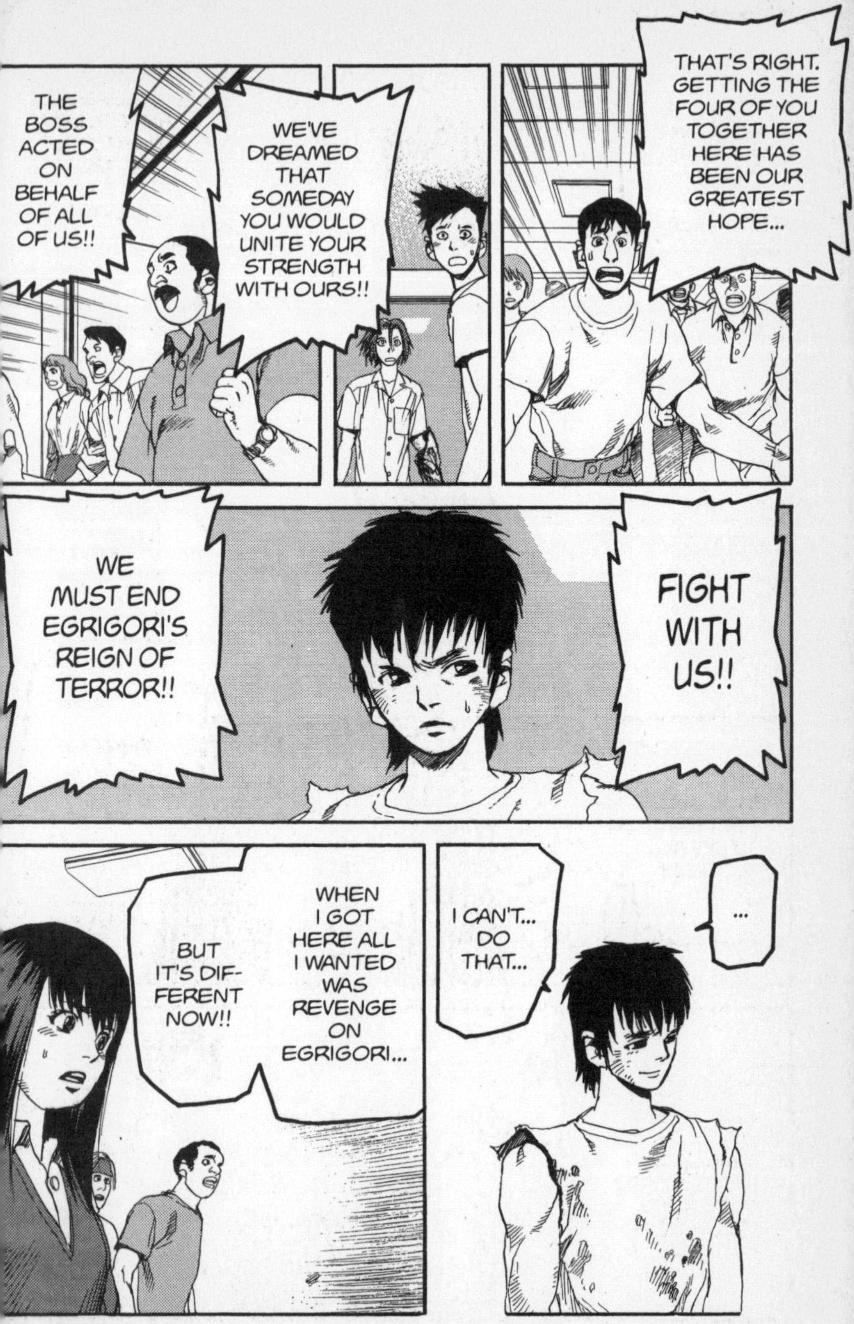
THAT'S RIGHT. GETTING THE FOUR OF YOU TOGETHER HERE HAS BEEN OUR GREATEST HOPE...
WE'VE DREAMED THAT SOMEDAY YOU WOULD UNITE YOUR STRENGTH WITH OURS!!
THE BOSS ACTED ON BEHALF OF ALL OF US!!
FIGHT WITH US!!
WE MUST END EGRIGORI'S REIGN OF TERROR!!
...
I CAN'T... DO THAT...
WHEN I GOT HERE ALL I WANTED WAS REVENGE ON EGRIGORI...
BUT IT'S DIF-FERENT NOW!!

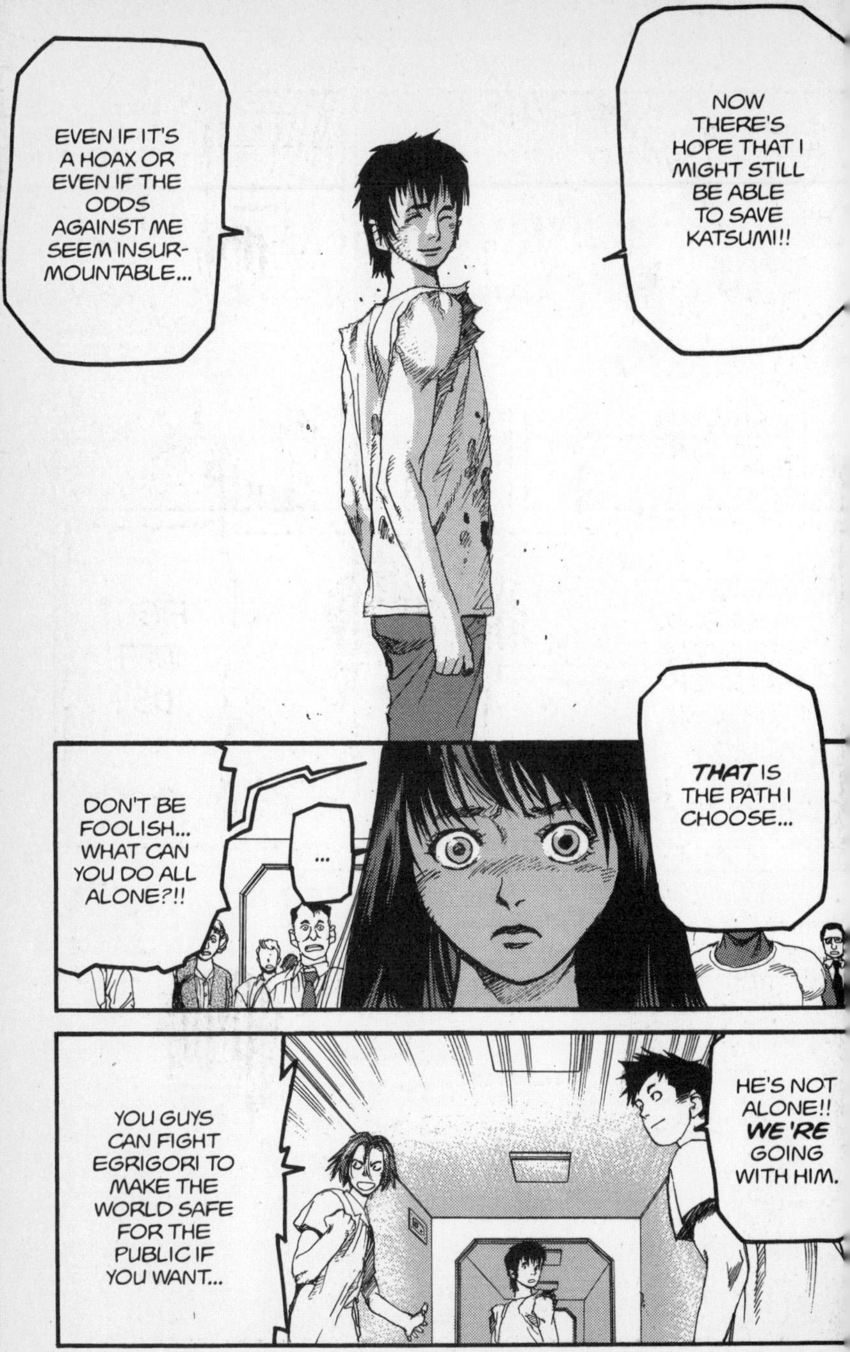
NOW THERE'S HOPE THAT I MIGHT STILL BE ABLE TO SAVE KATSUMI!!
EVEN IF IT'S A HOAX OR EVEN IF THE ODDS AGAINST ME SEEM INSUR-MOUNTABLE...
THAT IS THE PATH I CHOOSE...
DON'T BE FOOLISH... WHAT CAN YOU DO ALL ALONE?!!
...
HE'S NOT ALONE!! *WE'RE* GOING WITH HIM.
YOU GUYS CAN FIGHT EGRIGORI TO MAKE THE WORLD SAFE FOR THE PUBLIC IF YOU WANT...

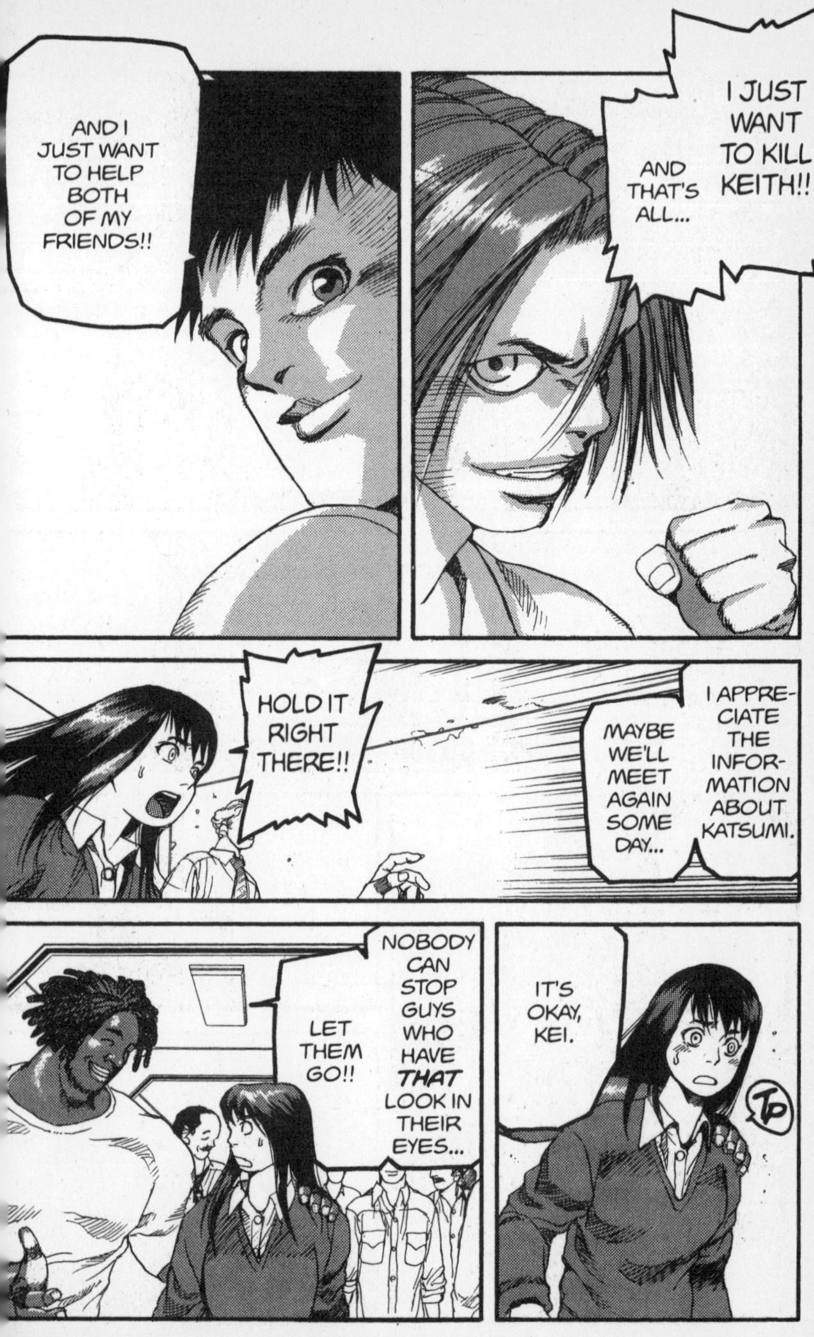
I JUST WANT TO KILL KEITH!!
AND THAT'S ALL...
AND I JUST WANT TO HELP BOTH OF MY FRIENDS!!
I APPRECIATE THE INFORMATION ABOUT KATSUMI.
MAYBE WE'LL MEET AGAIN SOME DAY...
HOLD IT RIGHT THERE!!
IT'S OKAY, KEI.
TP
NOBODY CAN STOP GUYS WHO HAVE *THAT* LOOK IN THEIR EYES...
LET THEM GO!!

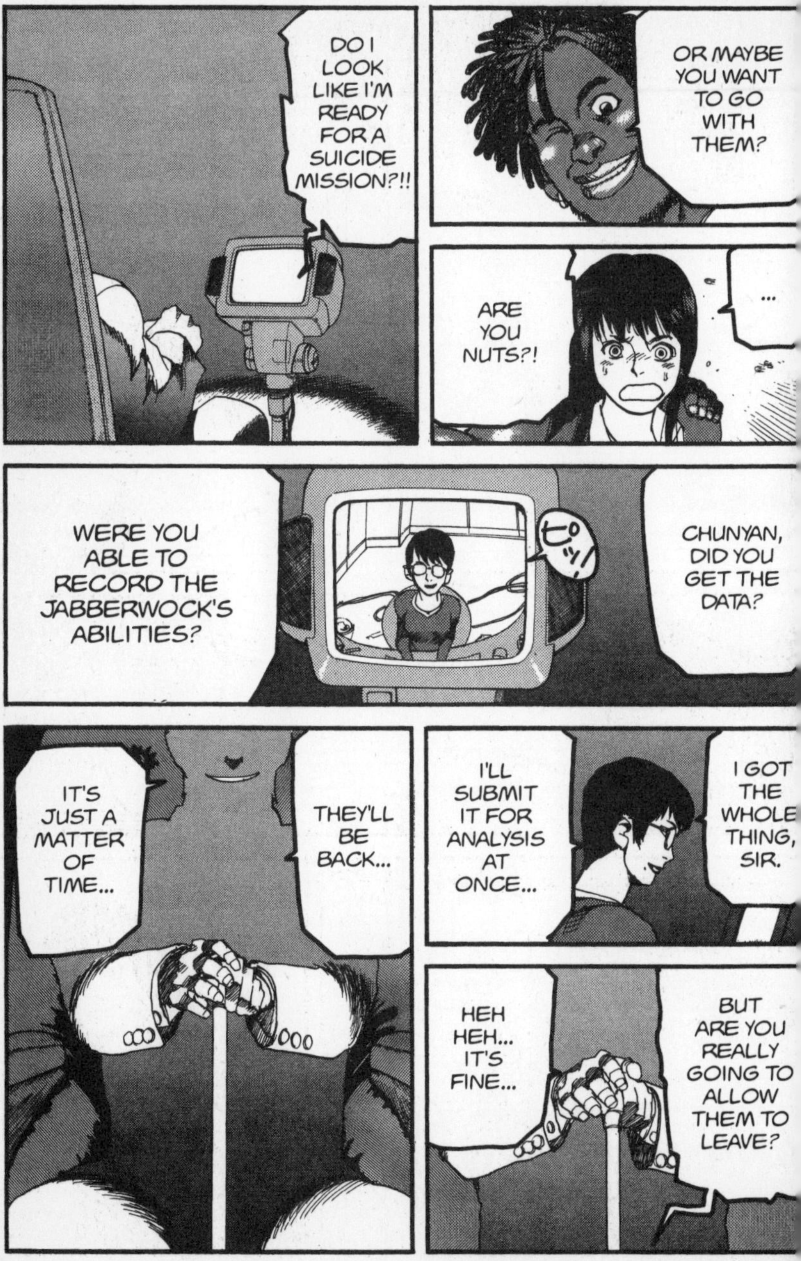
OR MAYBE YOU WANT TO GO WITH THEM?
...
ARE YOU NUTS?!
DO I LOOK LIKE I'M READY FOR A SUICIDE MISSION?!!
CHUNYAN, DID YOU GET THE DATA?
ピッ
WERE YOU ABLE TO RECORD THE JABBERWOCK'S ABILITIES?
I GOT THE WHOLE THING, SIR.
I'LL SUBMIT IT FOR ANALYSIS AT ONCE...
BUT ARE YOU REALLY GOING TO ALLOW THEM TO LEAVE?
HEH HEH... IT'S FINE...
THEY'LL BE BACK...
IT'S JUST A MATTER OF TIME...

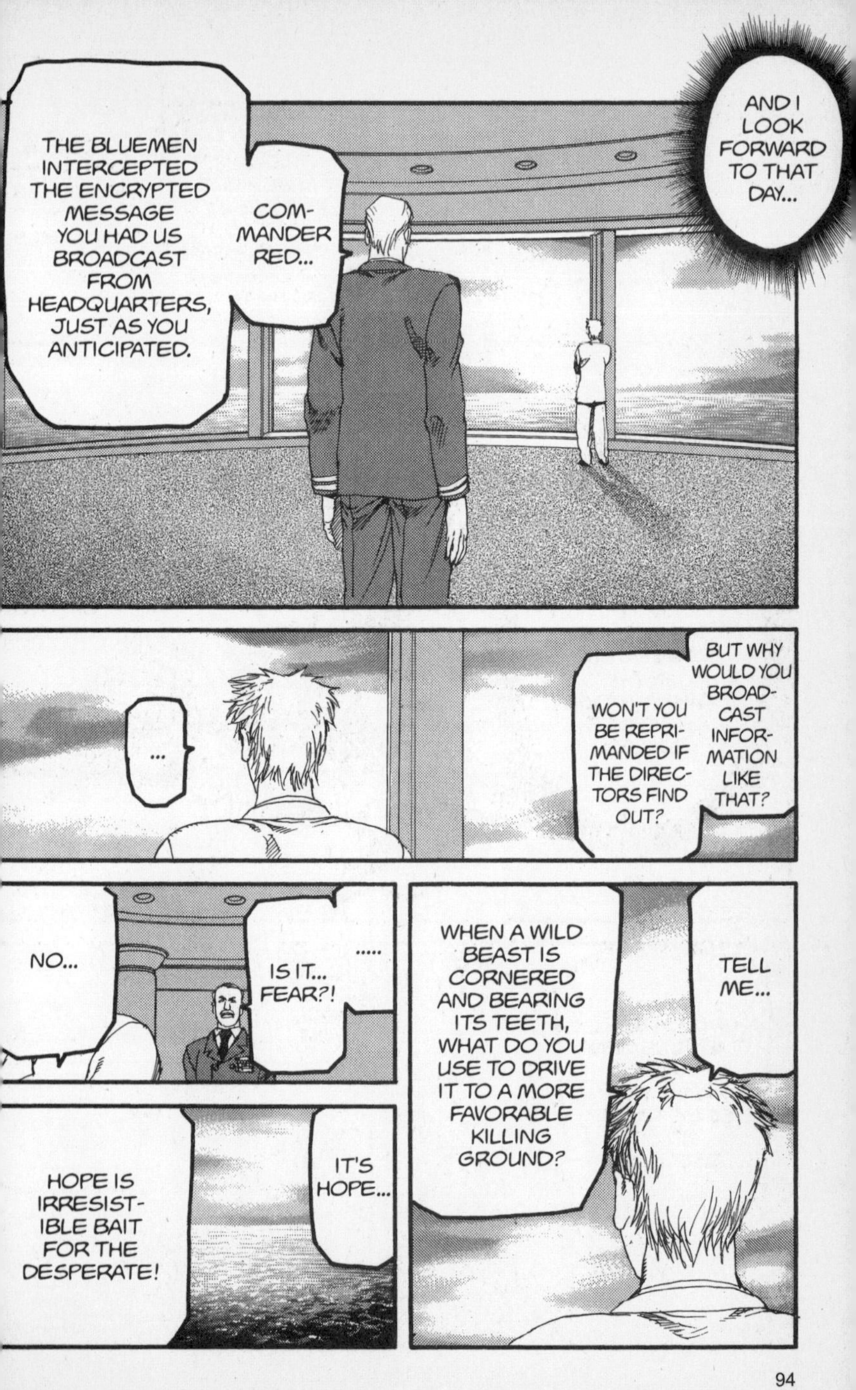
AND I LOOK FORWARD TO THAT DAY...
COM-MANDER RED...
THE BLUEMEN INTERCEPTED THE ENCRYPTED MESSAGE YOU HAD US BROADCAST FROM HEADQUARTERS, JUST AS YOU ANTICIPATED.
BUT WHY WOULD YOU BROAD-CAST INFOR-MATION LIKE THAT?
WON'T YOU BE REPRI-MANDED IF THE DIREC-TORS FIND OUT?
...
TELL ME...
WHEN A WILD BEAST IS CORNERED AND BEARING ITS TEETH, WHAT DO YOU USE TO DRIVE IT TO A MORE FAVORABLE KILLING GROUND?
.....
IS IT... FEAR?!
NO...
IT'S HOPE...
HOPE IS IRRESIST-IBLE BAIT FOR THE DESPERATE!

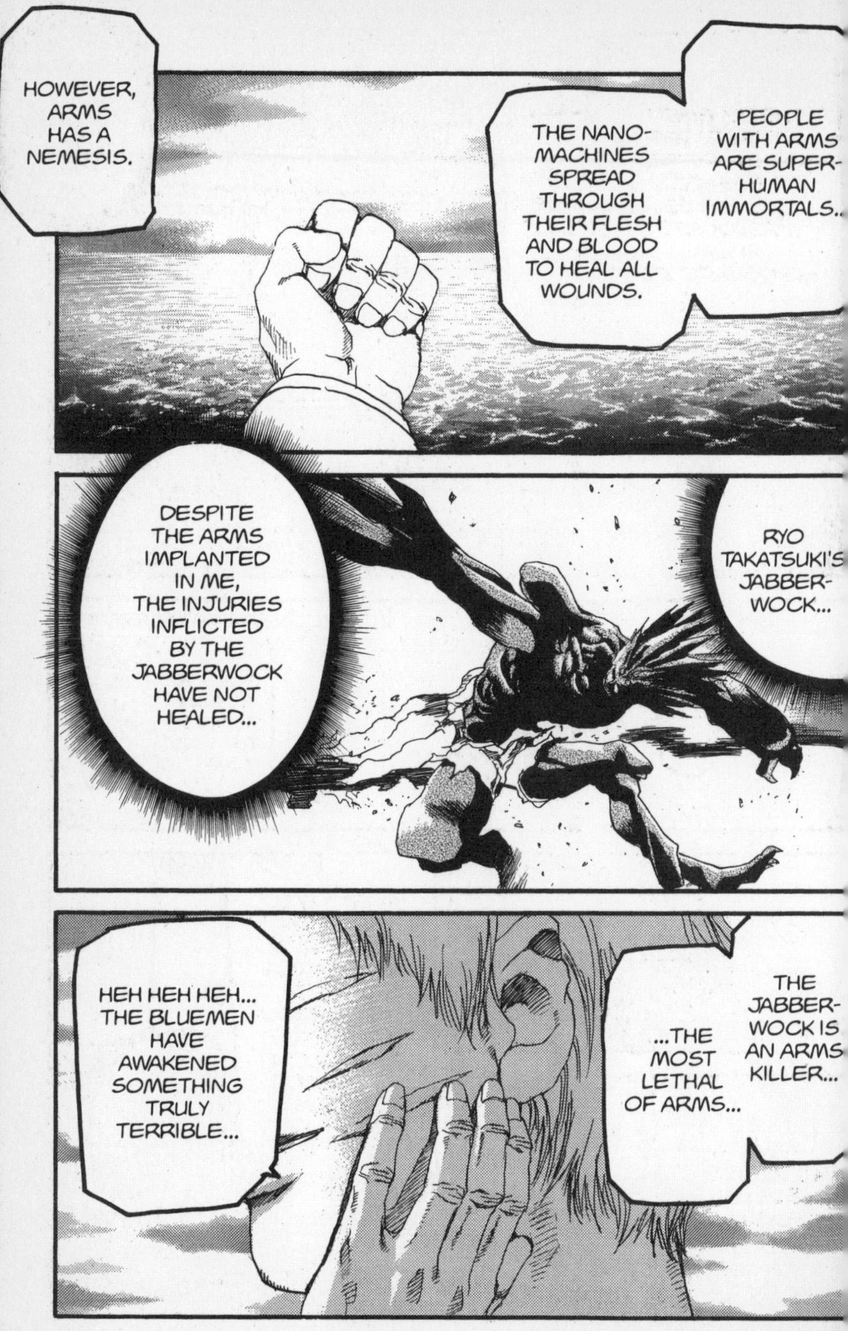
PEOPLE WITH ARMS ARE SUPER-HUMAN IMMORTALS..
THE NANO-MACHINES SPREAD THROUGH THEIR FLESH AND BLOOD TO HEAL ALL WOUNDS.
HOWEVER, ARMS HAS A NEMESIS.
RYO TAKATSUKI'S JABBER-WOCK...
DESPITE THE ARMS IMPLANTED IN ME, THE INJURIES INFLICTED BY THE JABBERWOCK HAVE NOT HEALED...
THE JABBER-WOCK IS AN ARMS KILLER...
...THE MOST LETHAL OF ARMS...
HEH HEH HEH... THE BLUEMEN HAVE AWAKENED SOMETHING TRULY TERRIBLE...

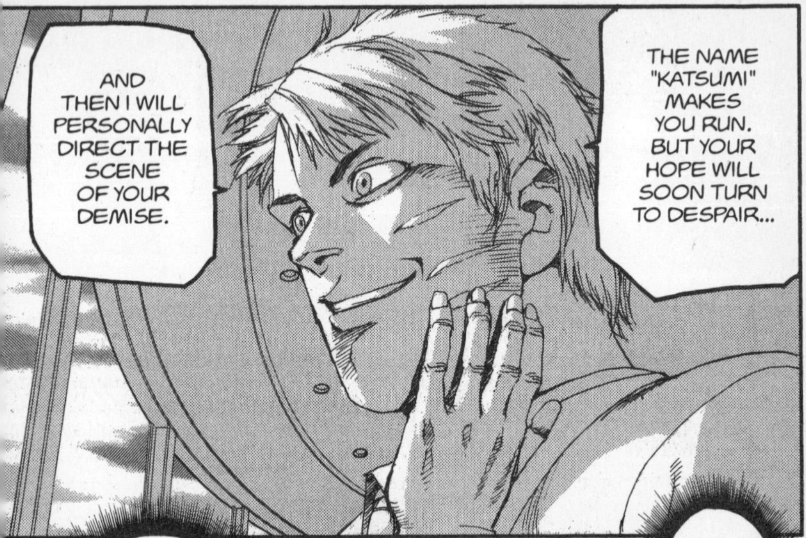
THE NAME "KATSUMI" MAKES YOU RUN. BUT YOUR HOPE WILL SOON TURN TO DESPAIR...
AND THEN I WILL PERSONALLY DIRECT THE SCENE OF YOUR DEMISE.

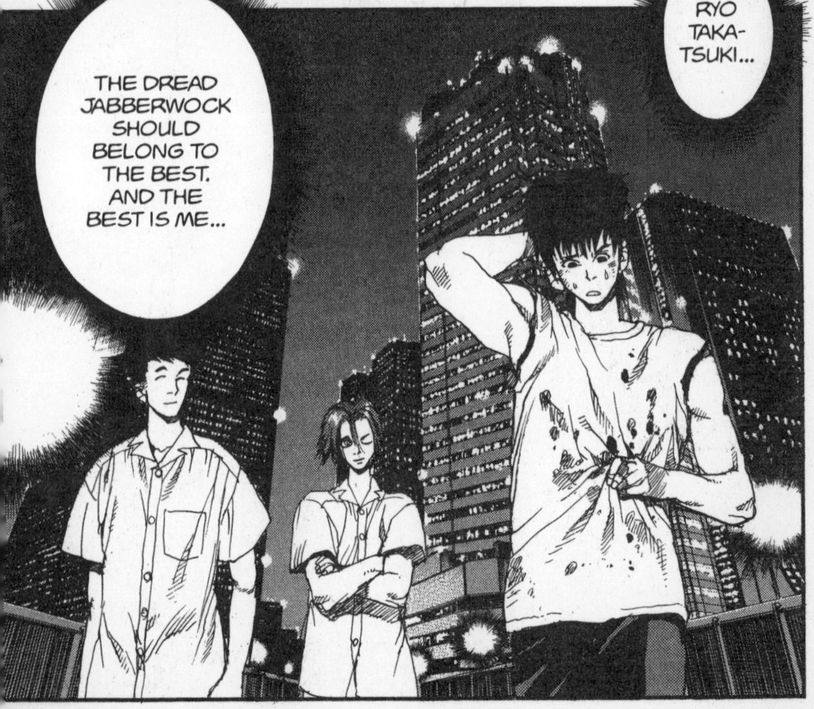
RYO TAKA-TSUKI...
THE DREAD JABBERWOCK SHOULD BELONG TO THE BEST. AND THE BEST IS ME...

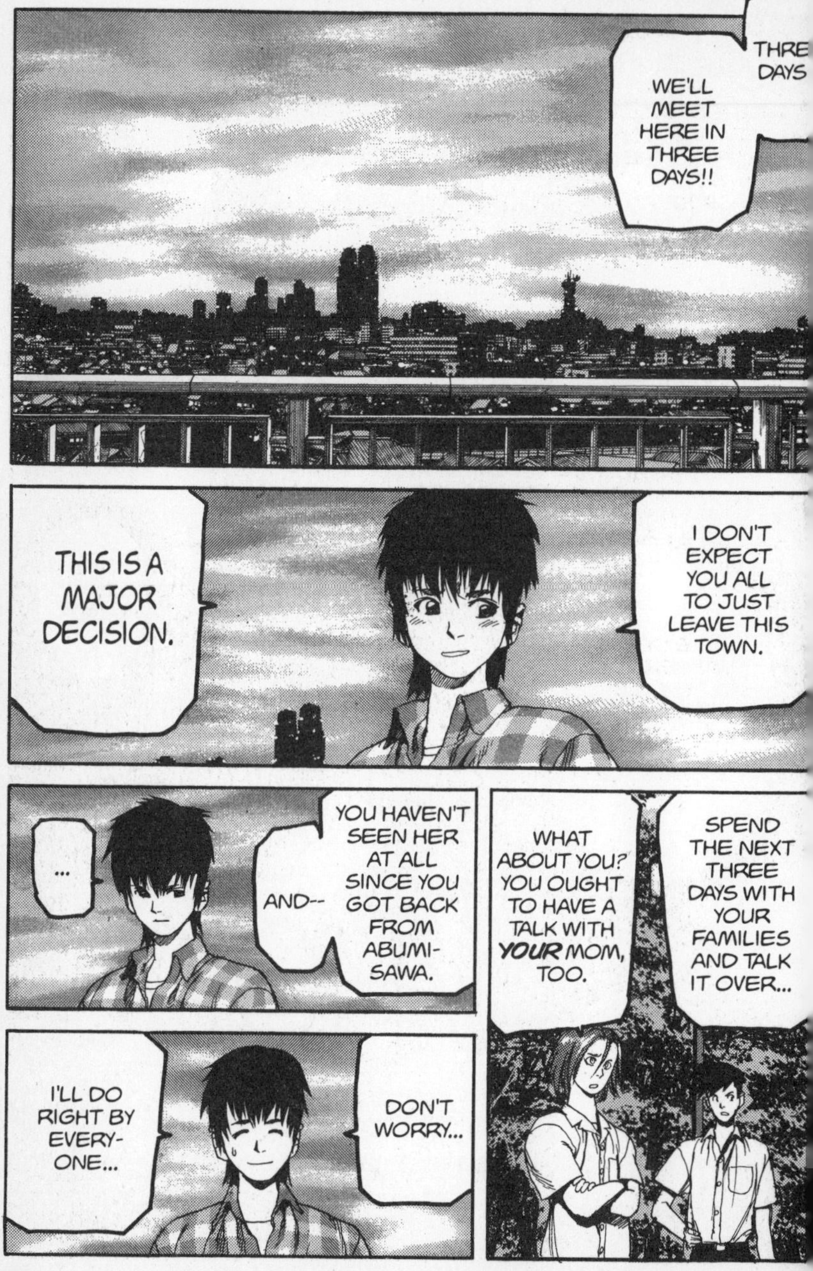
THRE DAYS
WE'LL MEET HERE IN THREE DAYS!!
I DON'T EXPECT YOU ALL TO JUST LEAVE THIS TOWN.
THIS IS A MAJOR DECISION.
SPEND THE NEXT THREE DAYS WITH YOUR FAMILIES AND TALK IT OVER...
WHAT ABOUT YOU? YOU OUGHT TO HAVE A TALK WITH ***YOUR*** MOM, TOO.
AND-- YOU HAVEN'T SEEN HER AT ALL SINCE YOU GOT BACK FROM ABUMI-SAWA.
...
DON'T WORRY...
I'LL DO RIGHT BY EVERY-ONE...

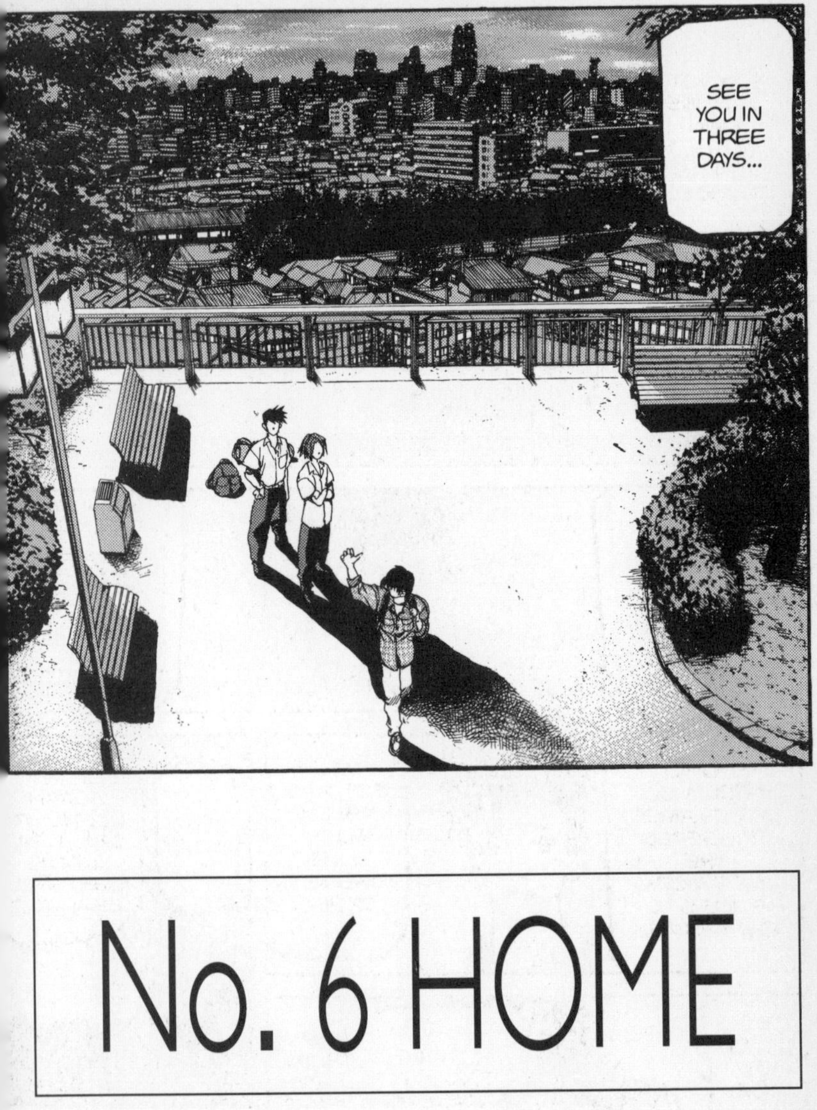
SEE YOU IN THREE DAYS...

No. 6 HOME

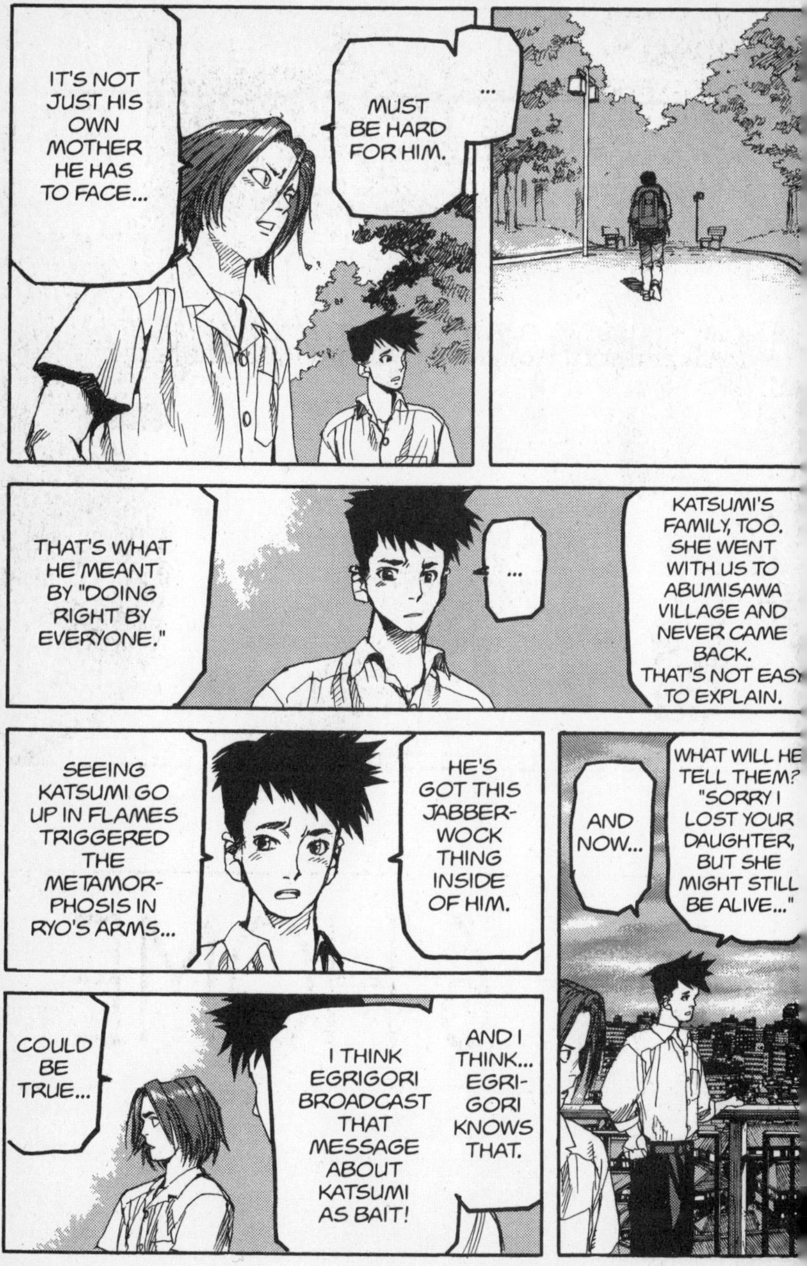
...
MUST BE HARD FOR HIM.
IT'S NOT JUST HIS OWN MOTHER HE HAS TO FACE...
KATSUMI'S FAMILY, TOO. SHE WENT WITH US TO ABUMISAWA VILLAGE AND NEVER CAME BACK. THAT'S NOT EASY TO EXPLAIN.
...
THAT'S WHAT HE MEANT BY "DOING RIGHT BY EVERYONE."
WHAT WILL HE TELL THEM? "SORRY I LOST YOUR DAUGHTER, BUT SHE MIGHT STILL BE ALIVE..."
AND NOW...
HE'S GOT THIS JABBER-WOCK THING INSIDE OF HIM.
SEEING KATSUMI GO UP IN FLAMES TRIGGERED THE METAMOR-PHOSIS IN RYO'S ARMS...
AND I THINK... EGRI-GORI KNOWS THAT.
I THINK EGRIGORI BROADCAST THAT MESSAGE ABOUT KATSUMI AS BAIT!
COULD BE TRUE...

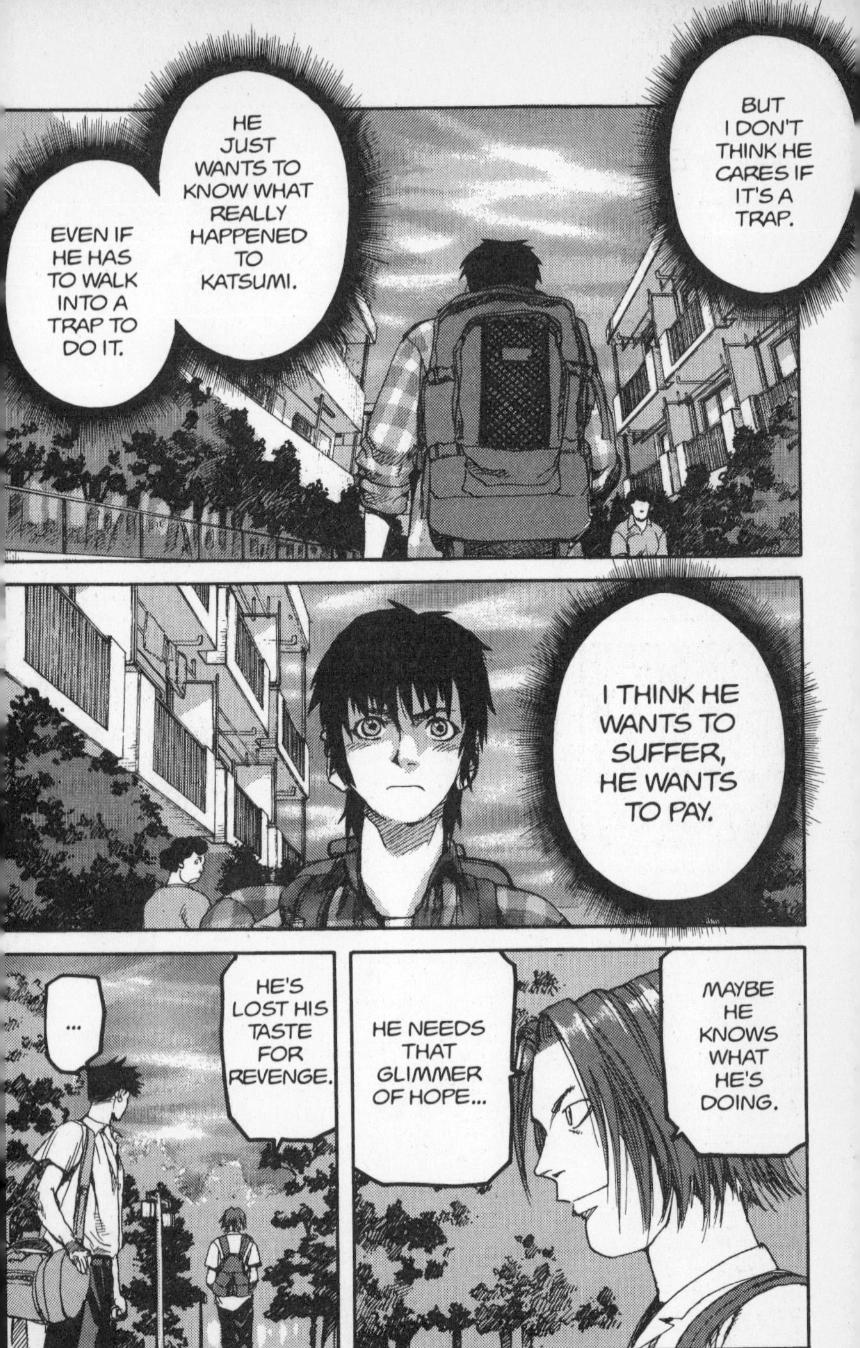
BUT I DON'T THINK HE CARES IF IT'S A TRAP.
HE JUST WANTS TO KNOW WHAT REALLY HAPPENED TO KATSUMI.
EVEN IF HE HAS TO WALK INTO A TRAP TO DO IT.
I THINK HE WANTS TO SUFFER, HE WANTS TO PAY.
MAYBE HE KNOWS WHAT HE'S DOING.
HE NEEDS THAT GLIMMER OF HOPE...
HE'S LOST HIS TASTE FOR REVENGE.
...

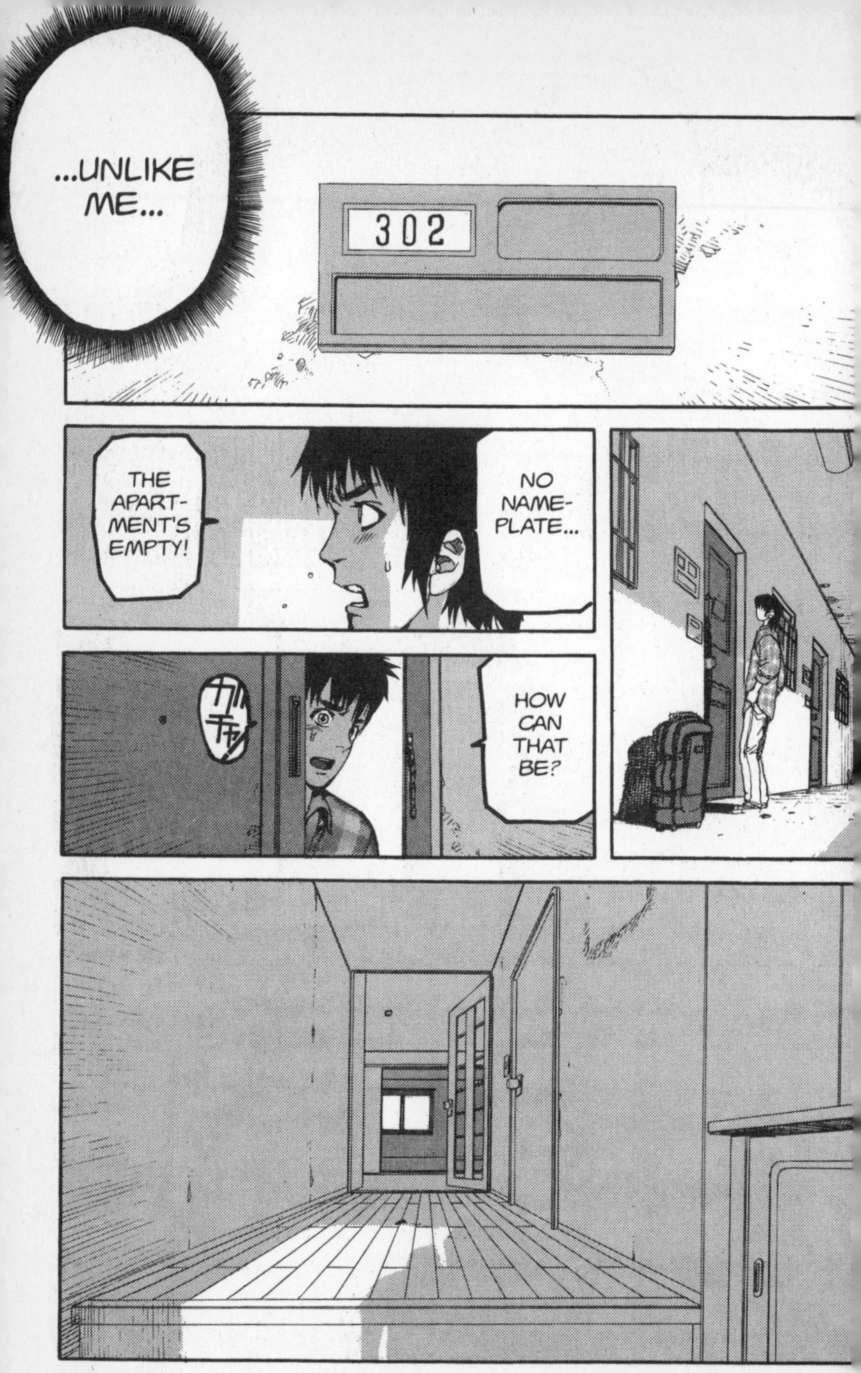
...UNLIKE ME...
302
NO NAME-PLATE...
THE APART-MENT'S EMPTY!
HOW CAN THAT BE?

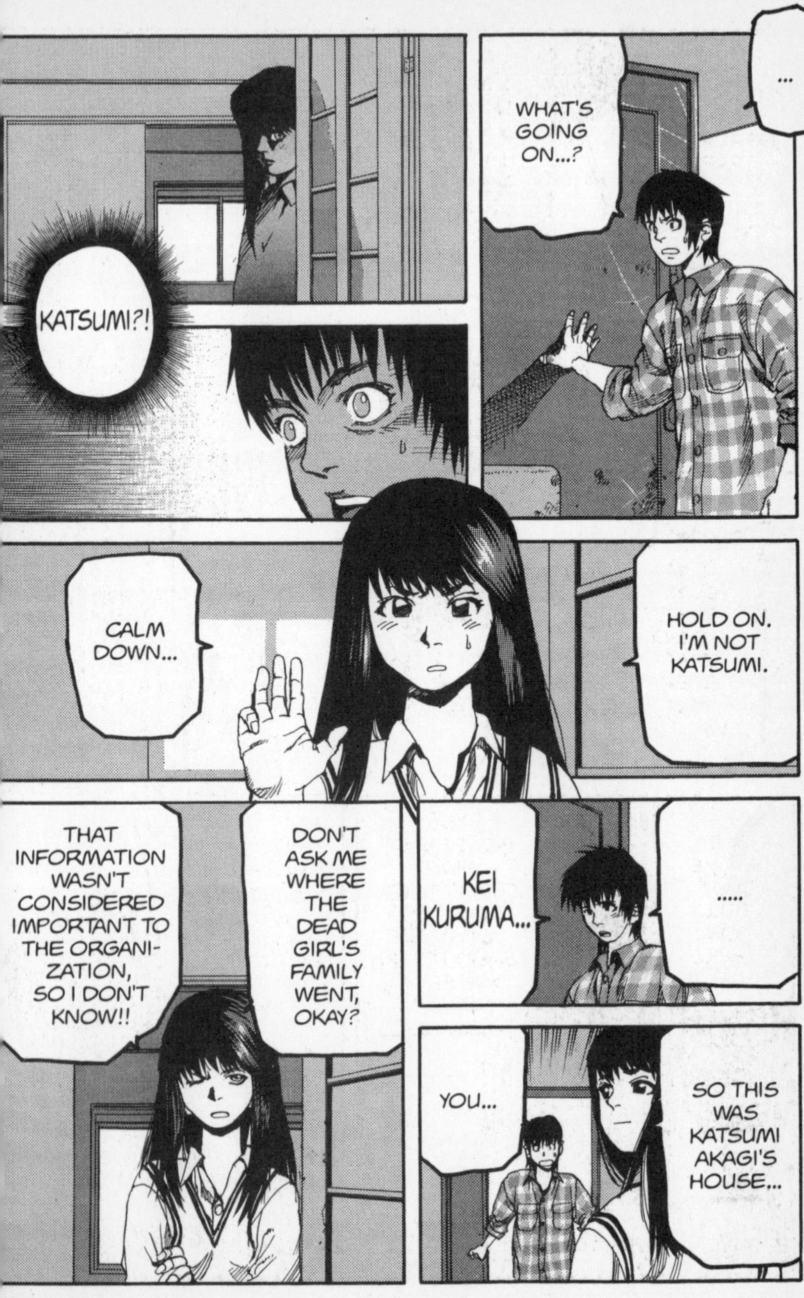
...
WHAT'S GOING ON...?
KATSUMI?!
HOLD ON. I'M NOT KATSUMI.
CALM DOWN...
.....
KEI KURUMA...
SO THIS WAS KATSUMI AKAGI'S HOUSE...
YOU...
DON'T ASK ME WHERE THE DEAD GIRL'S FAMILY WENT, OKAY?
THAT INFORMATION WASN'T CONSIDERED IMPORTANT TO THE ORGANI-ZATION, SO I DON'T KNOW!!

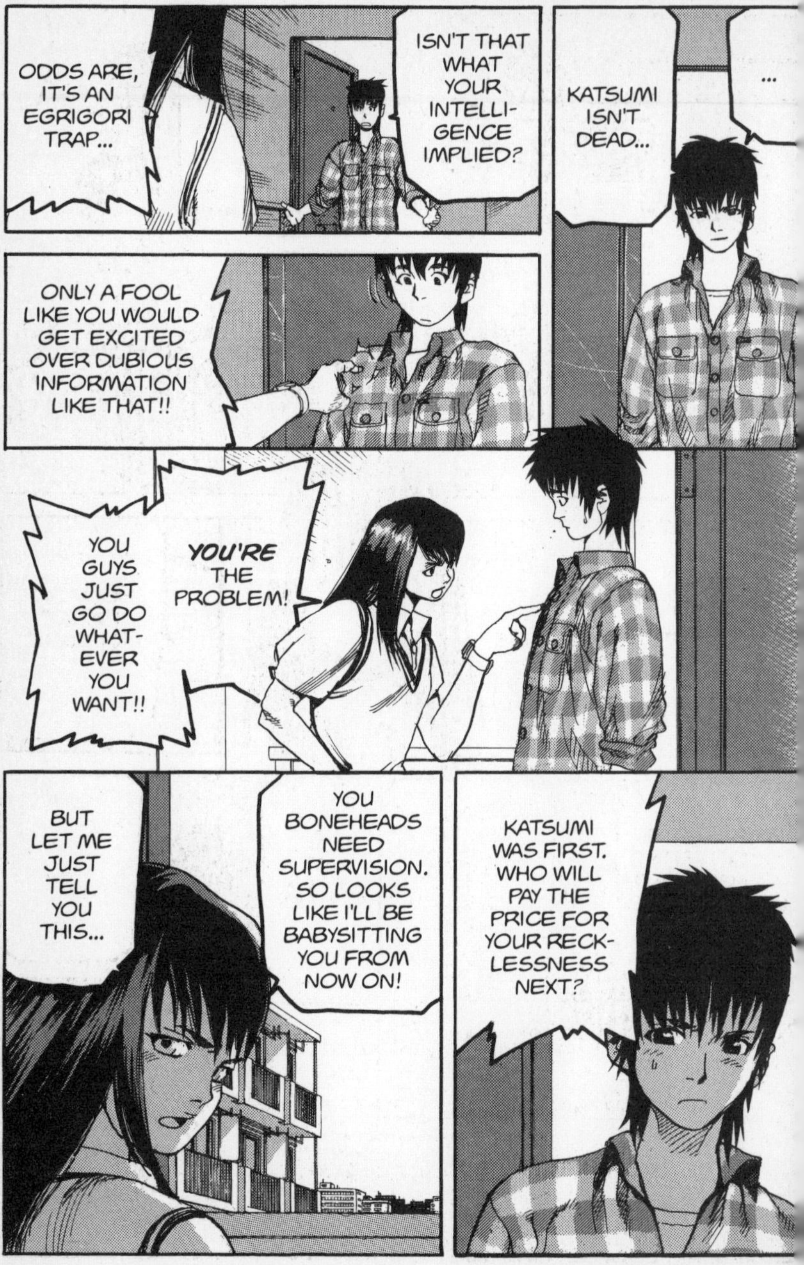
ODDS ARE, IT'S AN EGRIGORI TRAP...
ISN'T THAT WHAT YOUR INTELLI-GENCE IMPLIED?
KATSUMI ISN'T DEAD...
...
ONLY A FOOL LIKE YOU WOULD GET EXCITED OVER DUBIOUS INFORMATION LIKE THAT!!
YOU GUYS JUST GO DO WHAT-EVER YOU WANT!!
YOU'RE THE PROBLEM!
BUT LET ME JUST TELL YOU THIS...
YOU BONEHEADS NEED SUPERVISION. SO LOOKS LIKE I'LL BE BABYSITTING YOU FROM NOW ON!
KATSUMI WAS FIRST. WHO WILL PAY THE PRICE FOR YOUR RECK-LESSNESS NEXT?

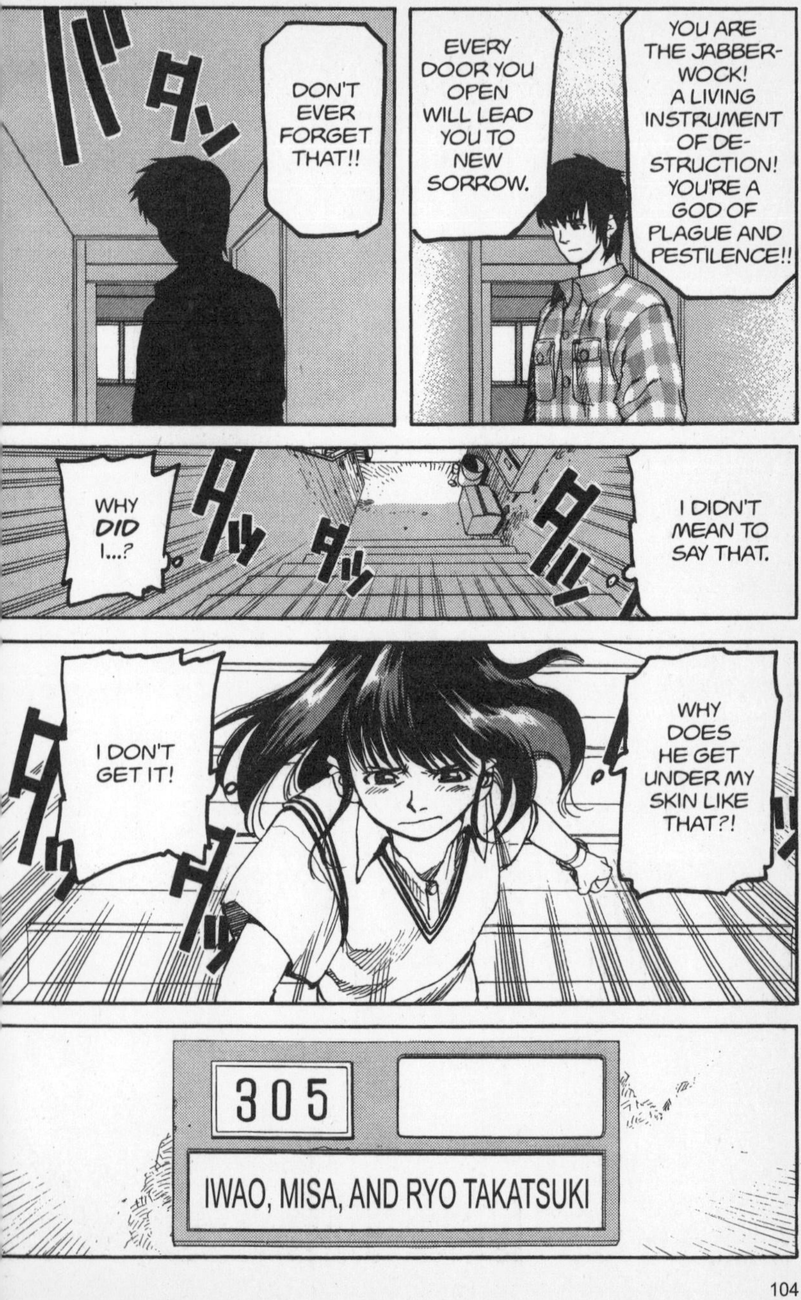
YOU ARE THE JABBER-WOCK! A LIVING INSTRUMENT OF DE-STRUCTION! YOU'RE A GOD OF PLAGUE AND PESTILENCE!!
EVERY DOOR YOU OPEN WILL LEAD YOU TO NEW SORROW.
DON'T EVER FORGET THAT!!
バタン
I DIDN'T MEAN TO SAY THAT.
ダッ
ダッ
ダッ
WHY *DID* I...?
WHY DOES HE GET UNDER MY SKIN LIKE THAT?!
I DON'T GET IT!
ダッ
ダッ
305
IWAO, MISA, AND RYO TAKATSUKI

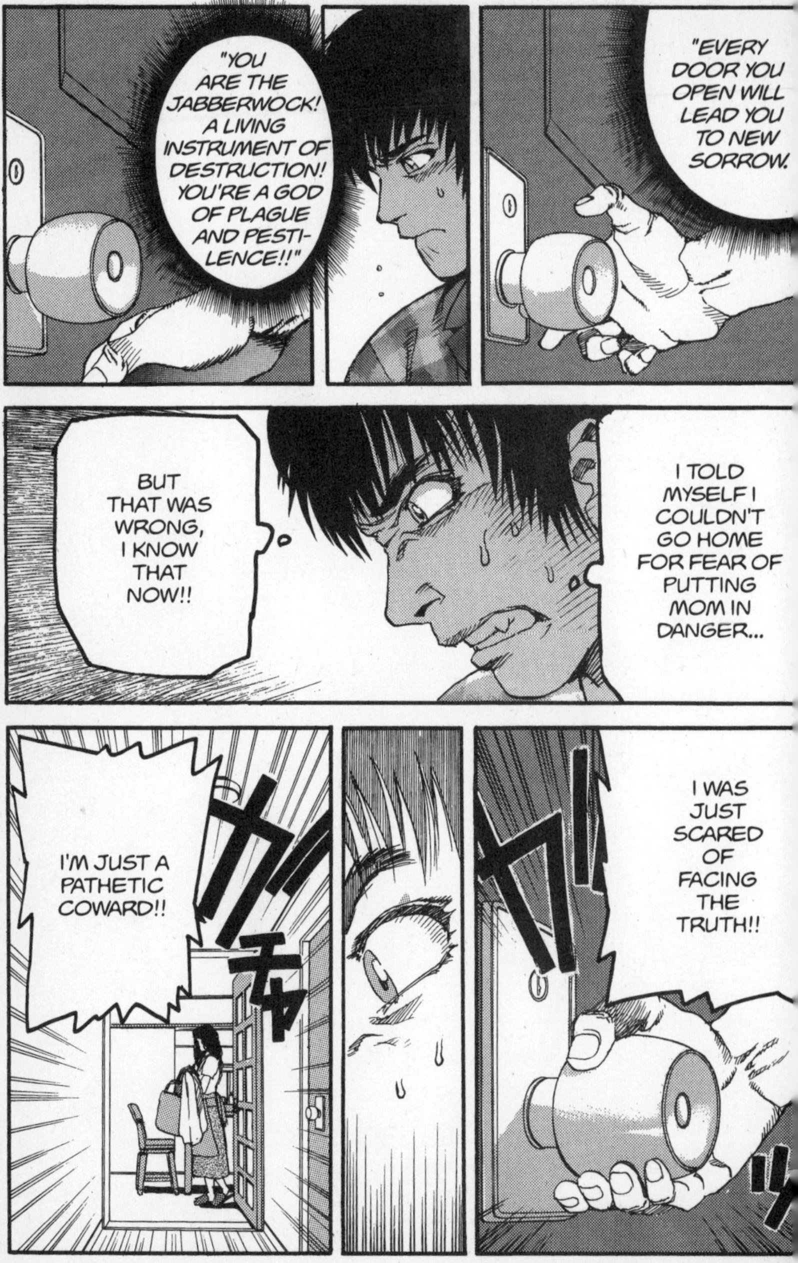
"EVERY DOOR YOU OPEN WILL LEAD YOU TO NEW SORROW.
"YOU ARE THE JABBERWOCK! A LIVING INSTRUMENT OF DESTRUCTION! YOU'RE A GOD OF PLAGUE AND PESTI-LENCE!!"
I TOLD MYSELF I COULDN'T GO HOME FOR FEAR OF PUTTING MOM IN DANGER...
BUT THAT WAS WRONG, I KNOW THAT NOW!!
I WAS JUST SCARED OF FACING THE TRUTH!!
I'M JUST A PATHETIC COWARD!!

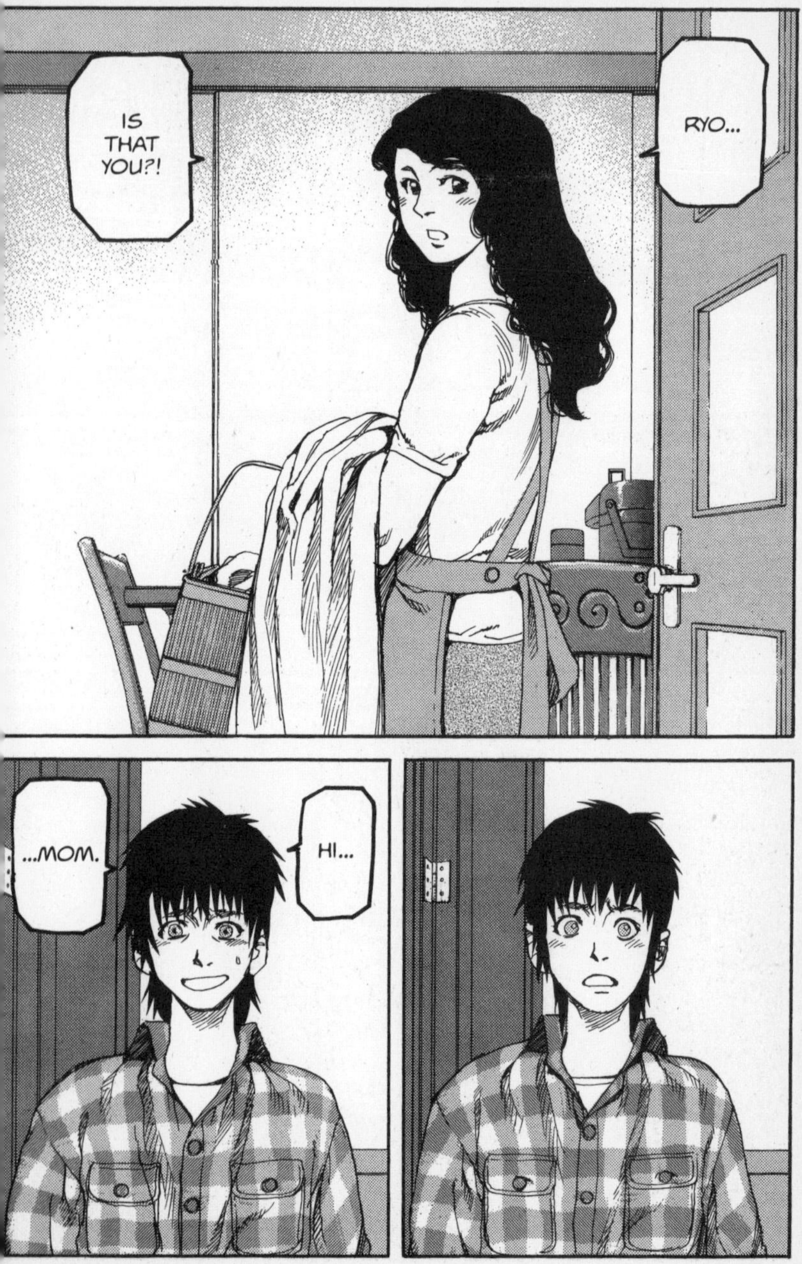
RYO...
IS THAT YOU?!
HI...
...MOM.

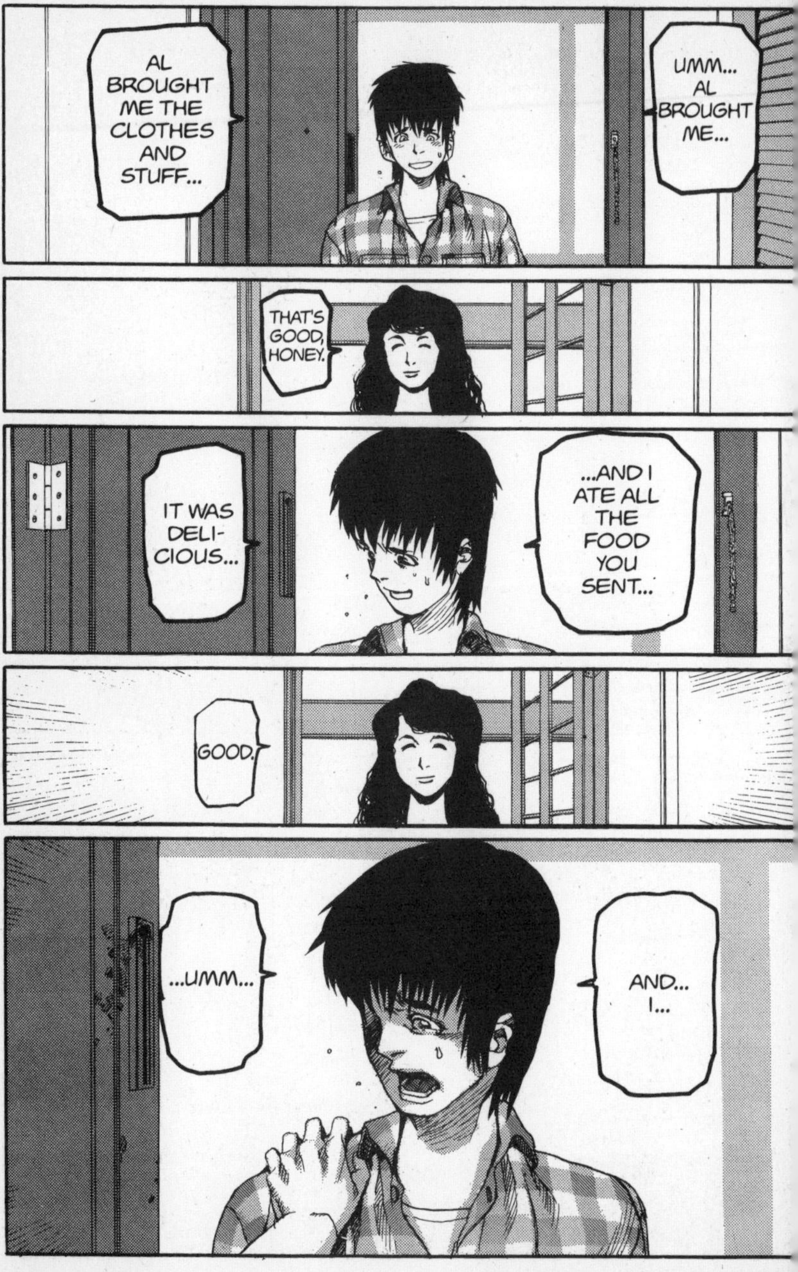
UMM... AL BROUGHT ME...
AL BROUGHT ME THE CLOTHES AND STUFF...
THAT'S GOOD, HONEY.
...AND I ATE ALL THE FOOD YOU SENT...
IT WAS DELICIOUS...
GOOD.
AND... I...
...UMM...

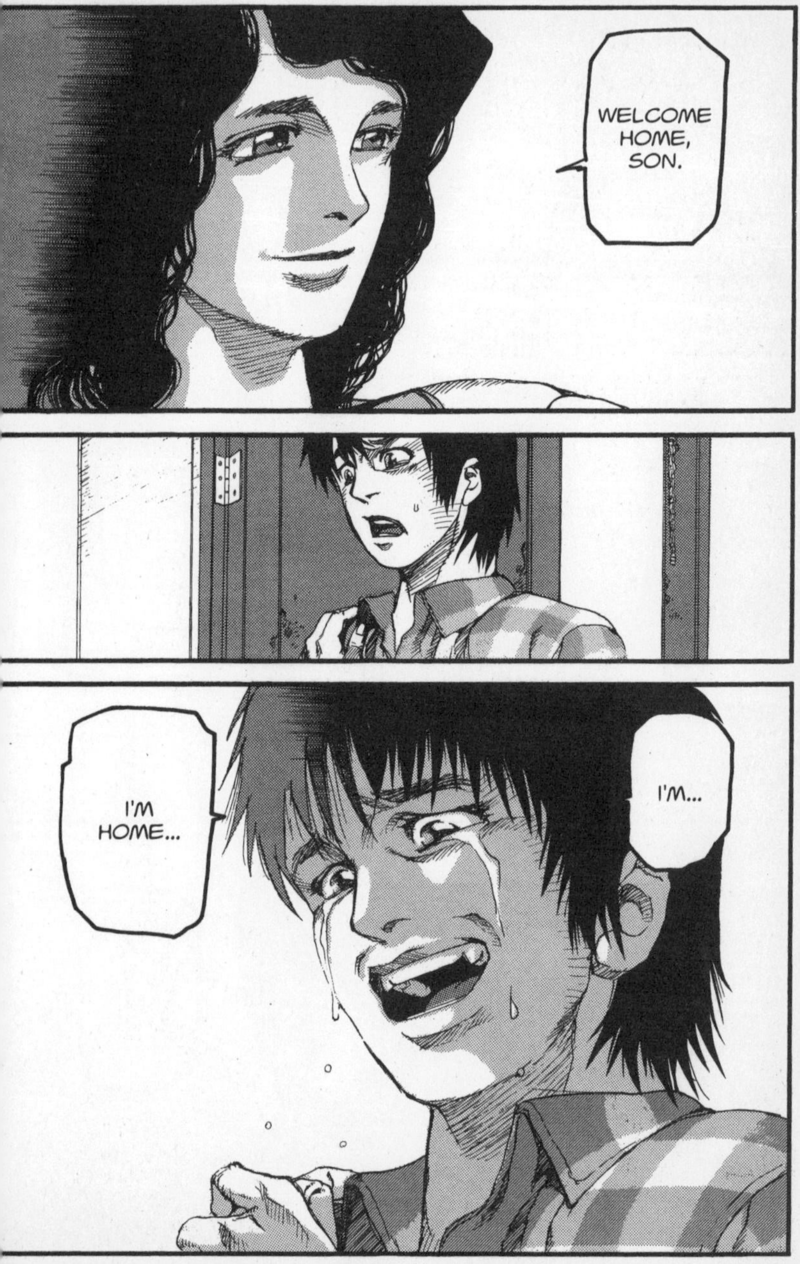
WELCOME HOME, SON.
I'M...
I'M HOME...

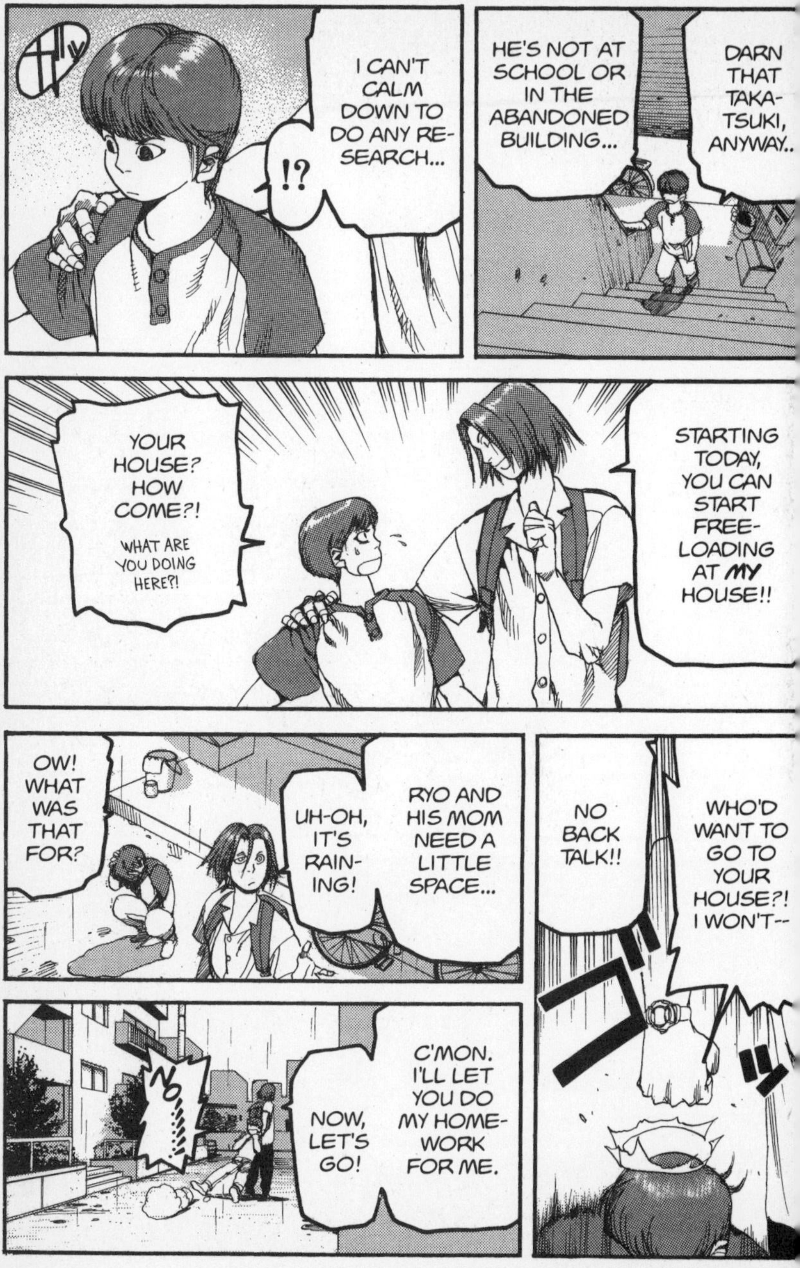
DARN THAT TAKA-TSUKI, ANYWAY..
HE'S NOT AT SCHOOL OR IN THE ABANDONED BUILDING...
I CAN'T CALM DOWN TO DO ANY RE-SEARCH...
!?
STARTING TODAY, YOU CAN START FREE-LOADING AT MY HOUSE!!
YOUR HOUSE? HOW COME?!
WHAT ARE YOU DOING HERE?!
WHO'D WANT TO GO TO YOUR HOUSE?! I WON'T--
NO BACK TALK!!
RYO AND HIS MOM NEED A LITTLE SPACE...
UH-OH, IT'S RAINING!
OW! WHAT WAS THAT FOR?
C'MON. I'LL LET YOU DO MY HOME-WORK FOR ME.
NOW, LET'S GO!
NO...!!!

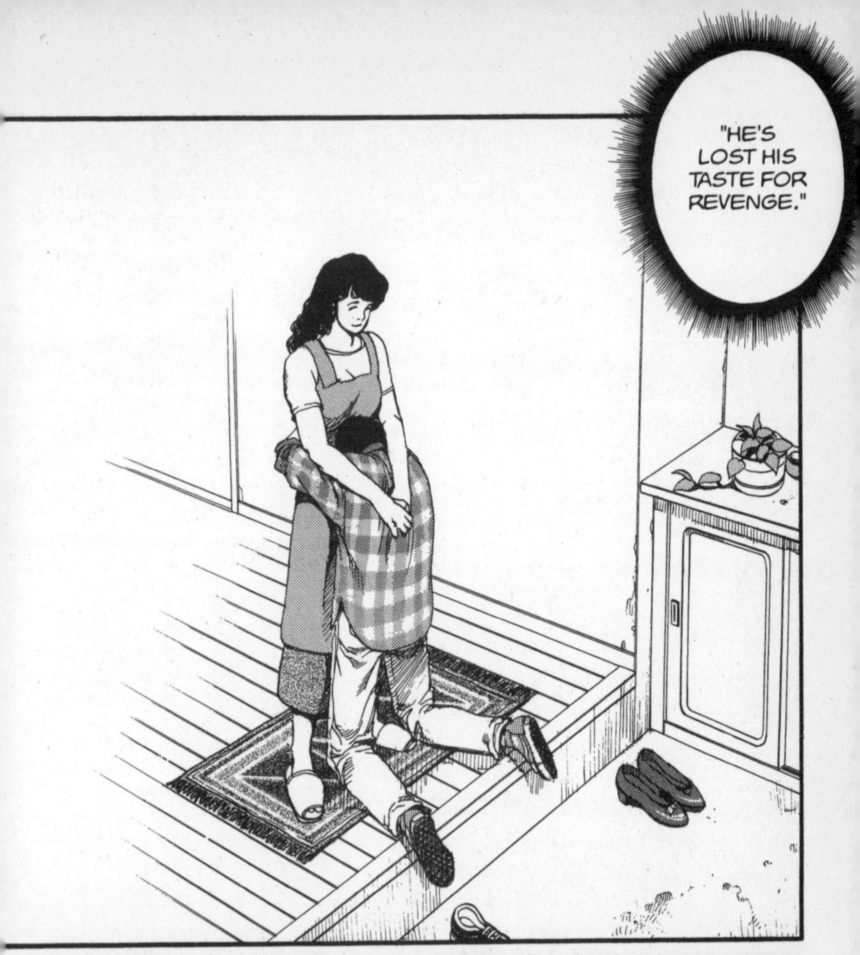
"HE'S LOST HIS TASTE FOR REVENGE."
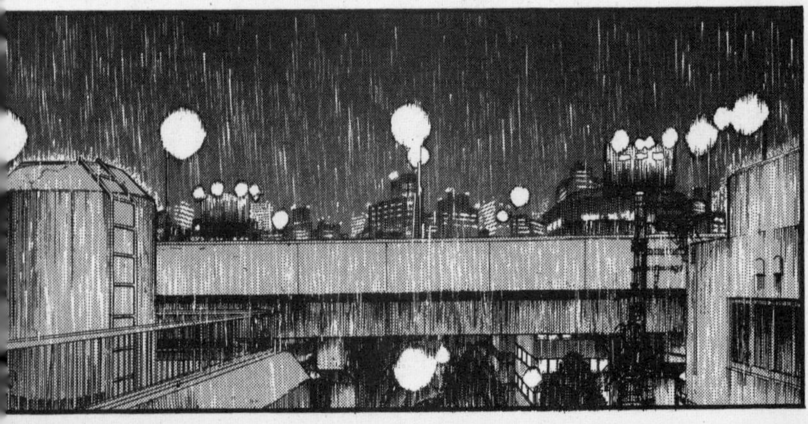

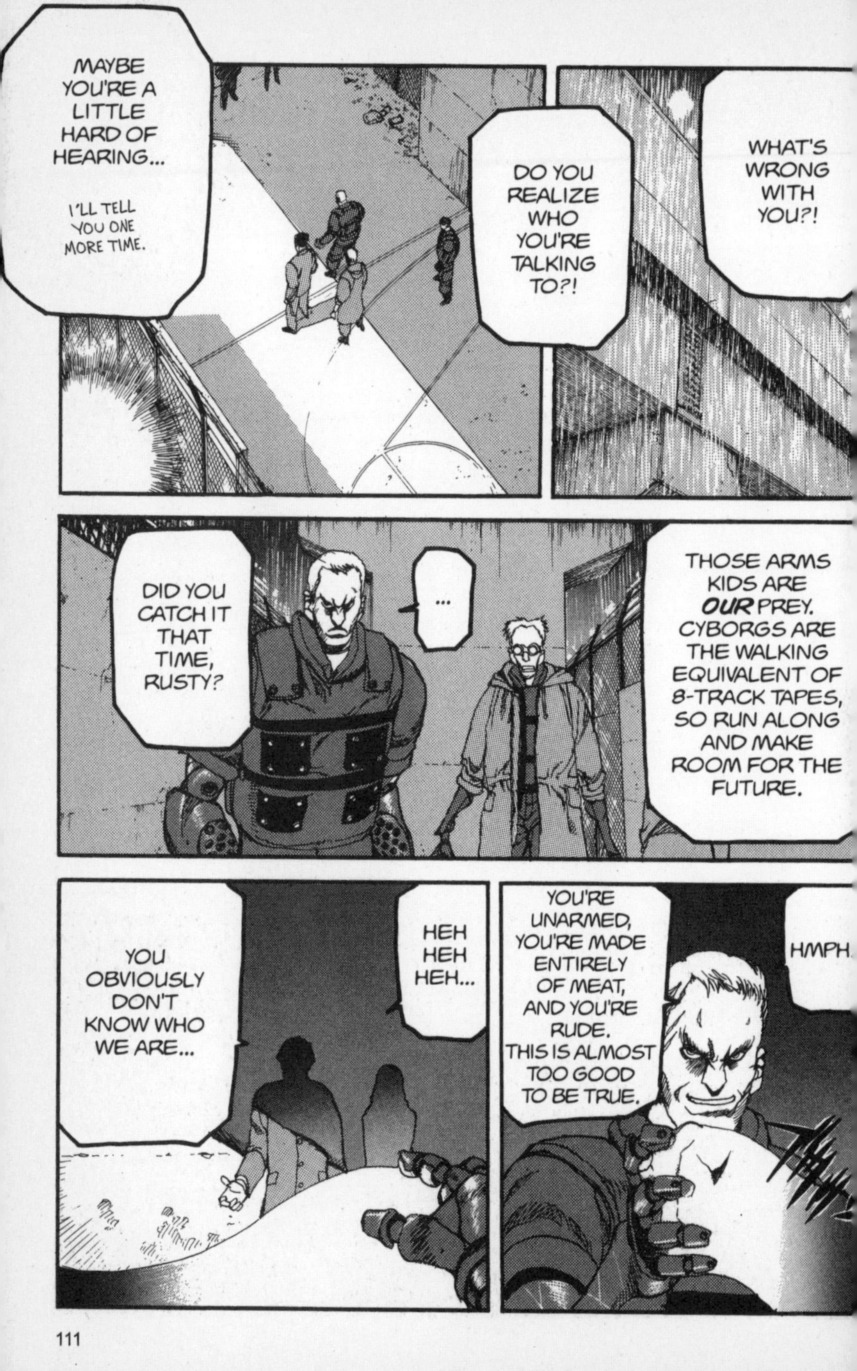
WHAT'S WRONG WITH YOU?!
DO YOU REALIZE WHO YOU'RE TALKING TO?!
MAYBE YOU'RE A LITTLE HARD OF HEARING...
I'LL TELL YOU ONE MORE TIME.
THOSE ARMS KIDS ARE ***OUR*** PREY. CYBORGS ARE THE WALKING EQUIVALENT OF 8-TRACK TAPES, SO RUN ALONG AND MAKE ROOM FOR THE FUTURE.
...
DID YOU CATCH IT THAT TIME, RUSTY?
HMPH.
YOU'RE UNARMED, YOU'RE MADE ENTIRELY OF MEAT, AND YOU'RE RUDE. THIS IS ALMOST TOO GOOD TO BE TRUE.
HEH HEH HEH...
YOU OBVIOUSLY DON'T KNOW WHO WE ARE...

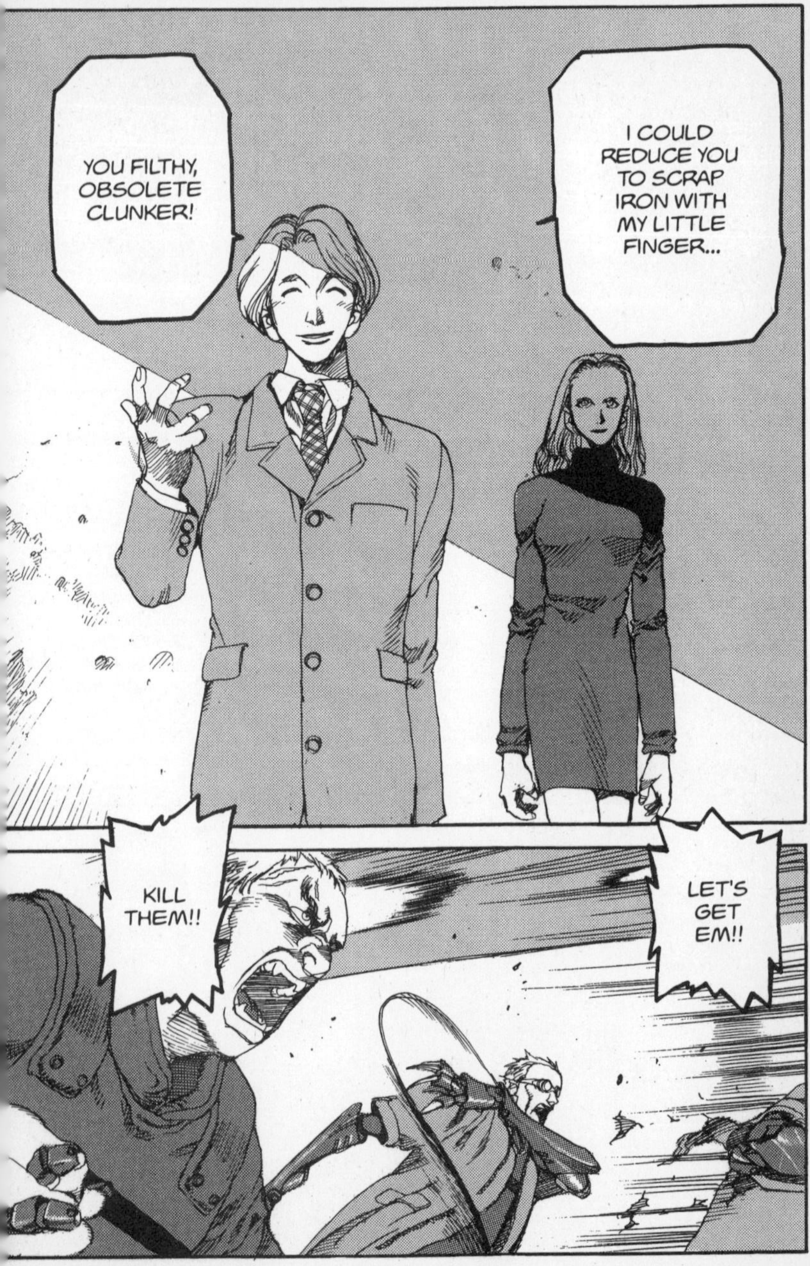
YOU FILTHY, OBSOLETE CLUNKER!
I COULD REDUCE YOU TO SCRAP IRON WITH MY LITTLE FINGER...
KILL THEM!!
LET'S GET EM!!

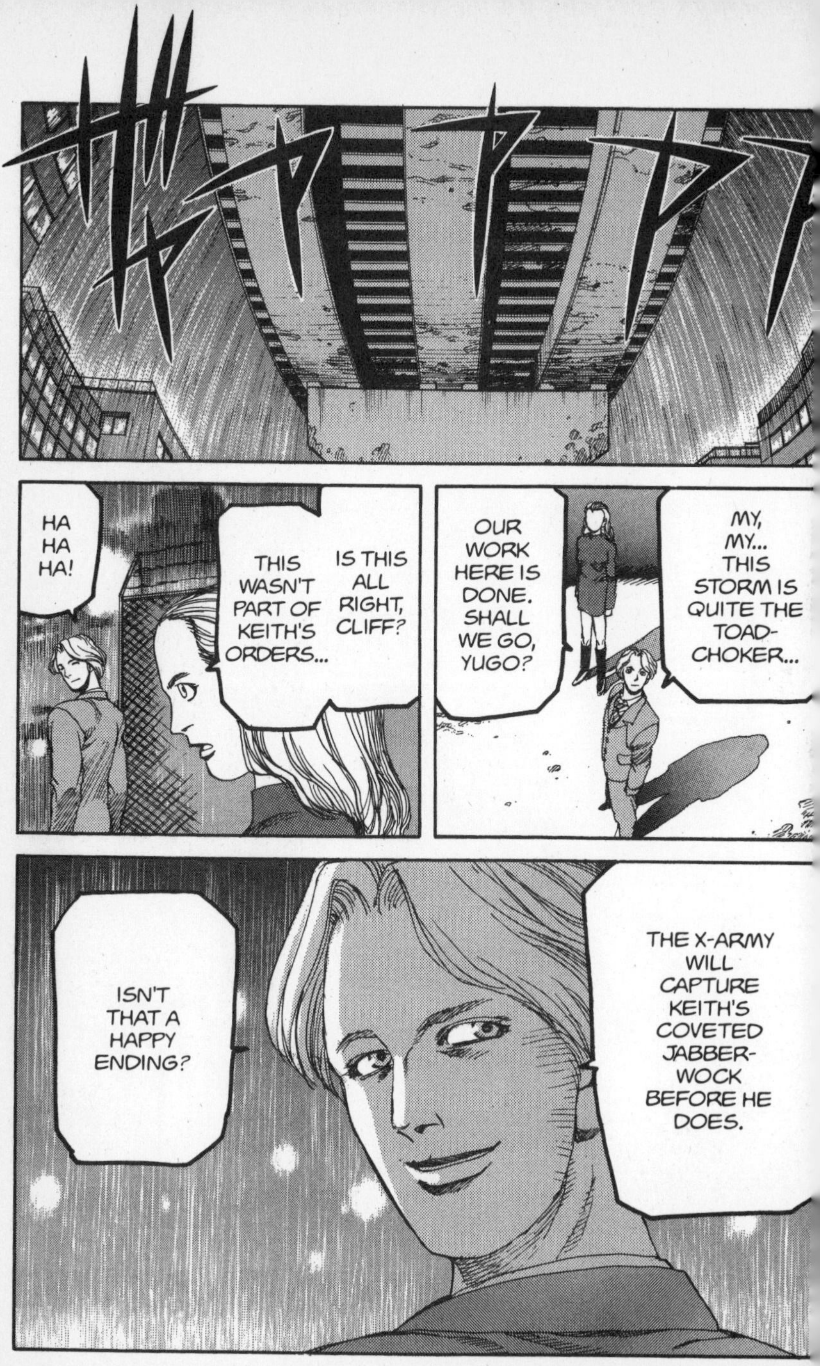
MY, MY... THIS STORM IS QUITE THE TOAD-CHOKER...
OUR WORK HERE IS DONE. SHALL WE GO, YUGO?
IS THIS ALL RIGHT, CLIFF?
THIS WASN'T PART OF KEITH'S ORDERS...
HA HA HA!
THE X-ARMY WILL CAPTURE KEITH'S COVETED JABBER-WOCK BEFORE HE DOES.
ISN'T THAT A HAPPY ENDING?

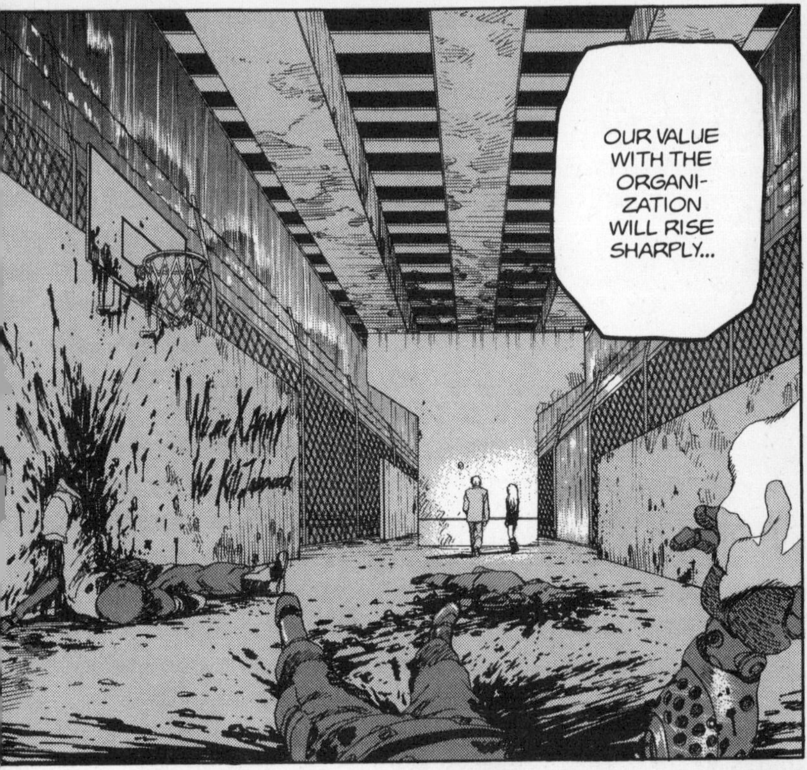
OUR VALUE WITH THE ORGANI-ZATION WILL RISE SHARPLY...
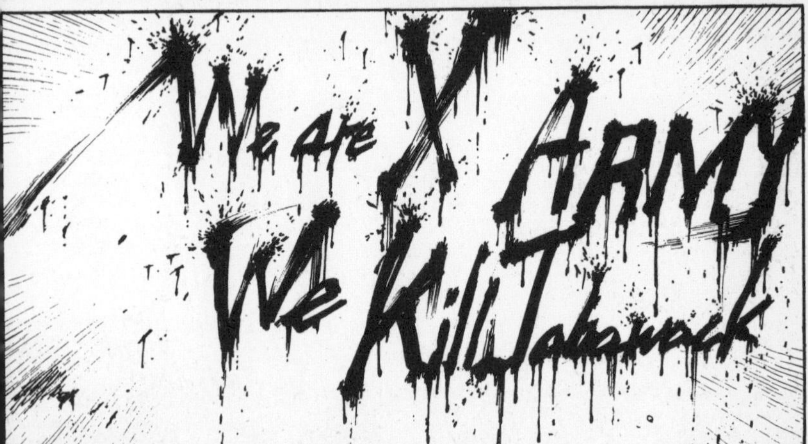
We are X ARMY
We Kill Jaberwock

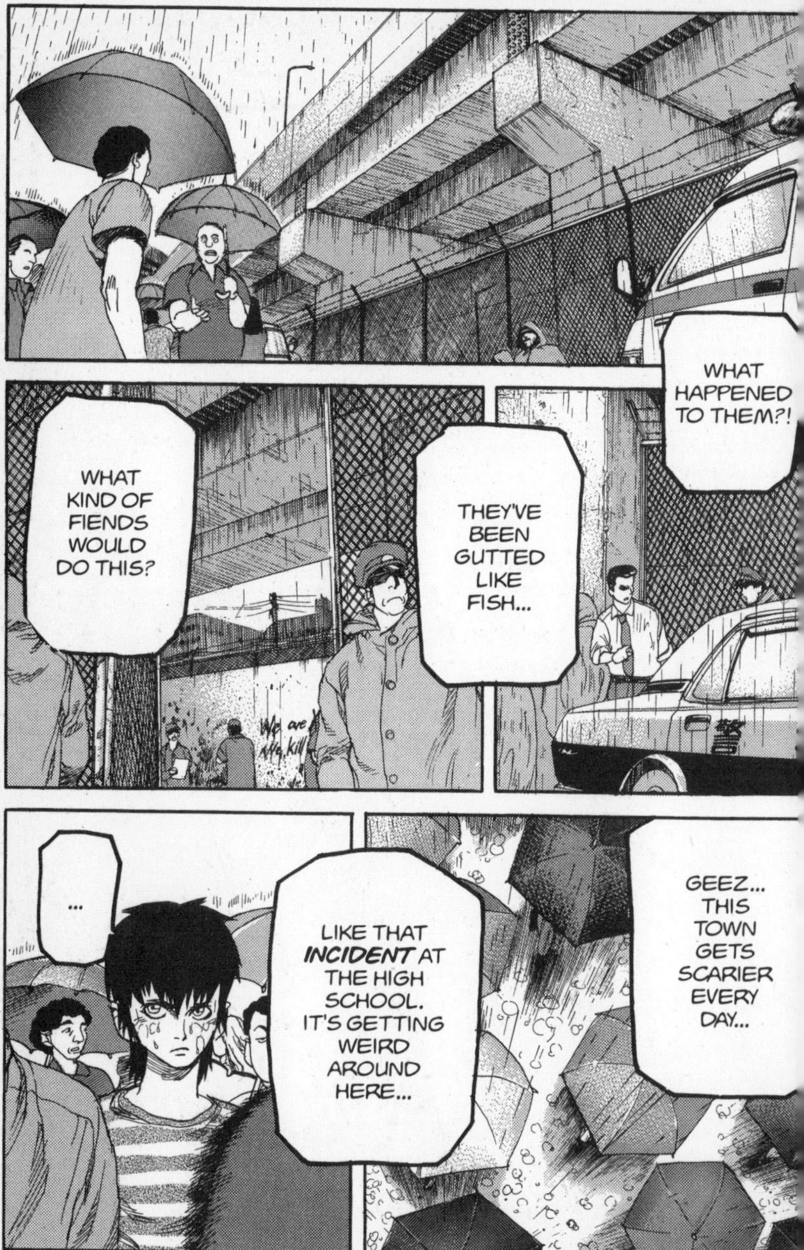
WHAT HAPPENED TO THEM?!
THEY'VE BEEN GUTTED LIKE FISH...
WHAT KIND OF FIENDS WOULD DO THIS?
GEEZ... THIS TOWN GETS SCARIER EVERY DAY...
LIKE THAT INCIDENT AT THE HIGH SCHOOL. IT'S GETTING WEIRD AROUND HERE...
...

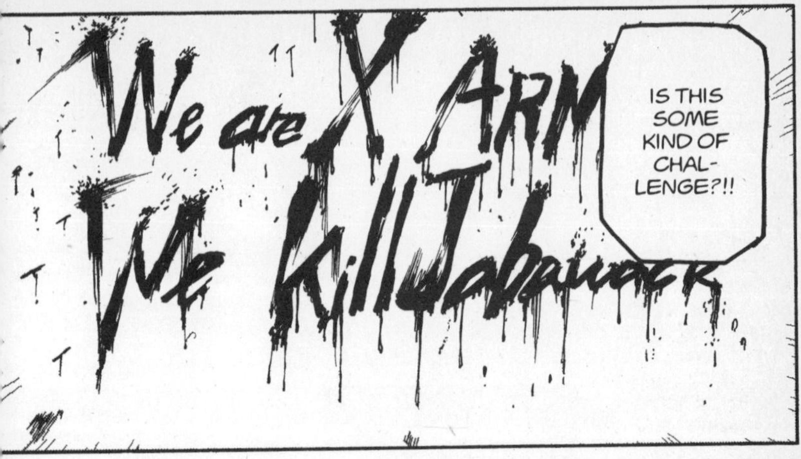
We are X ARM
IS THIS SOME KIND OF CHAL- LENGE?!!

No. 7 X-ARMY

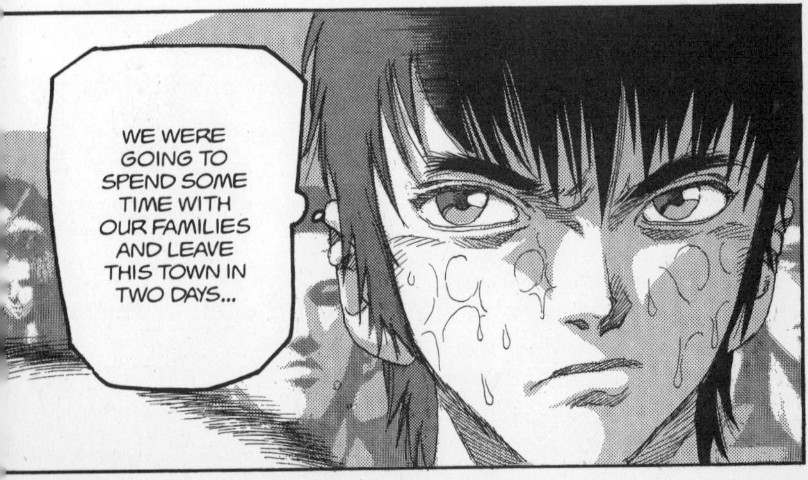
WE WERE GOING TO SPEND SOME TIME WITH OUR FAMILIES AND LEAVE THIS TOWN IN TWO DAYS...

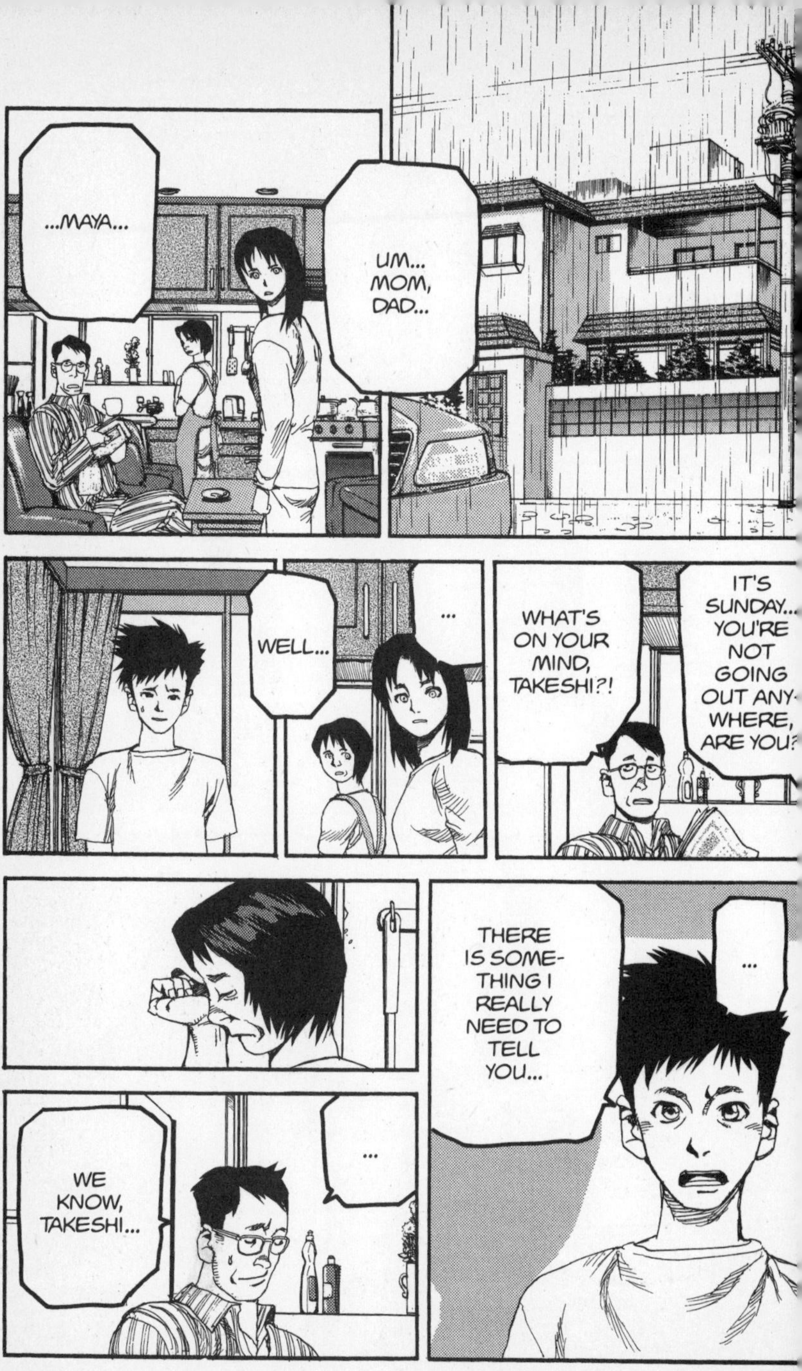
UM... MOM, DAD...
...MAYA...
IT'S SUNDAY... YOU'RE NOT GOING OUT ANY-WHERE, ARE YOU?
WHAT'S ON YOUR MIND, TAKESHI?!
...
WELL...
...
THERE IS SOME-THING I REALLY NEED TO TELL YOU...
...
WE KNOW, TAKESHI...

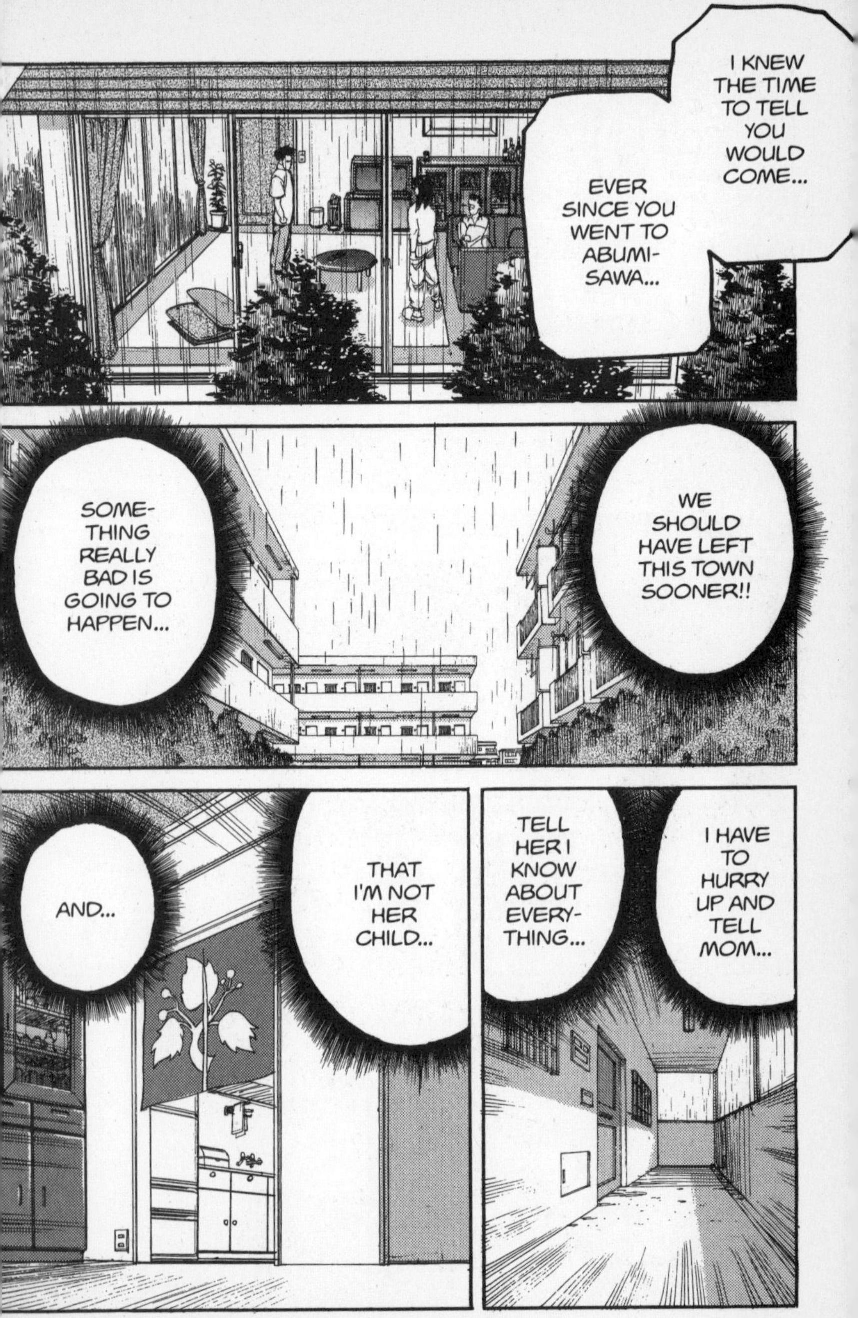
I KNEW THE TIME TO TELL YOU WOULD COME...
EVER SINCE YOU WENT TO ABUMI-SAWA...
WE SHOULD HAVE LEFT THIS TOWN SOONER!!
SOME-THING REALLY BAD IS GOING TO HAPPEN...
I HAVE TO HURRY UP AND TELL MOM...
TELL HER I KNOW ABOUT EVERY-THING...
THAT I'M NOT HER CHILD...
AND...

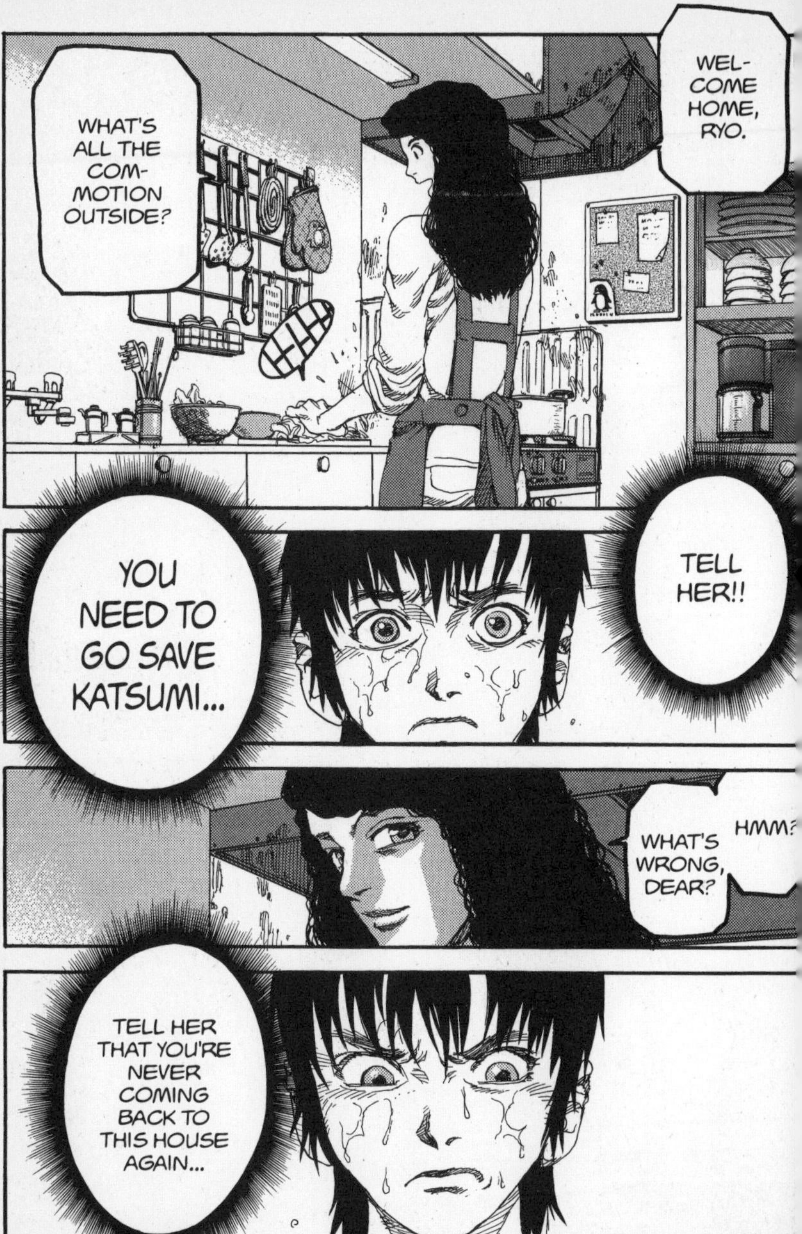
WEL-COME HOME, RYO.
WHAT'S ALL THE COM-MOTION OUTSIDE?
TELL HER!!
YOU NEED TO GO SAVE KATSUMI...
HMM?
WHAT'S WRONG, DEAR?
TELL HER THAT YOU'RE NEVER COMING BACK TO THIS HOUSE AGAIN...

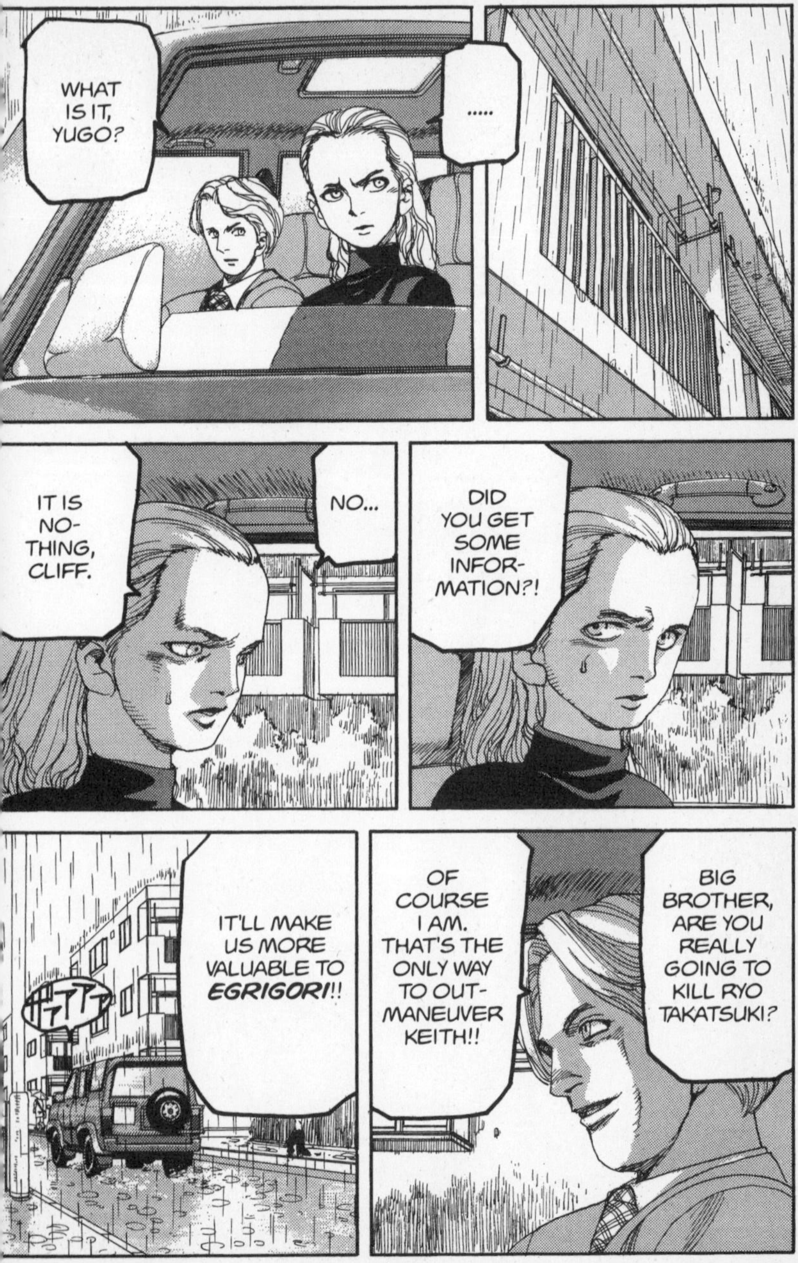
.....
WHAT IS IT, YUGO?
DID YOU GET SOME INFORMATION?!
NO...
IT IS NO-THING, CLIFF.
BIG BROTHER, ARE YOU REALLY GOING TO KILL RYO TAKATSUKI?
OF COURSE I AM. THAT'S THE ONLY WAY TO OUT-MANEUVER KEITH!!
IT'LL MAKE US MORE VALUABLE TO ***EGRIGORI***!!
ザァァァ

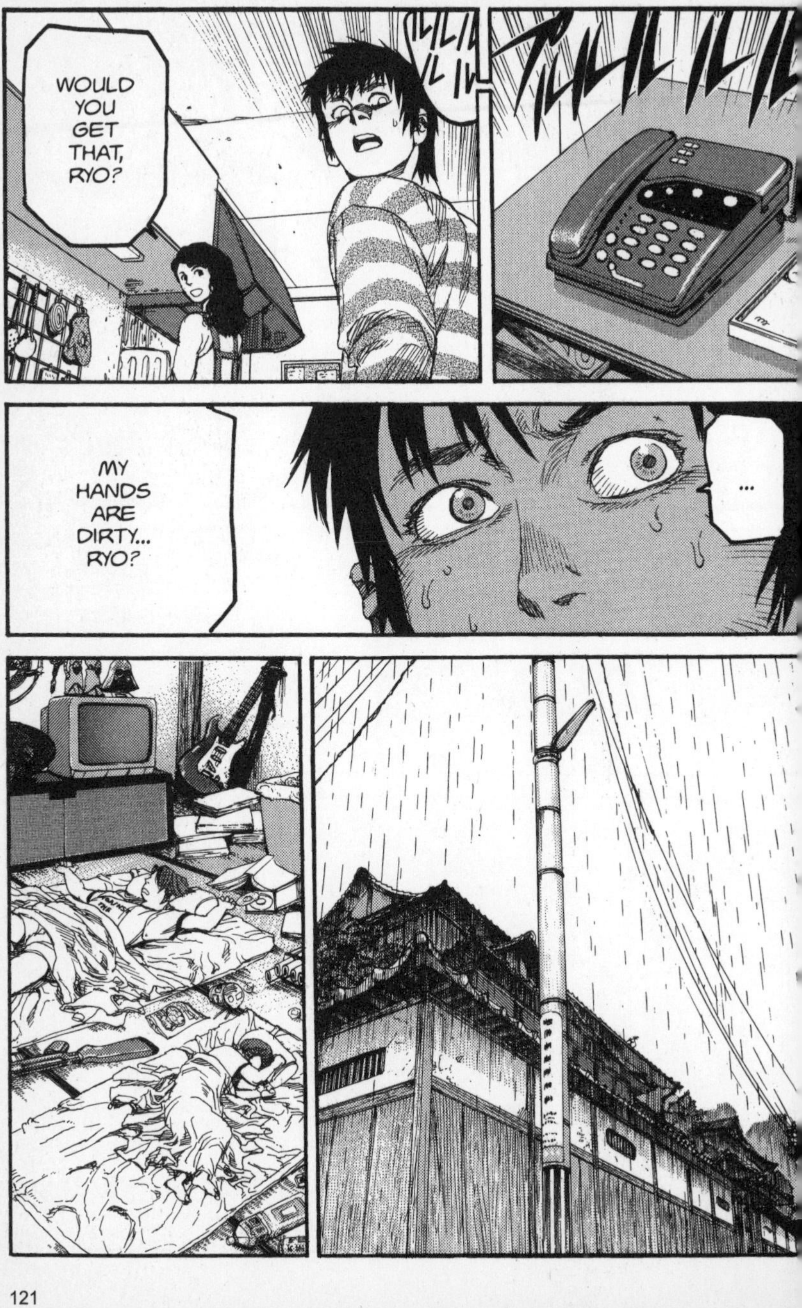
WOULD YOU GET THAT, RYO?
...
MY HANDS ARE DIRTY... RYO?

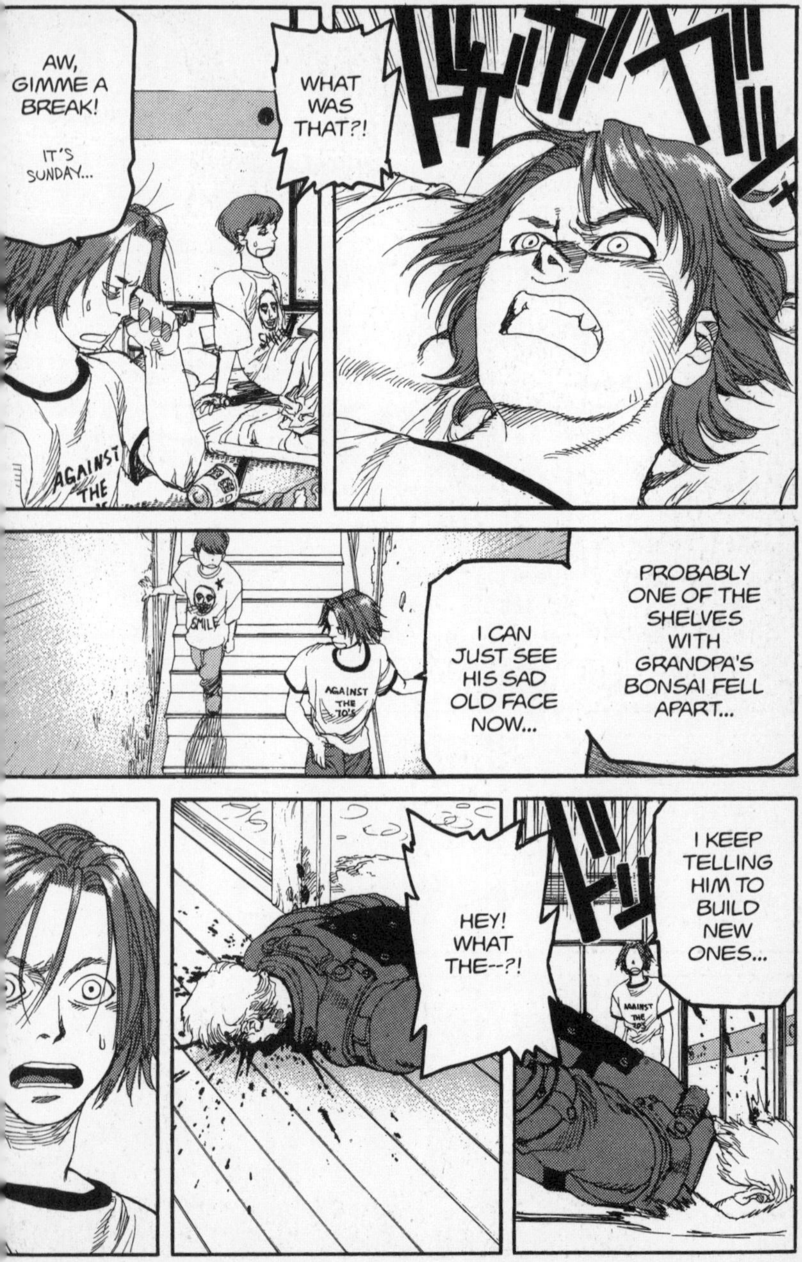
WHAT WAS THAT?!
AW, GIMME A BREAK!
IT'S SUNDAY...
PROBABLY ONE OF THE SHELVES WITH GRANDPA'S BONSAI FELL APART...
I CAN JUST SEE HIS SAD OLD FACE NOW...
I KEEP TELLING HIM TO BUILD NEW ONES...
HEY! WHAT THE--?!

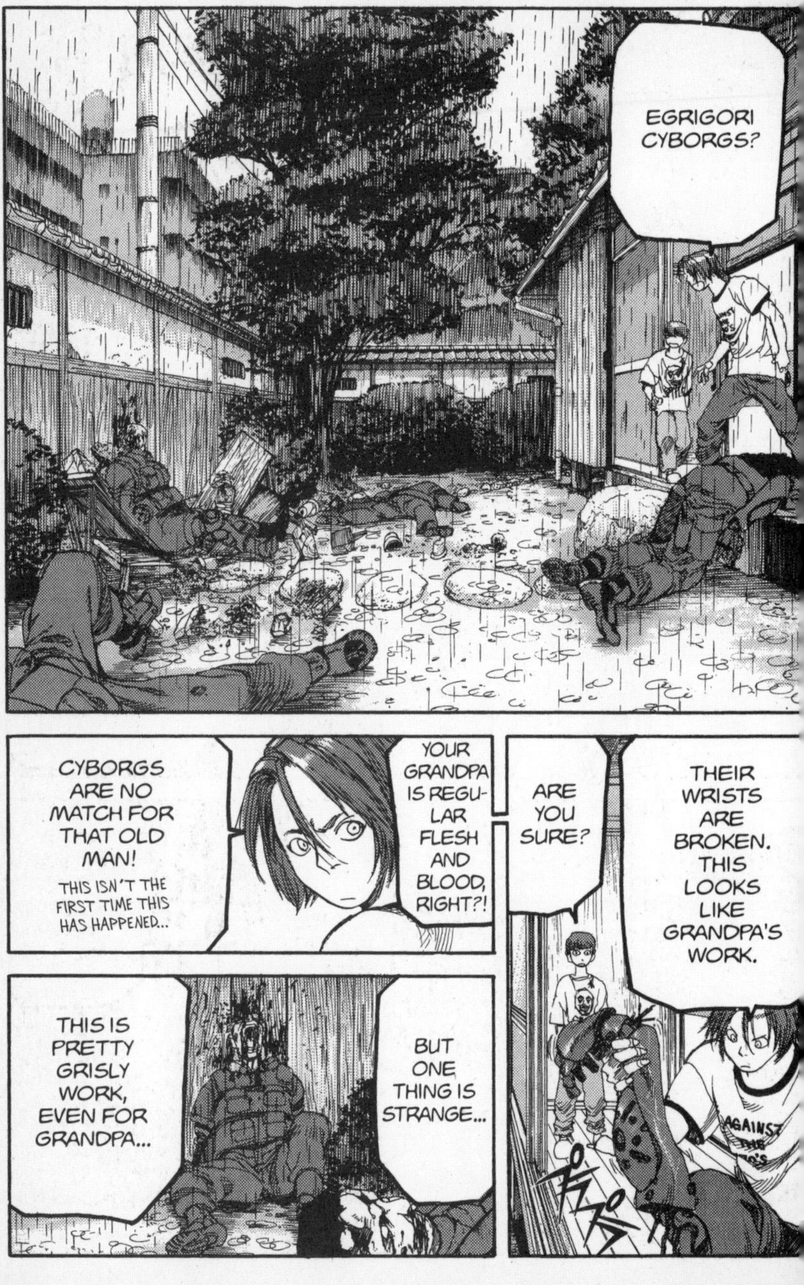
EGRIGORI CYBORGS?
THEIR WRISTS ARE BROKEN. THIS LOOKS LIKE GRANDPA'S WORK.
ARE YOU SURE?
YOUR GRANDPA IS REGU-LAR FLESH AND BLOOD, RIGHT?!
CYBORGS ARE NO MATCH FOR THAT OLD MAN!
THIS ISN'T THE FIRST TIME THIS HAS HAPPENED...
BUT ONE THING IS STRANGE...
THIS IS PRETTY GRISLY WORK, EVEN FOR GRANDPA...

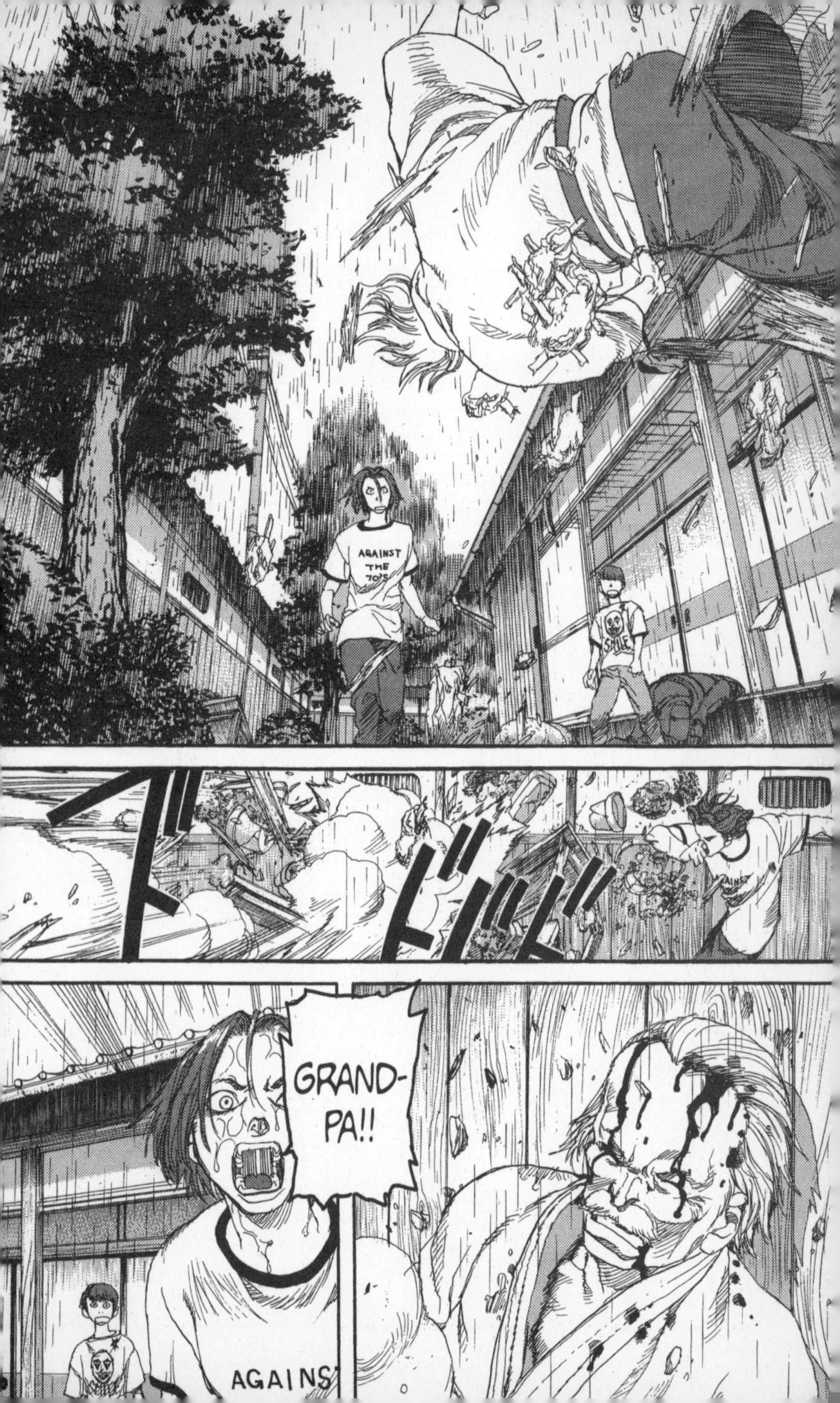
AGAINST THE 70'S
SMILE
ドドドッ
GRAND-PA!!
AGAINST

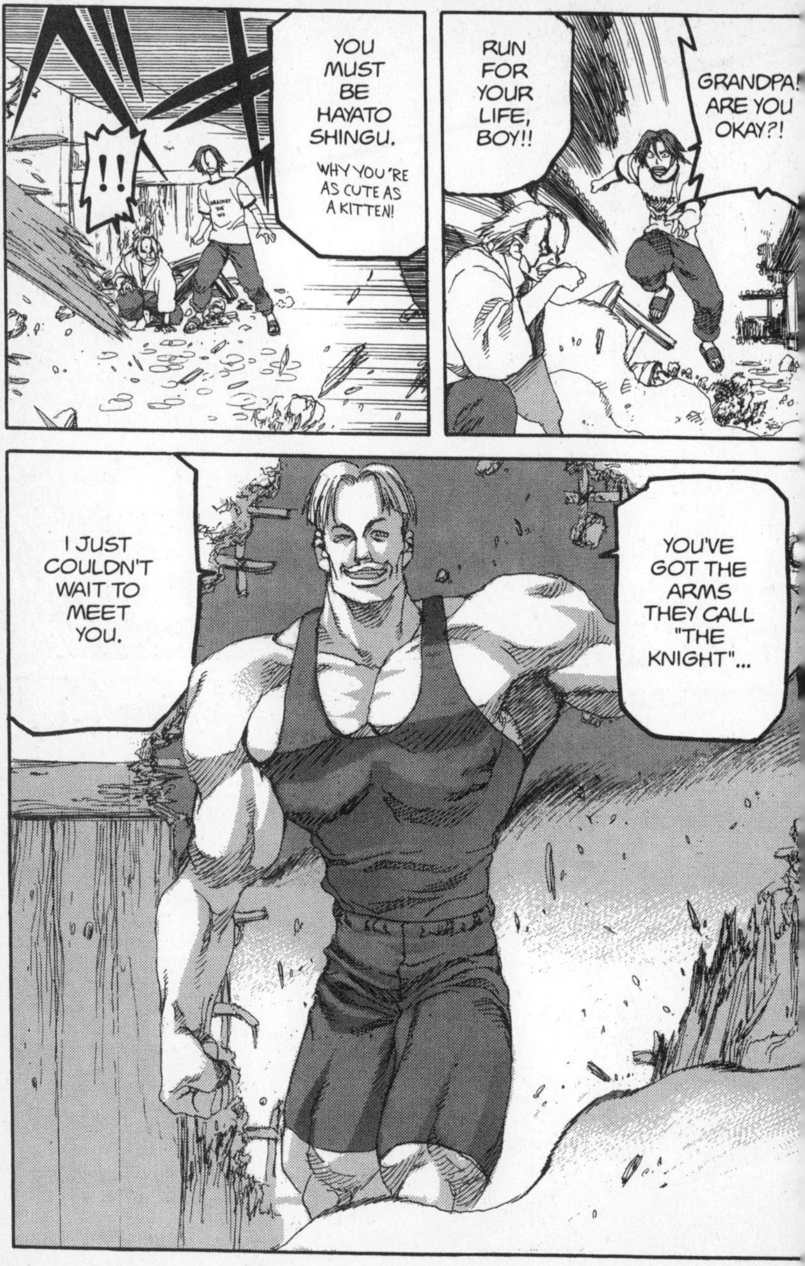
RUN FOR YOUR LIFE, BOY!!
GRANDPA! ARE YOU OKAY?!
YOU MUST BE HAYATO SHINGU.
WHY YOU'RE AS CUTE AS A KITTEN!
!!
YOU'VE GOT THE ARMS THEY CALL "THE KNIGHT"...
I JUST COULDN'T WAIT TO MEET YOU.

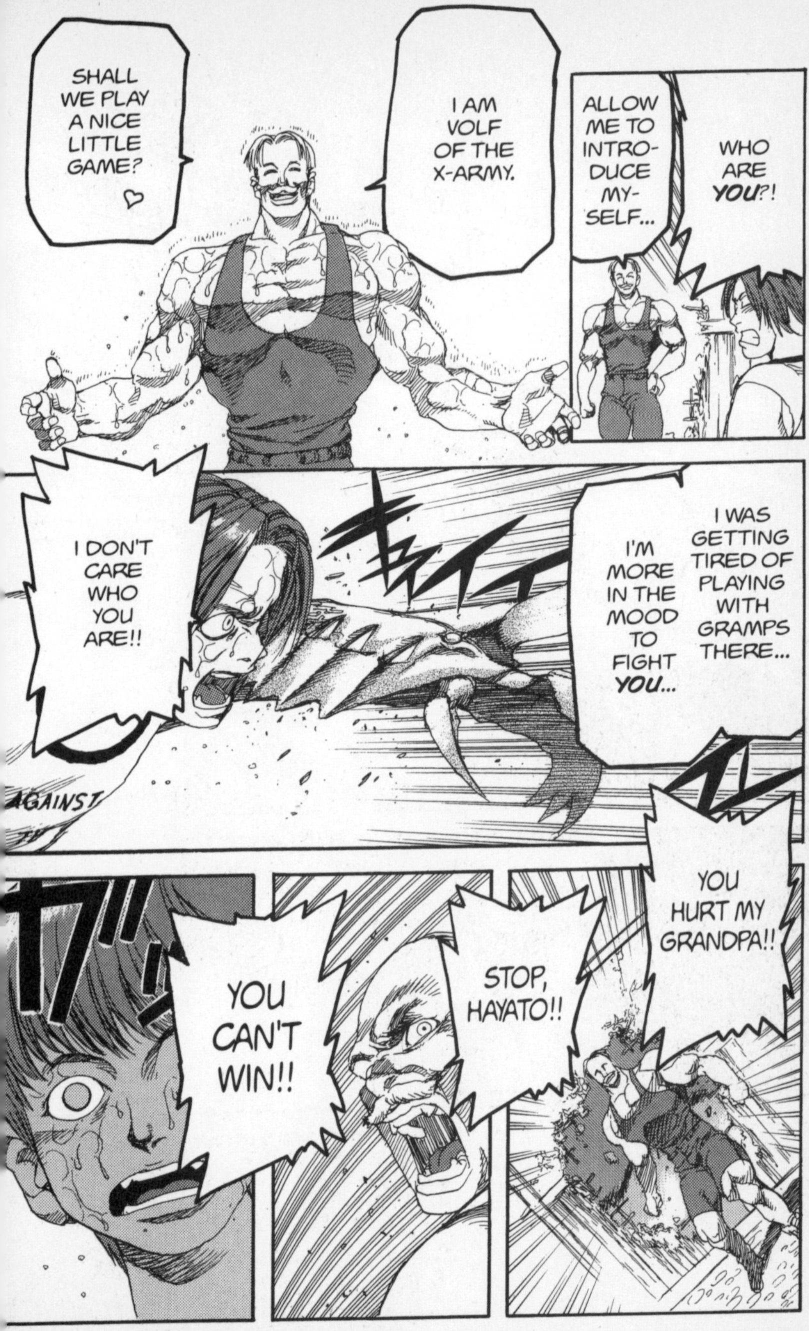
WHO ARE YOU?!
ALLOW ME TO INTRODUCE MYSELF...
I AM VOLF OF THE X-ARMY.
SHALL WE PLAY A NICE LITTLE GAME? ♡
I WAS GETTING TIRED OF PLAYING WITH GRAMPS THERE...
I'M MORE IN THE MOOD TO FIGHT YOU...
I DON'T CARE WHO YOU ARE!!
AGAINST
YOU HURT MY GRANDPA!!
STOP, HAYATO!!
YOU CAN'T WIN!!

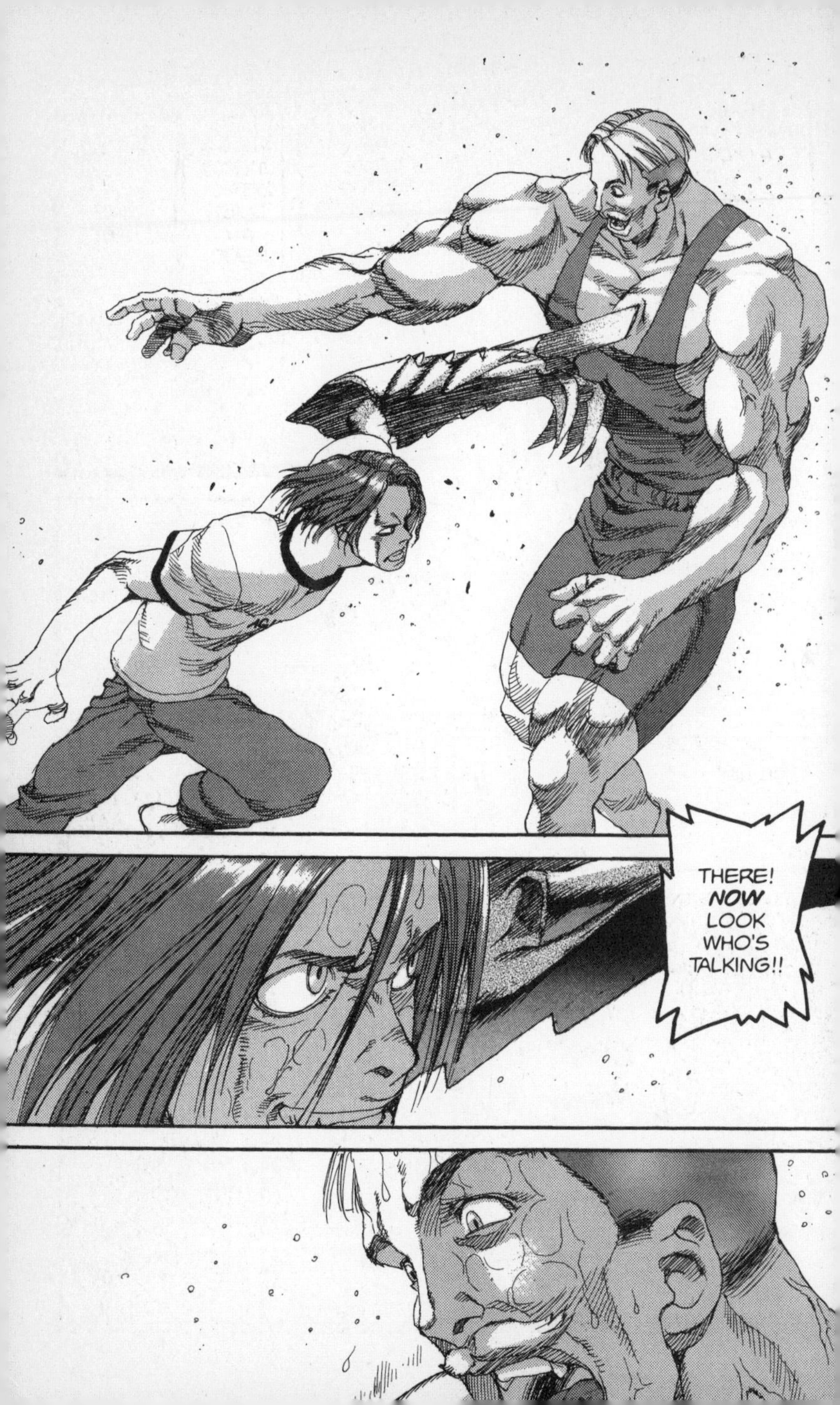
THERE! ***NOW*** LOOK WHO'S TALKING!!

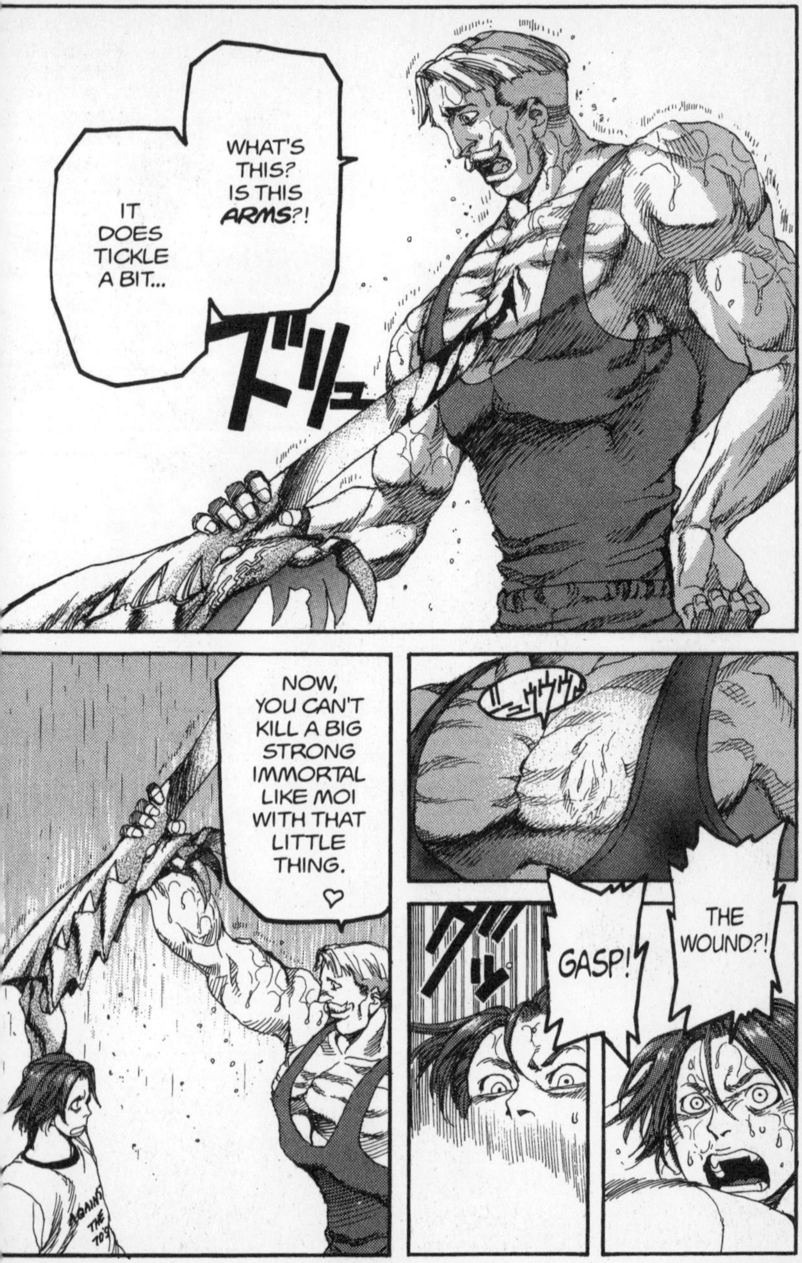
WHAT'S THIS? IS THIS ARMS?!
IT DOES TICKLE A BIT...
ドリュ
THE WOUND?!
GASP!
NOW, YOU CAN'T KILL A BIG STRONG IMMORTAL LIKE MOI WITH THAT LITTLE THING. ♡

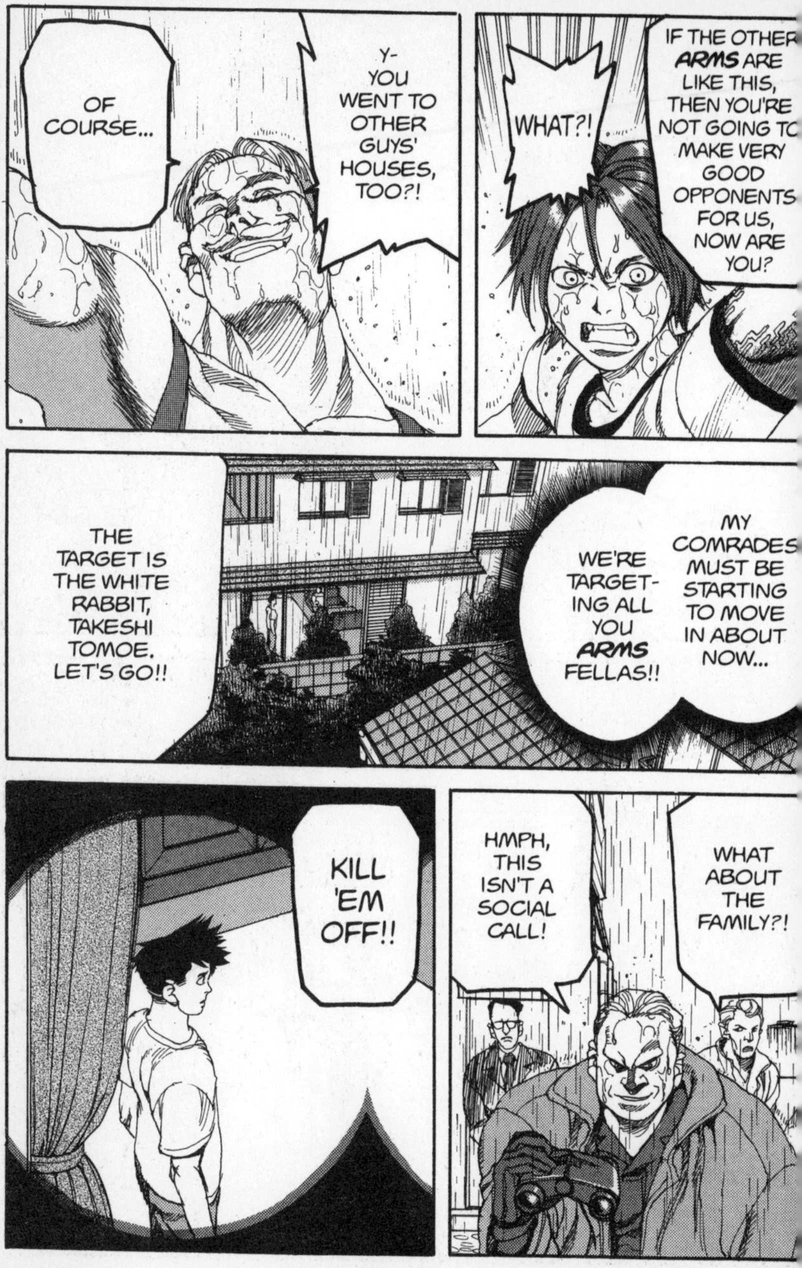
IF THE OTHER ARMS ARE LIKE THIS, THEN YOU'RE NOT GOING TO MAKE VERY GOOD OPPONENTS FOR US, NOW ARE YOU?
WHAT?!
Y- YOU WENT TO OTHER GUYS' HOUSES, TOO?!
OF COURSE...
MY COMRADES MUST BE STARTING TO MOVE IN ABOUT NOW...
WE'RE TARGETING ALL YOU ARMS FELLAS!!
THE TARGET IS THE WHITE RABBIT, TAKESHI TOMOE. LET'S GO!!
WHAT ABOUT THE FAMILY?!
HMPH, THIS ISN'T A SOCIAL CALL!
KILL 'EM OFF!!

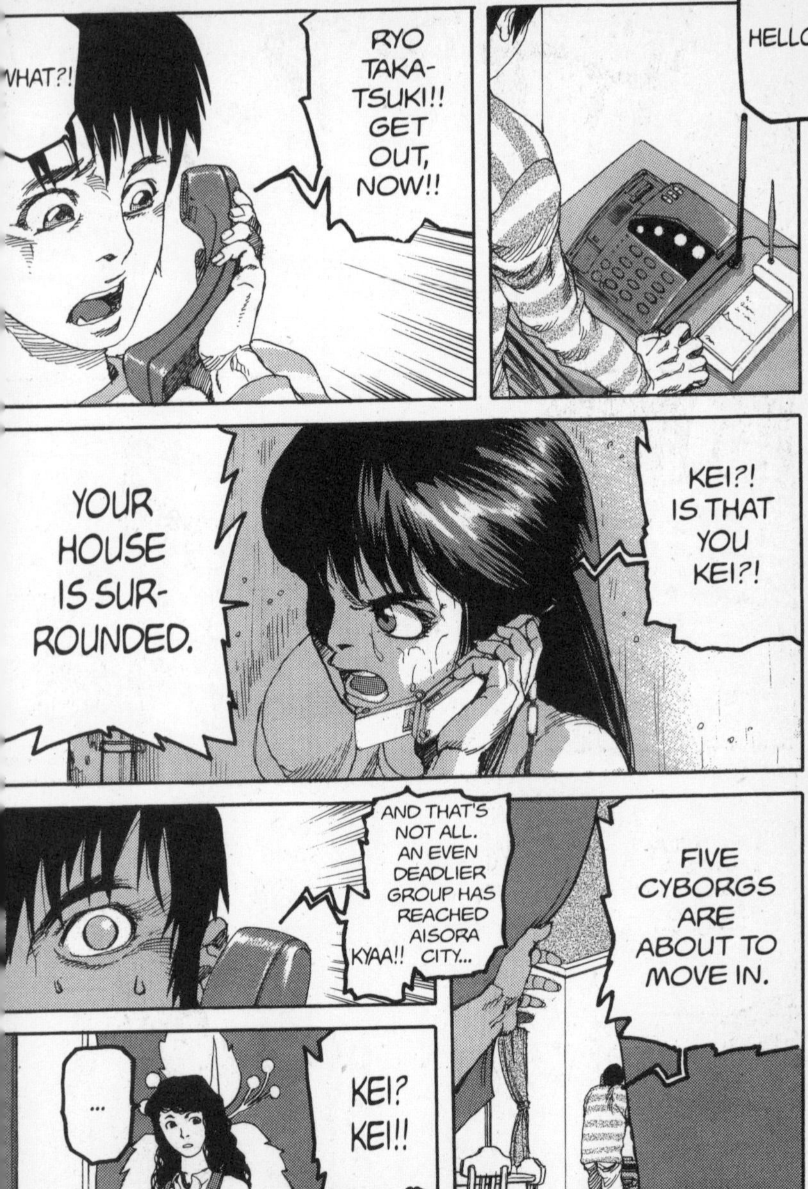
HELLO...?
RYO TAKA-TSUKI!! GET OUT, NOW!!
WHAT?!
KEI?! IS THAT YOU KEI?!
YOUR HOUSE IS SUR-ROUNDED.
FIVE CYBORGS ARE ABOUT TO MOVE IN.
AND THAT'S NOT ALL. AN EVEN DEADLIER GROUP HAS REACHED AISORA CITY...
KYAA!!
KEI? KEI!!
...

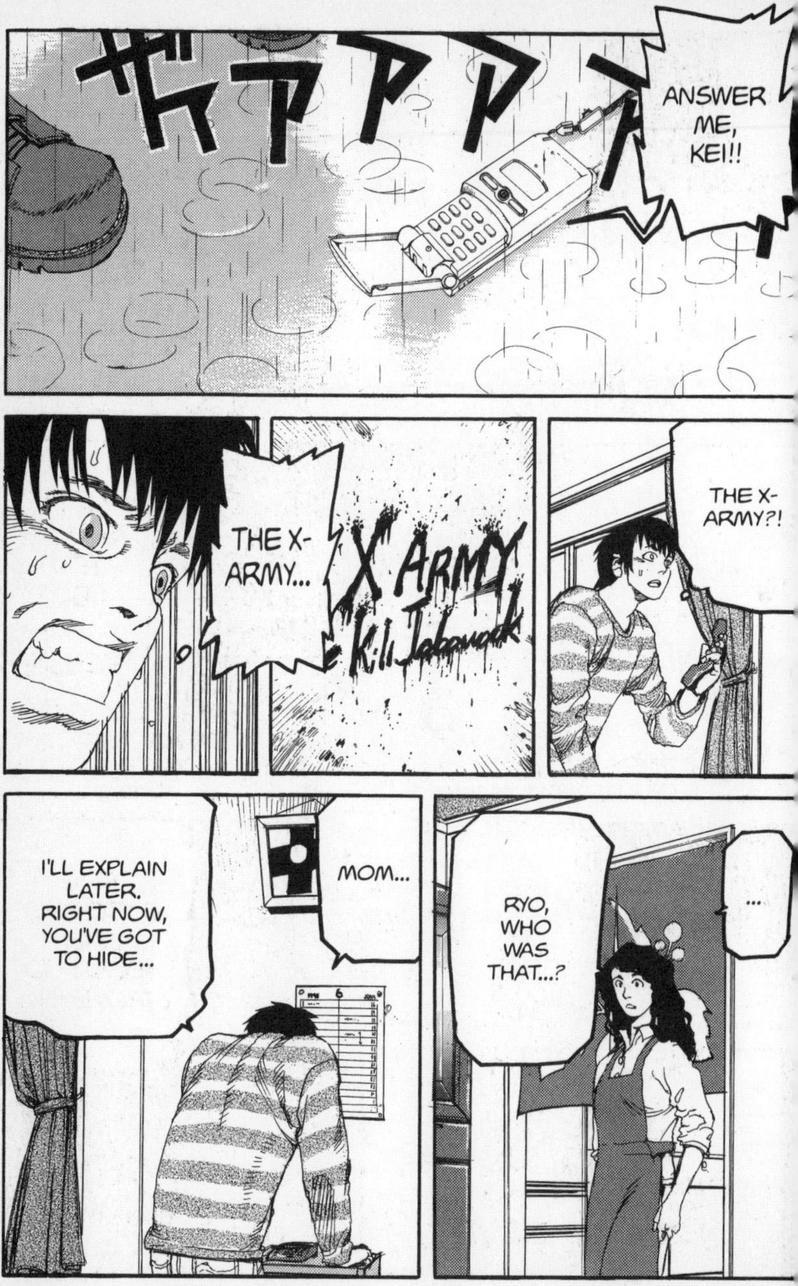
ANSWER ME, KEI!!
THE X-ARMY?!
X ARMY
THE X-ARMY...
...
RYO, WHO WAS THAT...?
MOM...
I'LL EXPLAIN LATER. RIGHT NOW, YOU'VE GOT TO HIDE...

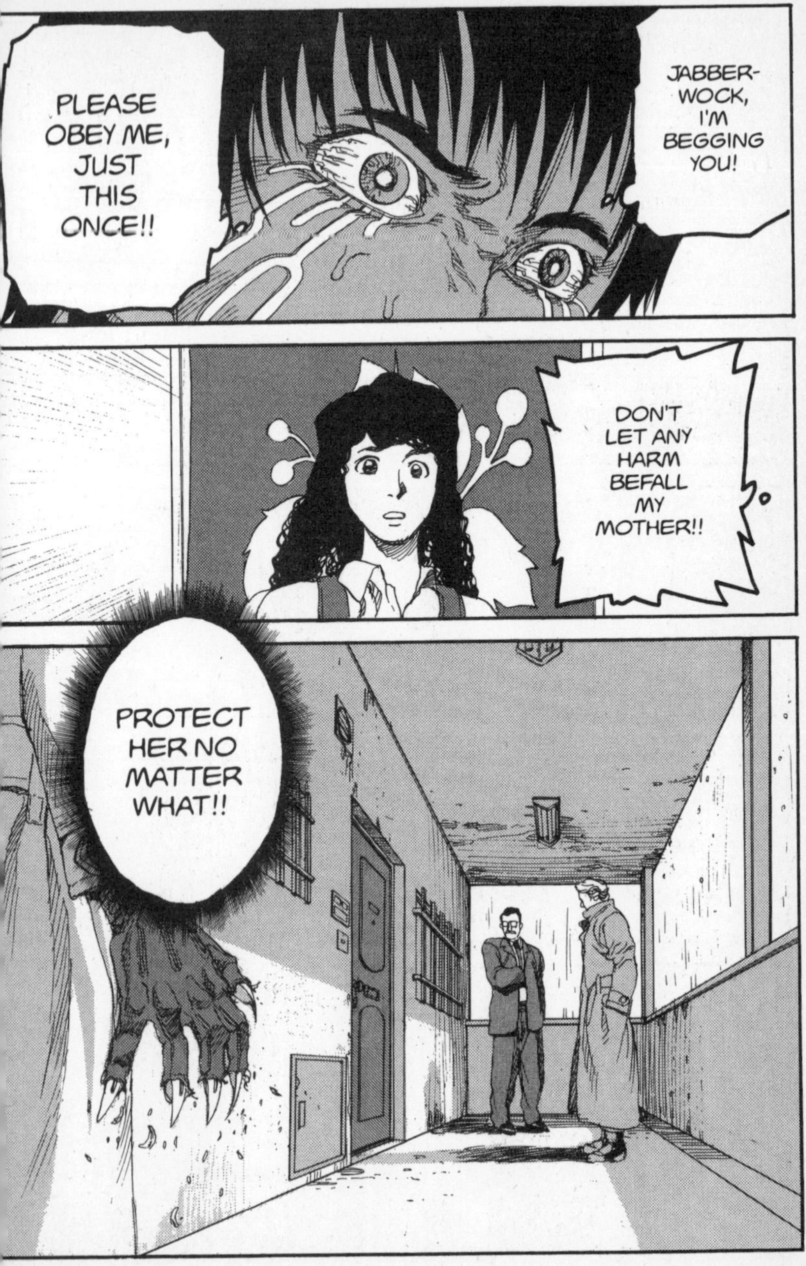
JABBER-WOCK, I'M BEGGING YOU!
PLEASE OBEY ME, JUST THIS ONCE!!
DON'T LET ANY HARM BEFALL MY MOTHER!!
PROTECT HER NO MATTER WHAT!!

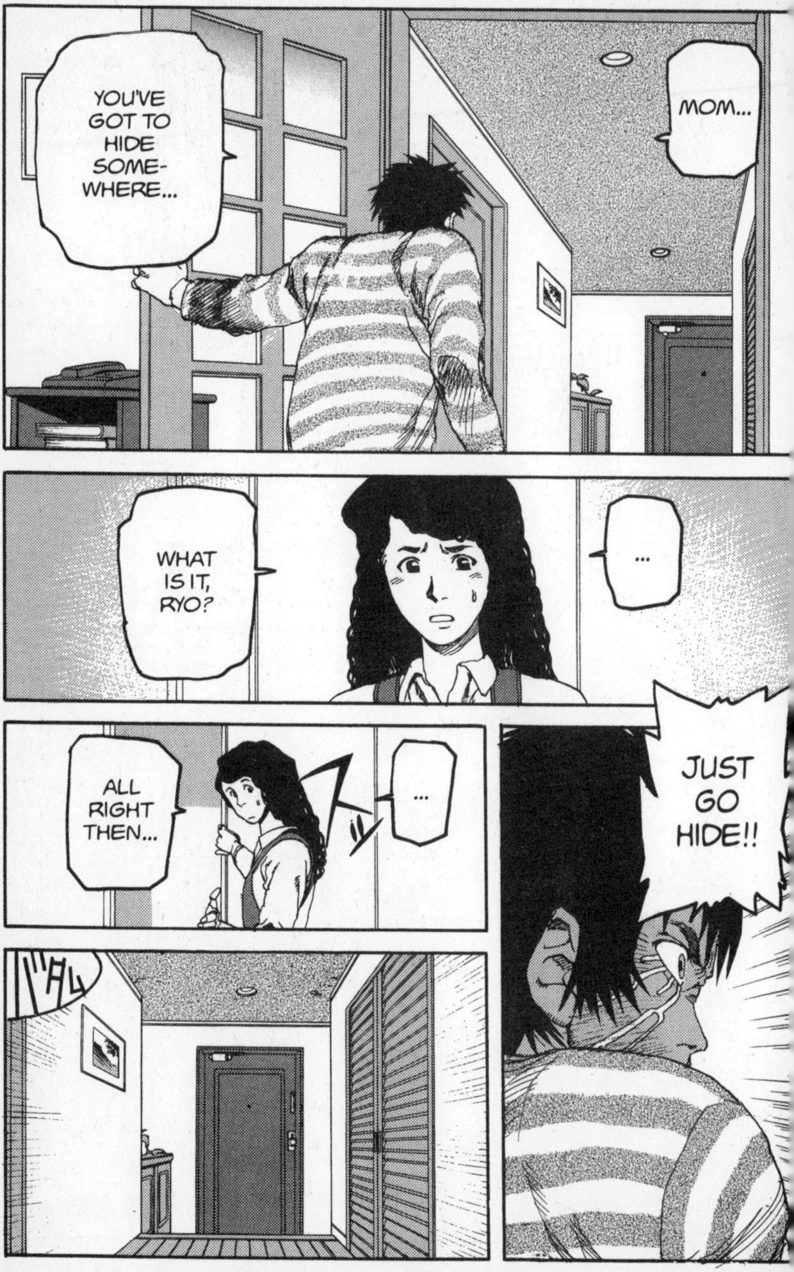
MOM...
YOU'VE GOT TO HIDE SOMEWHERE...
...
WHAT IS IT, RYO?
JUST GO HIDE!!
...
ALL RIGHT THEN...

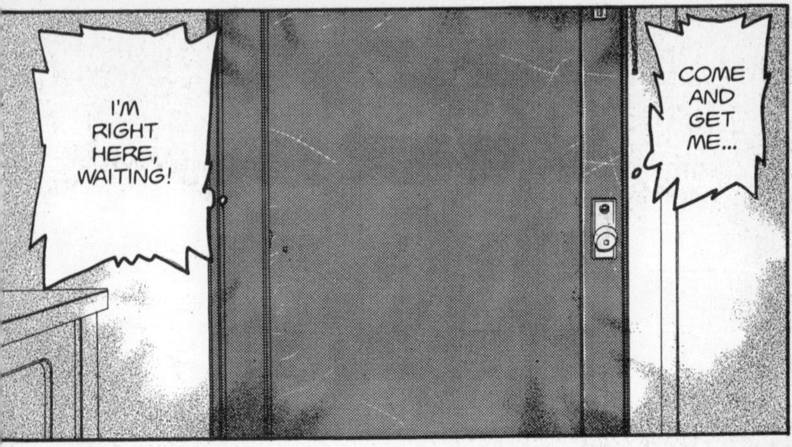
I'M RIGHT HERE, WAITING!
COME AND GET ME...

NO. 8 MUTANT

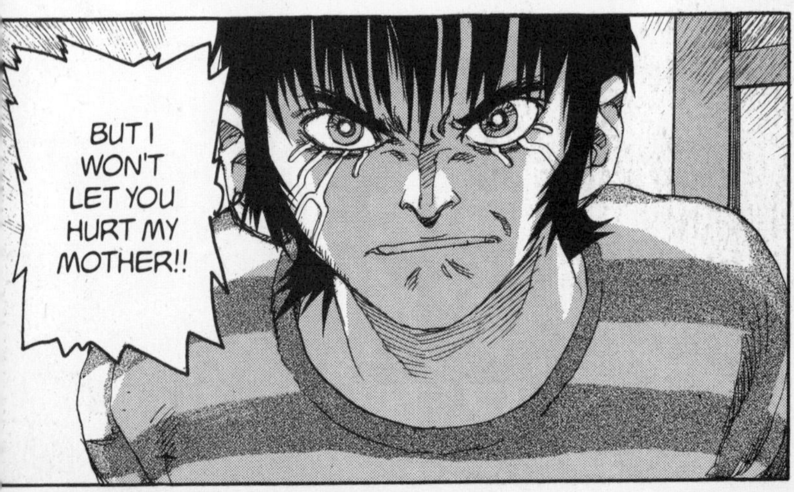
BUT I WON'T LET YOU HURT MY MOTHER!!

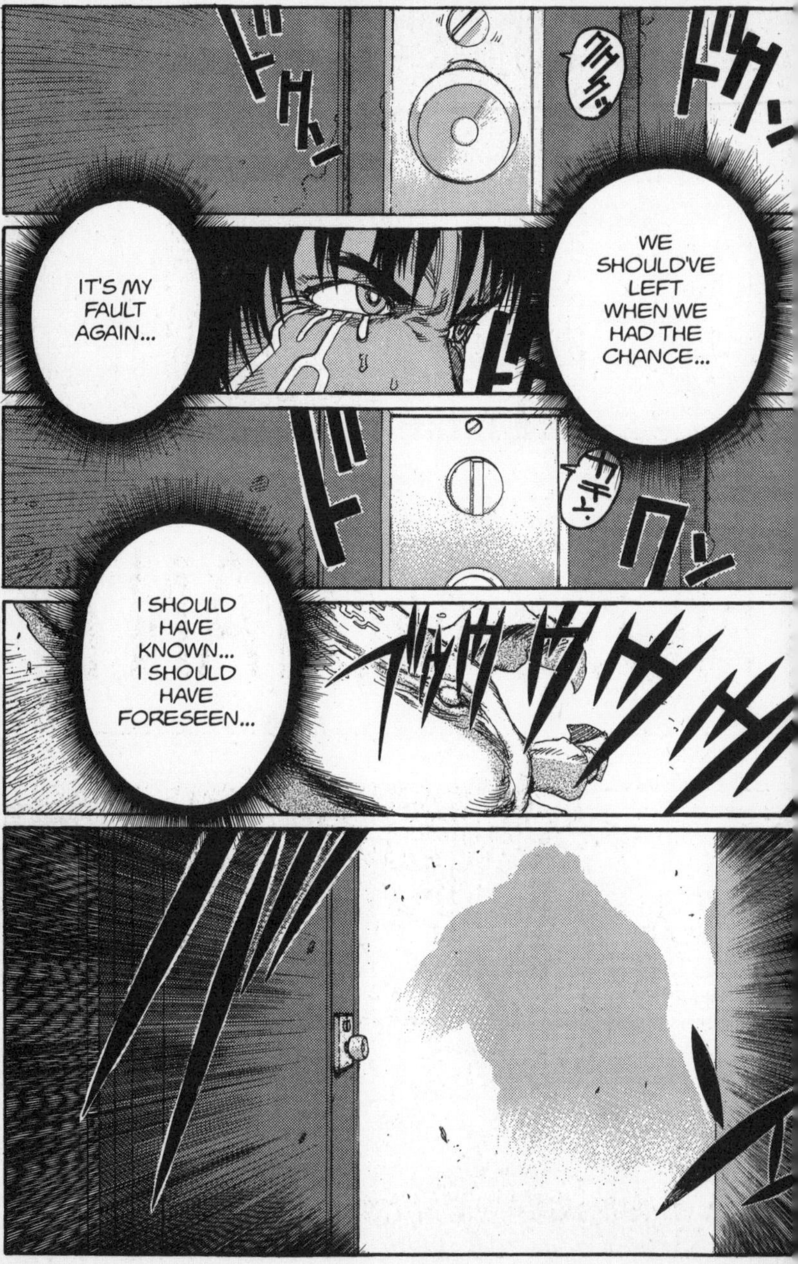
WE SHOULD'VE LEFT WHEN WE HAD THE CHANCE...
IT'S MY FAULT AGAIN...
I SHOULD HAVE KNOWN... I SHOULD HAVE FORESEEN...

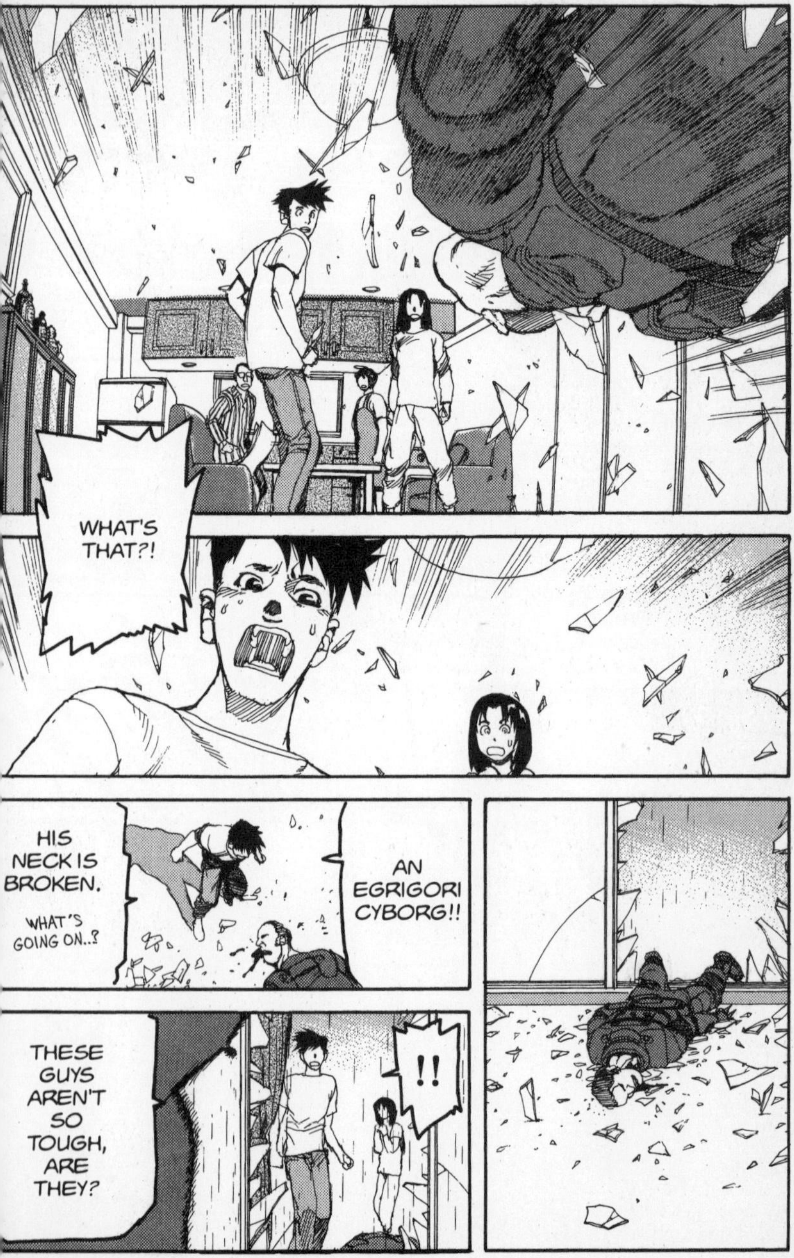
WHAT'S THAT?!
AN EGRIGORI CYBORG!!
HIS NECK IS BROKEN.
WHAT'S GOING ON..?
!!
THESE GUYS AREN'T SO TOUGH, ARE THEY?

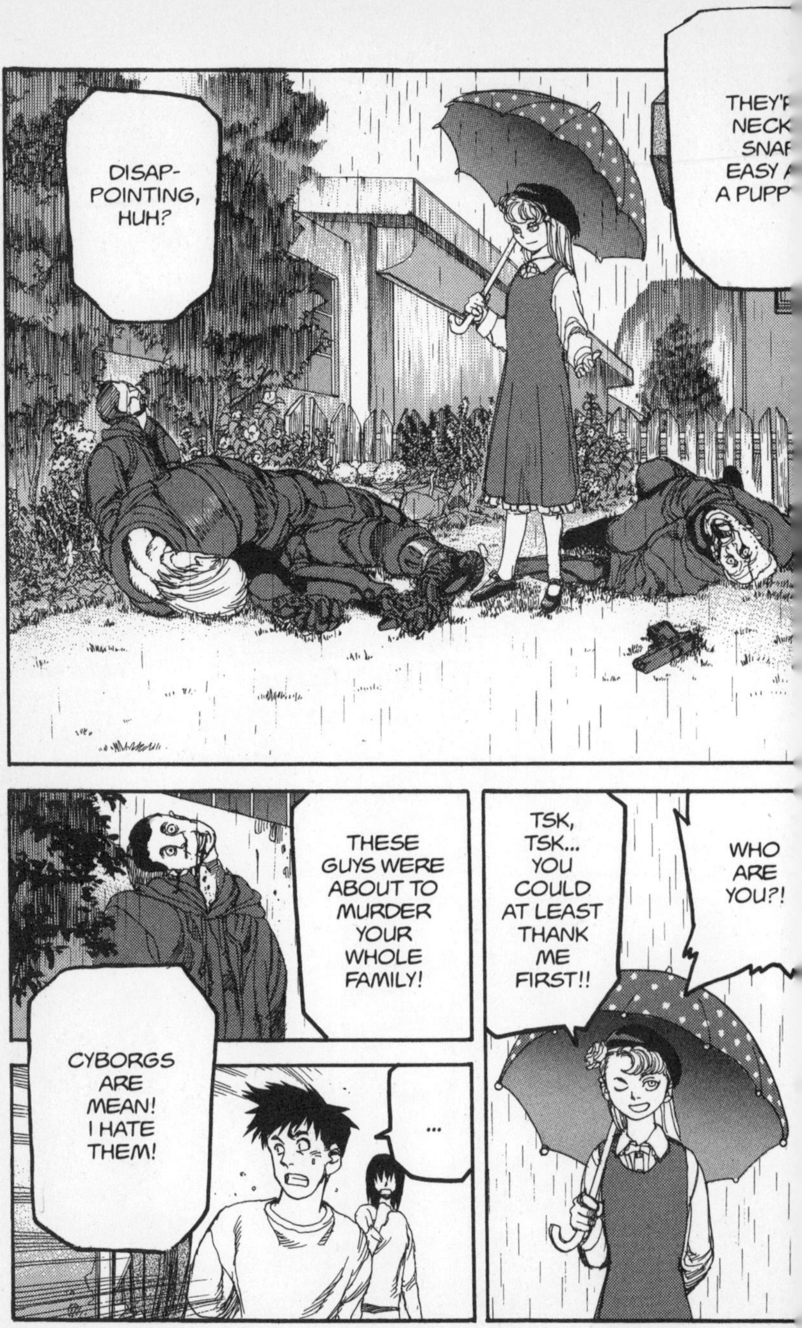
THEY' NECK SNA EASY A PUPP
DISAP-POINTING, HUH?
WHO ARE YOU?!
TSK, TSK... YOU COULD AT LEAST THANK ME FIRST!!
THESE GUYS WERE ABOUT TO MURDER YOUR WHOLE FAMILY!
...
CYBORGS ARE MEAN! I HATE THEM!

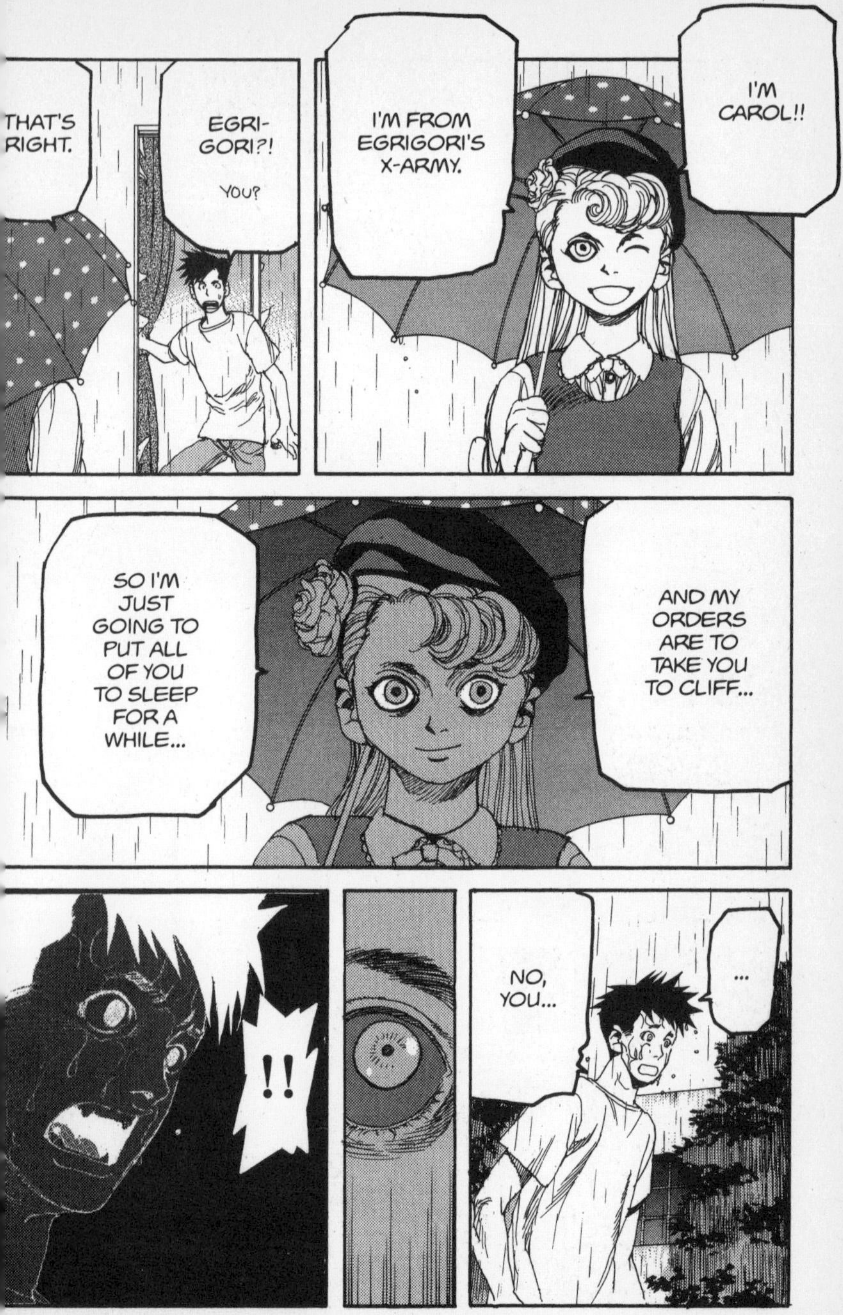
I'M CAROL!!
I'M FROM EGRIGORI'S X-ARMY.
EGRI-GORI?!
YOU?
THAT'S RIGHT.
AND MY ORDERS ARE TO TAKE YOU TO CLIFF...
SO I'M JUST GOING TO PUT ALL OF YOU TO SLEEP FOR A WHILE...
...
NO, YOU...
!!

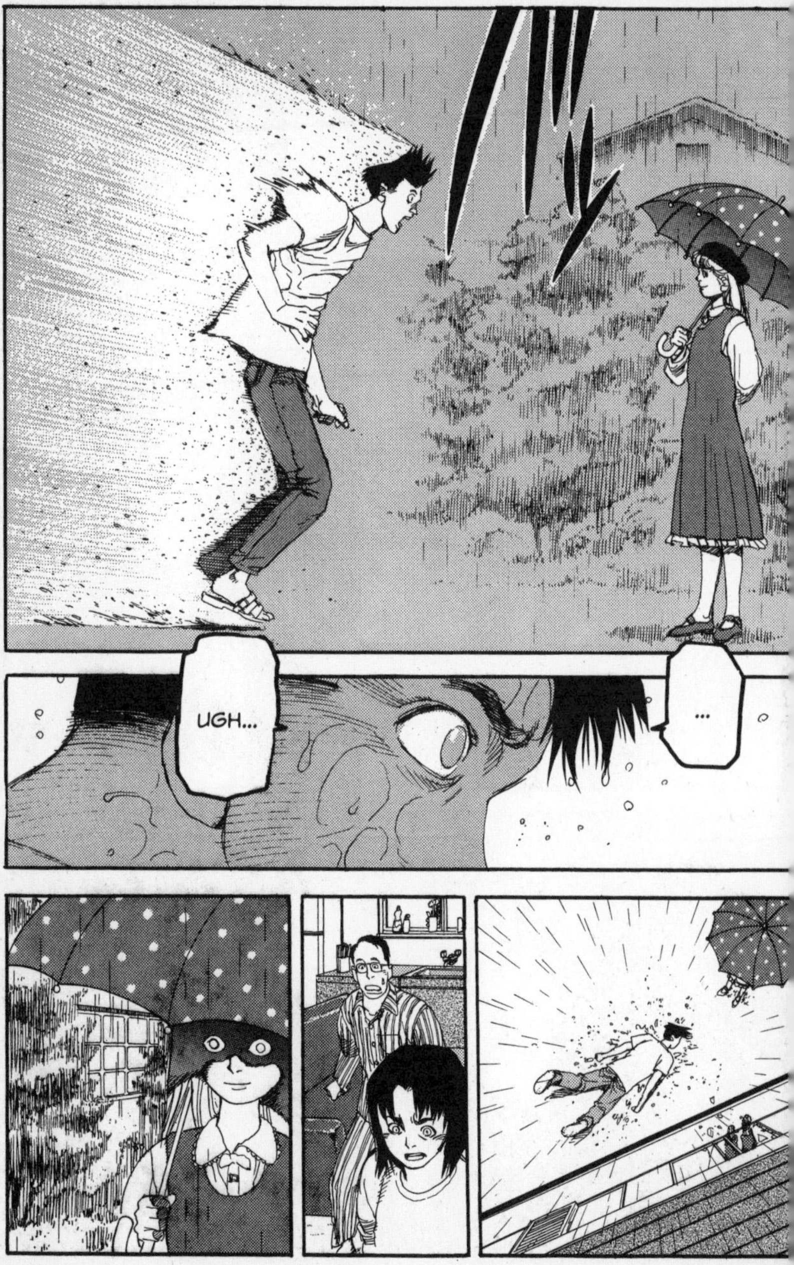
...
UGH...

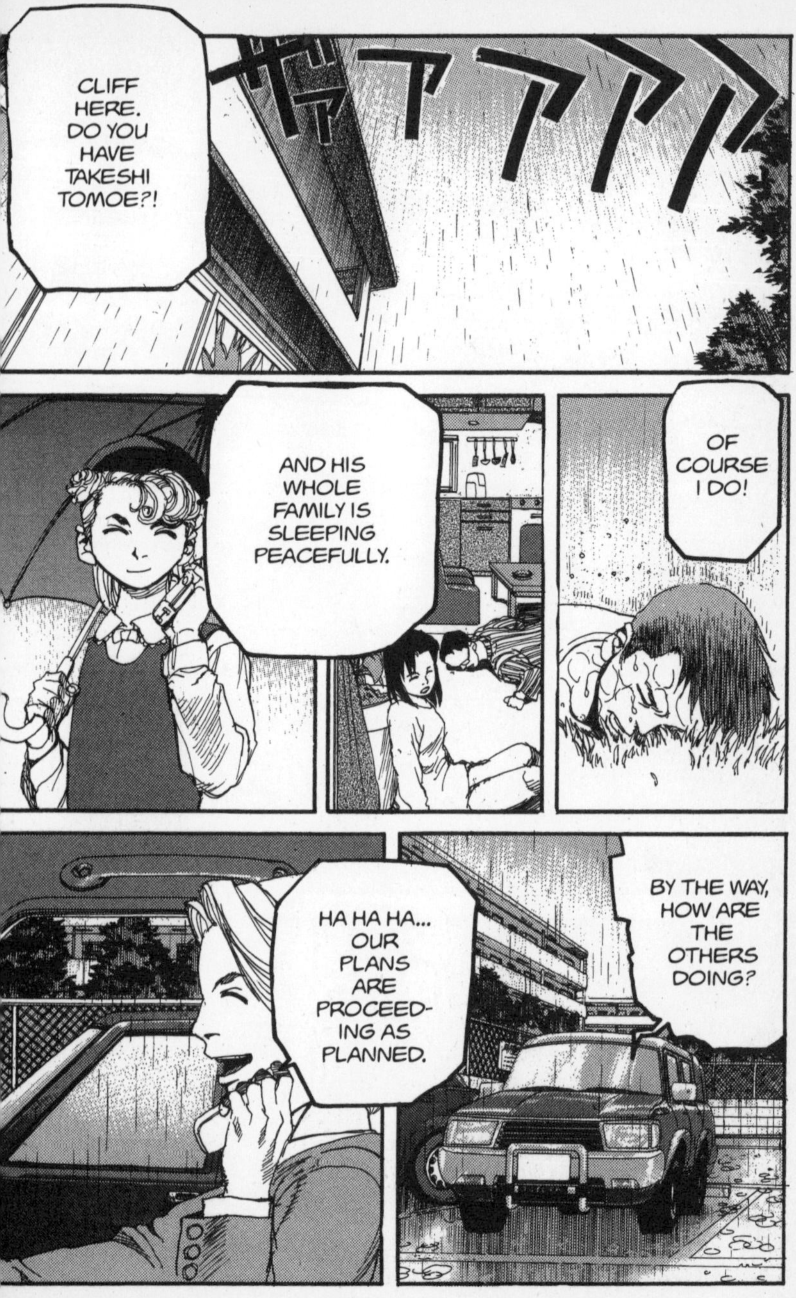
CLIFF HERE. DO YOU HAVE TAKESHI TOMOE?!
OF COURSE I DO!
AND HIS WHOLE FAMILY IS SLEEPING PEACEFULLY.
BY THE WAY, HOW ARE THE OTHERS DOING?
HA HA HA... OUR PLANS ARE PROCEED-ING AS PLANNED.

THE INVINCIBLE-- YET GRACEFUL-- VOLF GOT HAYATO SHINGU...

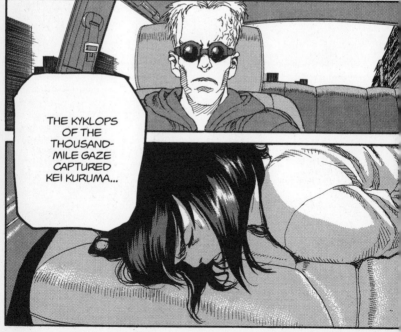

THE KYKLOPS OF THE THOUSAND-MILE GAZE CAPTURED KEI KURUMA...

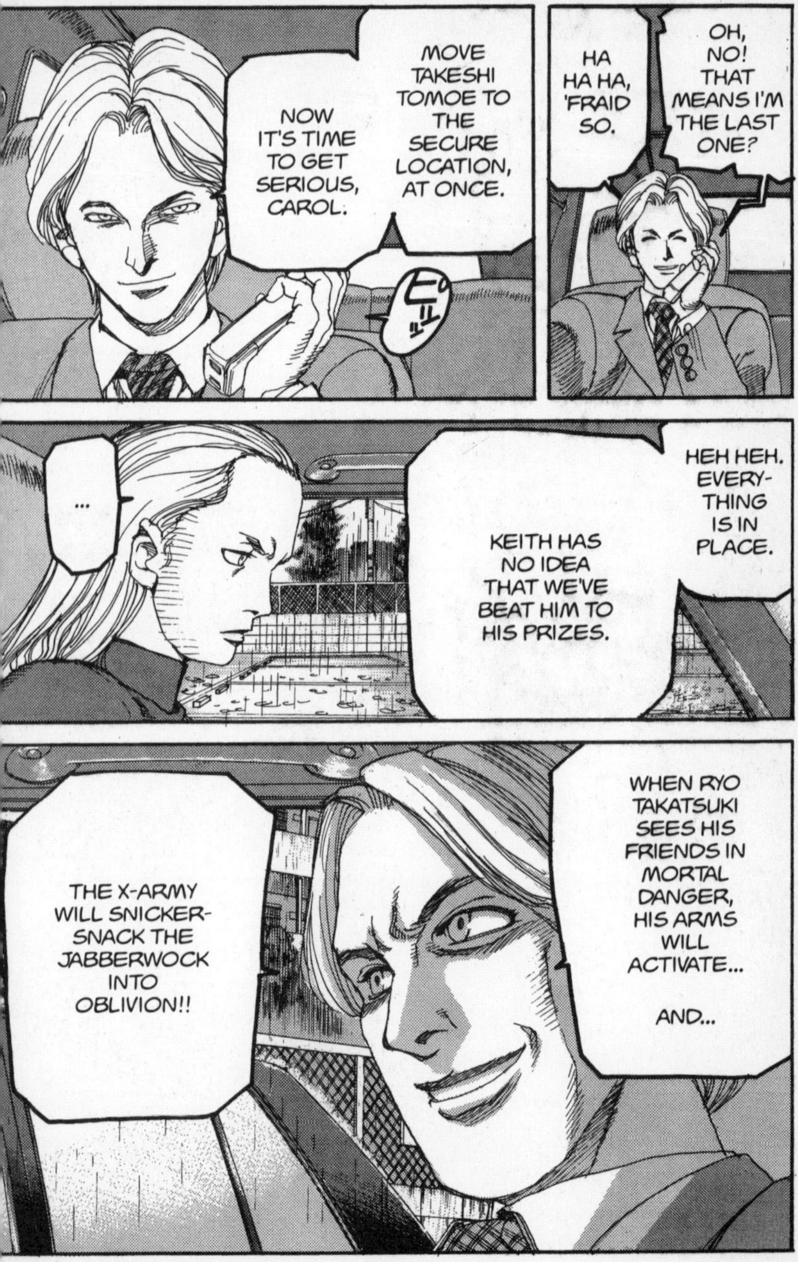
OH, NO! THAT MEANS I'M THE LAST ONE?
HA HA HA, 'FRAID SO.
MOVE TAKESHI TOMOE TO THE SECURE LOCATION, AT ONCE.
NOW IT'S TIME TO GET SERIOUS, CAROL.
ピッ
HEH HEH. EVERY-THING IS IN PLACE.
KEITH HAS NO IDEA THAT WE'VE BEAT HIM TO HIS PRIZES.
...
WHEN RYO TAKATSUKI SEES HIS FRIENDS IN MORTAL DANGER, HIS ARMS WILL ACTIVATE...
AND...
THE X-ARMY WILL SNICKER-SNACK THE JABBERWOCK INTO OBLIVION!!

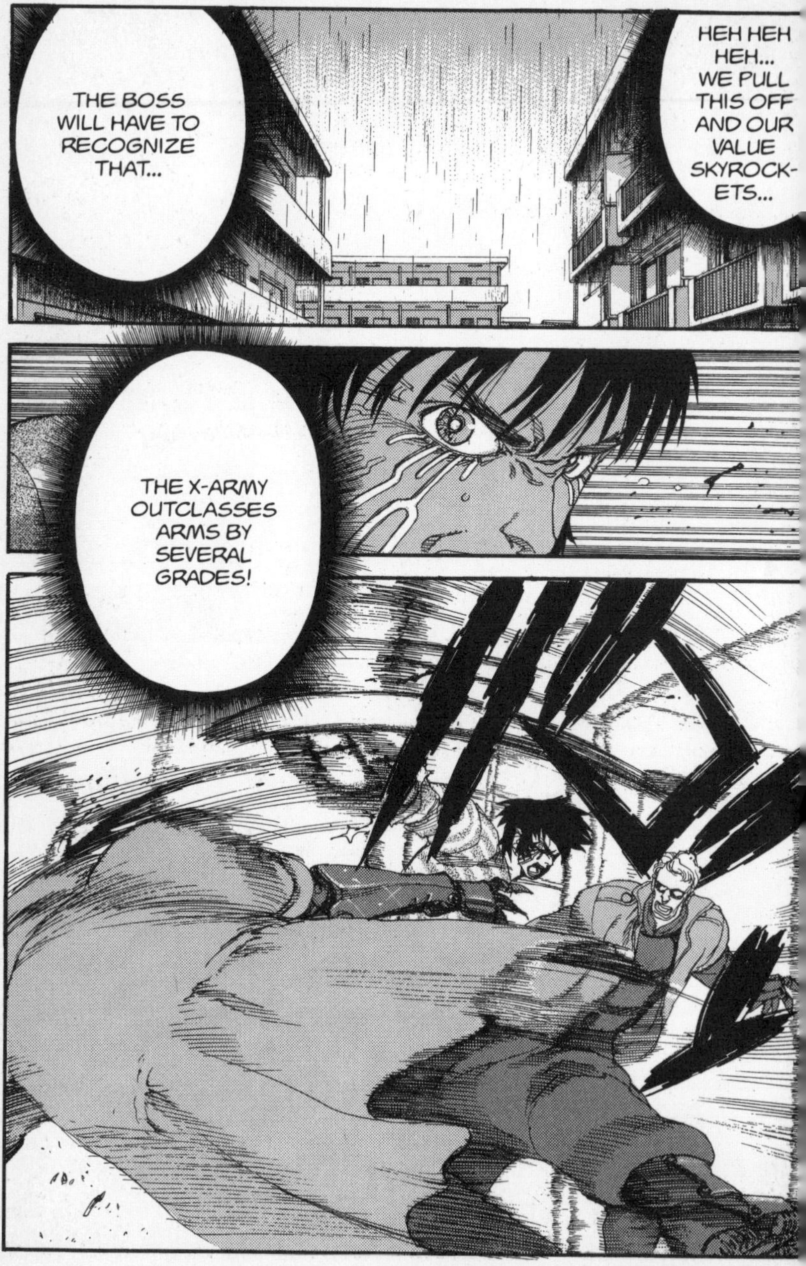
HEH HEH HEH... WE PULL THIS OFF AND OUR VALUE SKYROCK-ETS...
THE BOSS WILL HAVE TO RECOGNIZE THAT...
THE X-ARMY OUTCLASSES ARMS BY SEVERAL GRADES!

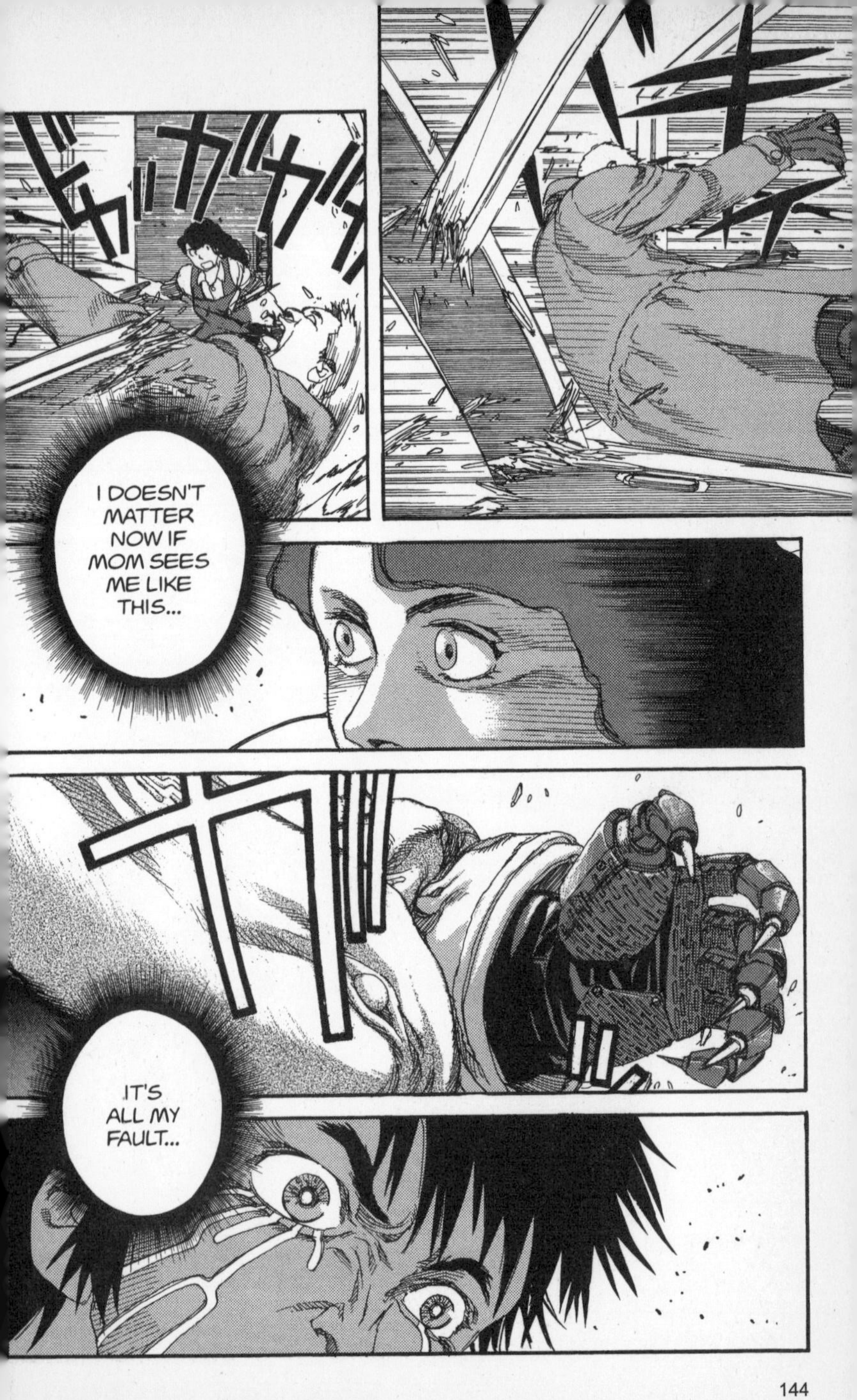
I DOESN'T MATTER NOW IF MOM SEES ME LIKE THIS...
IT'S ALL MY FAULT...

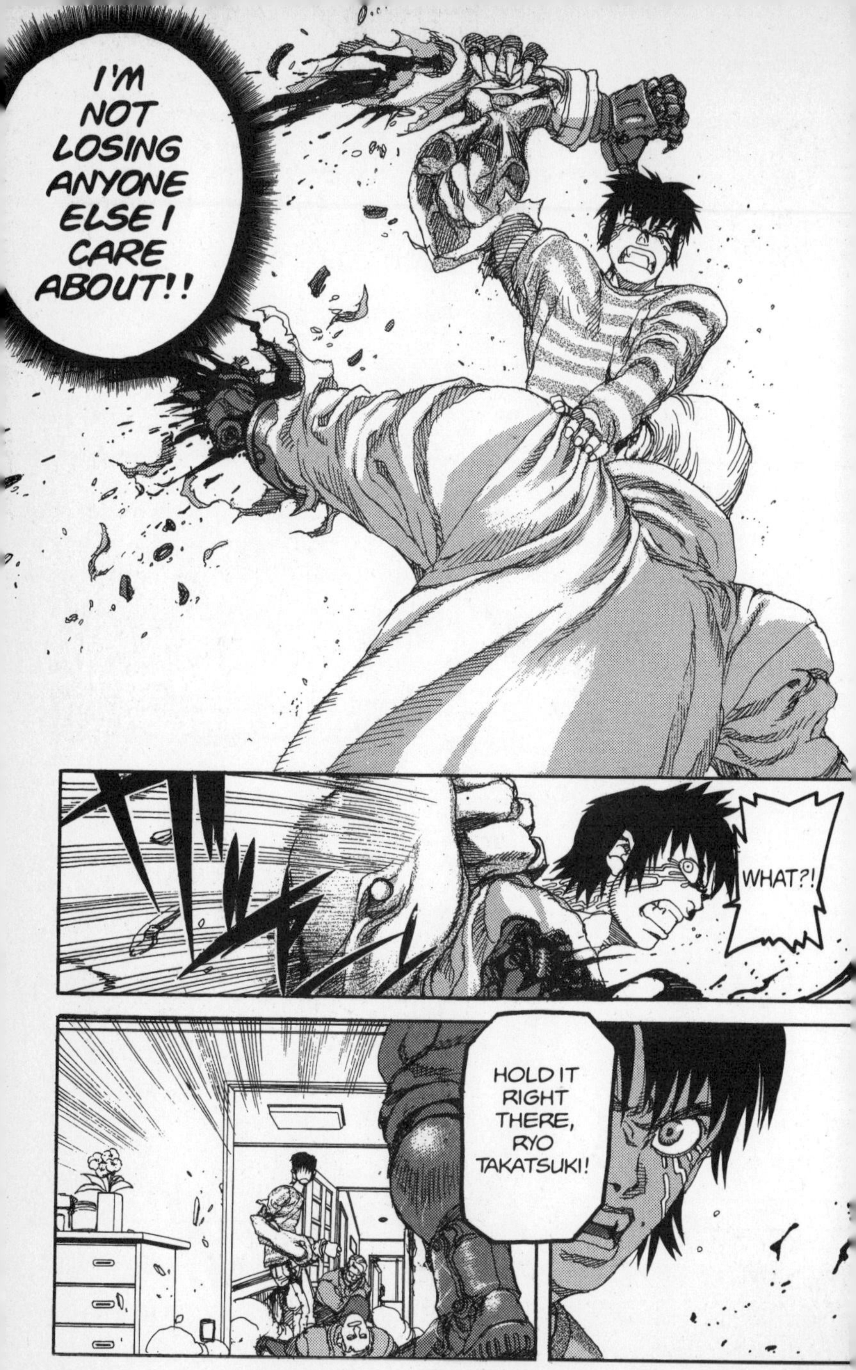
I'M NOT LOSING ANYONE ELSE I CARE ABOUT!!
WHAT?!
HOLD IT RIGHT THERE, RYO TAKATSUKI!

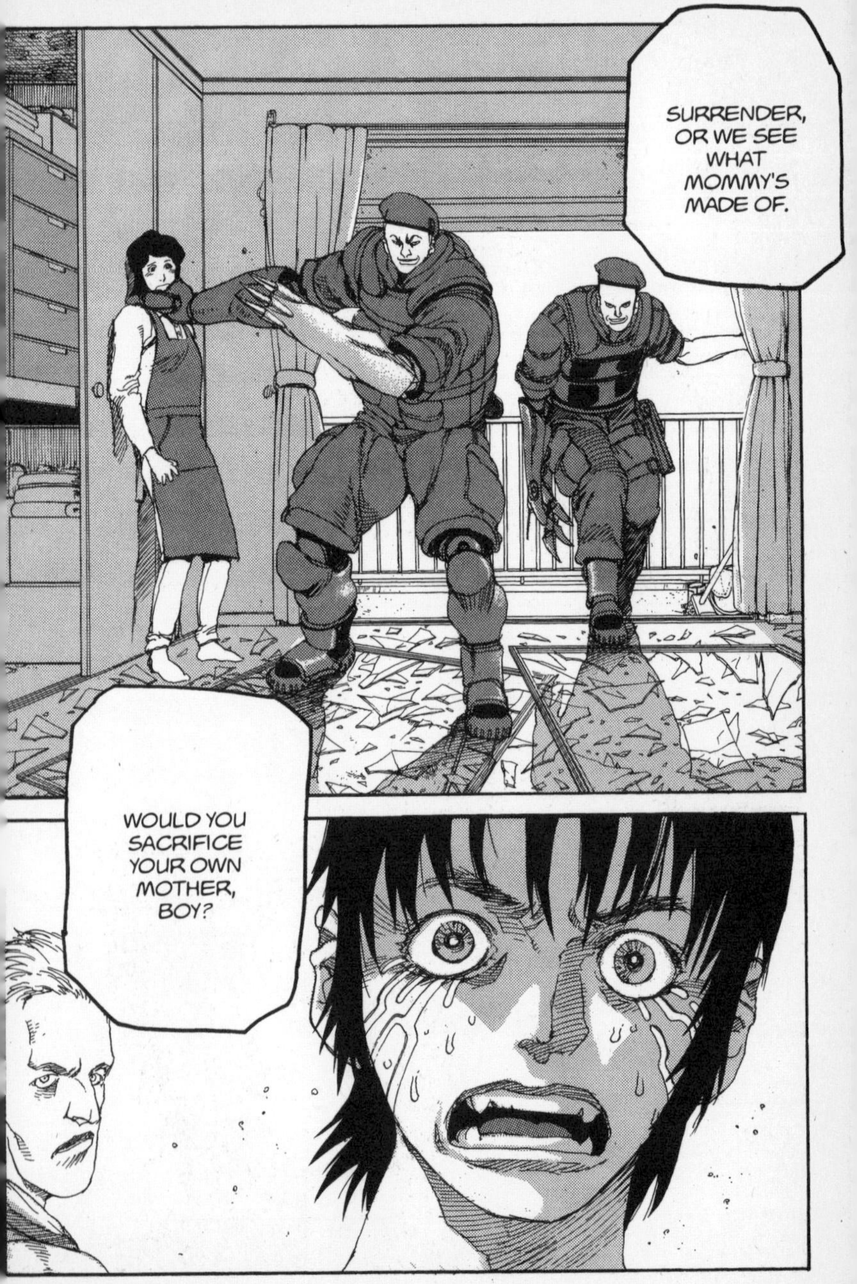
SURRENDER, OR WE SEE WHAT MOMMY'S MADE OF.
WOULD YOU SACRIFICE YOUR OWN MOTHER, BOY?

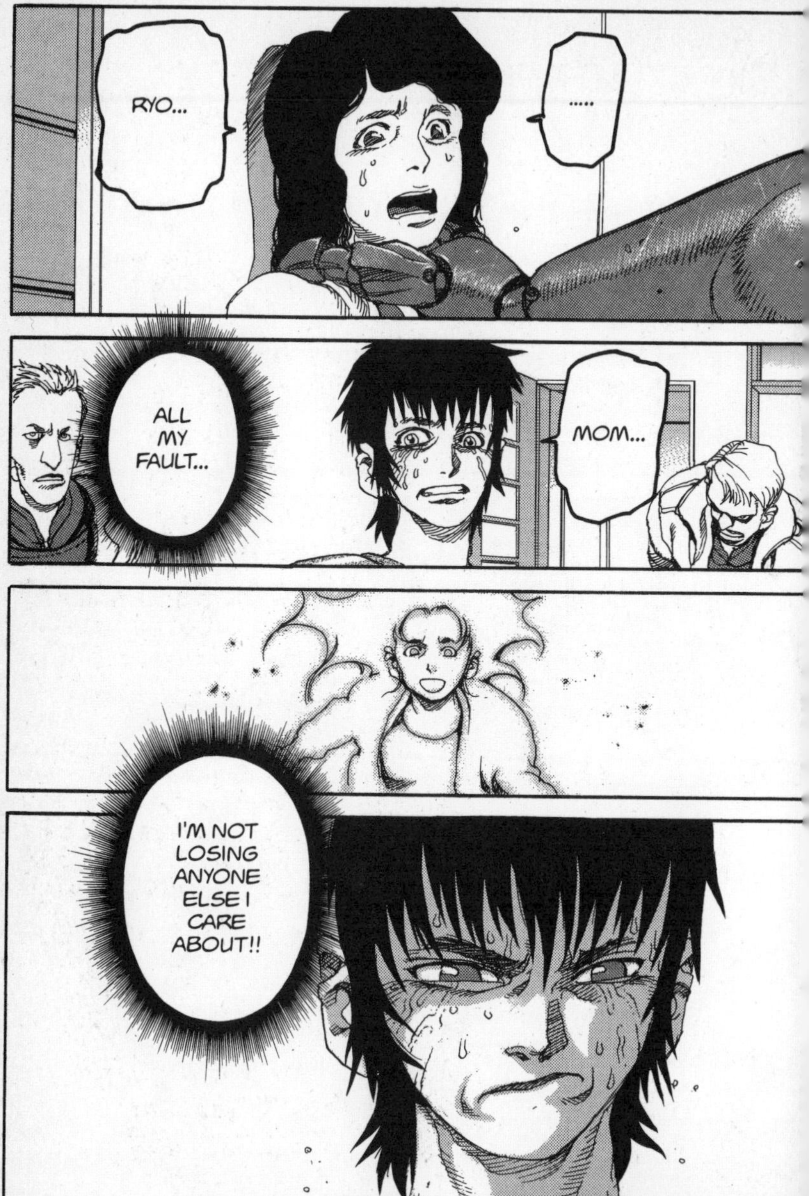
.....
RYO...
MOM...
ALL MY FAULT...
I'M NOT LOSING ANYONE ELSE I CARE ABOUT!!

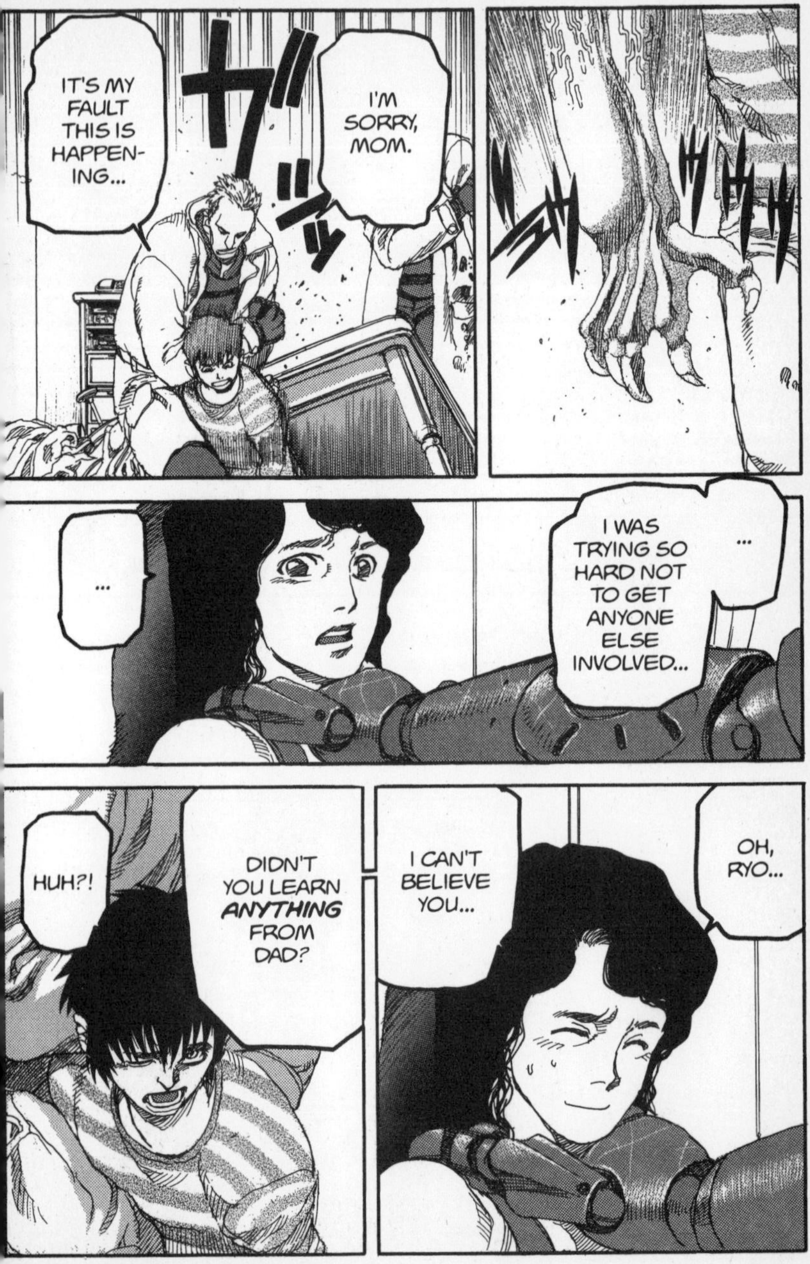
I'M SORRY, MOM.
IT'S MY FAULT THIS IS HAPPEN-ING...
...
I WAS TRYING SO HARD NOT TO GET ANYONE ELSE INVOLVED...
...
OH, RYO...
I CAN'T BELIEVE YOU...
DIDN'T YOU LEARN **ANYTHING** FROM DAD?
HUH?!

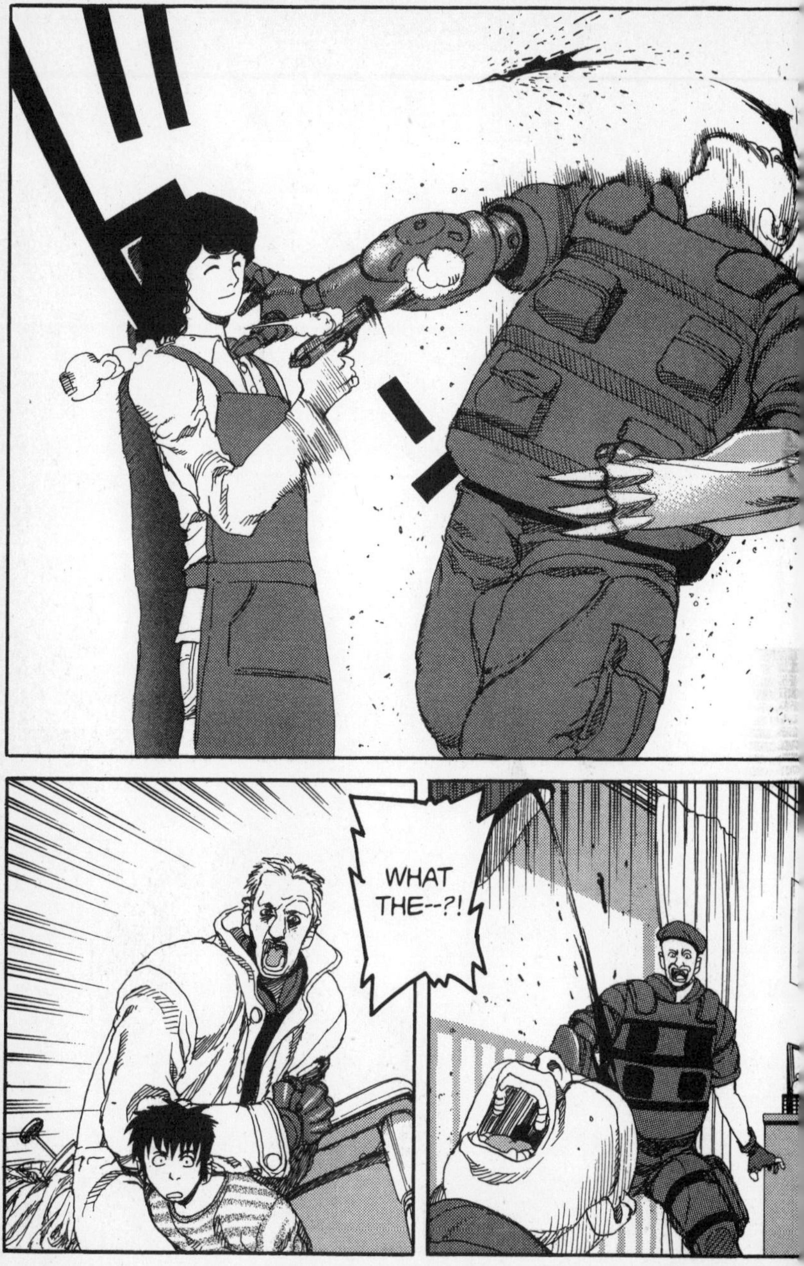
WHAT THE--?!

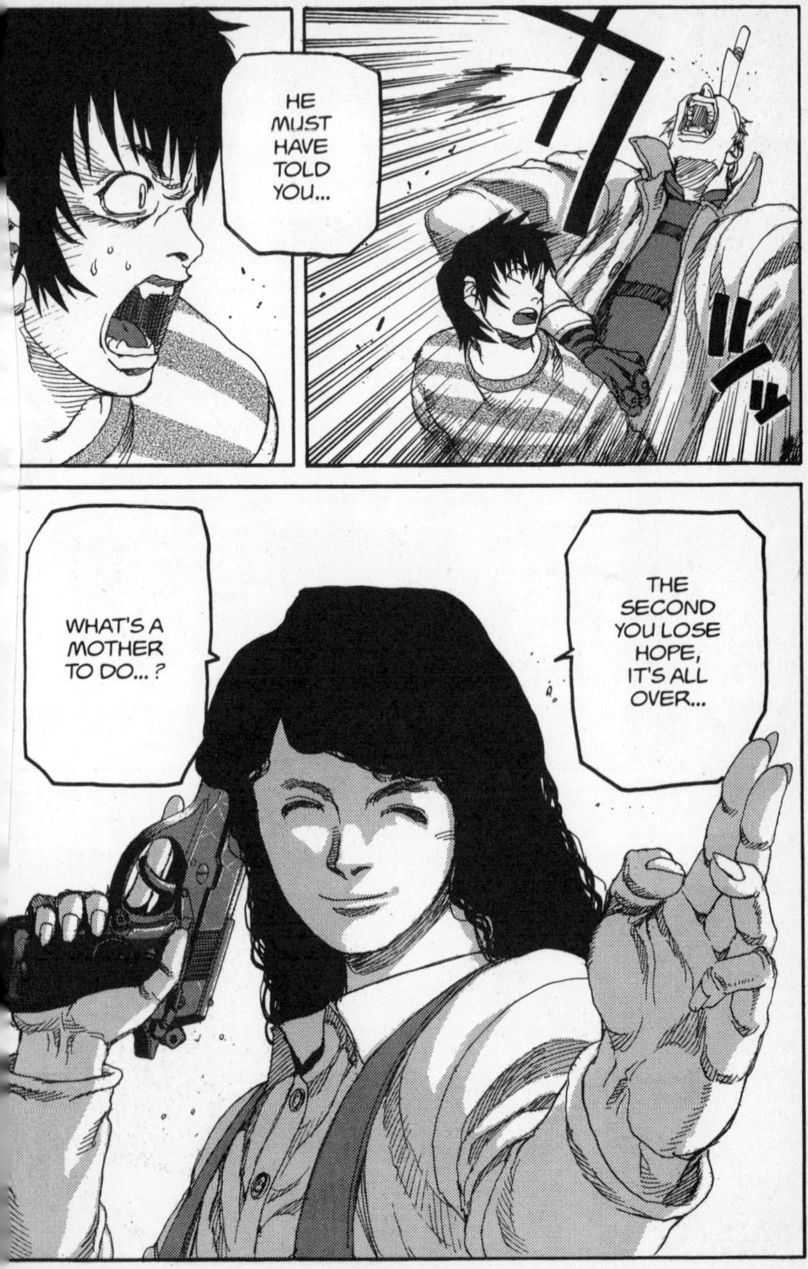
HE MUST HAVE TOLD YOU...
THE SECOND YOU LOSE HOPE, IT'S ALL OVER...
WHAT'S A MOTHER TO DO...?

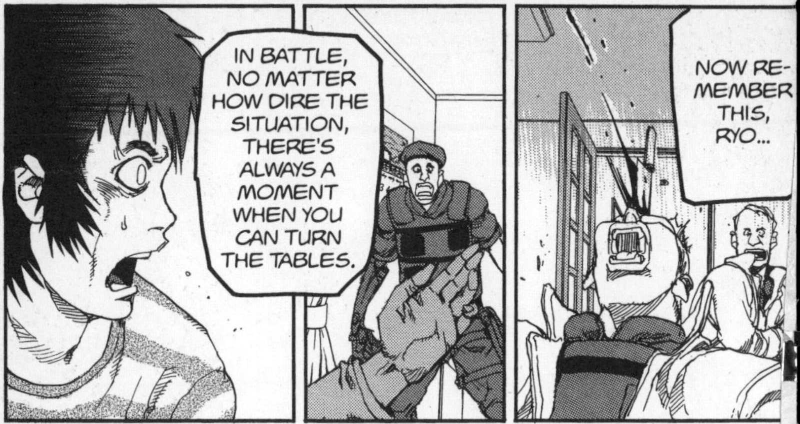
NOW RE-MEMBER THIS, RYO...
IN BATTLE, NO MATTER HOW DIRE THE SITUATION, THERE'S ALWAYS A MOMENT WHEN YOU CAN TURN THE TABLES.

No. 9 MOTHER

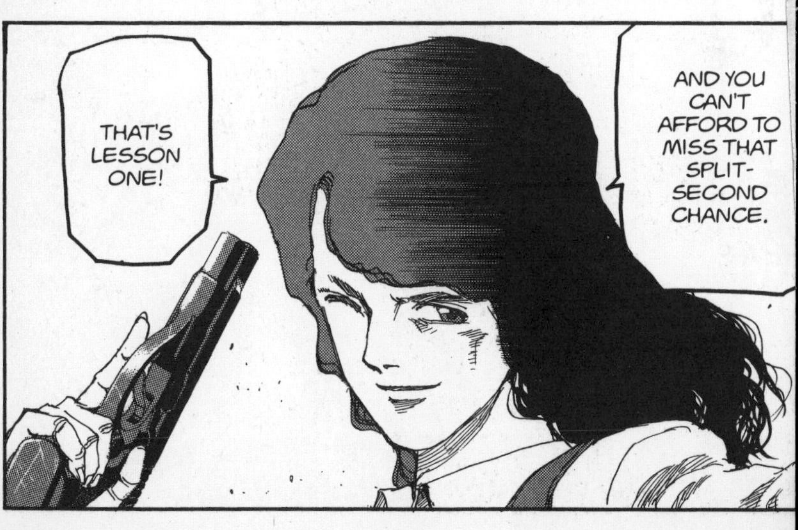
AND YOU CAN'T AFFORD TO MISS THAT SPLIT-SECOND CHANCE.
THAT'S LESSON ONE!

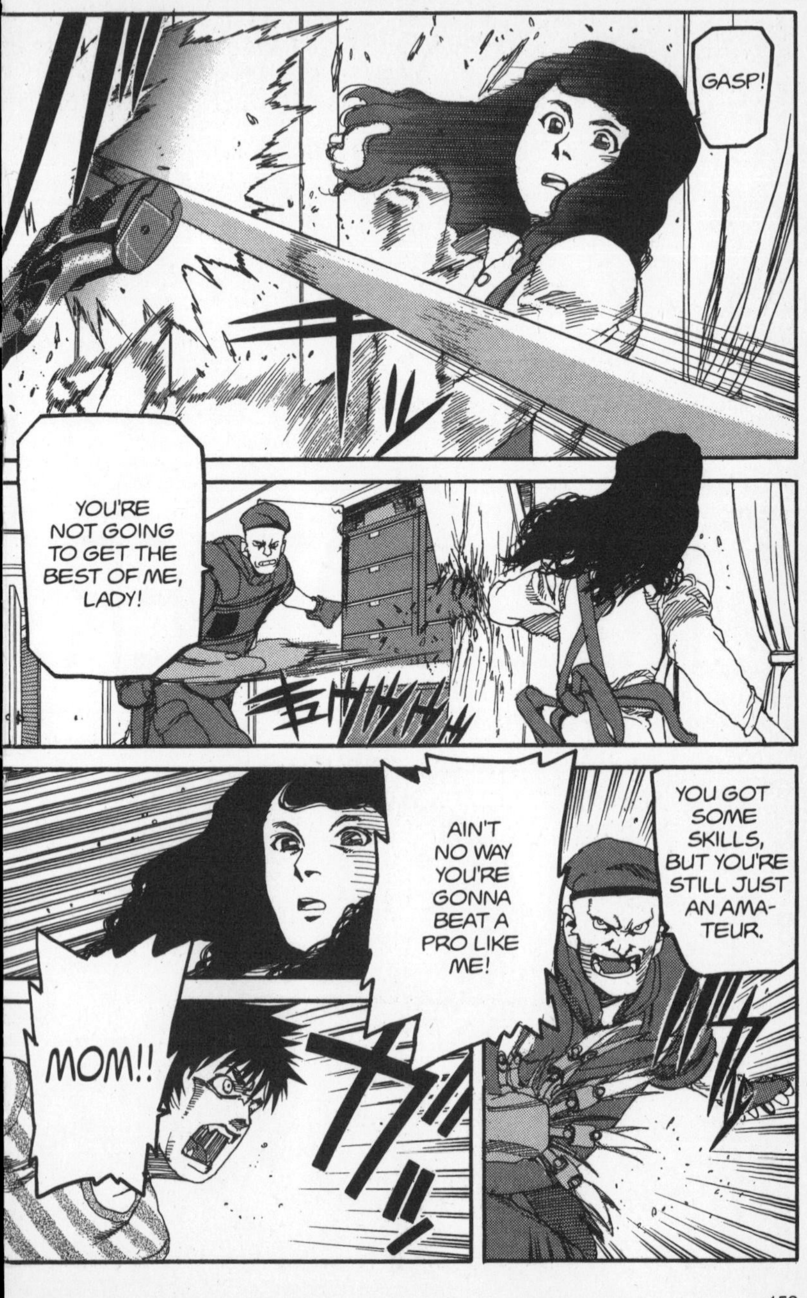
GASP!
YOU'RE NOT GOING TO GET THE BEST OF ME, LADY!
YOU GOT SOME SKILLS, BUT YOU'RE STILL JUST AN AMA-TEUR.
AIN'T NO WAY YOU'RE GONNA BEAT A PRO LIKE ME!
MOM!!

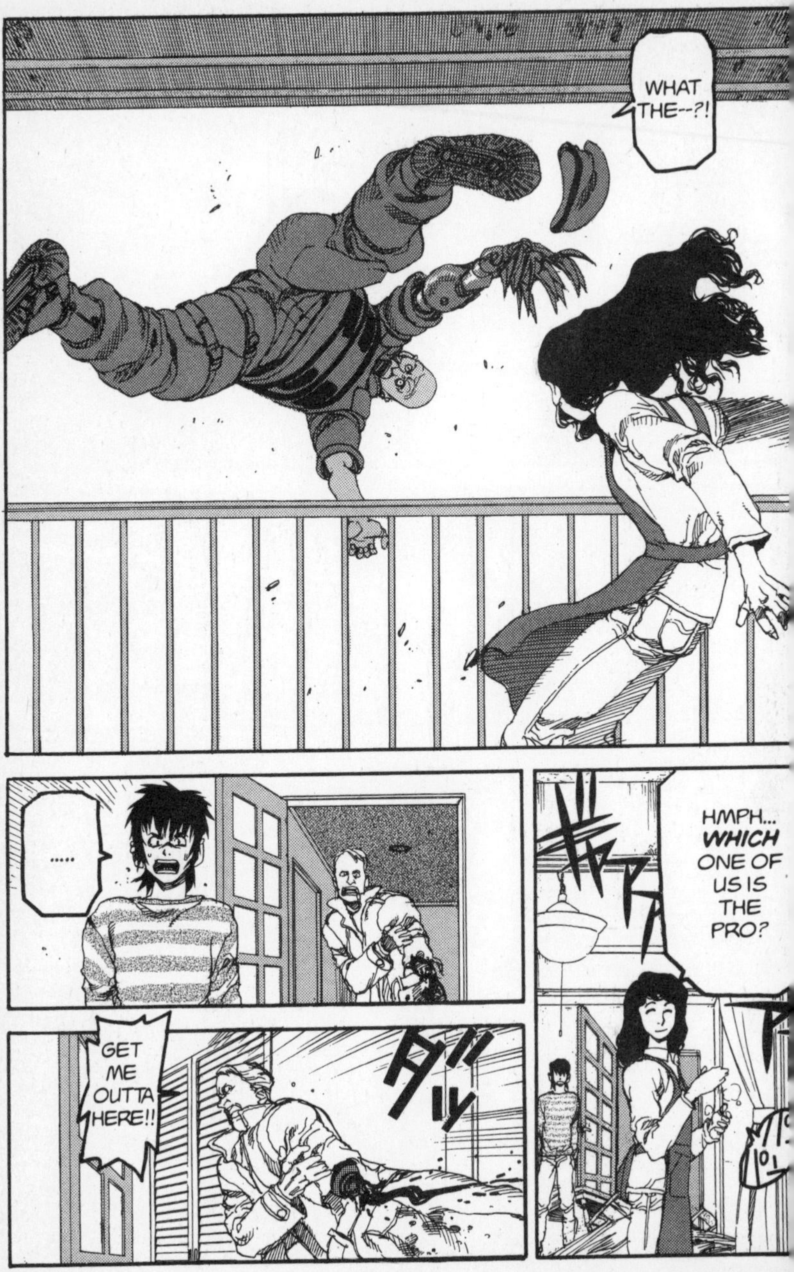
WHAT THE--?!
HMPH... **WHICH** ONE OF US IS THE PRO?
.....
GET ME OUTTA HERE!!

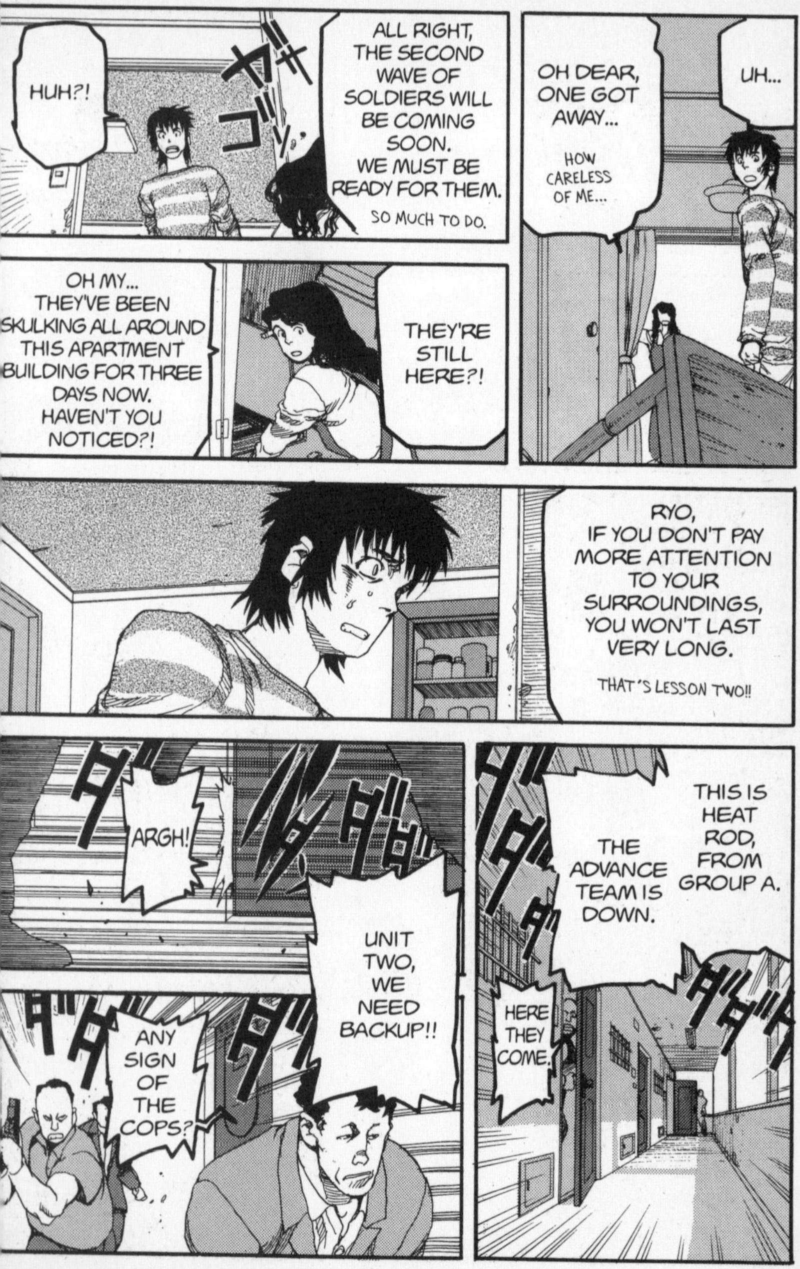
UH...
OH DEAR, ONE GOT AWAY...
HOW CARELESS OF ME...
ALL RIGHT, THE SECOND WAVE OF SOLDIERS WILL BE COMING SOON. WE MUST BE READY FOR THEM.
SO MUCH TO DO.
HUH?!
THEY'RE STILL HERE?!
OH MY... THEY'VE BEEN SKULKING ALL AROUND THIS APARTMENT BUILDING FOR THREE DAYS NOW. HAVEN'T YOU NOTICED?!
RYO, IF YOU DON'T PAY MORE ATTENTION TO YOUR SURROUNDINGS, YOU WON'T LAST VERY LONG.
THAT'S LESSON TWO!!
THIS IS HEAT ROD, FROM GROUP A.
THE ADVANCE TEAM IS DOWN.
HERE THEY COME.
ARGH!
UNIT TWO, WE NEED BACKUP!!
ANY SIGN OF THE COPS?

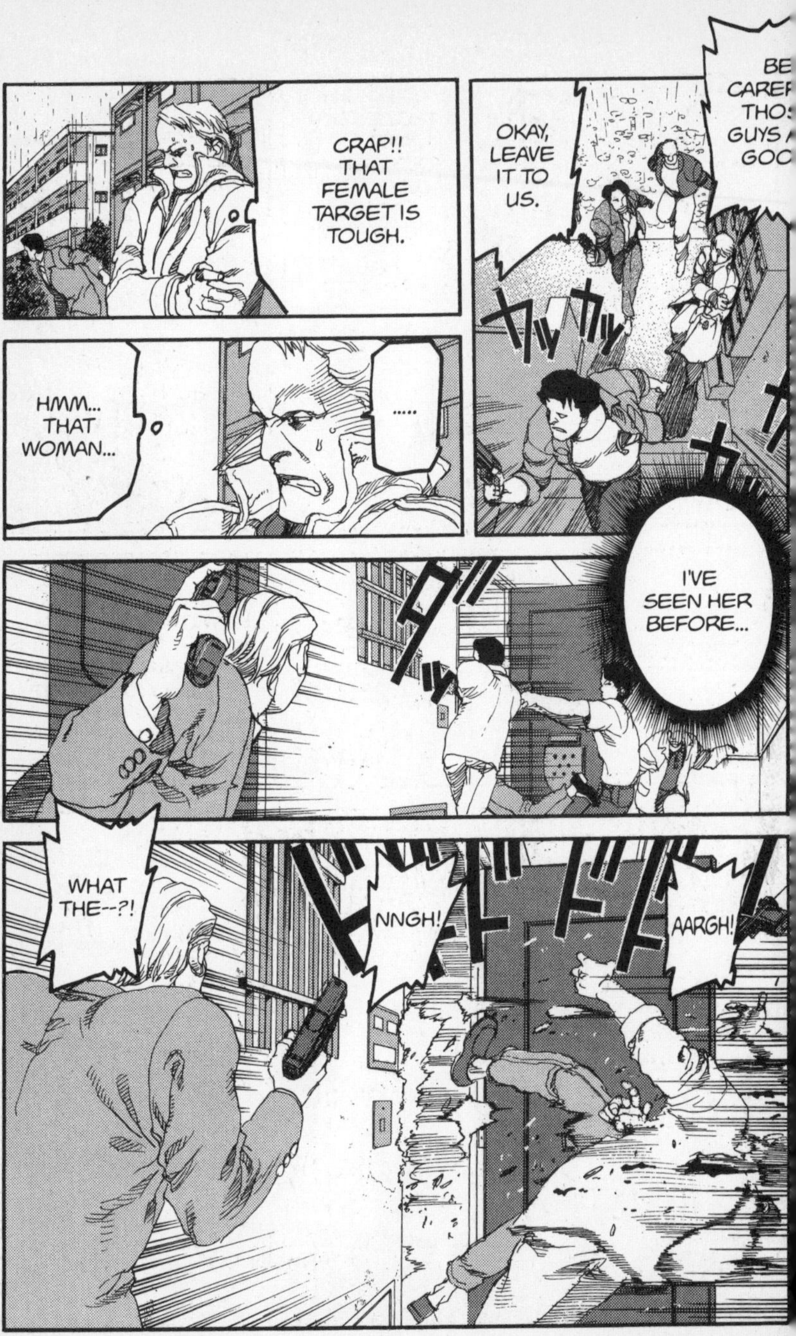
BE CAREF THOS GUYS GOO
OKAY, LEAVE IT TO US.
CRAP!! THAT FEMALE TARGET IS TOUGH.
.....
HMM... THAT WOMAN...
I'VE SEEN HER BEFORE...
AARGH!
NNGH!
WHAT THE--?!

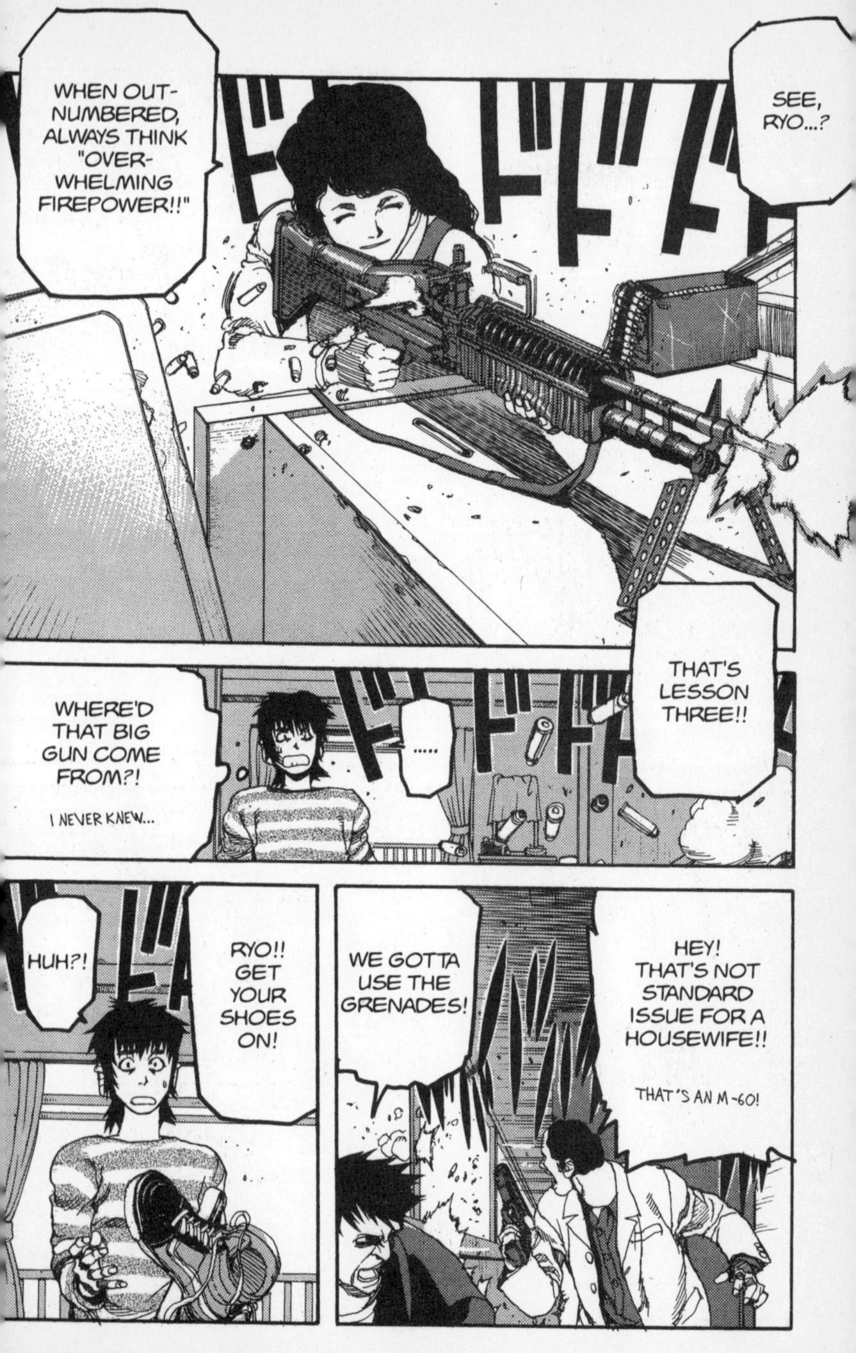
SEE, RYO...?
WHEN OUT-NUMBERED, ALWAYS THINK "OVER-WHELMING FIREPOWER!!"
THAT'S LESSON THREE!!
.....
WHERE'D THAT BIG GUN COME FROM?!
I NEVER KNEW...
HEY! THAT'S NOT STANDARD ISSUE FOR A HOUSEWIFE!!
THAT'S AN M-60!
WE GOTTA USE THE GRENADES!
RYO!! GET YOUR SHOES ON!
HUH?!

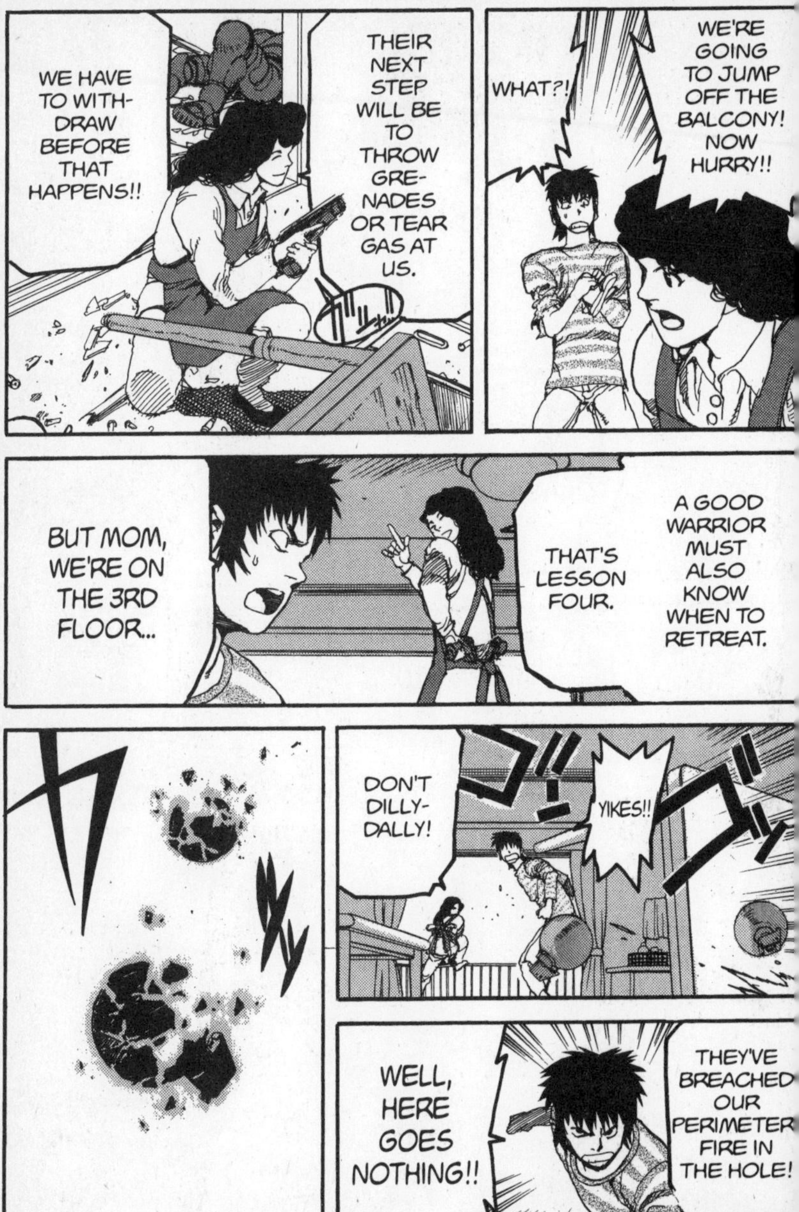
THEIR NEXT STEP WILL BE TO THROW GRE-NADES OR TEAR GAS AT US.
WE HAVE TO WITH-DRAW BEFORE THAT HAPPENS!!
WE'RE GOING TO JUMP OFF THE BALCONY! NOW HURRY!!
WHAT?!
BUT MOM, WE'RE ON THE 3RD FLOOR...
THAT'S LESSON FOUR.
A GOOD WARRIOR MUST ALSO KNOW WHEN TO RETREAT.
DON'T DILLY-DALLY!
YIKES!!
THEY'VE BREACHED OUR PERIMETER FIRE IN THE HOLE!
WELL, HERE GOES NOTHING!!

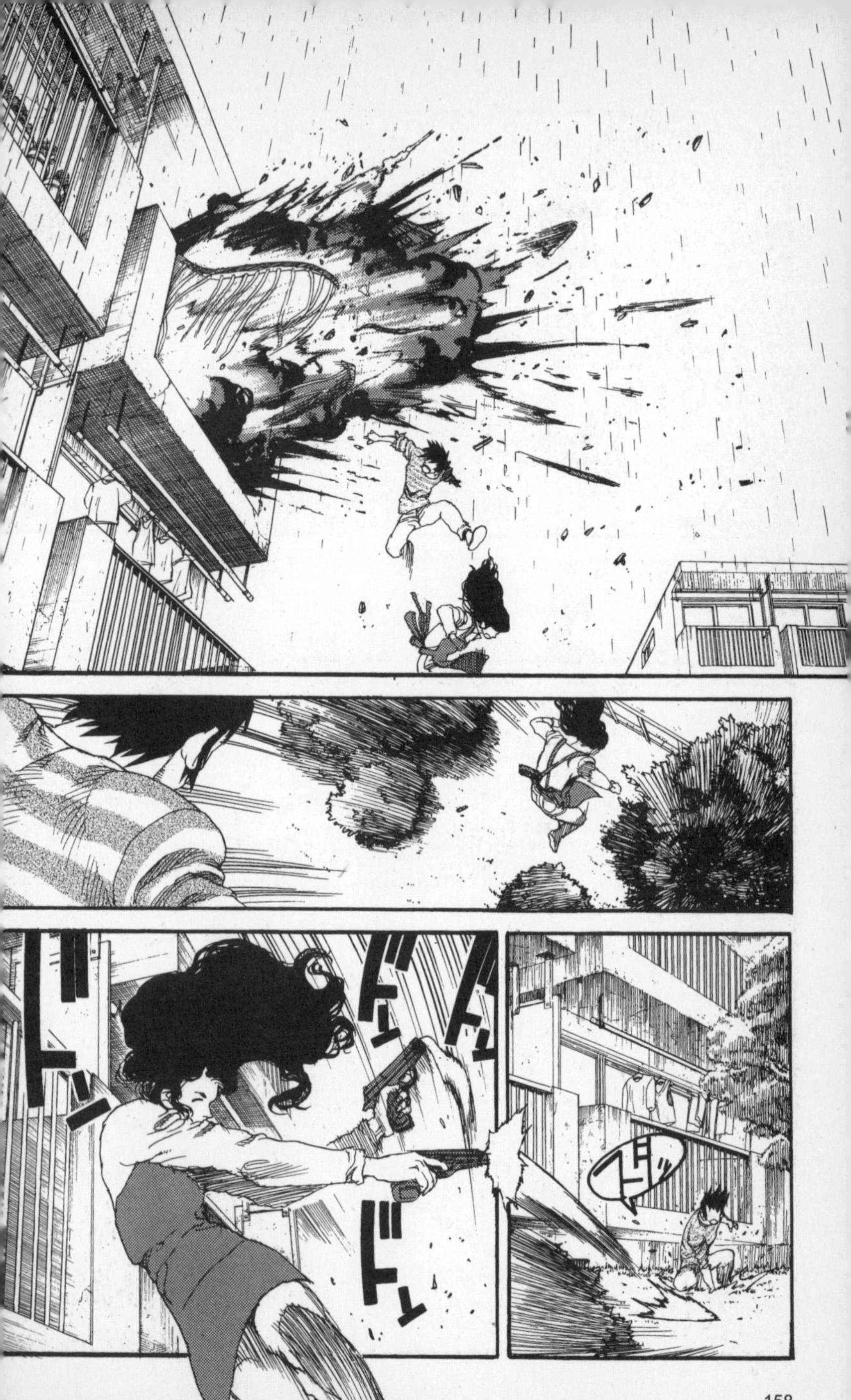
スタッ
ドュ
ドュ
ドュ
ドッ

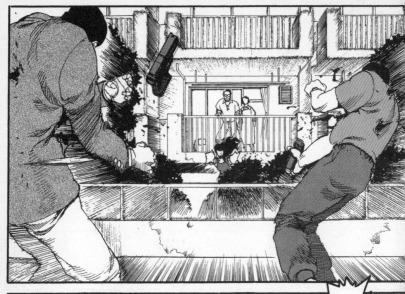

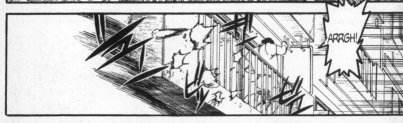

ARRGH!
PHEW! SHE'S LETHAL!
WHAT KIND OF HOUSE-WIFE IS SHE?!
.....
THOSE MOVES! THAT TWO-FISTED PISTOL ACTION!
WHO KNEW THAT SHE WAS STILL ALIVE...?

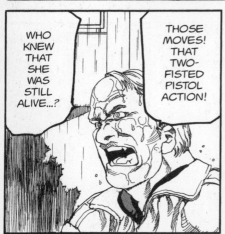

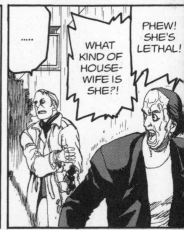

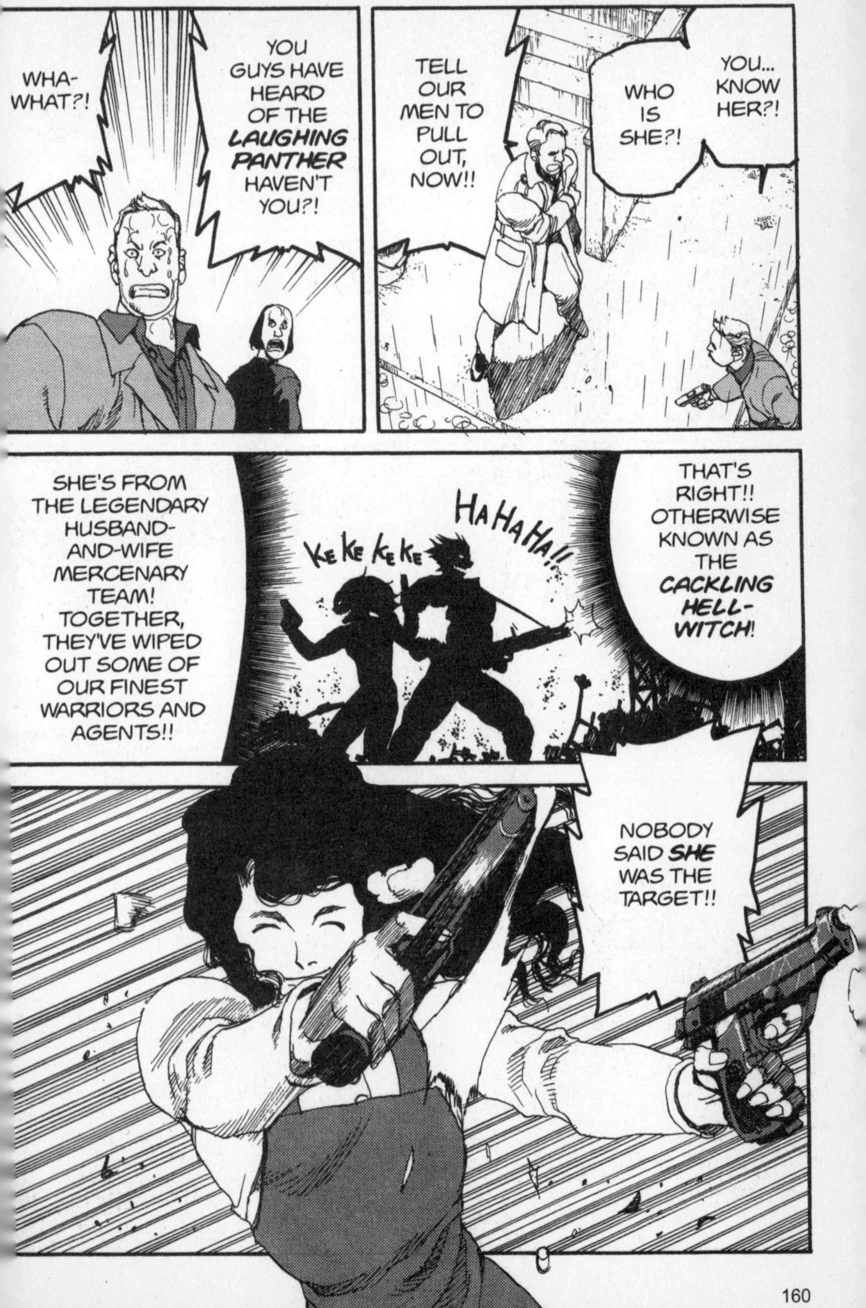
YOU... KNOW HER?!
WHO IS SHE?!
TELL OUR MEN TO PULL OUT, NOW!!
YOU GUYS HAVE HEARD OF THE LAUGHING PANTHER HAVEN'T YOU?!
WHA-WHAT?!
THAT'S RIGHT!! OTHERWISE KNOWN AS THE CACKLING HELL-WITCH!
HAHAHAHA!!
KEKEKEKEKE
SHE'S FROM THE LEGENDARY HUSBAND-AND-WIFE MERCENARY TEAM! TOGETHER, THEY'VE WIPED OUT SOME OF OUR FINEST WARRIORS AND AGENTS!!
NOBODY SAID SHE WAS THE TARGET!!

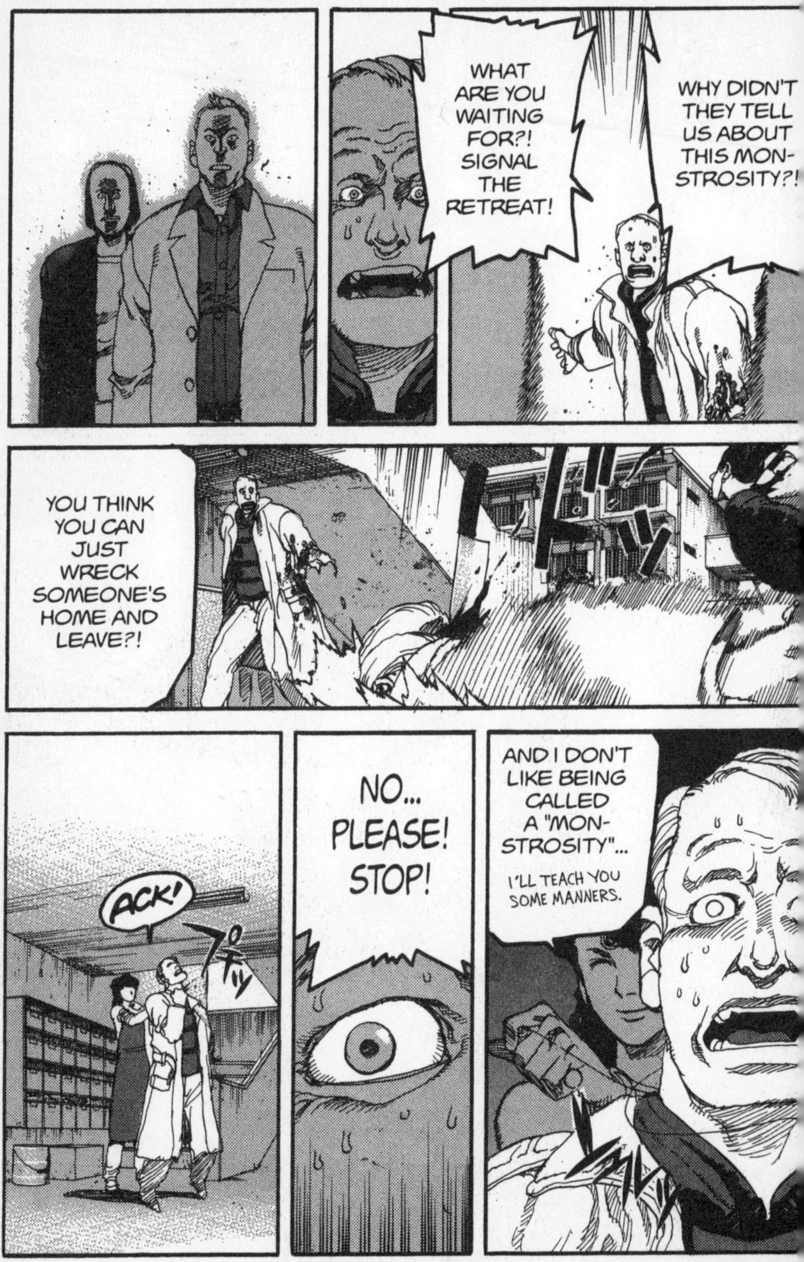
WHY DIDN'T THEY TELL US ABOUT THIS MON-STROSITY?!
WHAT ARE YOU WAITING FOR?! SIGNAL THE RETREAT!
YOU THINK YOU CAN JUST WRECK SOMEONE'S HOME AND LEAVE?!
AND I DON'T LIKE BEING CALLED A "MON-STROSITY"...
I'LL TEACH YOU SOME MANNERS.
NO... PLEASE! STOP!
ACK!

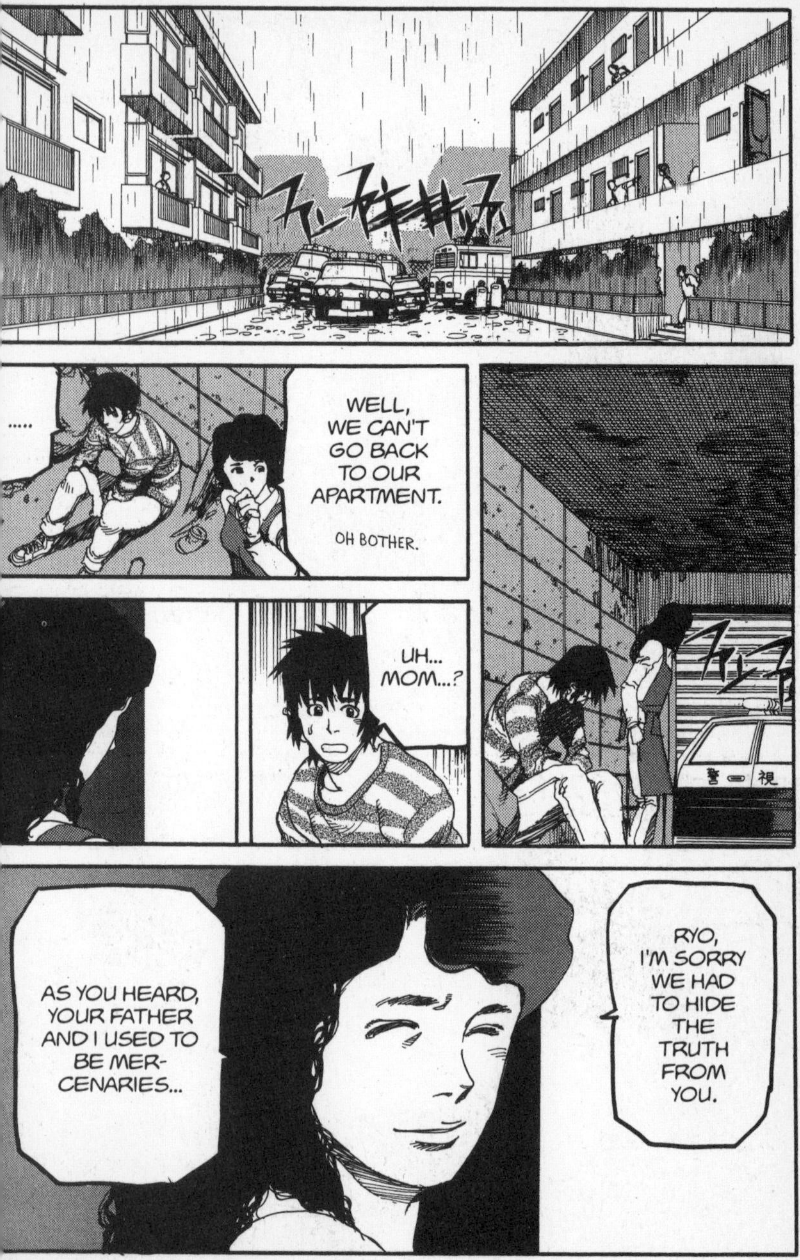
WELL, WE CAN'T GO BACK TO OUR APARTMENT.
OH BOTHER.
.....
UH... MOM...?
RYO, I'M SORRY WE HAD TO HIDE THE TRUTH FROM YOU.
AS YOU HEARD, YOUR FATHER AND I USED TO BE MER-CENARIES...

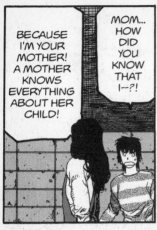

AND AS YOU LEARNED AT ABUMISAWA, I DID NOT GIVE BIRTH TO YOU.
.....
HUH?!
MOM... HOW DID YOU KNOW THAT I--?!
BECAUSE I'M YOUR MOTHER! A MOTHER KNOWS EVERYTHING ABOUT HER CHILD!
I KNOW THAT YOUR ARMS HAS ACTIVATED, THAT YOU'VE BEEN LIVING IN AN ABANDONED BUILDING SINCE YOU CAME BACK FROM ABUMISAWA VILLAGE, AND...
...THAT YOU'RE LEAVING HOME TO GO TO LOOK FOR KATSUMI.
.....
WHEN WE GOT YOU FROM THE BLUEMEN, WE GAVE UP OUR CAREERS AS MERCENARIES AND STARTED A NEW LIFE...

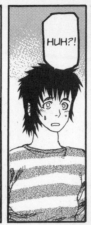

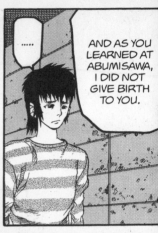

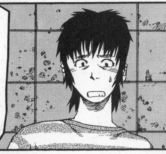

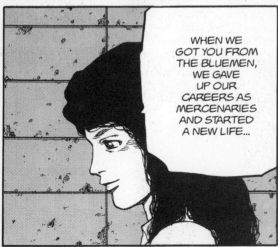

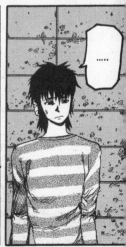

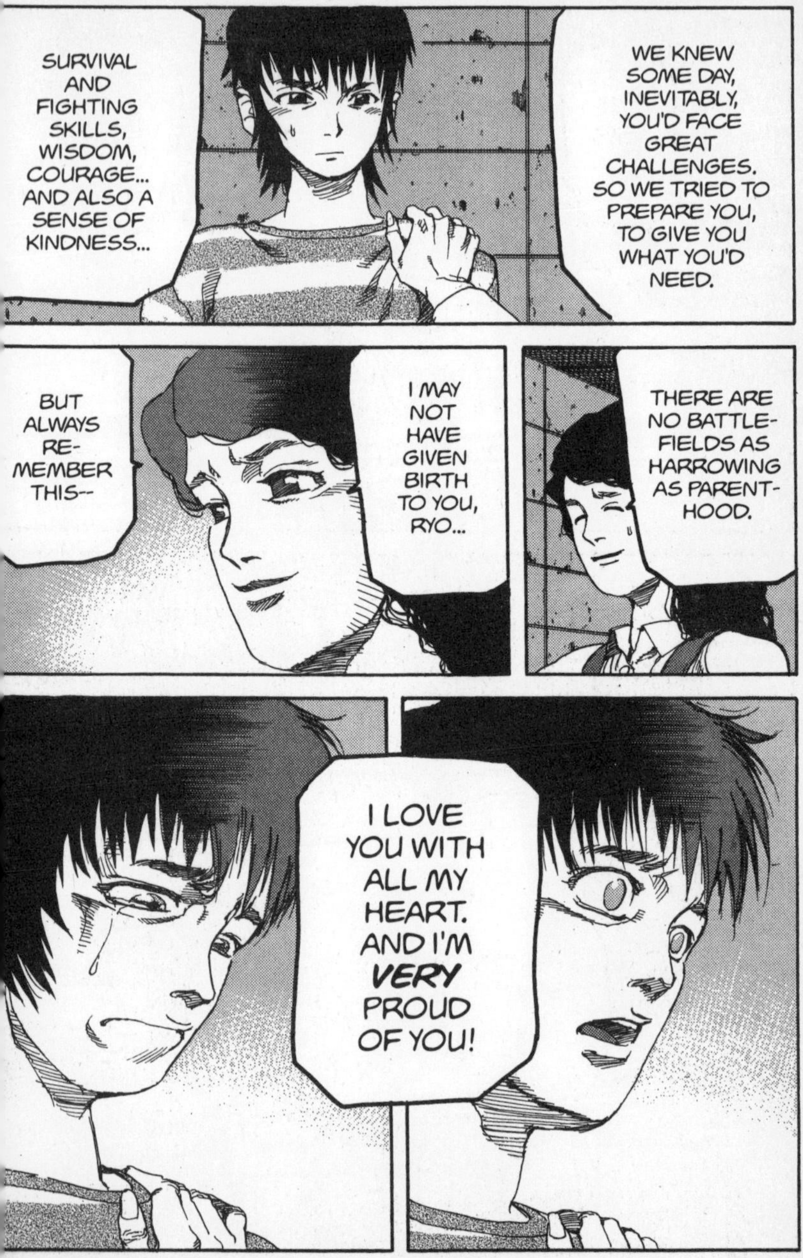
WE KNEW SOME DAY, INEVITABLY, YOU'D FACE GREAT CHALLENGES. SO WE TRIED TO PREPARE YOU, TO GIVE YOU WHAT YOU'D NEED.
SURVIVAL AND FIGHTING SKILLS, WISDOM, COURAGE... AND ALSO A SENSE OF KINDNESS...
THERE ARE NO BATTLE-FIELDS AS HARROWING AS PARENT-HOOD.
I MAY NOT HAVE GIVEN BIRTH TO YOU, RYO...
BUT ALWAYS RE-MEMBER THIS--
I LOVE YOU WITH ALL MY HEART. AND I'M ***VERY*** PROUD OF YOU!

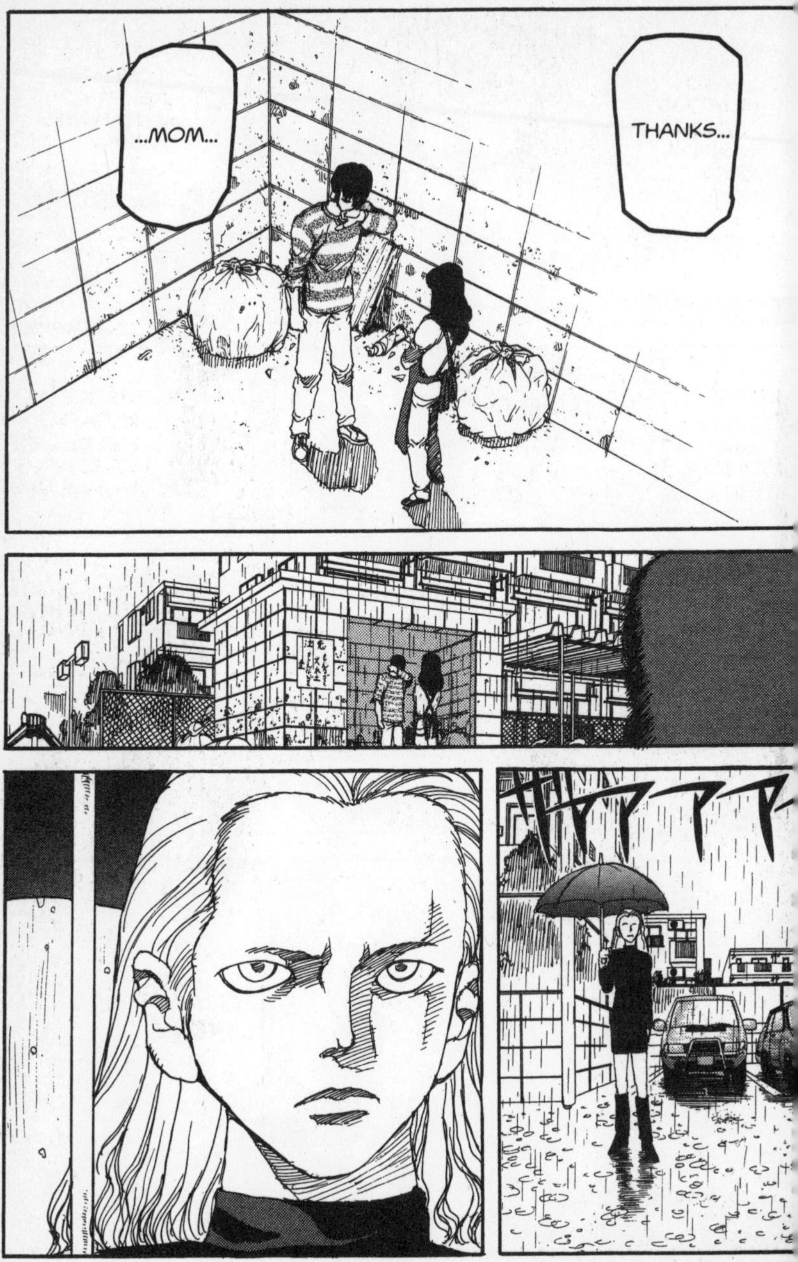
...MOM...
THANKS...

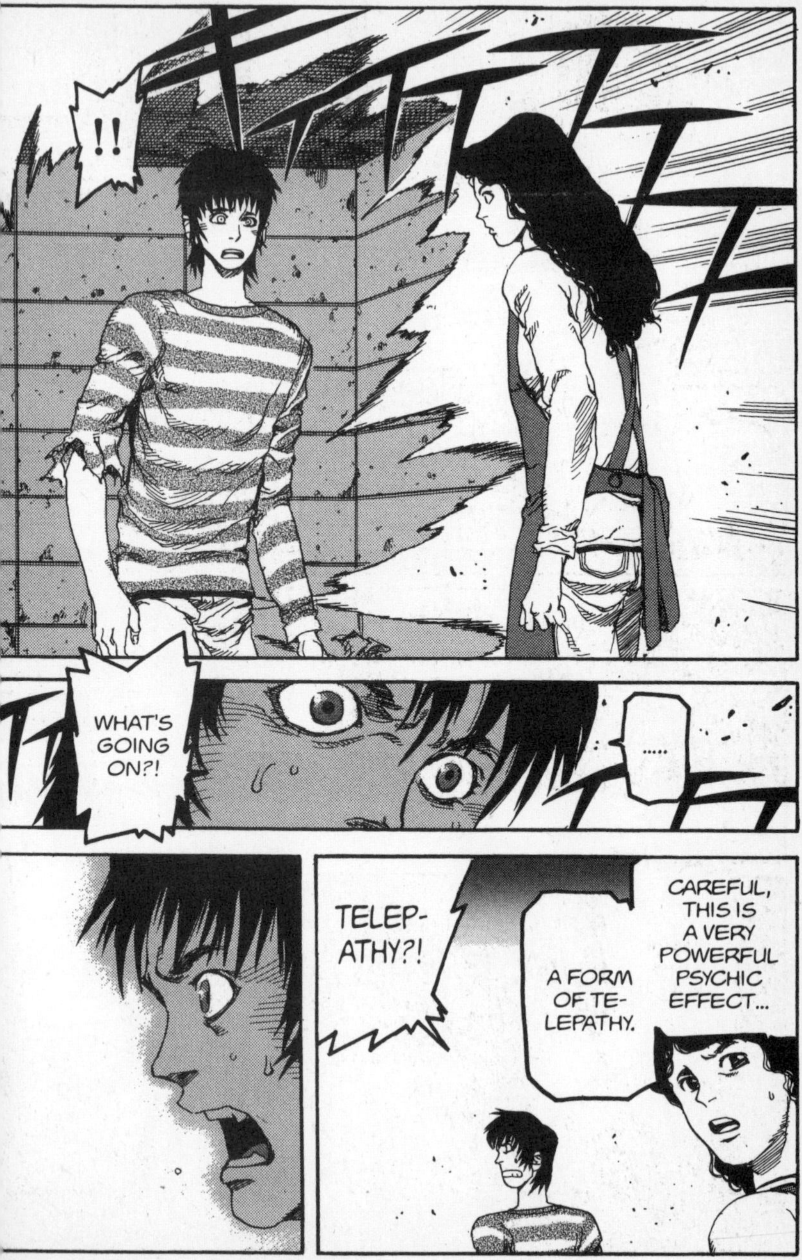
!!
.....
WHAT'S GOING ON?!
CAREFUL, THIS IS A VERY POWERFUL PSYCHIC EFFECT...
A FORM OF TE-LEPATHY.
TELEP-ATHY?!

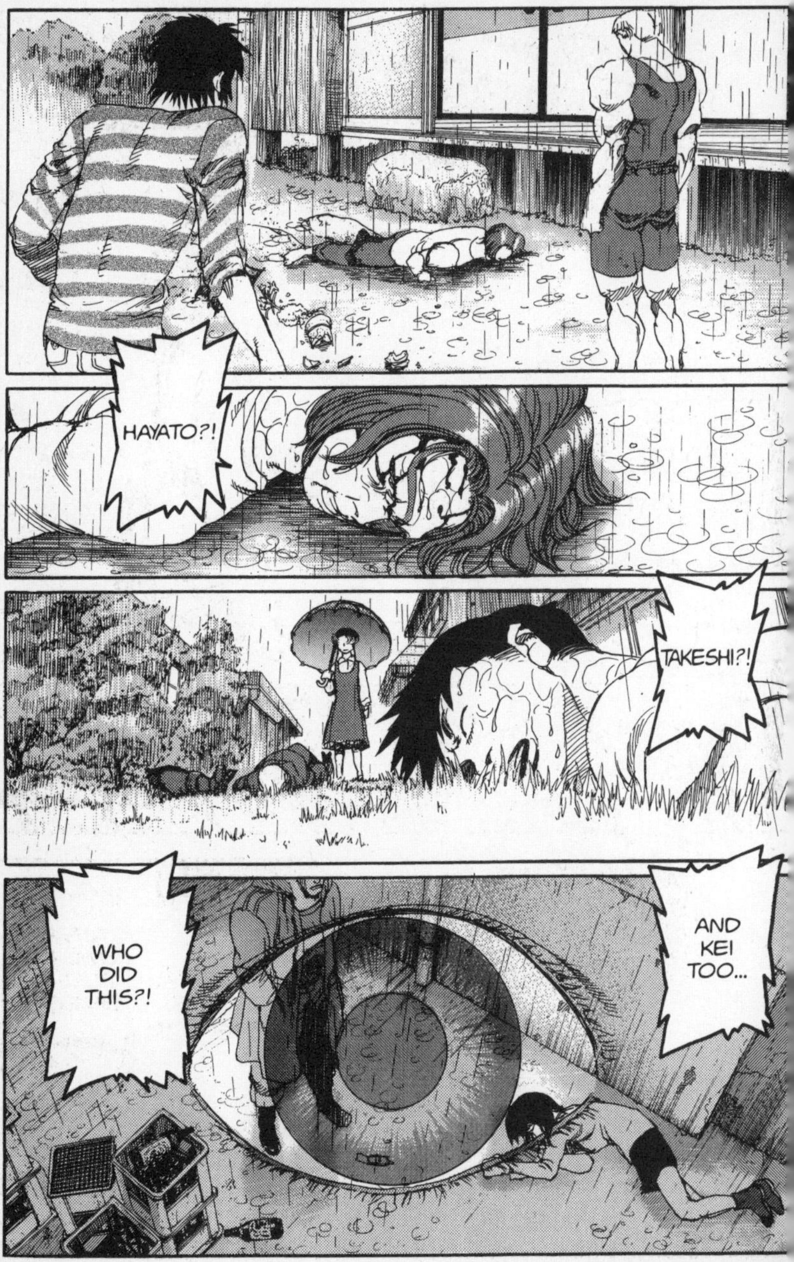
HAYATO?!
TAKESHI?!
AND KEI TOO...
WHO DID THIS?!

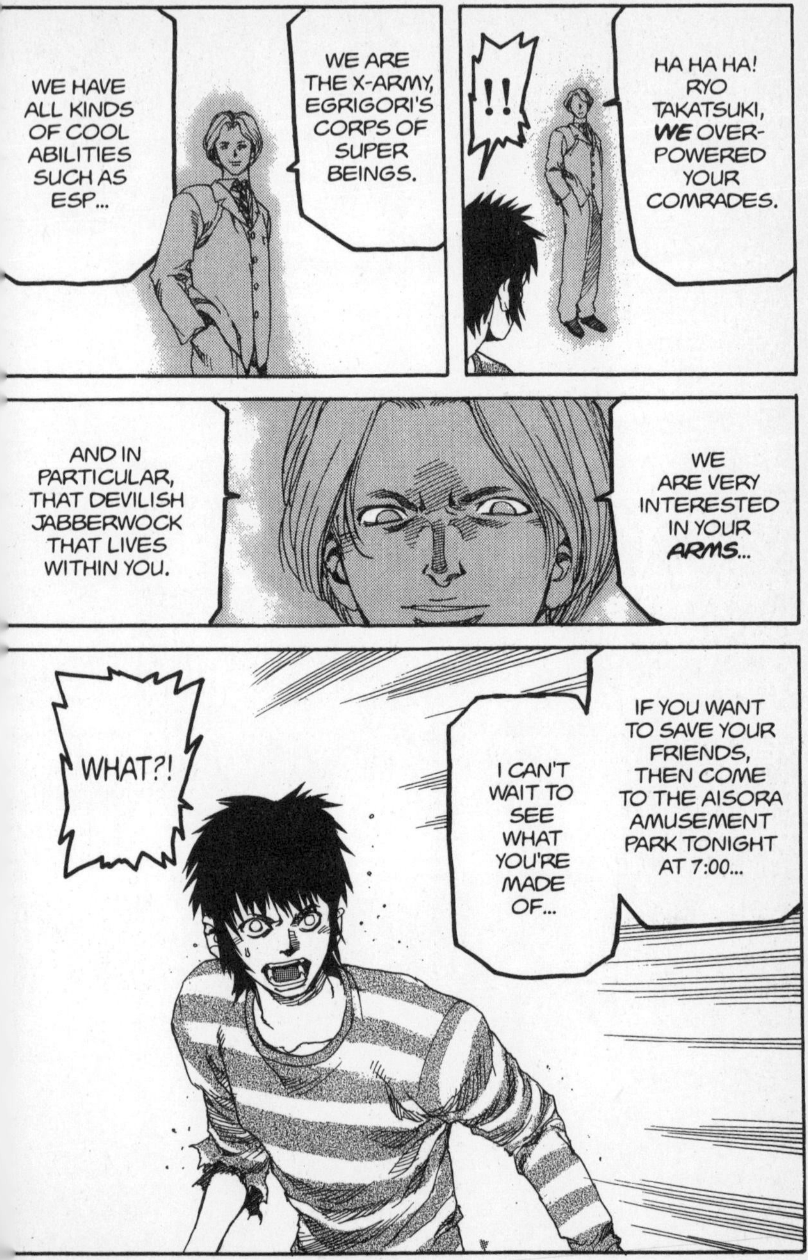
HA HA HA! RYO TAKATSUKI, WE OVER-POWERED YOUR COMRADES.
!!
WE ARE THE X-ARMY, EGRIGORI'S CORPS OF SUPER BEINGS.
WE HAVE ALL KINDS OF COOL ABILITIES SUCH AS ESP...
WE ARE VERY INTERESTED IN YOUR ARMS...
AND IN PARTICULAR, THAT DEVILISH JABBERWOCK THAT LIVES WITHIN YOU.
IF YOU WANT TO SAVE YOUR FRIENDS, THEN COME TO THE AISORA AMUSEMENT PARK TONIGHT AT 7:00...
I CAN'T WAIT TO SEE WHAT YOU'RE MADE OF...
WHAT?!

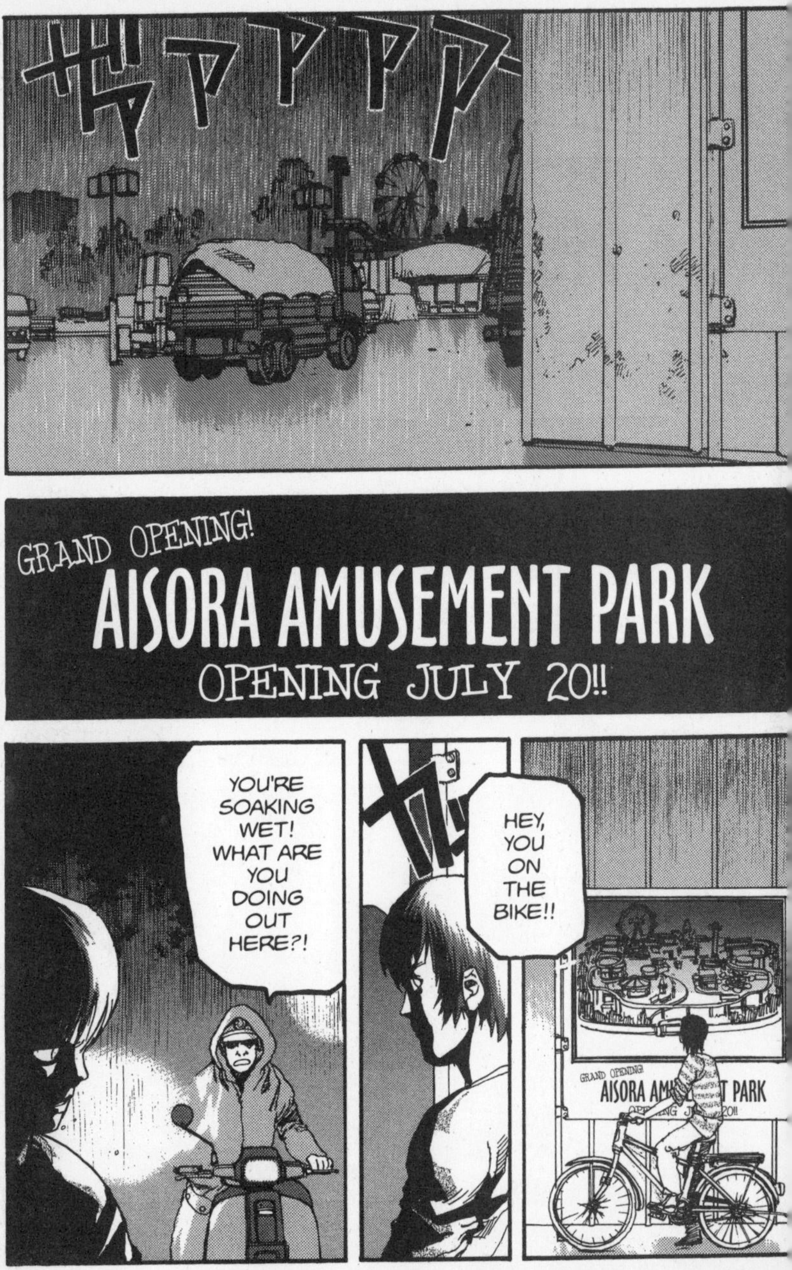
GRAND OPENING!
AISORA AMUSEMENT PARK
OPENING JULY 20!!
HEY, YOU ON THE BIKE!!
YOU'RE SOAKING WET! WHAT ARE YOU DOING OUT HERE?!

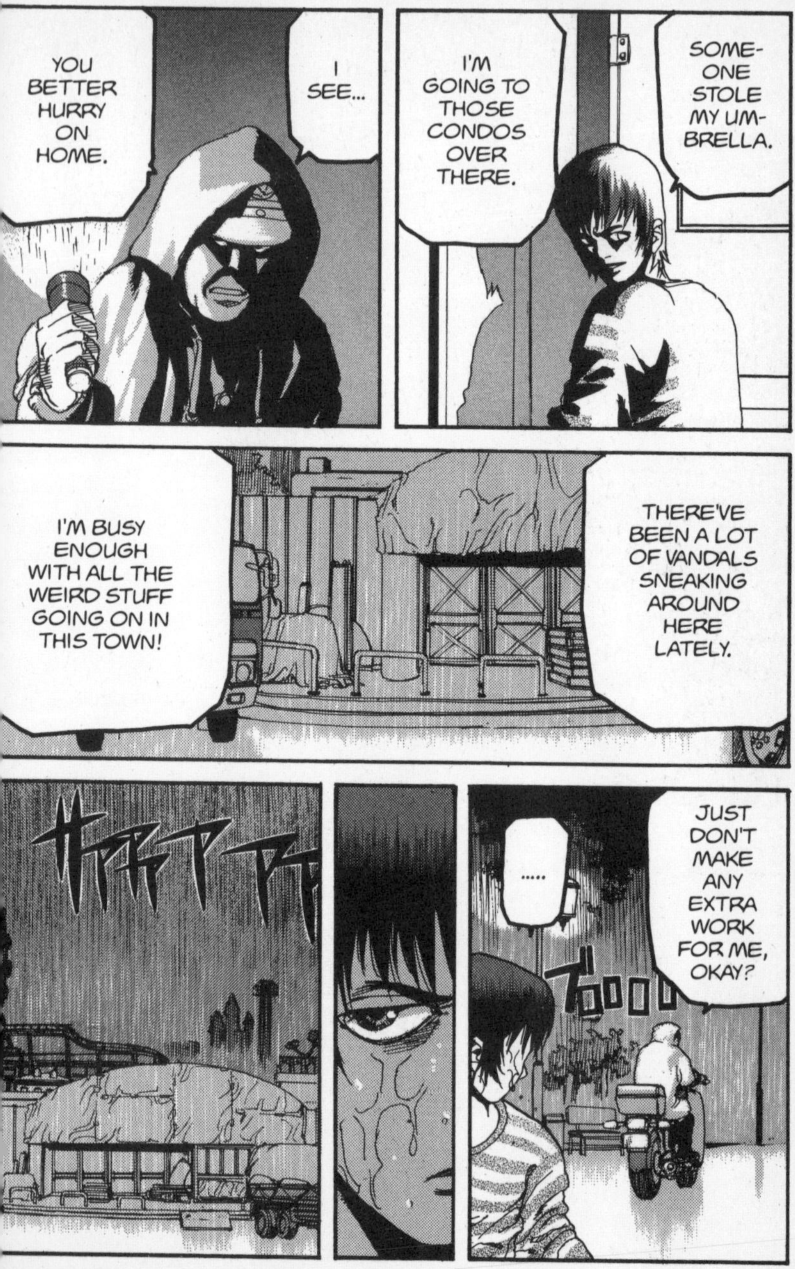
SOME-ONE STOLE MY UM-BRELLA.
I'M GOING TO THOSE CONDOS OVER THERE.
I SEE...
YOU BETTER HURRY ON HOME.
THERE'VE BEEN A LOT OF VANDALS SNEAKING AROUND HERE LATELY.
I'M BUSY ENOUGH WITH ALL THE WEIRD STUFF GOING ON IN THIS TOWN!
JUST DON'T MAKE ANY EXTRA WORK FOR ME, OKAY?
......

No. 10 THE ABUSEMENT PARK

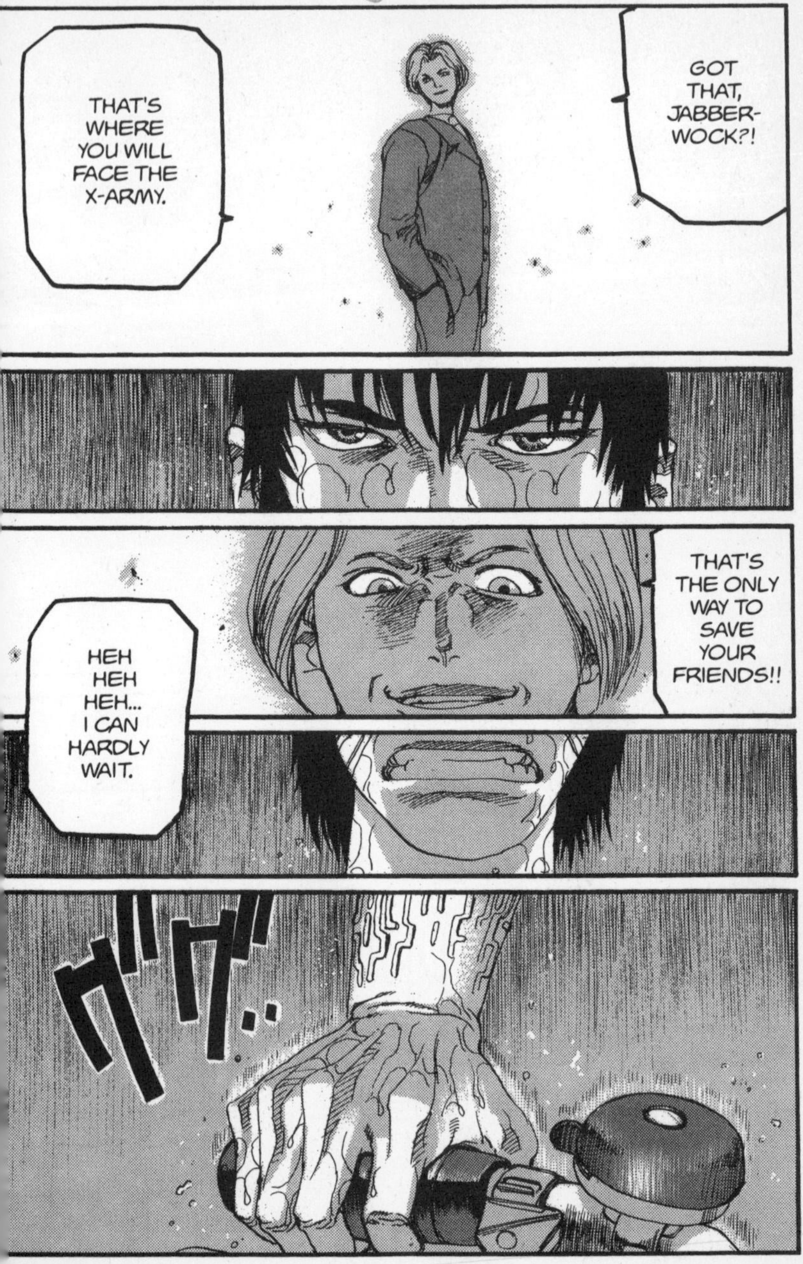
GOT THAT, JABBER-WOCK?!
THAT'S WHERE YOU WILL FACE THE X-ARMY.
THAT'S THE ONLY WAY TO SAVE YOUR FRIENDS!!
HEH HEH HEH... I CAN HARDLY WAIT.
グッ..

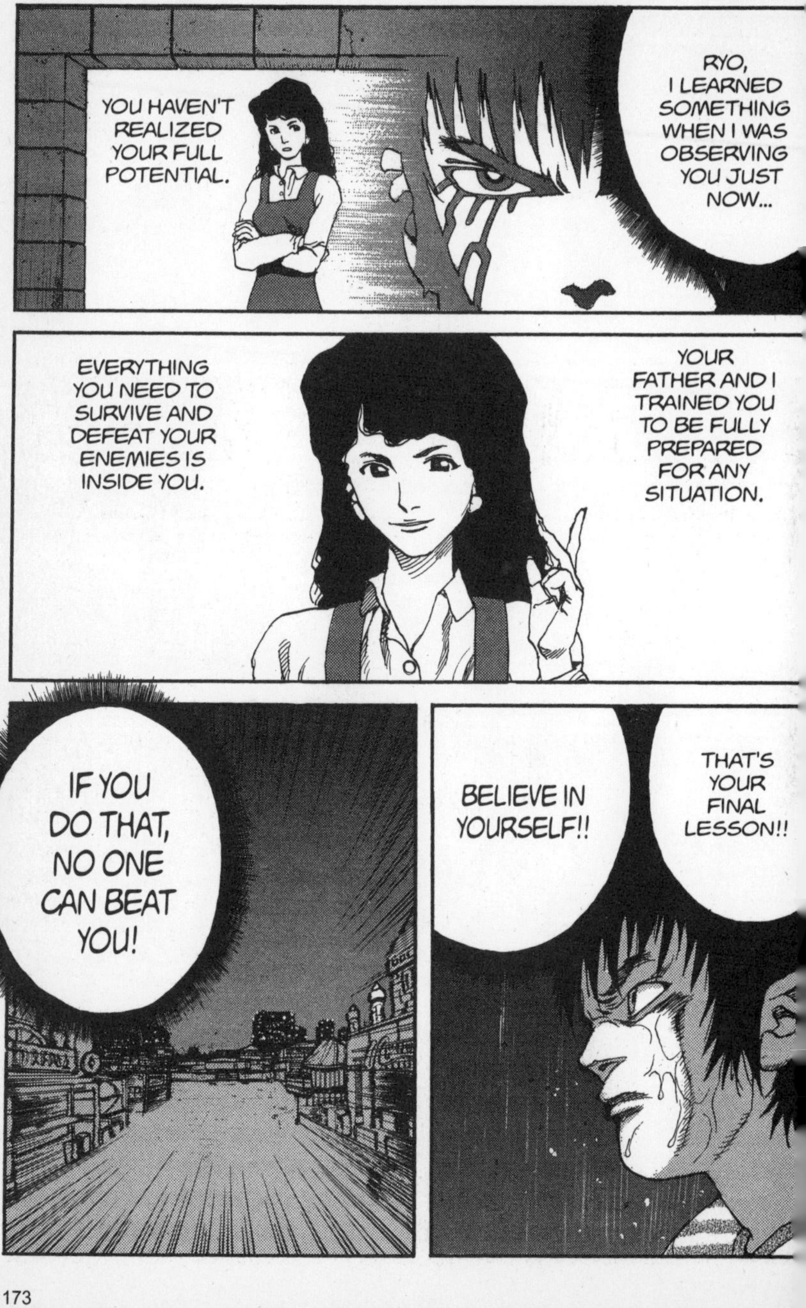
RYO, I LEARNED SOMETHING WHEN I WAS OBSERVING YOU JUST NOW...
YOU HAVEN'T REALIZED YOUR FULL POTENTIAL.
YOUR FATHER AND I TRAINED YOU TO BE FULLY PREPARED FOR ANY SITUATION.
EVERYTHING YOU NEED TO SURVIVE AND DEFEAT YOUR ENEMIES IS INSIDE YOU.
THAT'S YOUR FINAL LESSON!!
BELIEVE IN YOURSELF!!
IF YOU DO THAT, NO ONE CAN BEAT YOU!

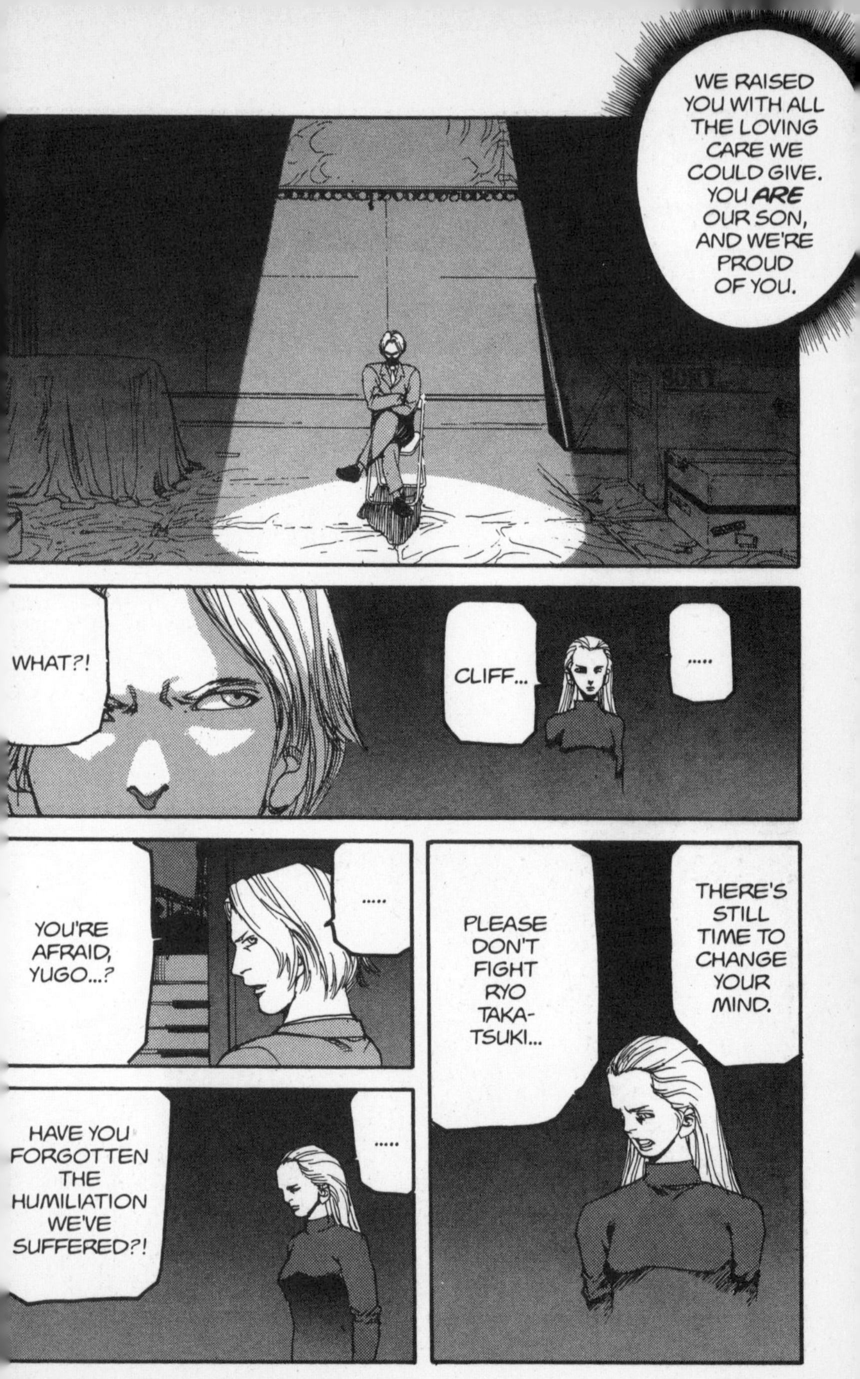
WE RAISED YOU WITH ALL THE LOVING CARE WE COULD GIVE. YOU ***ARE*** OUR SON, AND WE'RE PROUD OF YOU.
.....
CLIFF...
WHAT?!
THERE'S STILL TIME TO CHANGE YOUR MIND.
PLEASE DON'T FIGHT RYO TAKA-TSUKI...
.....
YOU'RE AFRAID, YUGO...?
.....
HAVE YOU FORGOTTEN THE HUMILIATION WE'VE SUFFERED?!

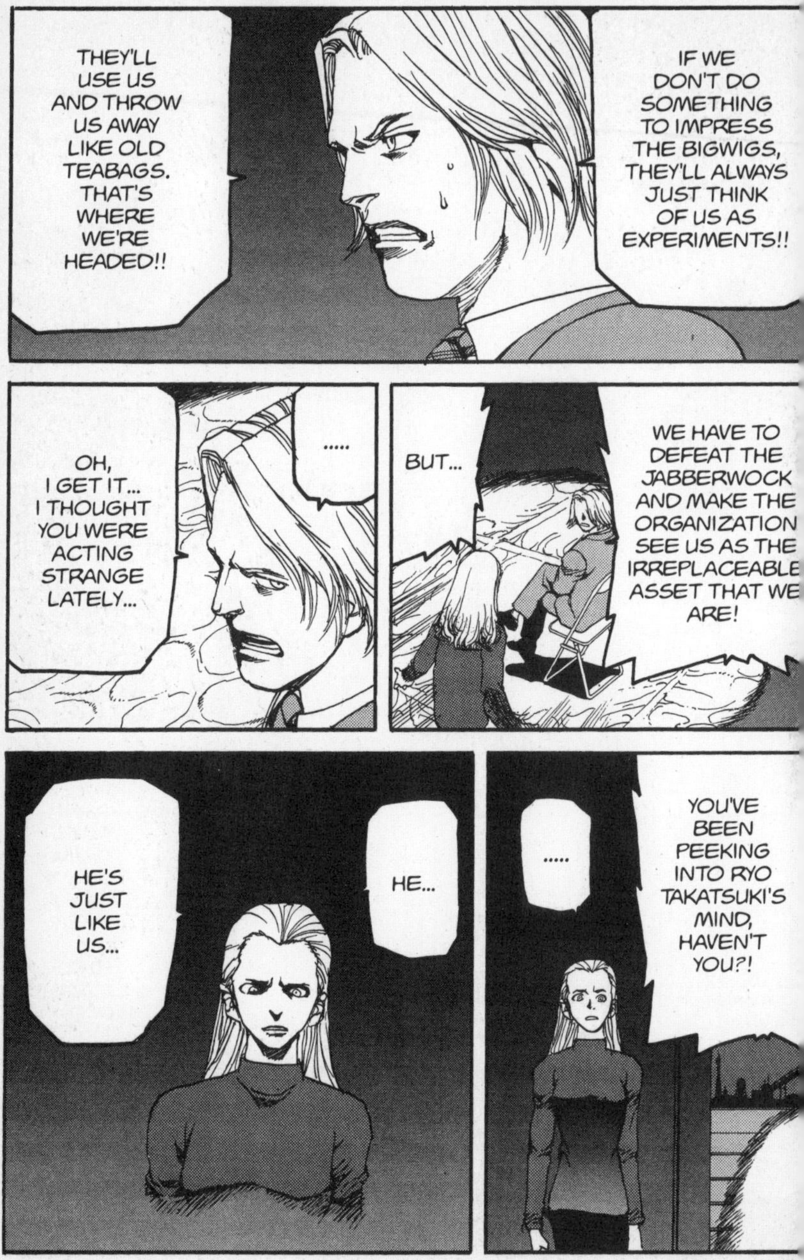
IF WE DON'T DO SOMETHING TO IMPRESS THE BIGWIGS, THEY'LL ALWAYS JUST THINK OF US AS EXPERIMENTS!!
THEY'LL USE US AND THROW US AWAY LIKE OLD TEABAGS. THAT'S WHERE WE'RE HEADED!!
WE HAVE TO DEFEAT THE JABBERWOCK AND MAKE THE ORGANIZATION SEE US AS THE IRREPLACEABLE ASSET THAT WE ARE!
BUT...
.....
OH, I GET IT... I THOUGHT YOU WERE ACTING STRANGE LATELY...
YOU'VE BEEN PEEKING INTO RYO TAKATSUKI'S MIND, HAVEN'T YOU?!
.....
HE...
HE'S JUST LIKE US...

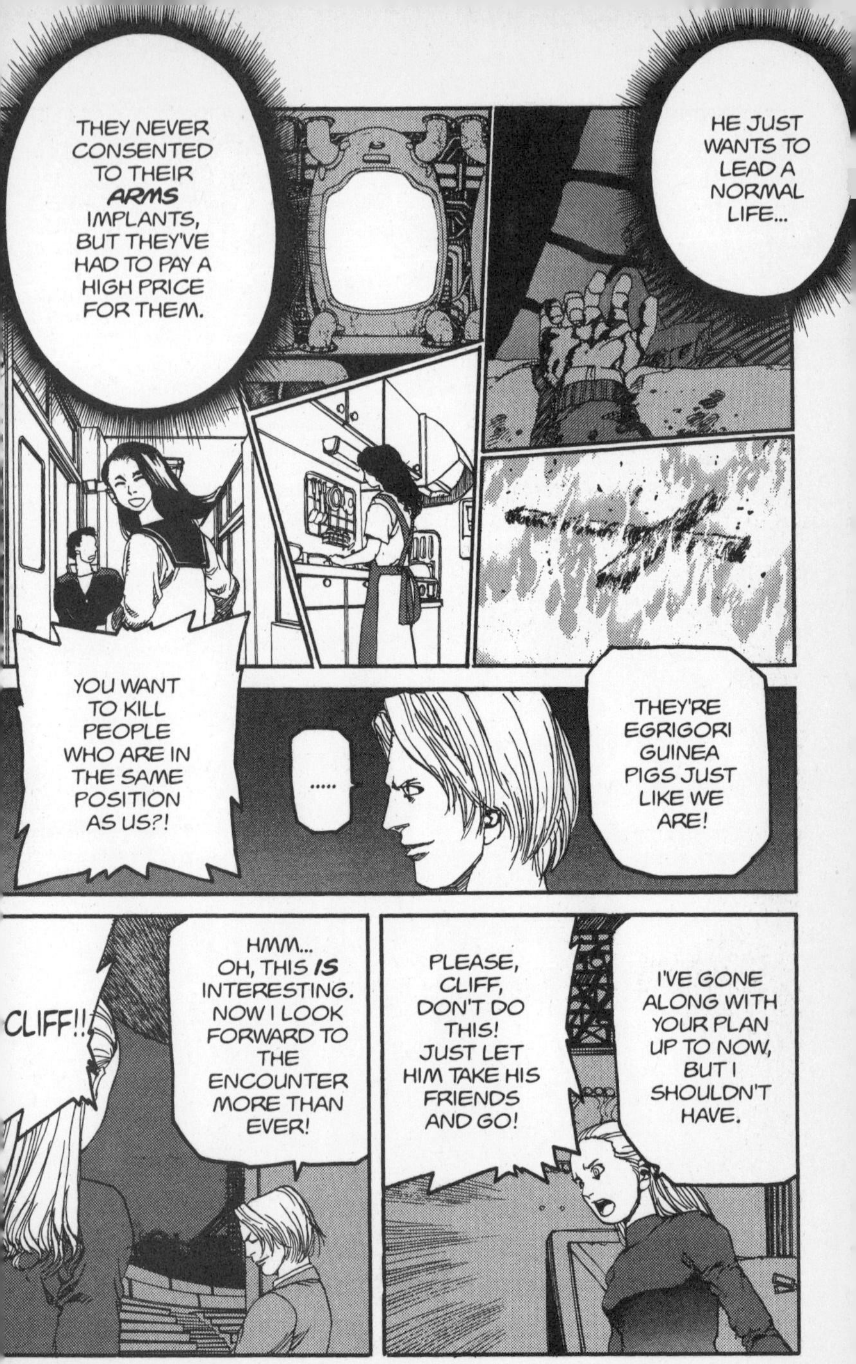
HE JUST WANTS TO LEAD A NORMAL LIFE...
THEY NEVER CONSENTED TO THEIR *ARMS* IMPLANTS, BUT THEY'VE HAD TO PAY A HIGH PRICE FOR THEM.
THEY'RE EGRIGORI GUINEA PIGS JUST LIKE WE ARE!
.....
YOU WANT TO KILL PEOPLE WHO ARE IN THE SAME POSITION AS US?!
I'VE GONE ALONG WITH YOUR PLAN UP TO NOW, BUT I SHOULDN'T HAVE.
PLEASE, CLIFF, DON'T DO THIS! JUST LET HIM TAKE HIS FRIENDS AND GO!
HMM... OH, THIS *IS* INTERESTING. NOW I LOOK FORWARD TO THE ENCOUNTER MORE THAN EVER!
CLIFF!!

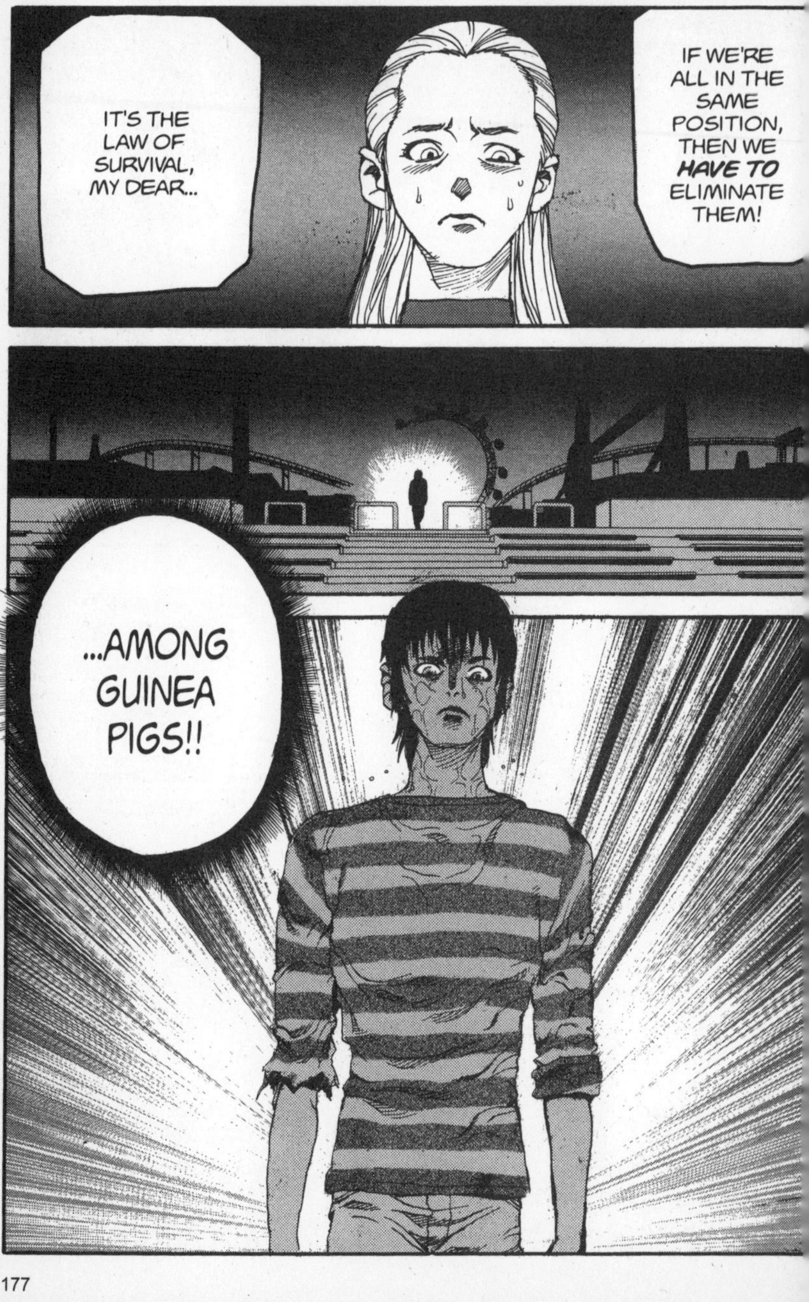
IF WE'RE ALL IN THE SAME POSITION, THEN WE **HAVE TO** ELIMINATE THEM!
IT'S THE LAW OF SURVIVAL, MY DEAR...
...AMONG GUINEA PIGS!!

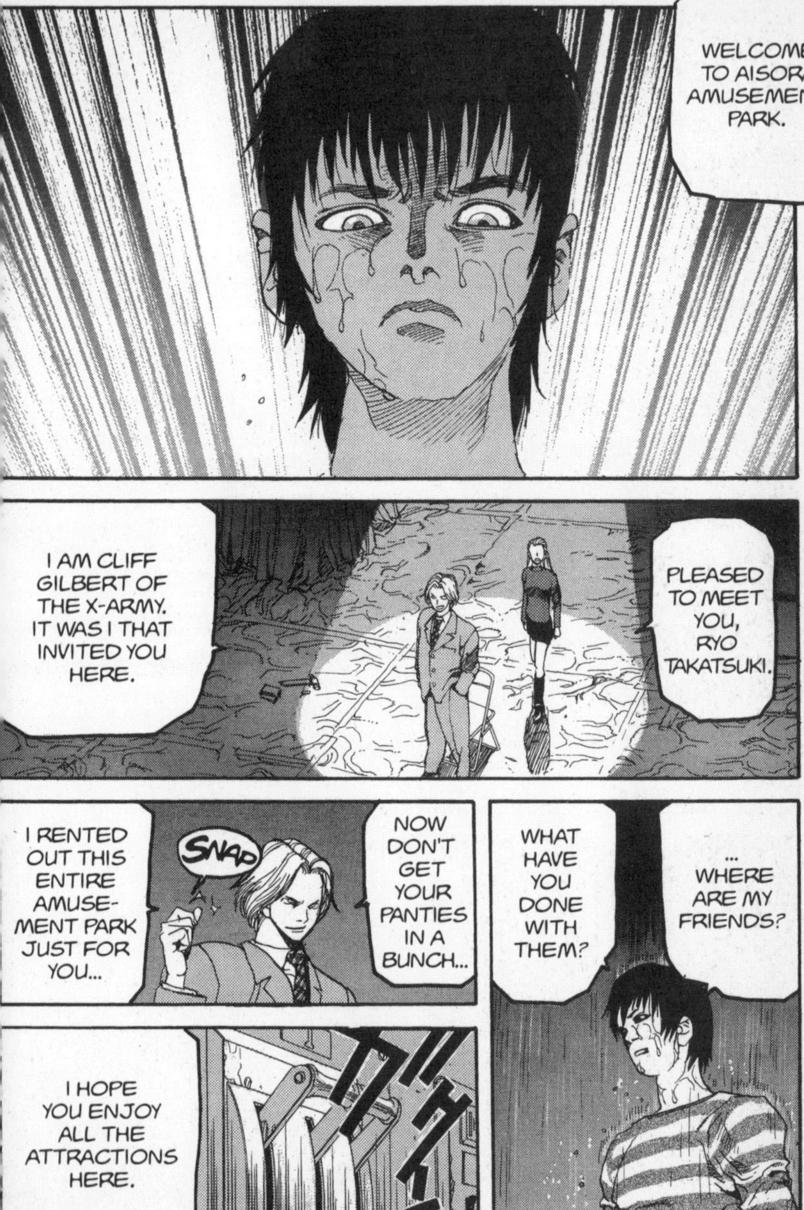
WELCOME TO AISORA AMUSEMENT PARK.
PLEASED TO MEET YOU, RYO TAKATSUKI.
I AM CLIFF GILBERT OF THE X-ARMY. IT WAS I THAT INVITED YOU HERE.
... WHERE ARE MY FRIENDS?
WHAT HAVE YOU DONE WITH THEM?
NOW DON'T GET YOUR PANTIES IN A BUNCH...
SNAP
I RENTED OUT THIS ENTIRE AMUSEMENT PARK JUST FOR YOU...
I HOPE YOU ENJOY ALL THE ATTRACTIONS HERE.

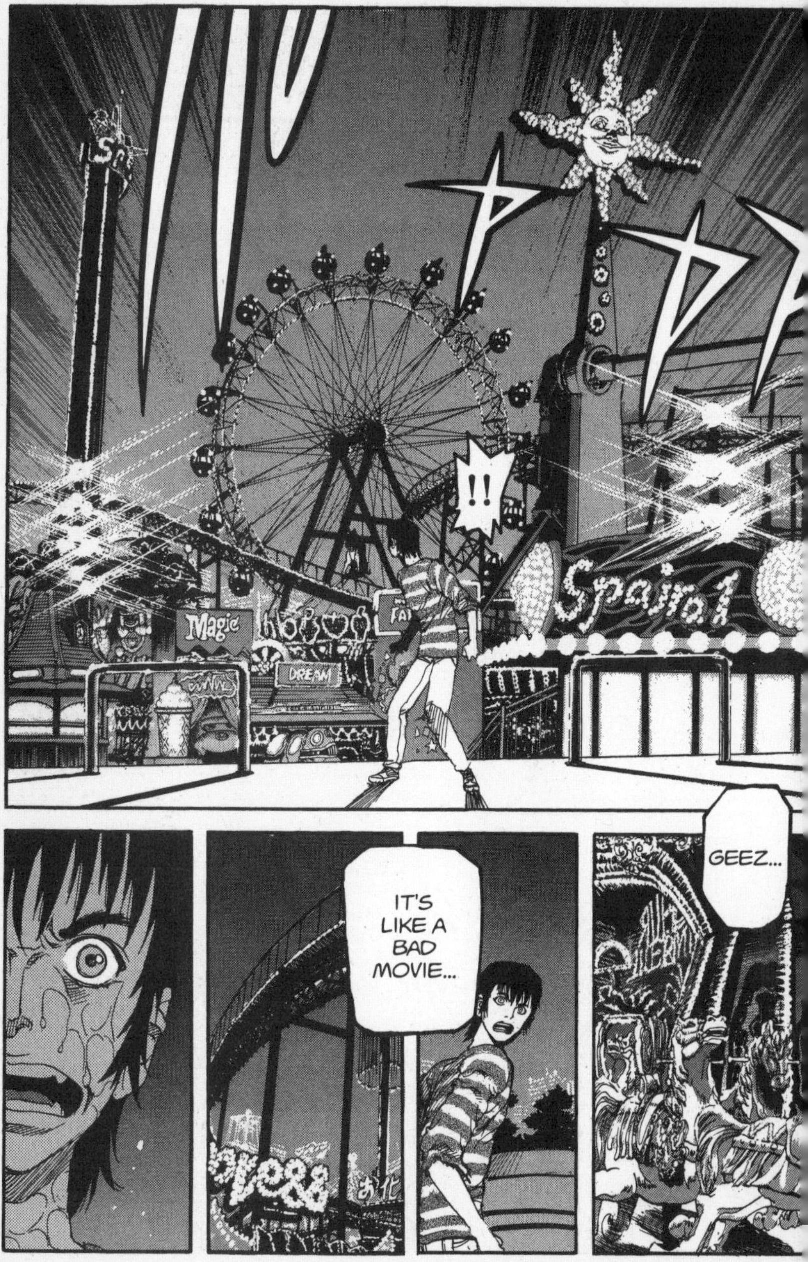
!!
Magic
DREAM
GEEZ...
IT'S LIKE A BAD MOVIE...

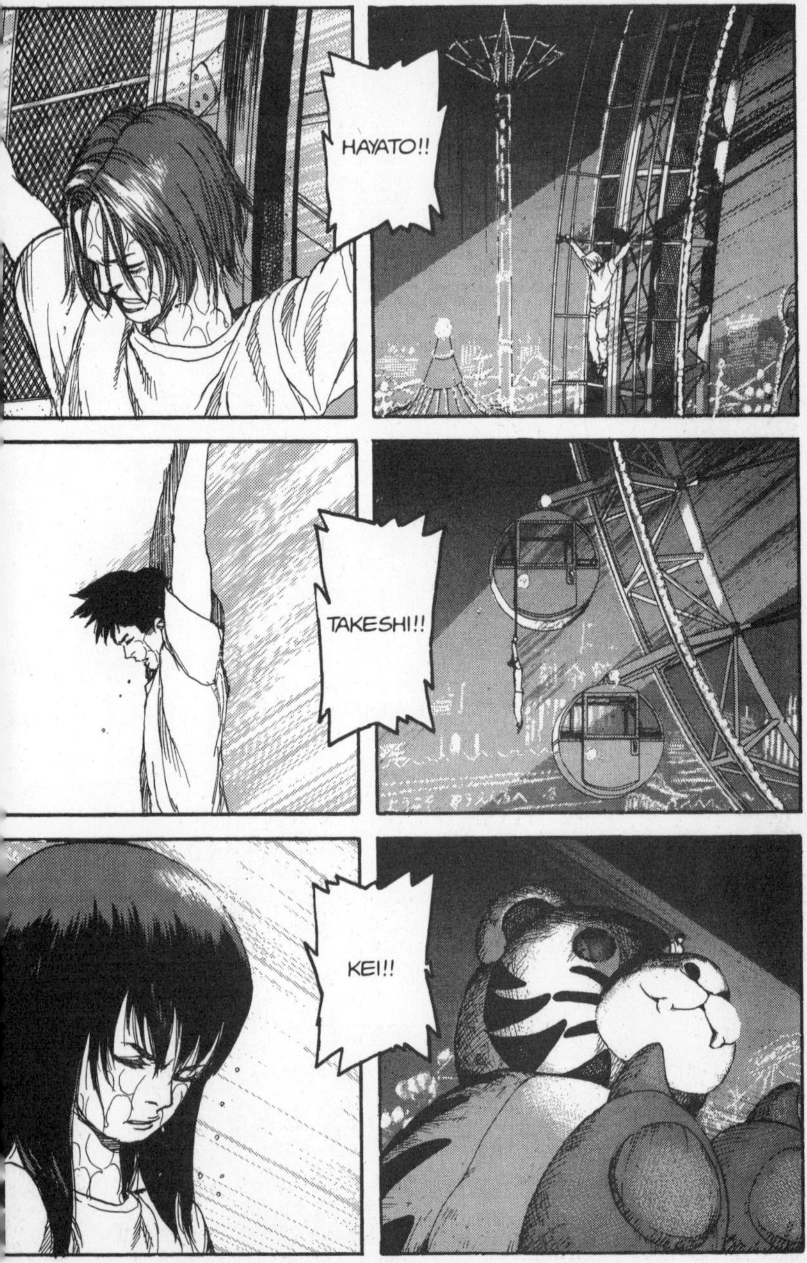
HAYATO!!
TAKESHI!!
KEI!!

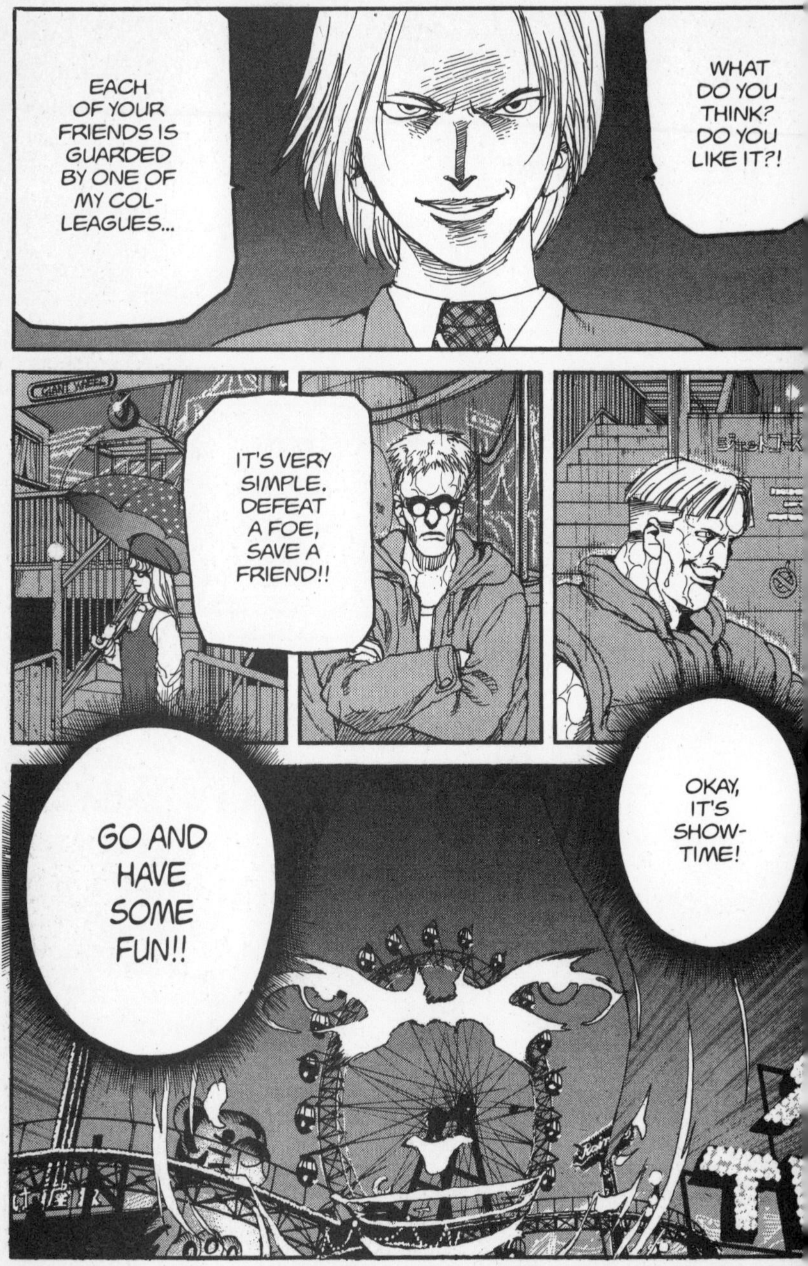
WHAT DO YOU THINK? DO YOU LIKE IT?!
EACH OF YOUR FRIENDS IS GUARDED BY ONE OF MY COL-LEAGUES...
IT'S VERY SIMPLE. DEFEAT A FOE, SAVE A FRIEND!!
GIANT WHEEL
OKAY, IT'S SHOW-TIME!
GO AND HAVE SOME FUN!!

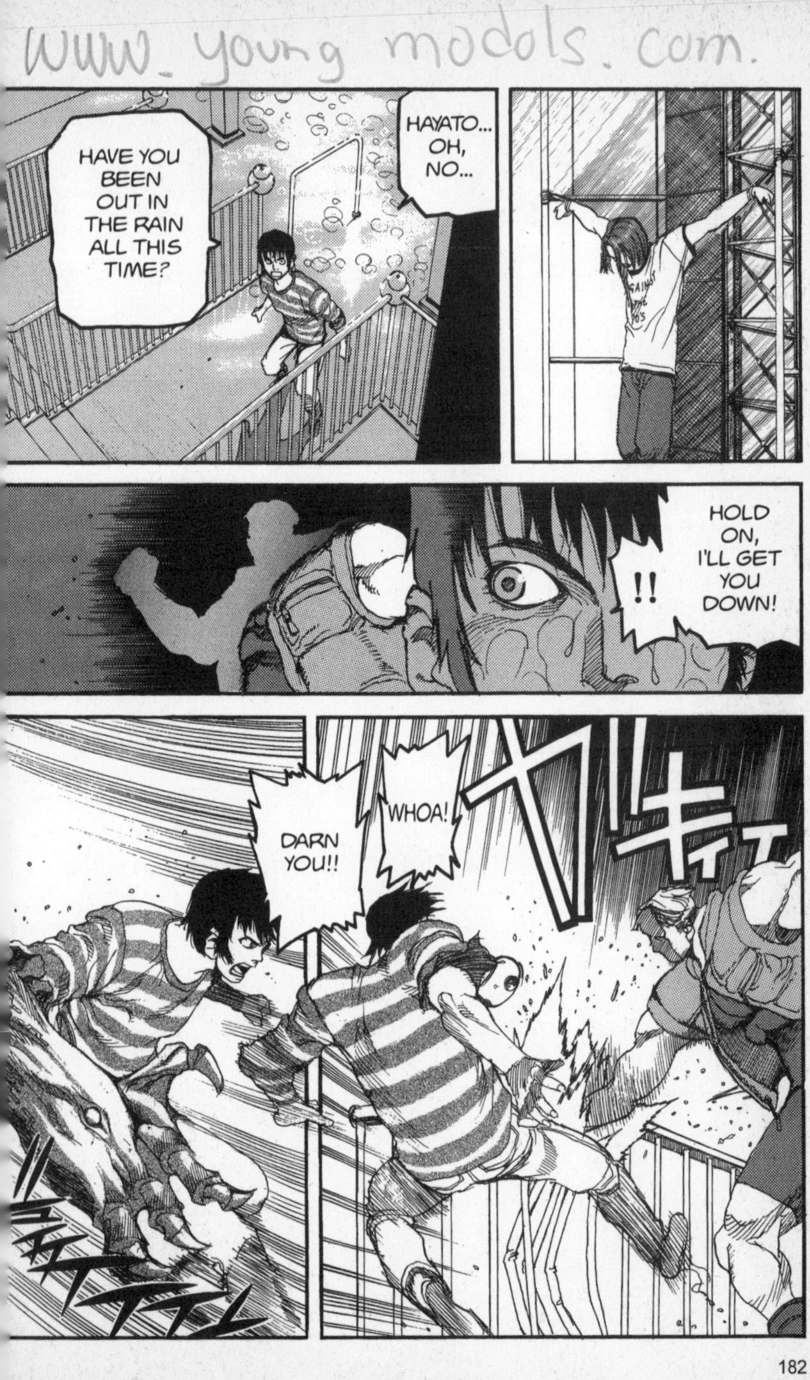
HAYATO... OH, NO...
HAVE YOU BEEN OUT IN THE RAIN ALL THIS TIME?
HOLD ON, I'LL GET YOU DOWN!
!!
WHOA!
DARN YOU!!

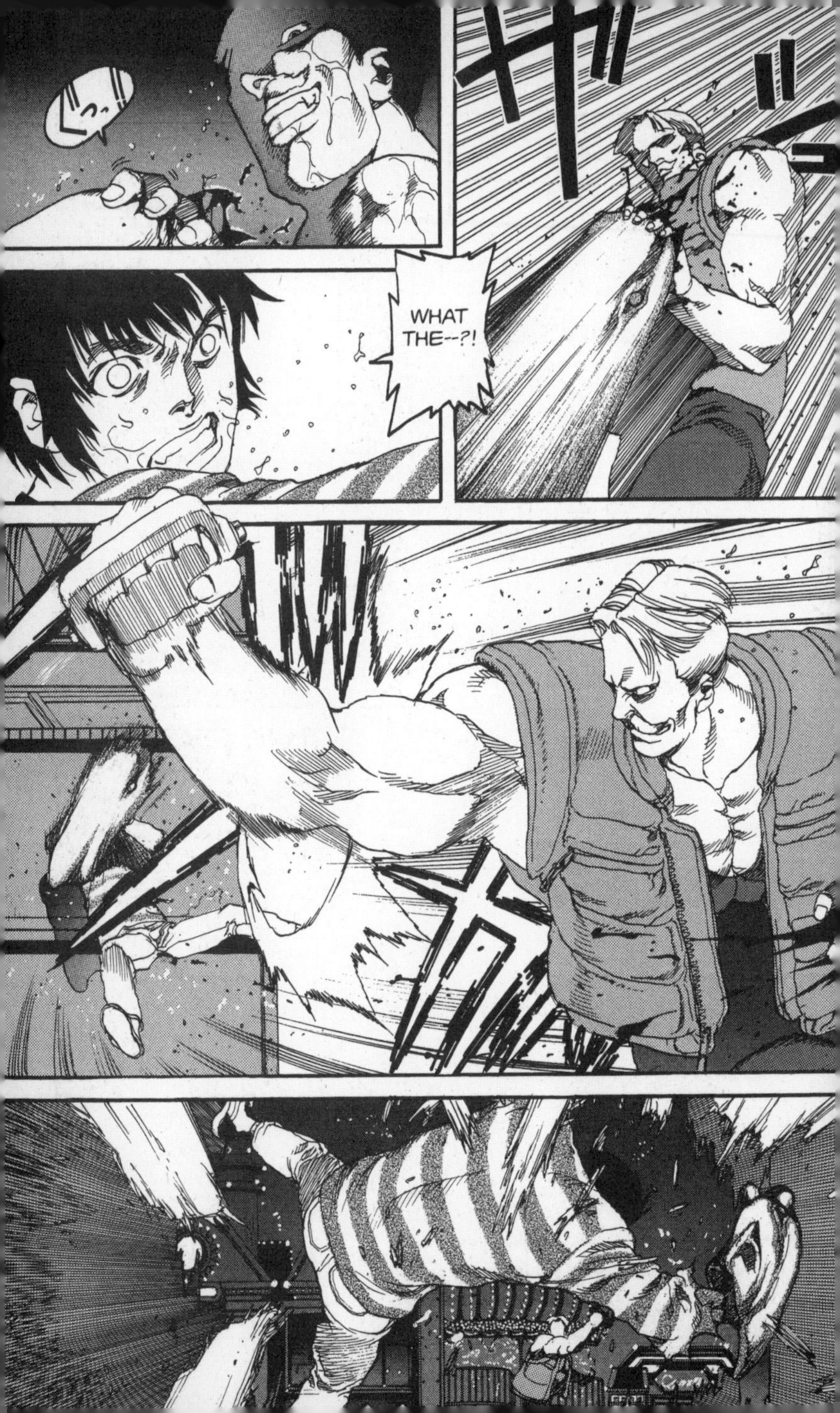
WHAT THE--?!

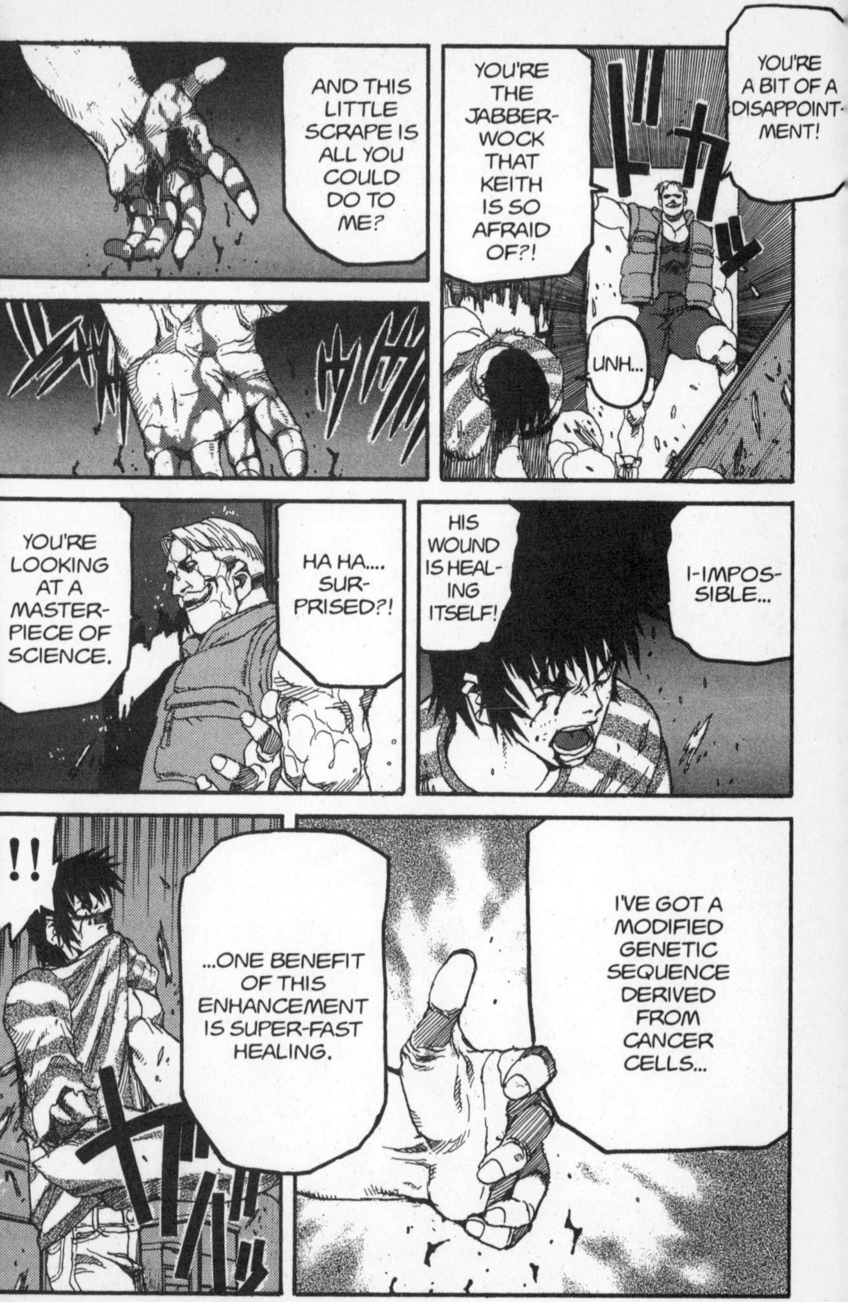
YOU'RE A BIT OF A DISAPPOINT-MENT!
YOU'RE THE JABBER-WOCK THAT KEITH IS SO AFRAID OF?!
UNH...
AND THIS LITTLE SCRAPE IS ALL YOU COULD DO TO ME?
I-IMPOS-SIBLE...
HIS WOUND IS HEAL-ING ITSELF!
HA HA.... SUR-PRISED?!
YOU'RE LOOKING AT A MASTER-PIECE OF SCIENCE.
I'VE GOT A MODIFIED GENETIC SEQUENCE DERIVED FROM CANCER CELLS...
...ONE BENEFIT OF THIS ENHANCEMENT IS SUPER-FAST HEALING.
!!

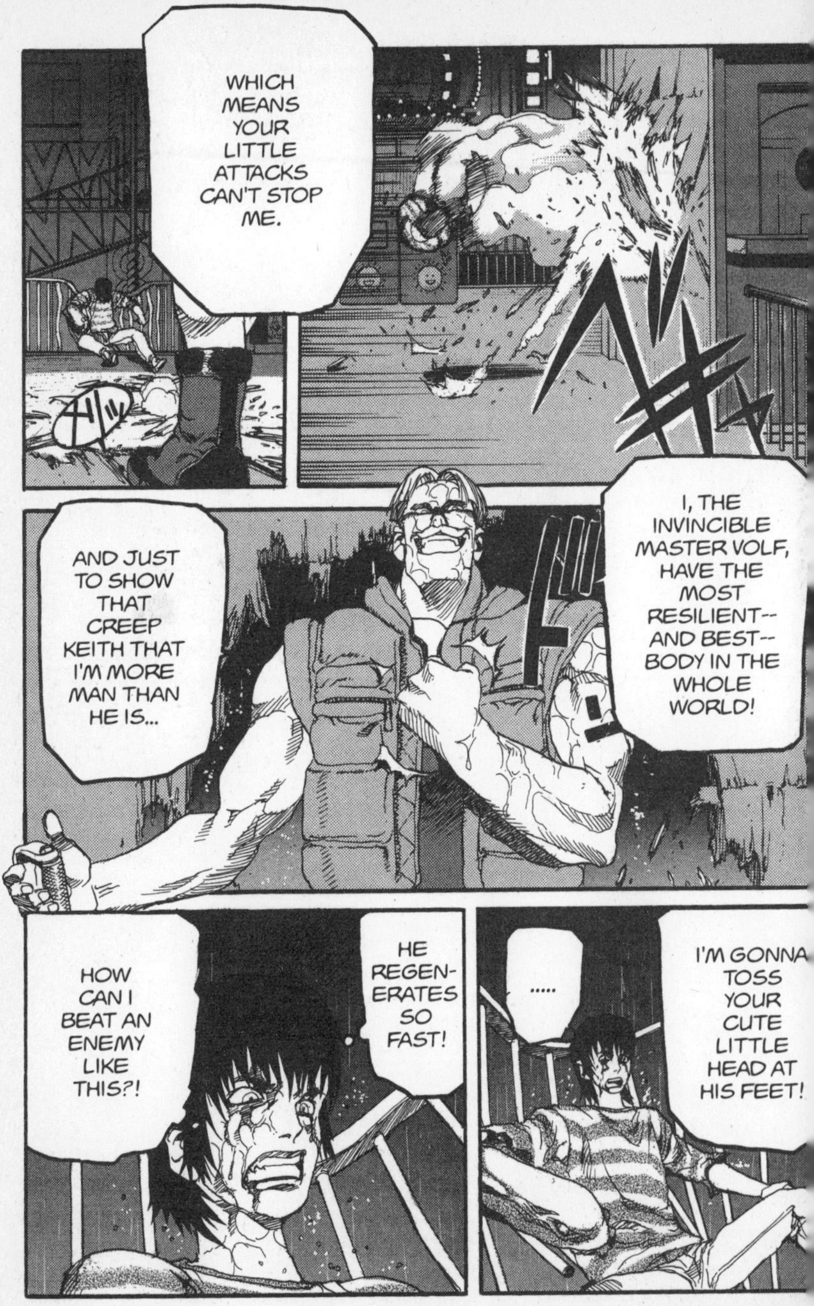
WHICH MEANS YOUR LITTLE ATTACKS CAN'T STOP ME.
I, THE INVINCIBLE MASTER VOLF, HAVE THE MOST RESILIENT--AND BEST--BODY IN THE WHOLE WORLD!
AND JUST TO SHOW THAT CREEP KEITH THAT I'M MORE MAN THAN HE IS...
I'M GONNA TOSS YOUR CUTE LITTLE HEAD AT HIS FEET!
.....
HE REGENERATES SO FAST!
HOW CAN I BEAT AN ENEMY LIKE THIS?!

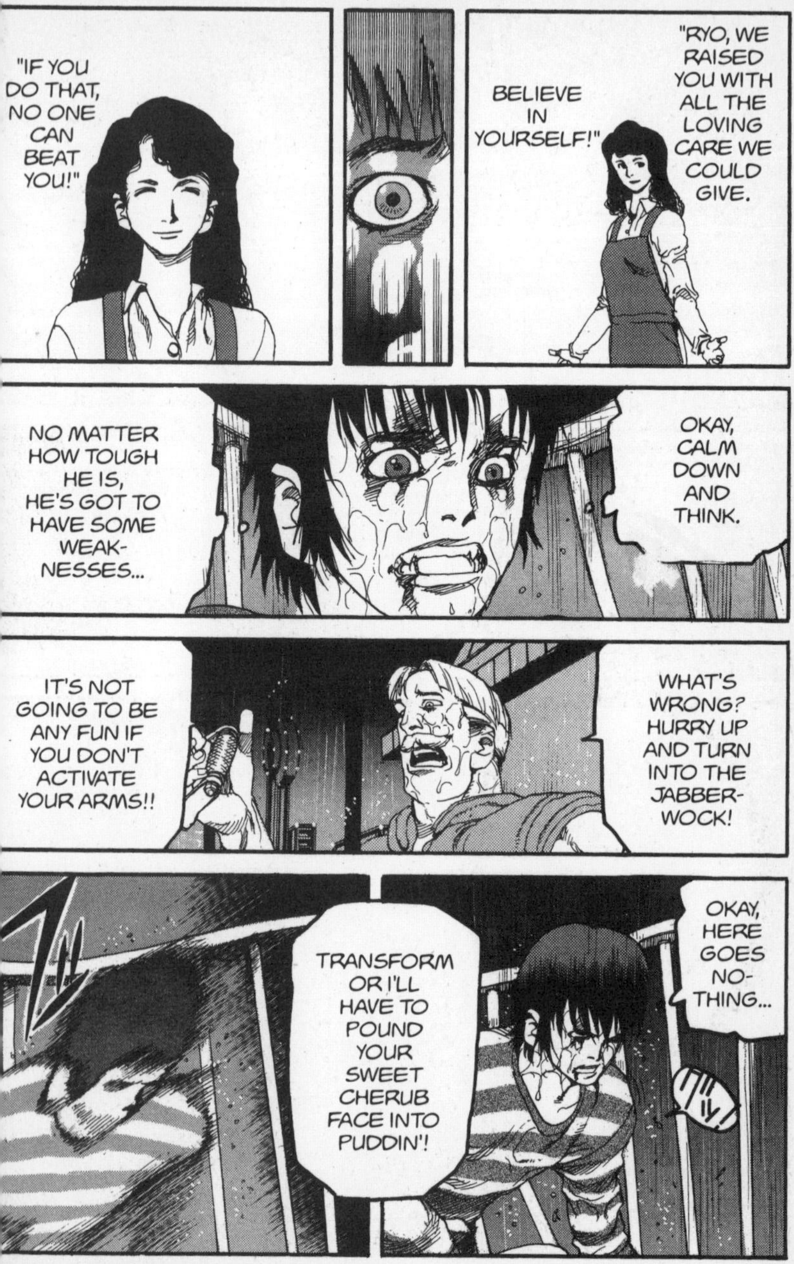
"RYO, WE RAISED YOU WITH ALL THE LOVING CARE WE COULD GIVE.
BELIEVE IN YOURSELF!"
"IF YOU DO THAT, NO ONE CAN BEAT YOU!"
OKAY, CALM DOWN AND THINK.
NO MATTER HOW TOUGH HE IS, HE'S GOT TO HAVE SOME WEAK-NESSES...
WHAT'S WRONG? HURRY UP AND TURN INTO THE JABBER-WOCK!
IT'S NOT GOING TO BE ANY FUN IF YOU DON'T ACTIVATE YOUR ARMS!!
OKAY, HERE GOES NO-THING...
TRANSFORM OR I'LL HAVE TO POUND YOUR SWEET CHERUB FACE INTO PUDDIN'!

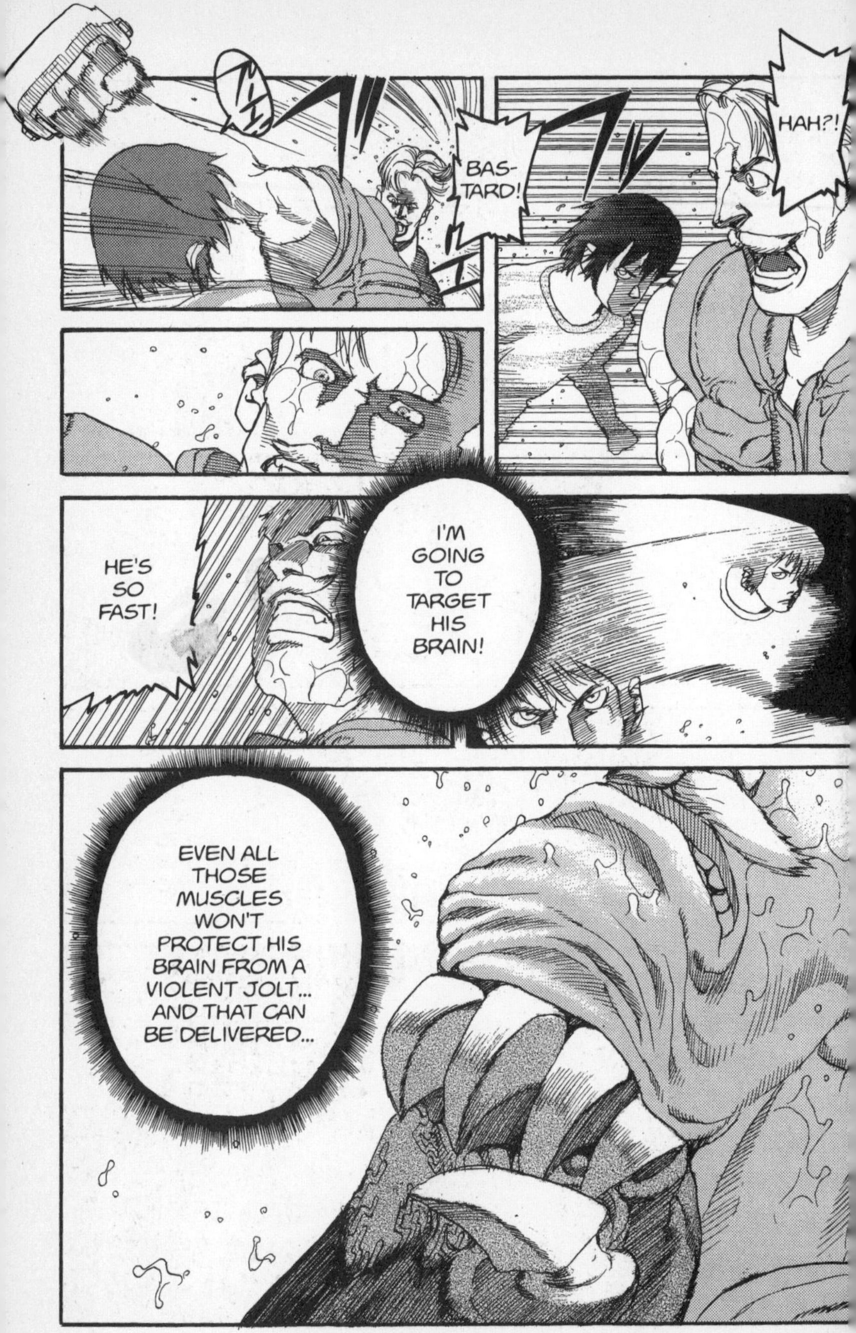
HAH?!
BAS-TARD!
I'M GOING TO TARGET HIS BRAIN!
HE'S SO FAST!
EVEN ALL THOSE MUSCLES WON'T PROTECT HIS BRAIN FROM A VIOLENT JOLT... AND THAT CAN BE DELIVERED...

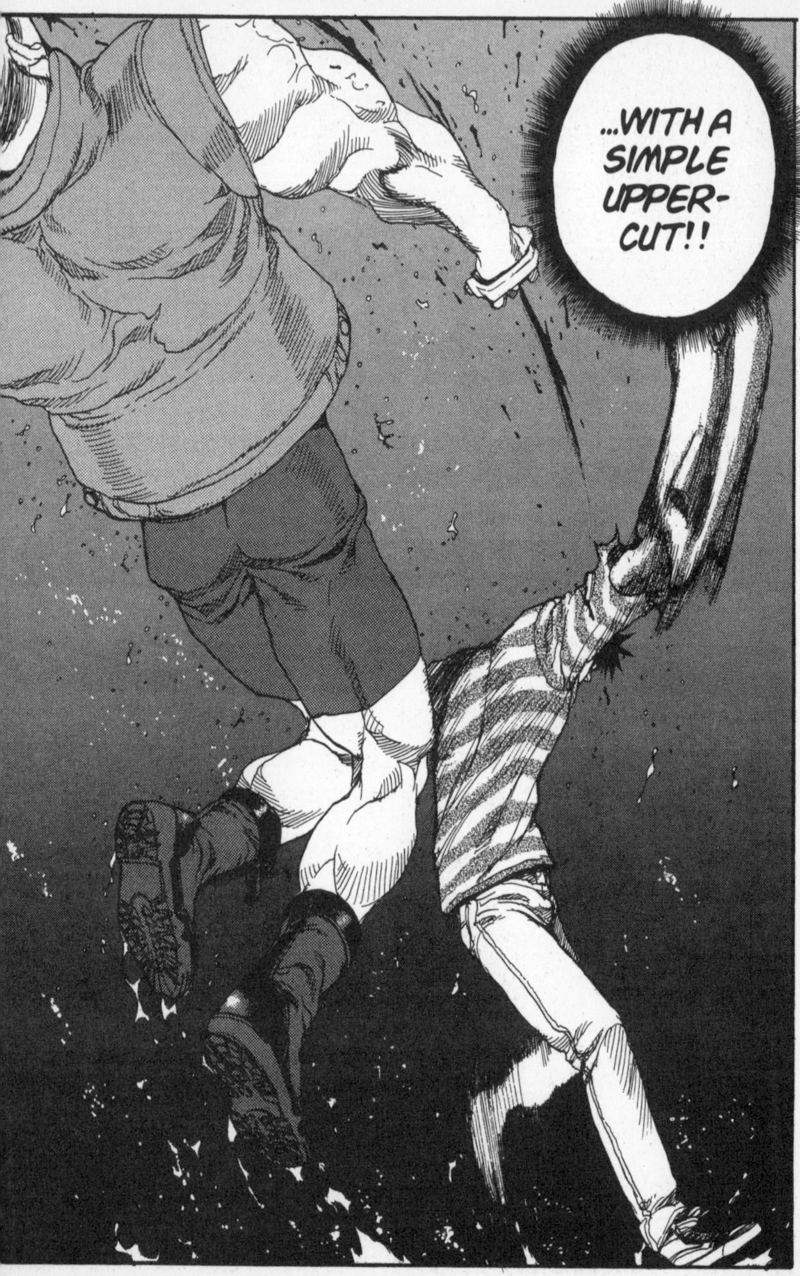
...WITH A SIMPLE UPPER-CUT!!

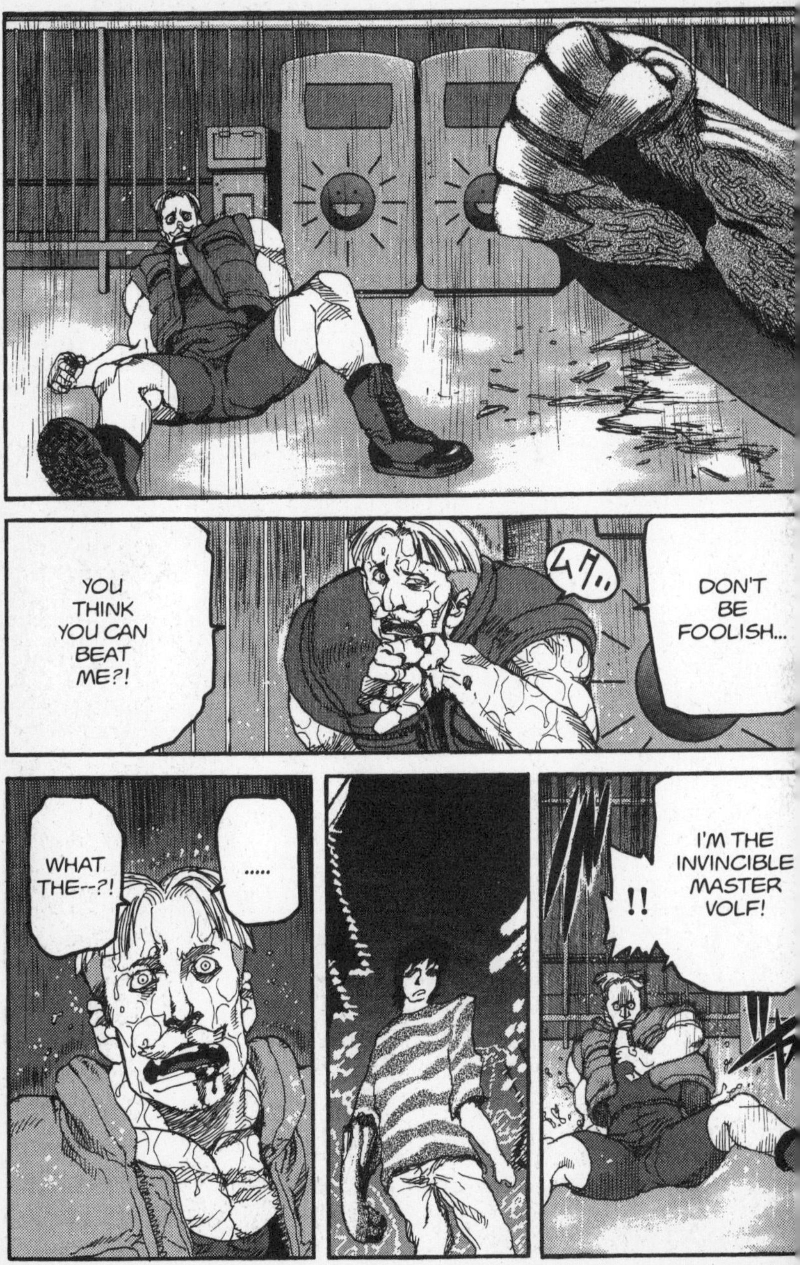
DON'T BE FOOLISH...
YOU THINK YOU CAN BEAT ME?!
I'M THE INVINCIBLE MASTER VOLF!
!!
.....
WHAT THE--?!

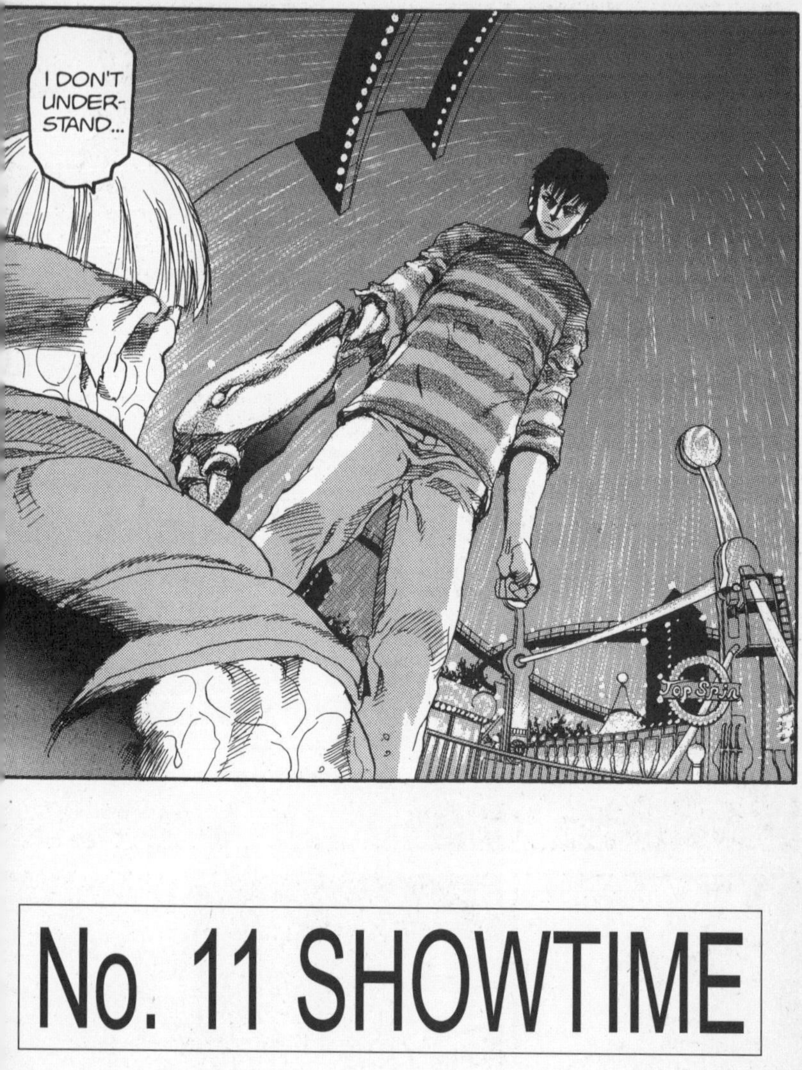
I DON'T UNDER-STAND...
Top Spin

No. 11 SHOWTIME

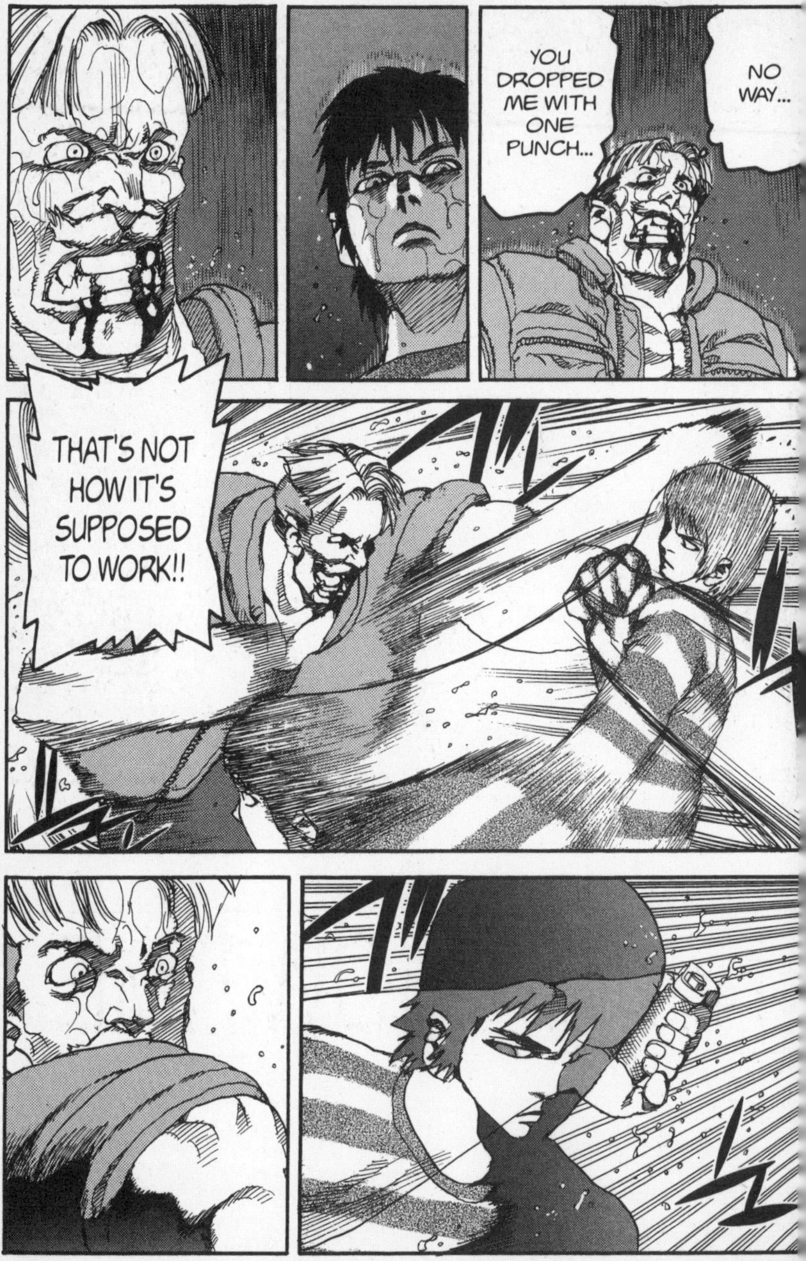
NO WAY...
YOU DROPPED ME WITH ONE PUNCH...
THAT'S NOT HOW IT'S SUPPOSED TO WORK!!

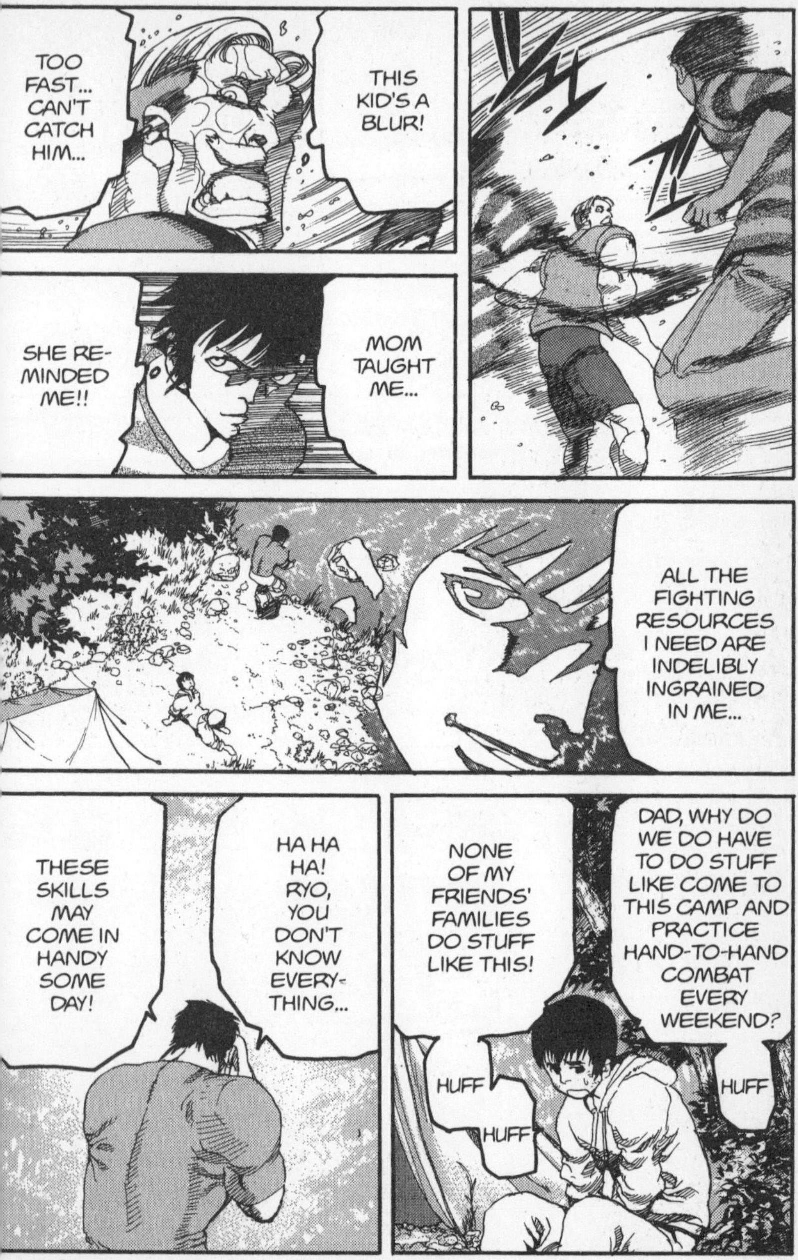
THIS KID'S A BLUR!
TOO FAST... CAN'T CATCH HIM...
MOM TAUGHT ME...
SHE RE-MINDED ME!!
ALL THE FIGHTING RESOURCES I NEED ARE INDELIBLY INGRAINED IN ME...
DAD, WHY DO WE DO HAVE TO DO STUFF LIKE COME TO THIS CAMP AND PRACTICE HAND-TO-HAND COMBAT EVERY WEEKEND?
NONE OF MY FRIENDS' FAMILIES DO STUFF LIKE THIS!
HUFF
HUFF
HUFF
HA HA HA! RYO, YOU DON'T KNOW EVERY-THING...
THESE SKILLS MAY COME IN HANDY SOME DAY!

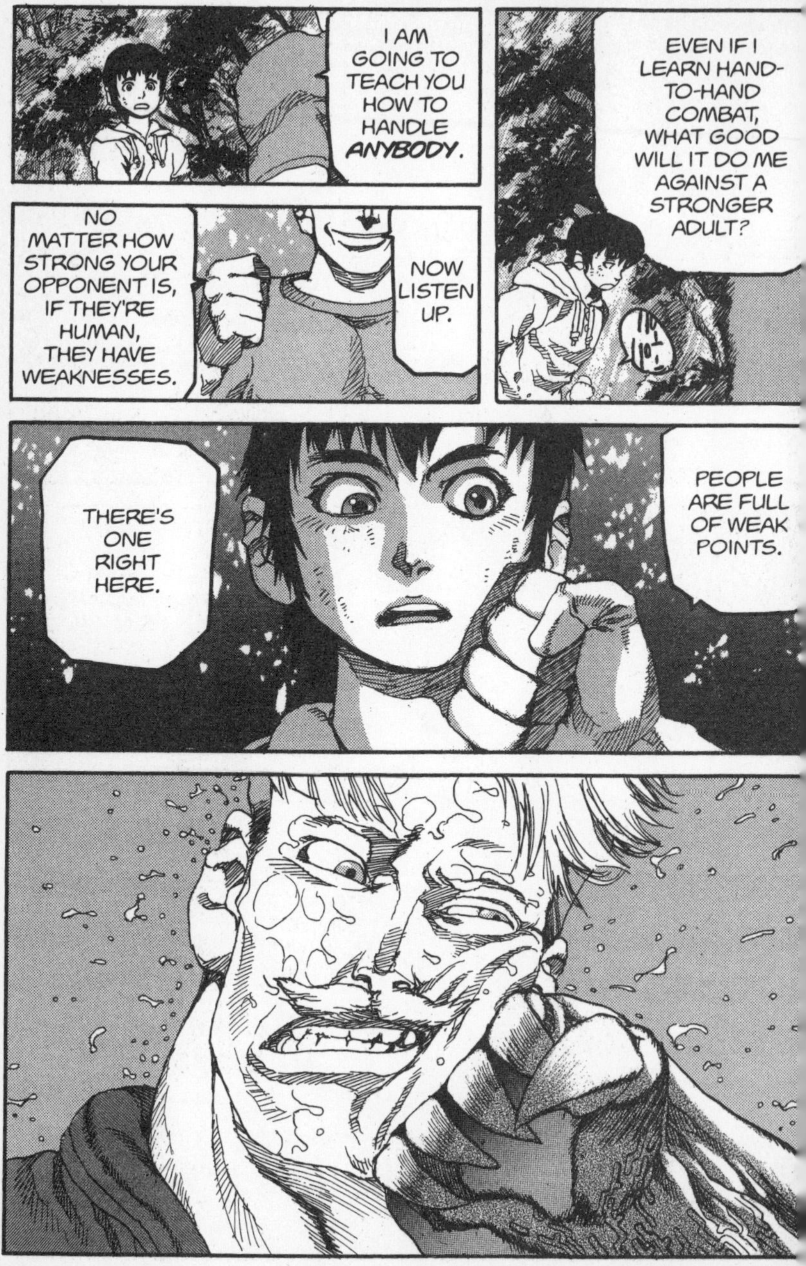
EVEN IF I LEARN HAND-TO-HAND COMBAT, WHAT GOOD WILL IT DO ME AGAINST A STRONGER ADULT?
I AM GOING TO TEACH YOU HOW TO HANDLE ANYBODY.
NOW LISTEN UP.
NO MATTER HOW STRONG YOUR OPPONENT IS, IF THEY'RE HUMAN, THEY HAVE WEAKNESSES.
PEOPLE ARE FULL OF WEAK POINTS.
THERE'S ONE RIGHT HERE.

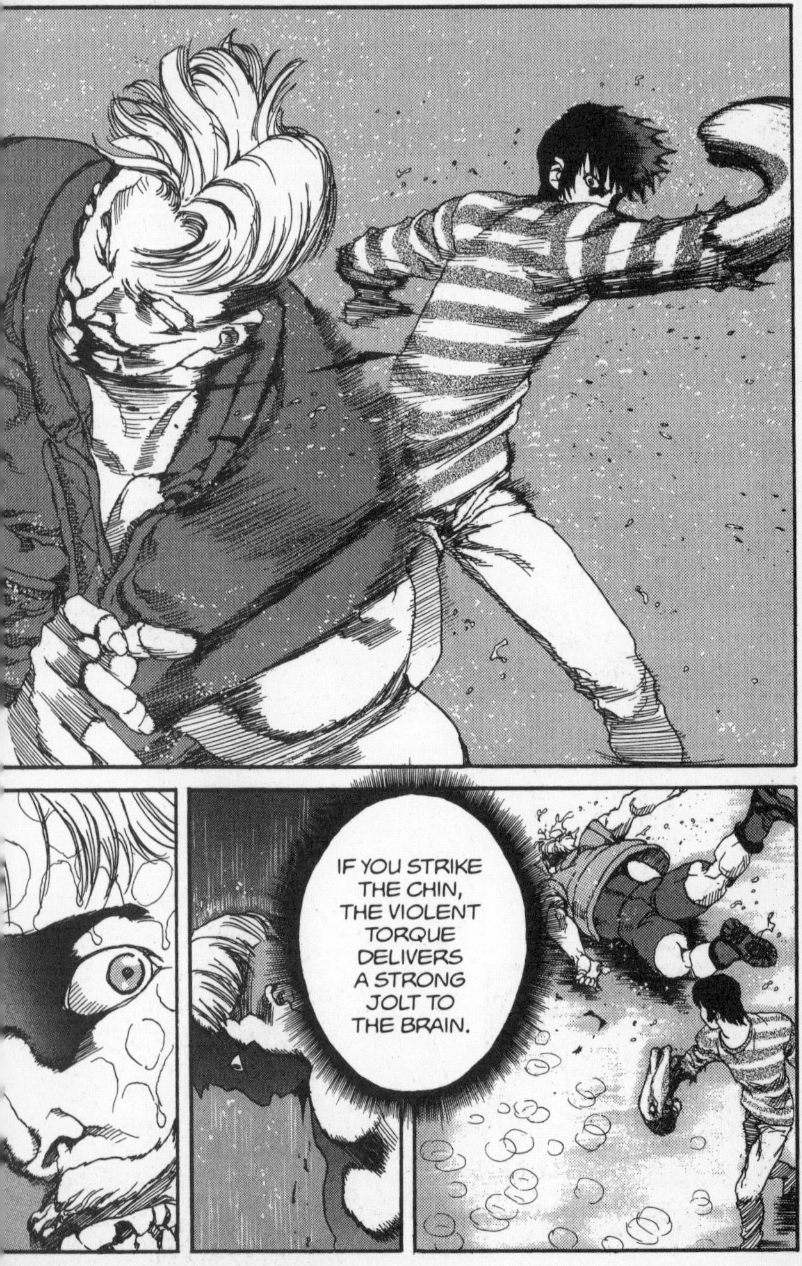
IF YOU STRIKE THE CHIN, THE VIOLENT TORQUE DELIVERS A STRONG JOLT TO THE BRAIN.

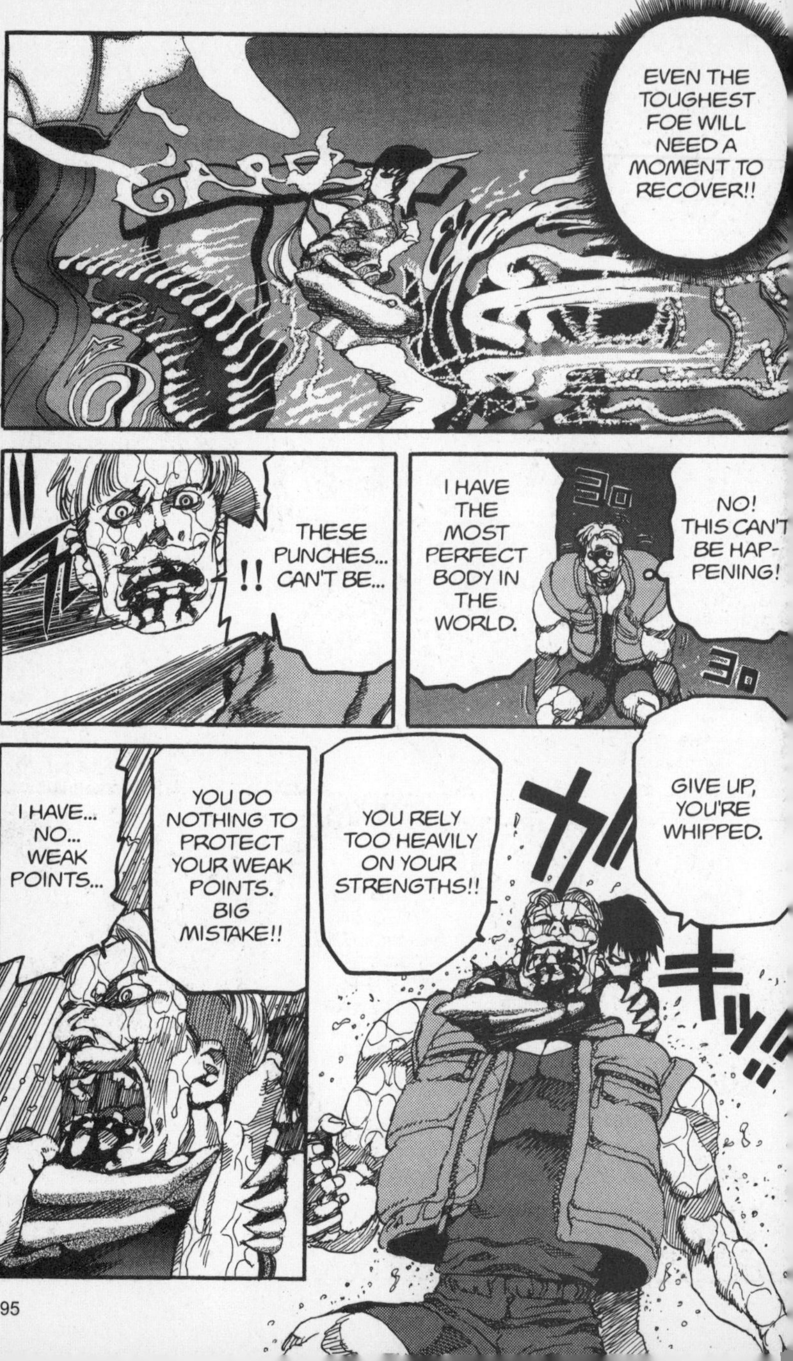
EVEN THE TOUGHEST FOE WILL NEED A MOMENT TO RECOVER!!
NO! THIS CAN'T BE HAP-PENING!
I HAVE THE MOST PERFECT BODY IN THE WORLD.
THESE PUNCHES... CAN'T BE...
!!
GIVE UP, YOU'RE WHIPPED.
YOU RELY TOO HEAVILY ON YOUR STRENGTHS!!
YOU DO NOTHING TO PROTECT YOUR WEAK POINTS. BIG MISTAKE!!
I HAVE... NO... WEAK POINTS...

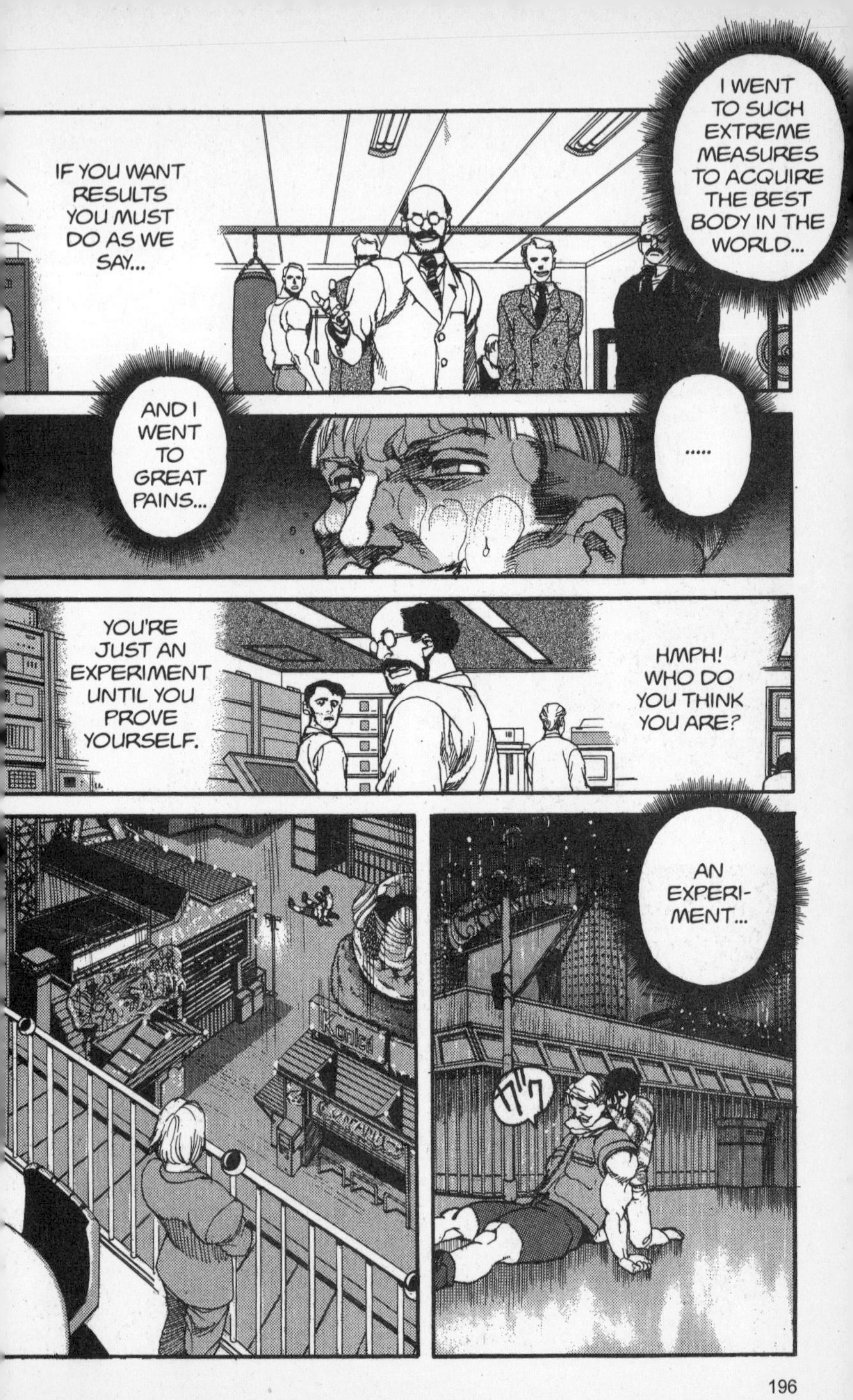
I WENT TO SUCH EXTREME MEASURES TO ACQUIRE THE BEST BODY IN THE WORLD...
IF YOU WANT RESULTS YOU MUST DO AS WE SAY...
.....
AND I WENT TO GREAT PAINS...
HMPH! WHO DO YOU THINK YOU ARE?
YOU'RE JUST AN EXPERIMENT UNTIL YOU PROVE YOURSELF.
AN EXPERI-MENT...
ガク

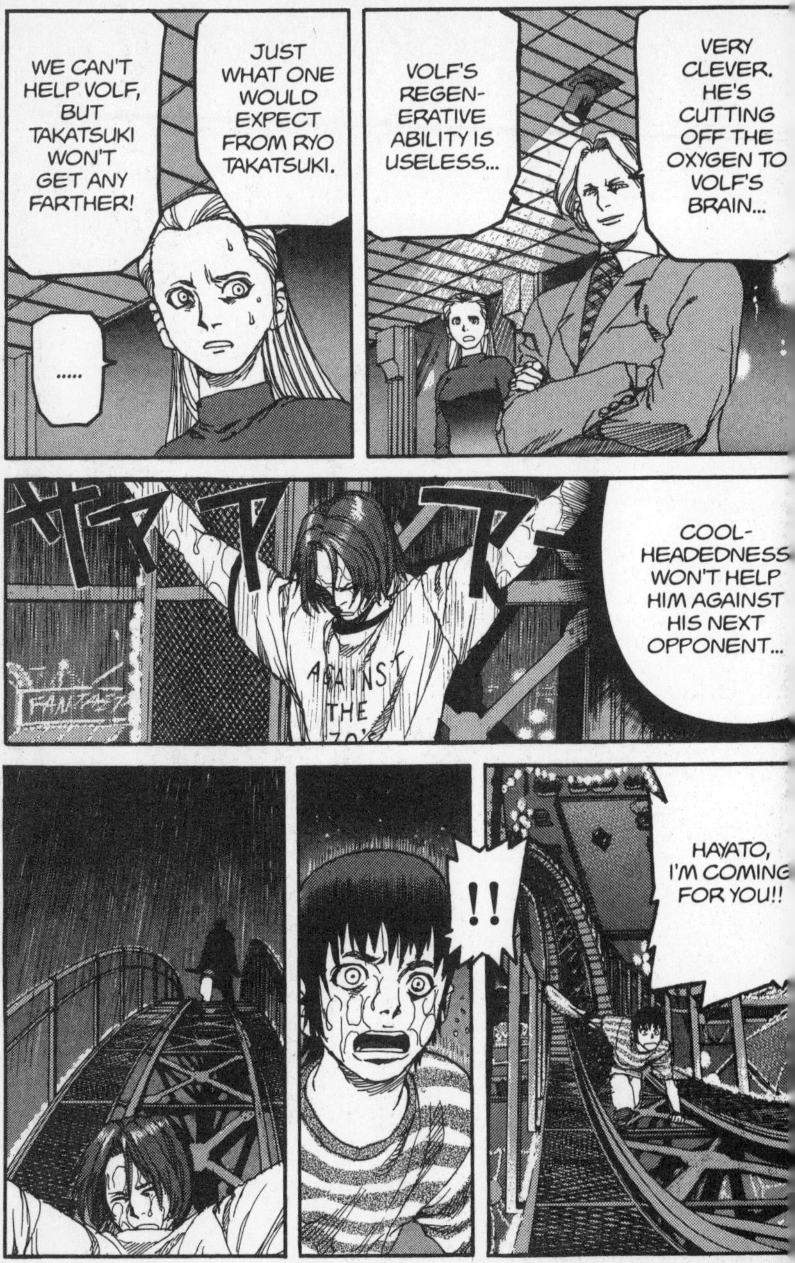
VERY CLEVER. HE'S CUTTING OFF THE OXYGEN TO VOLF'S BRAIN...
VOLF'S REGEN-ERATIVE ABILITY IS USELESS...
JUST WHAT ONE WOULD EXPECT FROM RYO TAKATSUKI.
WE CAN'T HELP VOLF, BUT TAKATSUKI WON'T GET ANY FARTHER!
......
COOL-HEADEDNESS WON'T HELP HIM AGAINST HIS NEXT OPPONENT...
AGAINST THE
HAYATO, I'M COMING FOR YOU!!
!!

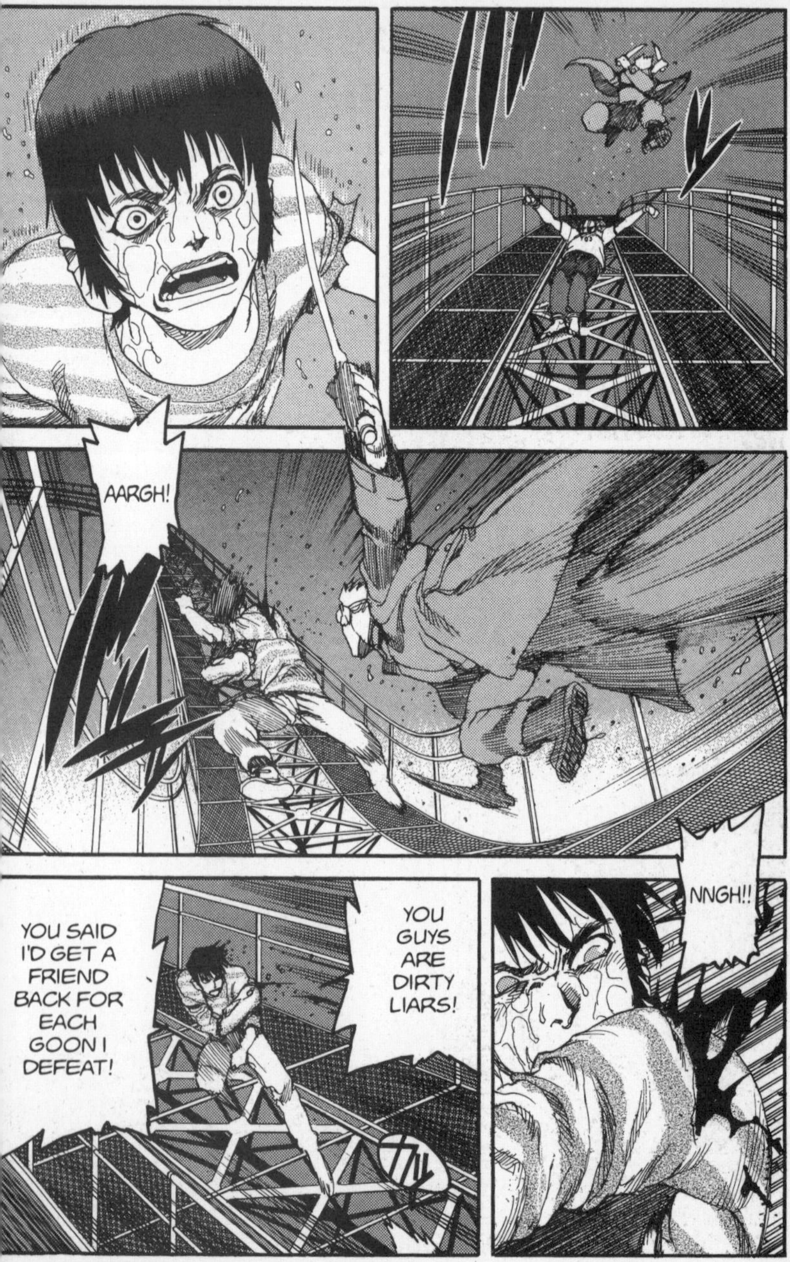
AARGH!
NNGH!!
YOU GUYS ARE DIRTY LIARS!
YOU SAID I'D GET A FRIEND BACK FOR EACH GOON I DEFEAT!

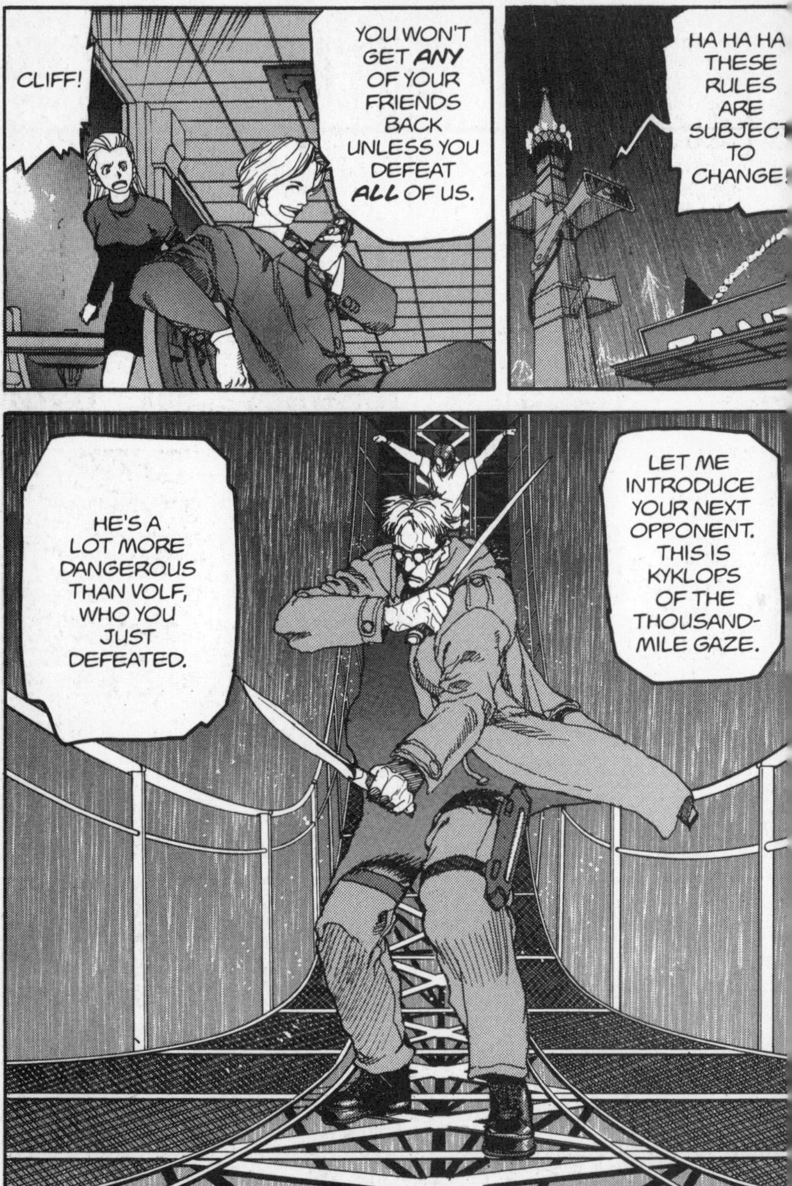
HA HA HA THESE RULES ARE SUBJECT TO CHANGE.
YOU WON'T GET **ANY** OF YOUR FRIENDS BACK UNLESS YOU DEFEAT **ALL** OF US.
CLIFF!
LET ME INTRODUCE YOUR NEXT OPPONENT. THIS IS KYKLOPS OF THE THOUSAND-MILE GAZE.
HE'S A LOT MORE DANGEROUS THAN VOLF, WHO YOU JUST DEFEATED.

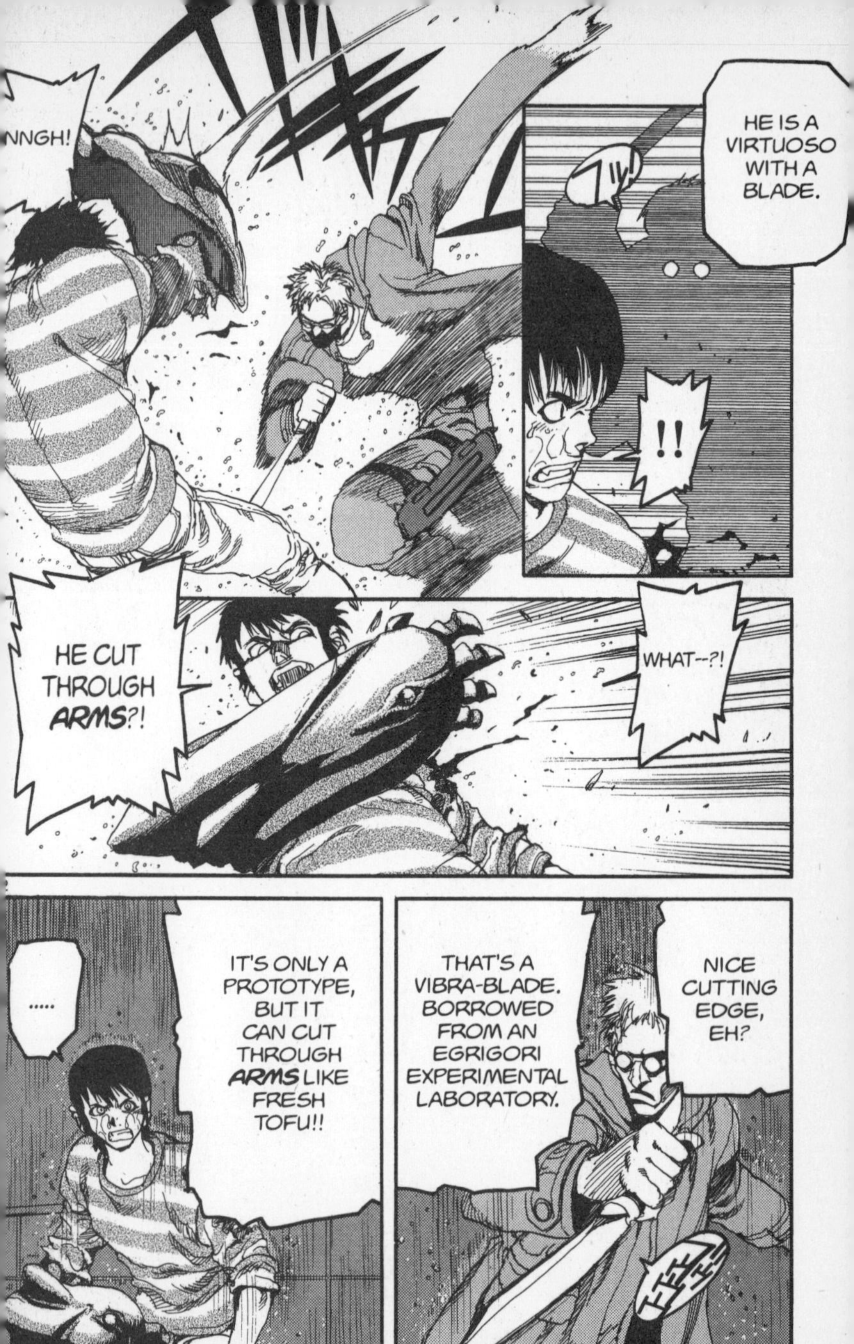
HE IS A VIRTUOSO WITH A BLADE.
!!
NNGH!
WHAT--?!
HE CUT THROUGH ARMS?!
NICE CUTTING EDGE, EH?
THAT'S A VIBRA-BLADE. BORROWED FROM AN EGRIGORI EXPERIMENTAL LABORATORY.
IT'S ONLY A PROTOTYPE, BUT IT CAN CUT THROUGH ARMS LIKE FRESH TOFU!!
.....

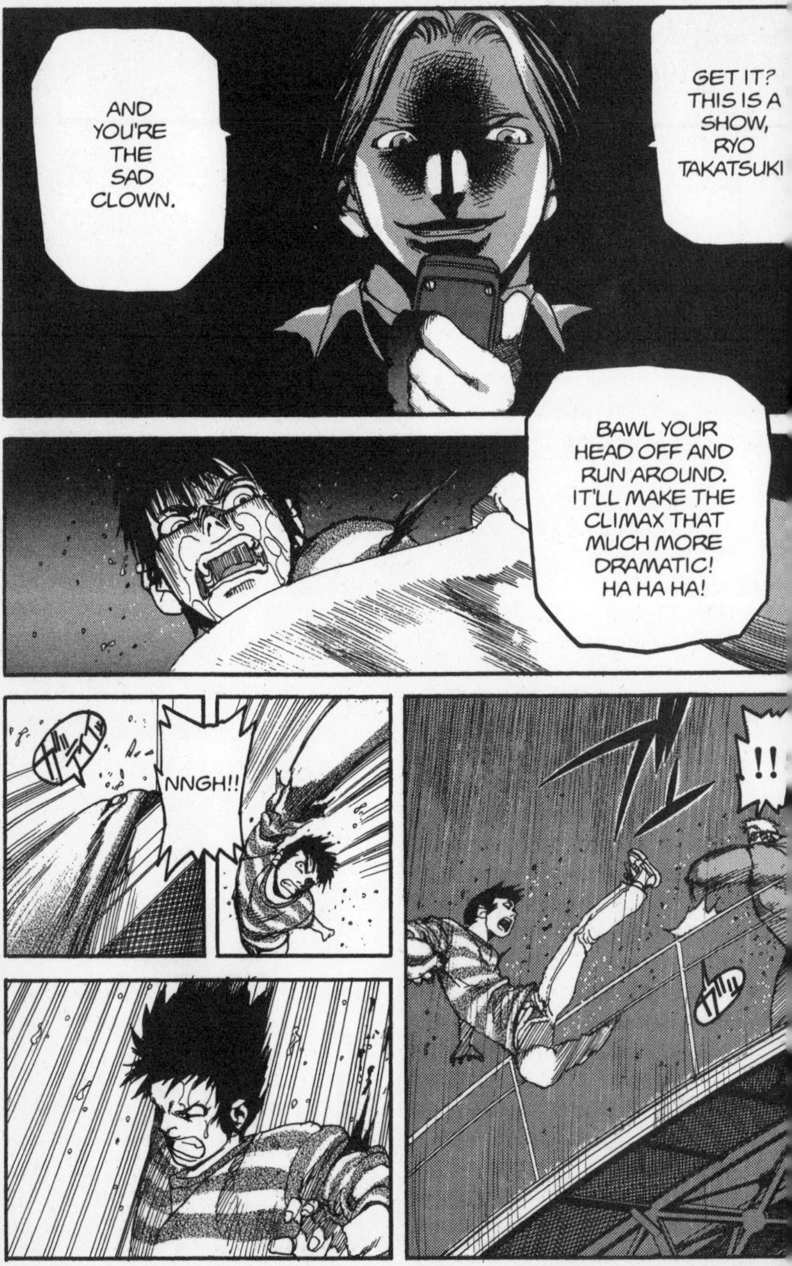
GET IT? THIS IS A SHOW, RYO TAKATSUKI
AND YOU'RE THE SAD CLOWN.
BAWL YOUR HEAD OFF AND RUN AROUND. IT'LL MAKE THE CLIMAX THAT MUCH MORE DRAMATIC! HA HA HA!
!!
NNGH!!

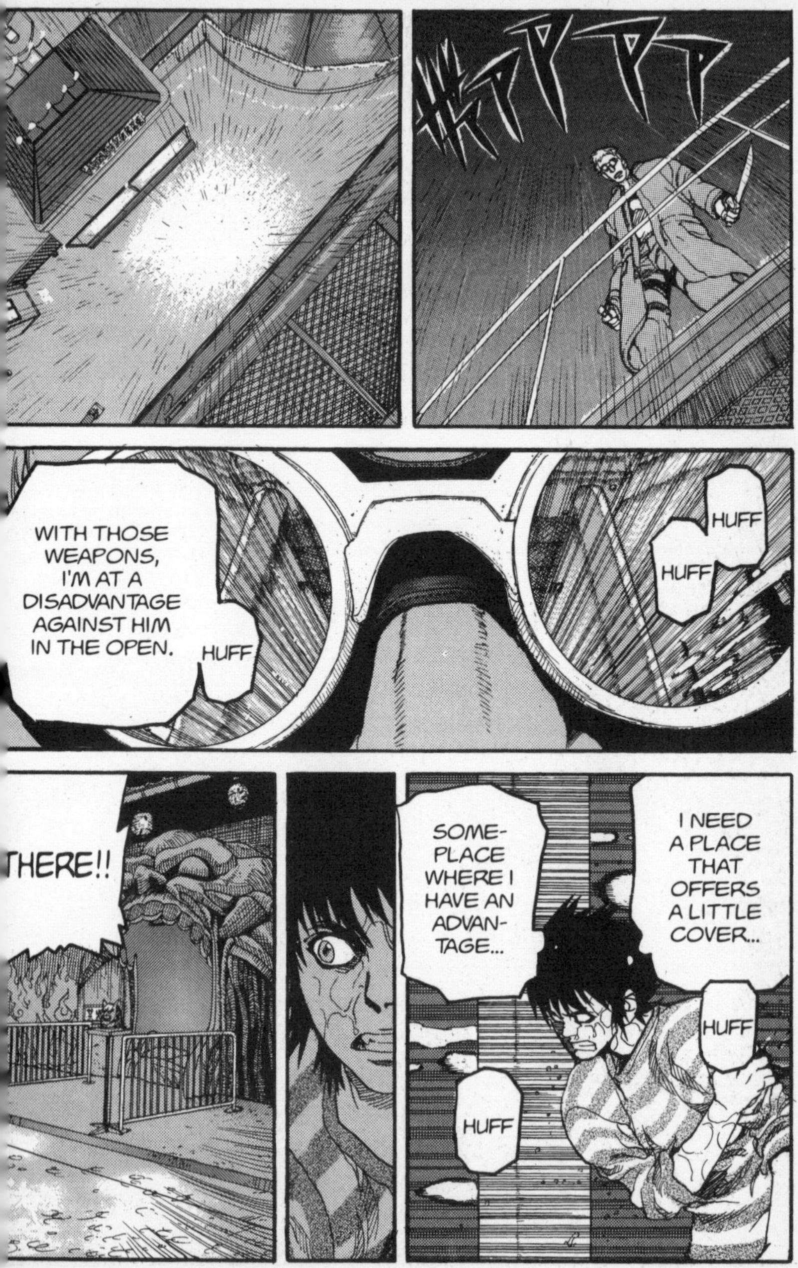
HUFF
HUFF
WITH THOSE WEAPONS, I'M AT A DISADVANTAGE AGAINST HIM IN THE OPEN.
HUFF
I NEED A PLACE THAT OFFERS A LITTLE COVER...
SOME-PLACE WHERE I HAVE AN ADVAN-TAGE...
HUFF
HUFF
THERE!!

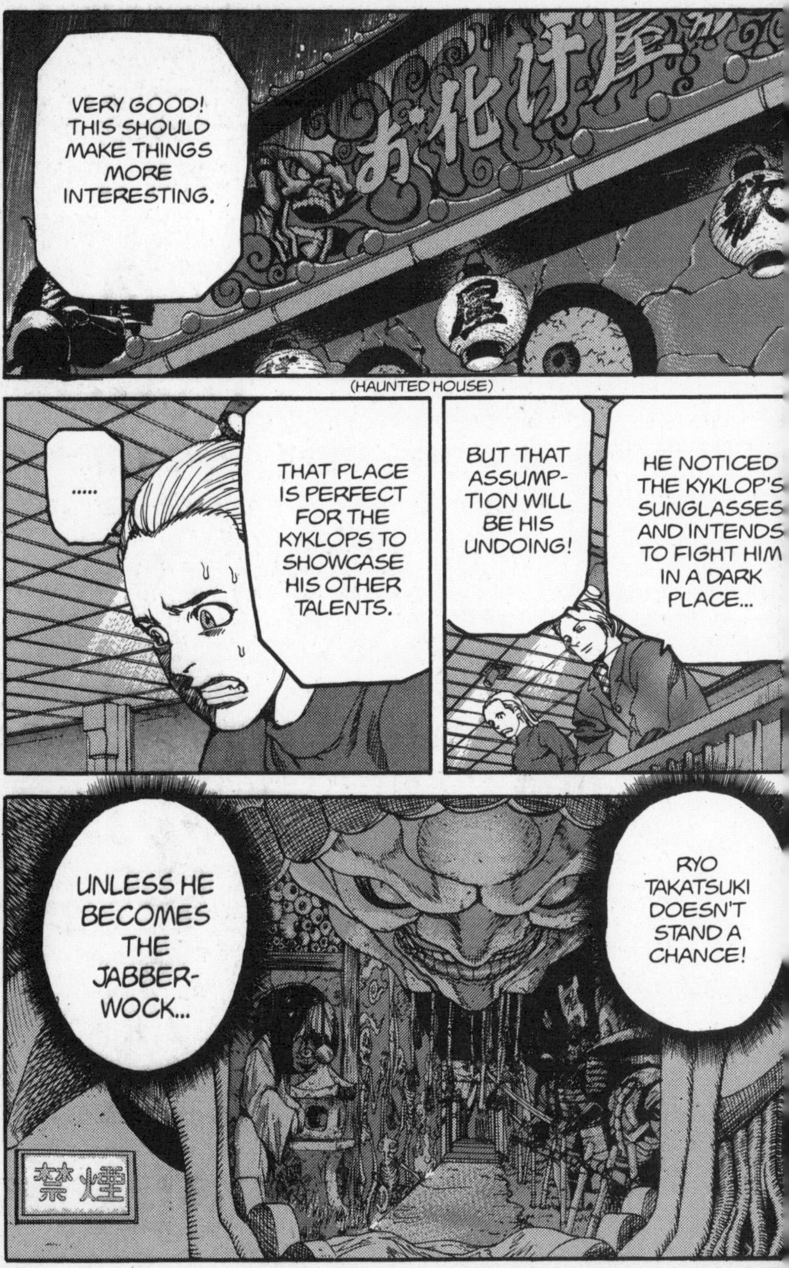
VERY GOOD! THIS SHOULD MAKE THINGS MORE INTERESTING.
(HAUNTED HOUSE)
HE NOTICED THE KYKLOP'S SUNGLASSES AND INTENDS TO FIGHT HIM IN A DARK PLACE...
BUT THAT ASSUMPTION WILL BE HIS UNDOING!
THAT PLACE IS PERFECT FOR THE KYKLOPS TO SHOWCASE HIS OTHER TALENTS.
.....
RYO TAKATSUKI DOESN'T STAND A CHANCE!
UNLESS HE BECOMES THE JABBERWOCK...
禁煙

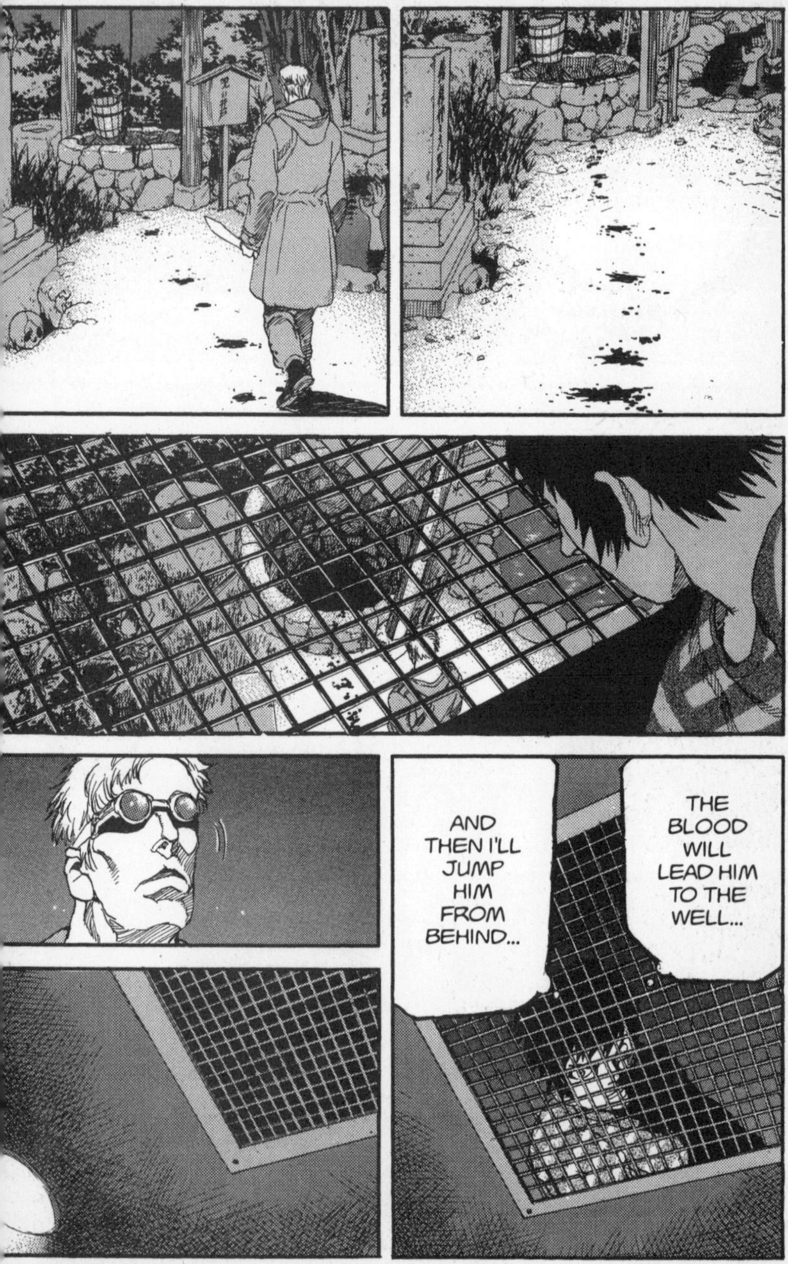
THE BLOOD WILL LEAD HIM TO THE WELL...
AND THEN I'LL JUMP HIM FROM BEHIND...

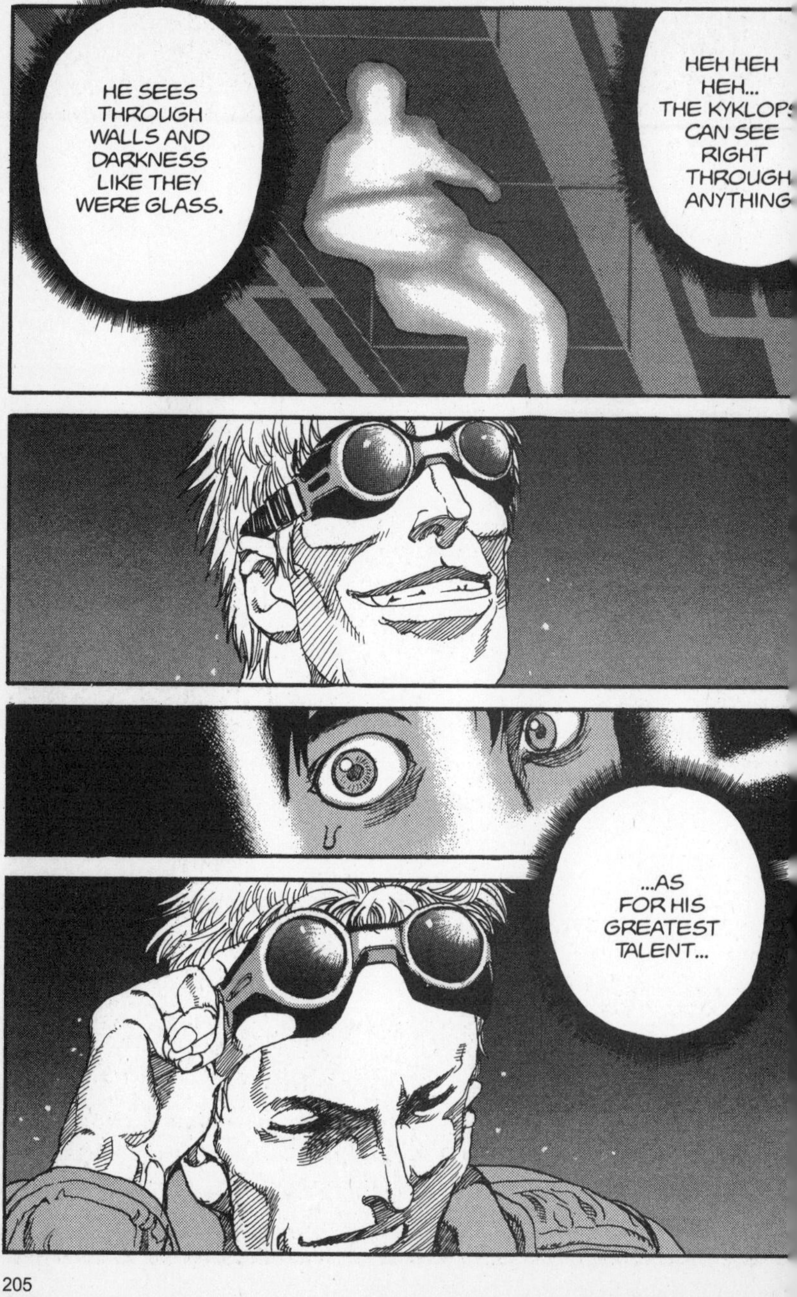
HEH HEH HEH... THE KYKLOP CAN SEE RIGHT THROUGH ANYTHING
HE SEES THROUGH WALLS AND DARKNESS LIKE THEY WERE GLASS.
...AS FOR HIS GREATEST TALENT...

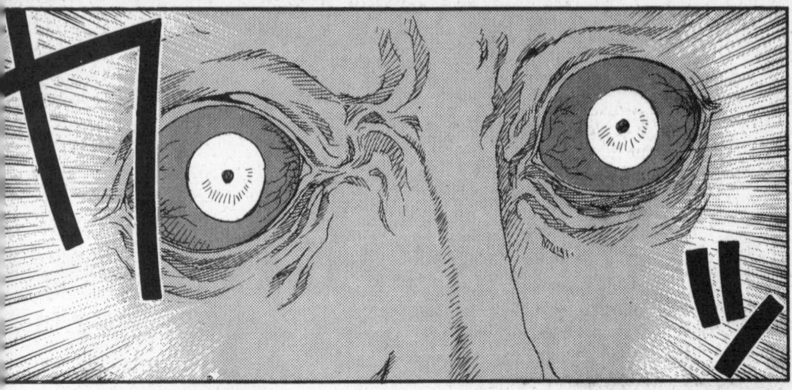

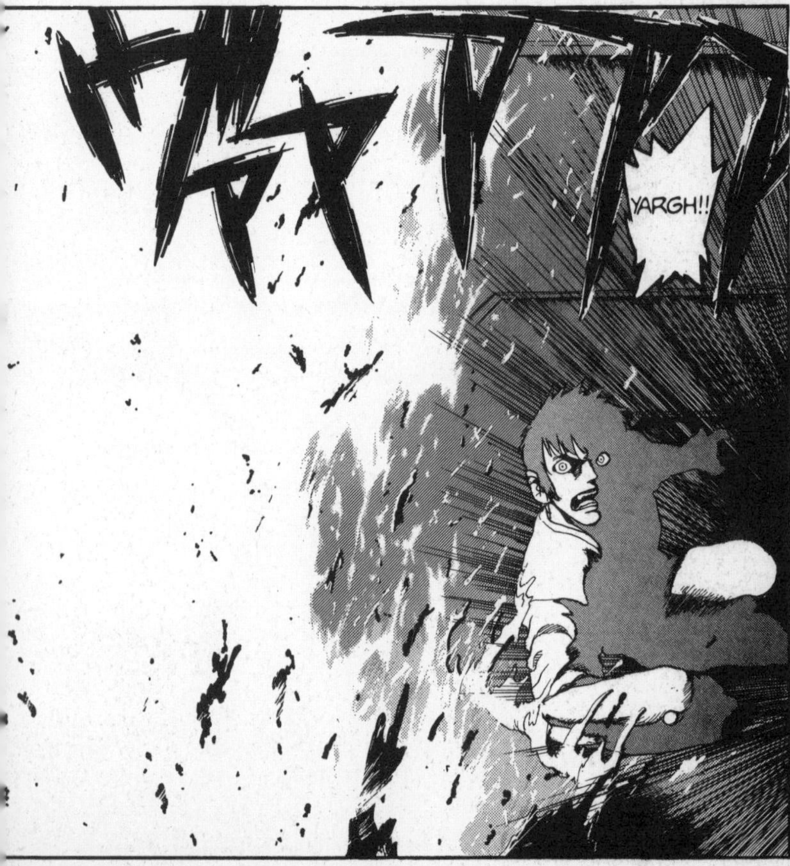
YARGH!!

More Manga!

If you like *Project Arms* here are some other manga you might be interested in:

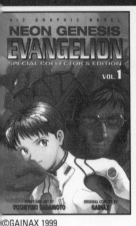

VIZ GRAPHIC NOVEL
NEON GENESIS
EVANGELION
SPECIAL COLLECTOR'S EDITION
VOL. 1
STORY AND ART BY
YOSHIYUKI SADAMOTO
ORIGINAL CONCEPT BY
GAINAX

CADENCE BOOKS GRAPHIC NOVEL
Adolf
A Tale of the Twentieth Century
STORY AND ART BY
OSAMU
TEZUKA

VIZ GRAPHIC NOVEL
STRIKER
VS.
THE THIRD REICH
get the manga that launched
SPRIGGAN
STORY BY
HIROSHI TAKASHIGE
ART BY
RYOJI MINAGAWA

Neon Genesis Evangelion
If secretive organizations with dubious agendas, lost technology of mysterious origins, and a story with incredible depth, replete with biblical references is your thing, then check out this seminal epic manga series—*Neon Genesis Evangelion.*

Adolf
Osamu "God of Manga" Tezuka's epic saga of World War II traces the lives of three men named Adolf, including Adolf Hitler, whose lives become interconnected. Adolf is a masterpiece example of Tezuka's amazing narrative manga skills. If you lke to read manga, if you like to read, or if you are able to read at all, this series is for you.

Striker
In the wrong hands, ancient technology and artifacts can have devastating consequences. It's Yu Ominae's mission to stop this from happening. Exciting action á la *Indiana Jones* depicted through Ryoji Minagawa's dynamic artwork!

A word from the editor...

You might be asking yourselves, "why aren't the sound effects translated and retouched?" Well, actually, they were translated and are included in the glossary. As to why they aren't retouched—we wanted to keep Ryoji Minagawa's dynamic artwork as close to the way it was originally published in Japan as possible. Occasionally, where the editor felt an effect or a sign was necessary to move the story forward, an editorial decision was made to go ahead and either retouch it or to include a note about it in between panels.

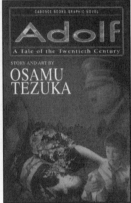

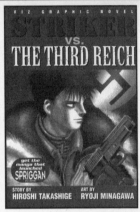

Glossary of Sound Effects, Signs, and other Miscellaneous Notes

Each entry includes: the location, indicated by page number and panel number (so 3.1 means page 3, panel number 1); the phonetic romanization of the original Japanese; and our English "translation"—we offer as close an English equivalent as we can.

Chapter 3

46.5	FX:	Byun (Arms transformation)
48.4	FX:	Zudo (thwack)
49.4	FX:	Su (tmp)
49.5	FX:	Byun (whoosh)
51.1	FX:	Pan Pan (pat pat)
53.1	FX:	Zuzazaza (skid)
54.4	FX:	Biin (Arms resonating)
55.1	FX:	Go (whoosh)
57.4	FX:	Dosha (blood spurting)

Chapter 4

64.3	FX:	Ka Ka Ka (footsteps)
65.2	FX:	Pi (beep)
65.3	FX:	Guun (vurr)
66.2	FX:	Pachi Pachi Pachi (clap clap)
66.3	FX:	Pachi Pachi (clap clap)
66.3	FX:	Hyu hyu (yahoo!)
68.1	FX:	Pan (pat)
69.3	FX:	Wai Wai Wai (crowd chatter)
70.2	FX:	Jiro (glare)
71.2	FX:	Pi Pi (beep beep)
71.3	FX:	Ka Ka Ka Ka (klak klak klak)
77.1	FX:	Bashiii (doors shutting)
77.2	FX:	Bashii (doors shutting)

Chapter 5

82.5	FX:	Bashin (zap)
82.6	FX:	Shuun (fizzle)
84.3	FX:	Bakii (zak)
88.4	FX:	Uiii (vreen)
89.1	FX:	Byuuu (Arms transformation noises)

Chapter 1

9.3	FX:	Basha Basha (splashing water)
10.5	FX:	Go (bonk)
13.10	FX:	Bun (Arms transformation noise)
14.1	FX:	Gata (skoot)
14.2	FX:	Biii (Arms transformation noise)
14.5	FX:	Bisha (door sliding)
14.6	FX:	Zawa Zawa Zawa (classroom noise reaction)
18.3	FX:	Gaba (grab)
20.1	FX:	Gu (grab)
20.4	FX:	Beki Meki Baki (crack rip crack)
21.1	FX:	Baki (rip)

Chapter 2

23.4	FX:	Beki Meri Meki (crack crunch)
24.1	FX:	Beki (crunch)
25.1	FX:	Bashu (fwoosh)
25.2	FX:	Zudo (boom)
25.3	FX:	Jakii (slik)
25.4	FX:	Zun (boot)
26.4	FX:	Don (thwak)
27.1	FX:	Bogo (crash)
27.2	FX:	Ga (grab)
28.9	FX:	Ga (klank)
30.1	FX:	Ka Ka Ka (footsteps)
31.4	FX:	Da (dash)
31.5	FX:	Ga (grab)
32.2	FX:	Yoro (moving back)
33.3	FX:	Gasha (fwump)
33.6	FX:	Da (dash)
35.3	FX:	Buuu (Arms humming)
39.5	FX:	Don (bump)

135.1—FX: Dokun Doku (heartbeats)

135.1—FX: Ku Ku Ku (rattle)

135.2—FX: Dokun (rattle)

135.3—FX: Dokun (rattle)

135.3—FX: Kachin (doorknob turning)

135.4—FX: Buuu (Arms transformation)

135.5—FX: Ban (door slamming open)

139.1—FX: Ba (fwoosh)

140.1—FX: Zaaa (rain)

142.2—FX: Pi (beep)

143.3—FX: Bagon (fwash)

144.1—FX: Baki (crash)

144.2—FX: Dogagaga (crash)

144.4—FX: Ga (grab)

145.2—FX: Gashan (glass shattering)

148.1—FX: Shuuu (Arms transformation noises)

148.2—FX: Gashi (grab)

149.6—FX: Don (bam)

150.1—FX: Ka (thok)

Chapter 9

152.1—FX: Baki (thwizz)

152.2—FX: Kyuuu (fwoosh)

152.3—FX: Baka (moving in)

152.5—FX: Ga (fwoosh)

153.2—FX: Gyaaaa (screaming)

153.2—FX: Pan Pan (pat pat)

153.4—FX: Da (dash)

154.2—FX: Gasa Goso (rustle rustle)

154.5—FX: Da Da Da Da Da (running)

154.6—FX: Da Bata Da Da (running and commotion)

154.7—FX: Da Da Da (running)

155.1—FX: Ka Ka Ka (footsteps)

155.4—FX: Da (dash)

155.5—FX: Do Do Do Do (rapid gunfire)

92.4—FX: Poso (tap)

93.4—FX: Pi (klik)

Chapter 6

101.4—FX: Gacha (creak)

104.2—FX: Batan (slam)

104.3—FX: Ta Ta Ta (tp tp tp)

104.4—FX:: Ta Ta Ta (tp tp tp)

105.5—FX: Ga (grab)

105.7—FX: Gacha (door opening)

109.2—FX: Ga (klap)

109.4—FX: Go (bonk)

111.4—FX: Bun (squeeze)

113.1—FX: Zaaaa (rain)

Chapter 7

119.1—FX: Totototototo (chop chop)

120.6—FX: Zaaa (rain)

121.1—FX: Pururu (phone ringing)

121.2—FX: Rururu (phone ringing)

122.1—FX: Dogagaga (thud crash)

122.4—FX: Do (thud)

123.2—FX: Pura Pura (fwump)

124.2—FX: Zudododo (crash skid)

125.2—FX: Beki (crash)

126.3—FX: Kiiii (Arms transformation noises)

126.6—FX: Ga (stab)

128.1—FX: Zuryu (shlik)

128.2—FX: Shuu (shlik)

128.4—FX: GU (grab)

131.1—FX: Zaaa (rain)

Chapter 8

133.4—FX: Su (door opening)

133.5—FX: Batan (slam)

156.1—FX: Do Do Do Do (rapid gunfire)

156.2—FX: Do Do Do Do (rapid gunfire)

156.3—FX: Ba Ba Ba (rapid fire)

156.4—FX: Do Do Do Do (rapid fire)

157.2—FX: Gasha (chak)

157.4—FX: Gon Gon (thud thud)

157.6—FX: Ka (beginning of explosion)

158.3—FX: Suta (tump)

158.4—FX: Don Don Don (bam bam bam)

159.2—FX: Shun Bi Gin Bin (bam ping tin)

161.4—FX: Do (thud)

161.5—FX: Shuru (swip)

161.7—FX: Puchi (squeeze)

162.1—FX: Fuan Fuan Kikiki (sirens and tire screeching)

162.2—FX: Fuan Fuan (sirens)

165.3—FX: Zaa (rain)

166.1—FX: Kiiii (high pitched sound)

166.2—FX: Kiii (high pitched sound)

Chapter 10

169.1—FX: Zaaa (rain)

169.4—FX: Ka (stopping)

170.4—FX: Burororo (vroom)

170.6—FX: Saaaa (rain)

171.1—FX: Saaa (rain)

172.5—FX: Gugu (grip)

178.5—FX: Gakun (pulling lever)

179.1—FX: Paaa (everything lighting up and turning on)

182.4—FX: Gakii (crash)

182.5—FX: Shuiii (Arms transformation noise)

183.1—FX: Gashu (grab)

183.2—FX: Gu (squeeze)

183.4—FX: Goka (bam)

184.1—FX: Doka (crash)

184.3—FX: Shuu (healing noise)

184.7—FX: Gaba (grab)

185.1—FX: Beki (crash)

185.2—FX: Meri (crunch)

185.3—FX: Don (thump)

186.6—FX: Gu (gearing up to attack)

186.7—FX: Fu (whoosh)

187.1—FX: Fu (whoosh)

187.2—FX: Bein (fwoosh)

187.2—FX: Pen (duck)

Chapter 11

189.2—FX: Muku (wipe)

189.3—FX: Basha (fwump)

191.4—FX: Bunn (punch missing)

191.5—FX: Bun (punch missing)

192.1—FX: Shuu Bun (whir whoosh)

193.1—FX: Pan Pan (pat pat)

195.2—FX: Yoro Yoro (unsteady feet)

195.3—FX: Shuka (fwish)

195.4—FX: Gaki (squeeze)

196.4—FX: Gaku (slump)

197.3—FX: Saaaa (rain)

198.1—FX: Ba (whoosh)

198.3—FX: Bashi (slish)

198.5—FX: Ka (klank)

200.1—FX; Fu (huf)

200.2—FX: Gakin (slash)

200.4—FX: Vuvuvu (vibrating blade)

201.3—FX: Bun (whoosh)

201.3—FX: Ga (klank)

201.5—FX: Gadii (grab)

202.1—FX: Zaaa (rain)

206.1—FX: Ka (opening eyes)

206.2—FX: Vaaa (fwoosh)

About the Authors

Ryoji Minagawa was born in Chiba Prefecture and made his manga debut in 1988 with *HEAVEN* published in *SHŌNEN SUNDAY*. Much heralded for his incredible artwork in *SPRIGGAN* (*STRIKER*), Minagawa received more acclaim with *ARMS* when it was the winner of the 44th Shogakukan Manga award. *ARMS* was originally serialized in *SHŌNEN SUNDAY* from 1997 to 2002. His most current work, *D-LIVE*, is about skilled drivers and fast machines and is also serialized in *SHŌNEN SUNDAY*.

Kyoichi Nanatsuki was born in Hokkaido. His credits as manga writer include *SAMURAI SHOWDOWN*, originally published in *SHŌNEN SUNDAY COMICS SPECIAL* and *HOTARU ROAD*, which was serialized in *YOUNG SUNDAY*. His most recent work, *YAMI NO AEGIS* (*AEGIS IN THE DARK*), about a tough bodyguard for hire, is currently being serialized in *YOUNG SUNDAY*.

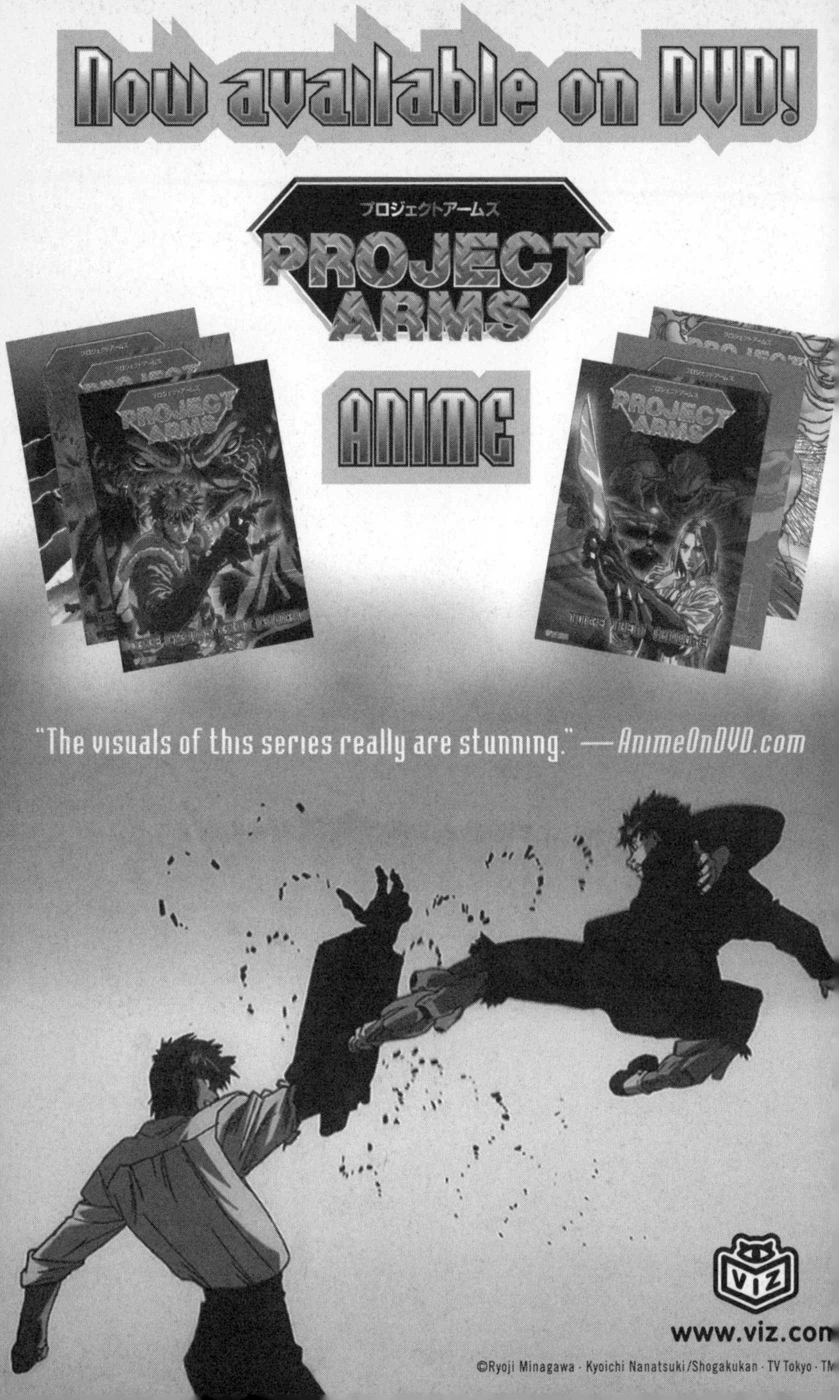

action

THE BATTLE BETWEEN GOOD AND EVIL

- The All-New Tenchi Muyô!
- Bastard!!
- Battle Angel Alita
- The Big O
- Di Gi Charat
- Excel Saga
- Firefighter! Daigo of Fire Company M
- Flame of Recca
- Gundam
- Inu-Yasha *
- Neon Genesis Evangelion
- Project Arms *
- Ranma 1/2 *
- Rahxephon
- Short Program
- Silent Möbius
- Steam Detectives
- No Need for Tenchi!
- Tuxedo Gin
- Video Girl Ai *
- Zoids *

START YOUR ACTION GRAPHIC
NOVEL COLLECTION TODAY!

STARTING @ **$8.95!**

*Also available on DVD from VIZ

1997 Ryoji Minagawa/Kyoichi Nanatsuki/Shogakukan, Inc.

www.viz.com